Foundations of Eastern Civilization

Craig G. Benjamin, Ph.D.

THE
GREAT
COURSES·

PUBLISHED BY:

THE GREAT COURSES
Corporate Headquarters
4840 Westfields Boulevard, Suite 500
Chantilly, Virginia 20151-2299
Phone: 1-800-832-2412
Fax: 703-378-3819
www.thegreatcourses.com

Craig G. Benjamin, Ph.D.
Associate Professor of History
Grand Valley State University

Professor Craig G. Benjamin is Associate Professor of History in the Frederik Meijer Honors College at Grand Valley State University (GVSU), where he teaches East Asian civilization, big history, ancient Central Asian history, and historiography to students at all levels, from freshmen to graduates. Professor Benjamin received his undergraduate education at The Australian National University in Canberra and Macquarie University in Sydney. In 2003, he was awarded his Ph.D. in Ancient History from Macquarie University for his dissertation on the migration of the Yuezhi, an ancient Central Asian nomadic confederation, and its impact on the establishment of the Silk Roads. In that same year, Professor Benjamin moved to the United States to take a position at GVSU in western Michigan, where he has taught ever since.

For the past six years, Professor Benjamin has taught a two-semester course on East Asian civilization in the Honors College at GVSU. He has also received several awards for teaching, including the 2012 Faculty of Distinction Award from Omicron Delta Kappa Society (a national leadership honor society) and the 2009 Student Award for Faculty Excellence from the GVSU Student Senate.

Professor Benjamin's primary research interest is in ancient Central Asia, specifically the relationship between the great nomadic confederations, such as the Scythians/Saka, Yuezhi, and Xiongnu, and the major civilizations of the period, including Han China and the Roman Empire. He is also involved with teaching and researching big history, a relatively new field that examines the past on the largest possible timescale, from the origins of the universe to the present day. Professor Benjamin has written more than 30 published papers, articles, and book chapters. He is the author of *The Yuezhi: Origin, Migration and the Conquest of Northern Bactria* and *Readings in the*

Historiography of World History and coauthor (with David Christian and Cynthia Stokes Brown) of *Big History: Between Nothing and Everything*. Professor Benjamin has coedited several volumes in the Brepols Silk Road Studies series and is editor of the *Cambridge History of the World*, volume 4, *A World with States, Empires, and Networks, 1200 BCE–900 CE*.

Professor Benjamin is vice-president (and president-elect) of the World History Association and treasurer of the International Big History Association. He is also a consultant for The College Board and a member of the SAT® World History Subject Committee and the Advanced Placement World History Development Committee. In addition to his many professional activities, Professor Benjamin has been featured on The History Channel. Before taking up an academic career, he was a professional musician and jazz educator for 25 years in Australia, playing flute and saxophone. In addition to pursuing his academic and musical interests, Professor Benjamin has spent much of his life hiking and climbing in the great mountain ranges of the world. ■

Table of Contents

Table of Contents

Table of Contents

Foundations of Eastern Civilization

Scope:

Much has been written about the foundations of Western civilization, from Greek and Roman antiquity through to the present day. Yet Eastern civilizations have also played a significant role in shaping our world, and to truly understand the modern world, it is essential to know something about the many extraordinary contributions Eastern civilization has made. Gaining this knowledge is even more imperative given the incredible dynamism of that region today. East Asia is home to two of the world's top three economies and about 22 percent of the world's population—it matters! As the process of globalization brings our world ever closer together, the foundational ideas of both Eastern and Western civilization are becoming more and more interwoven. Simply put, it is no longer enough to know just the "Western half" of the story; both Eastern and Western are critical to understanding our present and our future.

This course focuses on the history and core foundational achievements of the major cultures and regions of the Eastern Hemisphere, especially China, Japan, Korea, and Southeast Asia. It examines the origins and development of the philosophy, science, religion, economics, politics, and social life of these important cultures and measures their influence on other Eastern states, as well as their legacy to the contemporary world. One of the questions we will pursue throughout the course is: How did these nations build on their ancient roots to develop into such successful modern societies? To seek an answer, we must go back to the very beginning of Eastern civilization.

We begin our exploration in China with a consideration of the diverse geography of this, the third-largest nation on earth. We follow Chinese history and culture over thousands of years, from the migration of early foraging humans into the region to the appearance of the first sedentary agricultural communities. It is in the shadowy transition of these early communities into full-blown city-states and, eventually, imperial dynasties that we see the origins of cultural and philosophical ideas that evolved into the core foundational elements of Eastern civilization.

We follow the evolution of the Chinese dynasties and their fundamental political and philosophical ideas—such as the mandate of heaven, Confucianism, Daoism, and Legalism—from the first Xia dynasty through the Shang, Zhou, Qin, Han, and Tang. We also look at the Silk Roads in this section of the course, tracing connections that developed among Rome, India, the steppe-nomadic world, and East Asia that led to extraordinary levels of cultural exchange. Perhaps the most significant of these exchanges was the spread of Buddhism into China and East Asia, because this Indian spiritual philosophy quickly became another of the core foundational elements of Eastern civilization.

In the next part of the course, we explore the history and cultural development of three other Eastern regions: Korea, Japan, and Southeast Asia. Despite the powerful influence of China, these societies constructed their own fascinating and unique cultural traditions. We begin with the arrival of early human migrants into the Korean Peninsula and Japanese Archipelago and use the findings of archaeologists to tease out the origins of core cultural ideas that appeared in both regions. We then trace their evolution through to the fascinating Three Kingdoms and Silla periods in Korea and the sophisticated Nara and Heian periods in Japan. In Southeast Asia, we explore the long and complex relationship between China and Vietnam, which resulted in a rich blending of original and imported practices, and we follow the diffusion of Hinduism and Islam into Southeast Asia, which helped shape the extraordinary societies we see in the region today.

After this, we return to China under the creative and economically powerful Song dynasty, before the Mongols arrived to temporarily disrupt the flow of Eastern civilization. The Ming and Qing attempted to restore traditional Chinese cultural practices but were forced to do so in the face of an expansionist West. As China loses sovereignty to Western powers, we return to Korea and Japan to follow their complex relationship with each other—and the rest of the world—into the 20th century.

In the final four lectures of the course, we return to the question of how these nations built on their ancient roots to develop into such successful modern societies. And we ask how many of these foundational ideas still resonate in modern East Asia today. This course unfolds a 10,000-year-long story of triumph and tragedy without parallel in world history—a story of emperors and peasants, princesses and concubines, Confucians and Legalists, Daoists and Buddhists, camels and silkworms, revolutions, war and peace. We have much to explore, many fascinating people and ideas to encounter, and many historical and cultural threads to follow as we tease out the core elements of Eastern civilization and consider their role in the making of the modern world. ■

Korea—The Unified Silla
Lecture 25

A t the end of the last lecture, we saw that the Tang dynasty in China, after failing in its attempts to invade the Koguryo kingdom, decided to focus its Korean foreign policy on forging an alliance with the Silla kingdom. Eventually, the Silla, after dealing with some tricky Tang foreign policy intentions, successfully united most of the peninsula under its leadership. This unified Silla dynasty, which ruled much of Korea until 935 C.E., and its ongoing relationship with the Tang dynasty in China are the subjects of this lecture. This relationship was not only politically important for both states but also responsible for the further transmission of core Chinese civilizational ideas into Korean culture.

Silla Struggles for Control

- In the mid-7th century, the Koguryo kingdom in the north of Korea was engaged in repeated bloody conflicts with both the Sui and Tang dynasties. With its traditional foe distracted by these Chinese campaigns, the Paekche kingdom decided to attack the Silla in the south. The Silla kingdom was hard pressed to stave off the Paekche forces and sought a strategic alliance with the Chinese Tang dynasty.

- The two new allies agreed on a strategy: The Tang would join with the Silla to defeat Paekche, after which Koguryo would be attacked in a pincer movement by Tang forces from the north and Silla troops from the south.
  - Accordingly, in 660 C.E., a Tang invasion fleet landed troops near the Paekche capital, while a Silla army simultaneously attacked Paekche territory from the east. The capital of Paekche fell to the combined assault, and the Paekche kingdom was utterly defeated.

  - Over the next several years, Koguryo came under increasing pressure from Tang forces in the north and Silla forces in the south, and by 668, it had also been defeated.

- Now the Tang dynasty revealed its true intentions: to bring the entire Korean Peninsula under Chinese imperial control by establishing powerful military commanderies throughout the region and appointing a protector general to rule all of Korea, including the Silla.

- Silla was not prepared to accept Chinese hegemony and fought back against its recent allies, repeatedly sending armies into former Koguryo and Packche territory to defeat both revivalist forces and Tang armies. After almost a decade of struggle, Silla triumphed and, by 676, had forced the Tang to remove most of its forces and retreat. This victory over the Tang ensured that the Korean people, although heavily influenced by Chinese culture, were nonetheless able to retain their distinct cultural identity.

- Although the full name of the dynasty the Silla established is the Unified Silla, the kingdom was never able to control the entire peninsula. Émigrés from the defeated Koguryo kingdom established a new political entity they called Parhae, which gained control over much of the northern peninsula. At first, Silla attempted to bring Parhae under its control, but it eventually gave up and built a defensive wall along its northern border in the year 721.

- The relationship between China and all the Korean states remained strong, and eventually, both Silla and Parhae reconciled their differences with the Tang and went on to establish strong diplomatic and trade relations with the Chinese. In the end, both Parhae and Silla agreed to accept tributary status with the Middle Kingdom. Large-scale cultural exchange took place between Silla and Parhae and the Tang.

Silla Political Structure
- As royal authority increased under the Silla, members of what were called the "true-bone" clan lineages became the elites of Silla society. But as this elite group gained in power and prestige, the membership of the royal family came from an increasingly small section of the aristocracy.

- The exclusivity of access to the monarchy led to the undermining of claims to power from rival aristocratic families, creating an atmosphere of almost continuous tension between the ruling families and other nobles.

  o Tension existed also between the monarchy and a group of intellectuals who held the status known as "head-rank six," a sort of scholar class that was looked down on by the true-bone families.

  o Eventually, the royal family and the head-rank six families were reconciled and agreed to work together for the success of the state, although not without periodic outbreaks of conflict.

- Most of the aristocratic true-bone families lived in the great capital called Kyongju. References in Tang sources give us some idea of the immense wealth of these aristocratic families. Archaeological excavations of Kyongju have also revealed careful city planning and many large stone buildings and beautiful gardens. As the wealth and power of the aristocracy increased, however, the lives of the common people became increasingly impoverished.

- Despite the rigidly hierarchical nature of Korean society during this period, it is worth noting that everyone who lived in Unified Silla, rich or poor, was an ardent follower of Buddhism, which dominated the intellectual and cultural life of the state. Indeed, the only real rival to Buddhism as the orthodox system of thought in Silla was Confucianism, viewed as beneficial to the effective administration of the state.

- This deep penetration of Buddhism and Confucianism in Silla government and society is further evidence of the profound influence of Chinese civilization on Korean culture. A number of Silla intellectuals were concerned about this and did what they could to prevent Korean culture from being swamped by the Tang dynasty cultural juggernaut.

o The work of scholar Kim Tae-mun, for example, constantly emphasized native Silla cultural achievements in the face of a widespread obsession with Chinese civilization.

o And Kim Tae-mun had much to celebrate, including a superb astronomical observatory constructed by Silla intellectuals in Kyongju, advanced woodblock printing used to produce Buddhist and Confucian texts, the Bulguksa temple and other Buddhist architecture, the Seokguram Grotto, and the art of bronze bell making.

- As noted earlier, throughout the entire period of Silla unified rule in the south, the northern regions of the Korean Peninsula remained under the control of the Parhae state. Where the Silla had left many traditional Three Kingdoms aristocratic administrative structures in place, the Parhae created a new system of government that was more closely modeled on that of the Chinese Tang, and the design of the Parhae capital of Sanggyong was closely modeled on the Tang capital of Changan.

The names of various features of the Bulguksa temple—Cloud Bridge Stairway, Floating Shadow Pavilion—give some idea of the ethereal and refined nature of this complex.

Decline of the Silla

- Silla civilization reached its zenith during the reign of King Kyongdok (r. 742–765), yet the king faced renewed pressure from members of the true-bone aristocracy, who were determined to break the power of the throne and the ruling families that had dominated it for a century.

- Kyongdok tried to appease his rivals by introducing political reform based on the Tang dynasty model, but rebellion broke out and lasted on and off for the next 20 years, until the hereditary line of Silla's ruling family had been destroyed. With the throne undermined, aristocratic families turned on each other, assembling their own personal armies.

- Records show that the late Silla period was dominated by shifting alliances of aristocratic families who seized the throne, only to become the target for new rebellions and revenge. Twenty kings ruled during the 150-year period of Silla decline, and every single reign was marked by instability and conflict.

- Unrest among intellectuals came to a head late in the 9th century after a Silla candidate, Choe Chiwon, passed the difficult Tang dynasty Confucian exam and was appointed to an important administrative position in China. This leading scholar later submitted proposals to the Silla court for political reform, but he was ignored and retired in disgust. After this snub, head-rank six scholars began to actively work against the Silla government.

- At the same time, the struggle between the aristocratic clans abated somewhat in the mid-9th century, as certain powerful families gave up their aspirations for the throne and began to focus on getting rich through trade. These families dominated the maritime shipping lanes of the region and established themselves at the center of a flourishing trade system that connected Japan, Korea, and Tang China.

- As political rivalry flared up again late in the 9th century, powerful families abandoned the capital and set themselves up in fortified compounds near major population centers. They became known as castle lords and exercised authority over their own private armies, as well as the regions and peasants around their castles, in a manner similar to the nobles who would later operate in feudal Europe. This situation further weakened the central authority of the Silla kings and made it impossible for them to collect taxes.

- Peasants abandoned their farms in large numbers and wandered the land as rebels. Large-scale peasant revolts broke out in 889, which the government forces found difficult to put down.

- Three powerful castle lords emerged to take control of competing rebel forces, setting in motion a three-cornered contest for mastery of the Korean Peninsula.
    - One lord, Kyonhwon, sacked the Silla capital in 927 and killed the king, but the other two, Wang Kon and Kungye, prevented him from toppling the Silla state. Kungye was later killed by his own people, which meant that now there were just two lords competing for power.

    - Wang Kon, who came from a noble family in the northern Kaesong region, considered himself to be a successor of the old Koguryo kingdom and came up with a new name for the state he wished to construct to replace Silla: the Koryo.

    - Wang Kon built strong alliances with other northern nobility and shrewdly pursued a policy of friendship with the Silla king, partly to forge an alliance that would allow him to defeat his rival, Kyonhwon. In the end, Wang Kon's army crushed the army of Kyonwhon in 934 C.E.

- At about the same time, the Parhae kingdom in the north was defeated by militarized nomads out of Manchuria, and members of the Parhae ruling class fled to the new state of Koryo, where they received a warm welcome from Wang Kon. One year later, in 935 C.E., the last Silla king abdicated, allowing Wang Kon to quickly achieve complete reunification of the Korean Peninsula under his rule. Wang Kon (who is known today as King Taejo) now officially named this new era the Koryo dynasty; it would go on to rule for nearly 500 years.

Suggested Reading

Henthorn, *A History of Korea.*

Joe, *Traditional Korea.*

Questions to Consider

1. How were Buddhism and Confucianism reconciled to become the foundational ideologies of Korean civilization?

2. What internal and external tensions led eventually to the collapse of the Silla?

Korea—The Unified Silla
Lecture 25—Transcript

In our last lecture, I noted that archeology provides quite striking evidence of the violent and bitter conflict that characterized the Three Kingdoms Era of Korean history. Modern archaeologists have discovered scores of mountain fortresses in the remote mountain ranges located throughout the length of the Korean peninsula; tourists can visit the remains of some of these today, and perhaps some of you have done that. The literature from the period, both Korean and Chinese, also abounds with tales of epic campaigns and brutal warfare.

At the end of that last lecture, I also mentioned that next time we'd see how the Tang dynasty in China, after failing in its attempts to invade the Koguryo kingdom in the north, decided to instead focus its Korean foreign policy on forging an alliance with the Silla kingdom in the far southeast of the peninsula. Eventually, the Silla, after having to deal with some tricky Tang foreign policy machinations, was able to successfully unite most of the peninsula under its leadership. The dynasty of the Unified Silla, which went on to rule much of Korea until 935 C.E., and its ongoing relationship with the powerful Tang dynasty in China, is the subject of this lecture.

What we'll see, I think, is that this relationship wasn't only politically important for both states, but also responsible for the further transmission of core Chinese civilizational ideas into Korean culture, with profound implications for the future. You'll remember from last time that the Koguryo kingdom in the north was engaged in repeated bloody conflicts with both the Sui and Tang dynasties in the mid-seventh century. At this moment, with their traditional foe distracted by these Chinese campaigns, the king of the Paekche kingdom decided to attack Silla in the south. Silla was hard pressed to stave off the Paekche forces and decided to seek a strategic alliance with the Chinese Tang dynasty. The two new allies agreed on a strategy: The Tang would join forces with the Silla to help defeat Paekche, after which Koguryo would be attacked in a pincer movement by Tang forces coming in from the north and Silla troops driving up from the south. Accordingly, in 660 C.E., a Tang invasion fleet landed troops near the Paekche capital, while a Silla army simultaneously attacked Paekche territory from the east and south. The capital of Paekche fell to the combined assault, and the Paekche kingdom was utterly defeated. Now following up on the second part of their agreement, over the next several years Koguryo came under increasing pressure from Tang forces in the north and Silla forces in the south; and by 668, Koguryo had also been defeated.

But now the Chinese Tang dynasty revealed its true intentions: to bring the entire Korean peninsula under Chinese imperial control by establishing powerful military commanderies throughout the region and appointing a Protector General to rule all of Korea, including their new allies, the Silla. Silla wasn't prepared to accept Chinese hegemony and fought back against their recent allies, repeatedly sending armies north into former Koguryo and Paekche territory to defeat both revivalist forces there and also Tang dynasty armies. In the end, after almost a decade of quite bitter struggle, Silla triumphed, and by 676 had forced the Tang dynasty to remove most of their forces and retreat.

This victory of the Silla kingdom and their success in repulsing the Tang had immense historical consequences for Korea, not just politically and culturally but I think also culturally. In essence, this victory of 676 preserved the political and cultural independence of the Korean peninsula. This victory over the Tang ensured that the Korean people, although still heavily influenced by Chinese culture, were nonetheless able to retain their distinct cultural identity, which further enriched the complex tapestry of Eastern civilization. Although the full name of the dynasty the Silla established is the "Unified Silla," this is a misnomer: The Silla was never able to control the entire Korean peninsula. Émigrés from the defeated Koguryo kingdom established a new political entity in the north that they called Parhae, which gained control over much of the northern peninsula. This also was a good thing, particularly for the preservation of Korean culture, because the strong Parhae state in the north was able to keep Tang dynasty armies at bay, further protecting Silla in the south, and Silla culture particularly, from possible Chinese invasion.

At first Silla did attempt to bring Parhae under its control, but eventually gave up and instead built a strong defensive wall along its northern border in 721; this is an earlier version of the demilitarized zone that, of course, divides northern and southern Korea to this day. I want to return to this point later in the course, but it's certainly worth noting here that Korea has a long history of division between north and south, reinforced by influences in the north coming from China but also the steppe nomads; influences that didn't penetrate as deeply in the south.

But the relationship between China and all the Korean states remained strong, and eventually both Silla and Parhae reconciled their differences with the Tang and went on to establish very strong diplomatic and trade relationships with the Chinese. In the end, both Parhae and Silla agreed to formalize their relationship with the Tang and accept tributary status with the Middle Kingdom, a decision that was tremendously beneficial to both Korean kingdoms. I say this because large-scale cultural exchange now began to take place between both Silla and Parhae and the Tang. Monks and students traveled in their thousands to the great Tang capital of Changan to study Buddhism and Confucianism; you might remember we met several of them during on our visit to the great Tang capital of Changan in an earlier lecture. The impact of this exposure to sophisticated Tang civilization allowed the culture of both Silla and Parhae to blossom.

But let's turn now to the sort of political and structure that emerged in the Silla dynasty to see what sort of influence this continuing exposure to civilization had on Korean ideas about governance. As royal authority became more authoritarian, more centralized, under the Silla, members of what was called the "true-bone" clan lineage became the elites of Silla society. But as this elite true-bone group was gaining in power and prestige, membership of the royal family came from an increasingly smaller section of the aristocracy. One example of this is that all queens had to come traditionally from the house of Kim, and the exclusivity of access to the monarchy led to the undermining of claims to power from most of the other rival aristocratic families. This in turn created an atmosphere of almost continuous tension between the ruling families, the other nobility, and also with a third group, a particular group of highly educated intellectuals who held the status known as the "head-rank six." This is a sort of scholar class that was looked down upon by the true-bone noble families. Eventually the royal family and the head-rank six families were reconciled, and they agreed to work together for the success of the state, although not without periodic outbreaks of conflict.

Most of the aristocratic true-bone families now lived in the great capital the Silla constructed near Kyongju, which at that time had a different name, a very descriptive name, which translates as "city of gold." We have a pretty good idea of the immense wealth of the aristocratic true-bone families living in the Silla capital actually from Tang dynasty references. Let me quote one for you: "Wealth flows unceasingly into the house of the highest officials, who possess as many as 3,000 slaves, with corresponding numbers of weapons, cattle, horses and pigs." The same Tang sources note that there wasn't a single house with a thatched roof in Kyongju. This is important because thatched roofs were standard in the homes of common people in China and Korea; but elites could afford more substantial roofing materials, timber and tiles, for example. The Tang sources comment almost enviously that the sounds of music filled the streets of Kyongju night and day. Archaeological excavations of Kyongju have reinforced this Tang literary evidence by revealing very careful city panning with the city laid out on a grid pattern like Changan, plus many large stone buildings and beautiful planned gardens.

But these Tang references to the large numbers of slaves owned by the noble families also remind us that as the wealth and power of the aristocracy increased, so the lives of the common people were increasingly impoverished in Silla Korea. More and more peasants found themselves being sold into debt slavery, and even the laborers and highly skilled artisans who built this glorious capital city were probably slaves. Fortunately for historians, the Silla court carried out a census of rural villages and families every three years. These critically important records that were collected served to allow the state to extract as much as possible in terms of taxes but also conscripted labor from the peasants for the benefit of this elite Silla nobility.

Despite the rigidly hierarchical nature of Korean society during this period, it's worth noting that everyone who lived in so-called Unified Silla, rich or poor, had become an ardent follower of the religion of Buddhism, which utterly dominated the intellectual and cultural life of the state. As I mentioned just a few moment ago, thousands of monks and students studied in Changan in China, and many even traveled on to India, bringing back with them documents and ideologies of the various schools of Buddhism that were flourishing all over Eurasia, particularly in Tang China. The school of

Pure Land Buddhism was particularly popular with the common people in Korea because it didn't require literacy to appreciate it, simply the ability to memorize and chant the mantra "Homage to the Buddha of Infinite Light." Perhaps more than 80 percent of the population of Silla believed that regular recitation of this and a handful of other mantras would lead to rebirth in nirvana, rebirth in paradise.

The only real rival to Buddhism as the orthodox system of thought in Silla was, not surprisingly, Confucianism. Indeed, a Tang-style National Confucian College was established in the Silla capital in 682, where students studied the *Analects*, of course, and all the Zhou dynasty classics. Eventually the Silla adopted the Confucian state examination system in 788; but in a significant departure from the Chinese system, because Silla society was now so rigidly hierarchical and the elites wouldn't dream of sharing political power with the lesser classes, entrance to the Silla College and exam system was strictly reserved for members of the aristocracy. You remember, of course, a critical component of Confucius's definition of a gentleman—a *junzi*, a princeling—was that he could come from any class whatsoever so long as he achieved the necessary levels of intellectual and ethical cultivation. But such a definition wasn't recognized in the Silla dynasty of Korea. Despite this restriction—or more probably because of this restriction—the Confucian system was viewed as beneficial to the effective administration of the state, so was supported and sponsored by the royal families and all the other nobility.

This deep penetration of Buddhism and Confucianism in Silla government and Silla society is, of course, further evidence of just how profoundly Chinese civilization was now influencing Korean culture. But, very interesting, we also know that a number of Silla intellectuals were already pushing back. They were deeply concerned about this Chinese influence; they did what they could to prevent Korean culture from being swamped by the Tang dynasty cultural juggernaut. The work of scholar Kim Tae-mun, for example, constantly emphasized native Silla cultural achievements in the face of this widespread obsession with Chinese civilization. Frankly, Kim Tae-mun did have much to celebrate, including the construction of a superb astronomical observatory that was built by Silla intellectuals and architects in Kyongju. But ironically, I guess, the observatory actually grew out of a Silla obsession with another Chinese cultural invention, one we've explored several times in the course: the concept of yin and yang, and how to best establish a harmonious balance between the two. An eighth century Silla astronomer-astrologer mentioned in the Tang sources became a great student of yin-yang philosophy in China; and he returned to Korea, he was appointed by the Silla court as "Savant of the Celestial Phenomena." Part of his job was to use the astronomical data from the observatory to try and balance the celestial phenomena for the good of the state.

Not surprisingly, Silla intellectuals were also very advanced in mathematics. Their mathematical knowledge was theoretical certainly, but also practical, particularly in its application to the design and construction of quite magnificent Buddhist architecture. The superb temples and other buildings were very carefully designed by these mathematicians, in fact, particularly to provide for sufficient air circulation within the buildings to prevent damage from an excessive buildup of moisture.

The skill of woodblock printing was also highly advanced in Silla, where it was used mostly to print Buddhist and Confucian texts. In fact, a copy of the Buddhist *Dharani sutra*, printed before the completion of the Pagoda That Casts No Shadow in 751, may well be the oldest surviving printed document in all of world history.

Nowhere are Silla architectural skills and this fascination with yin yang more evident than in the construction of the refined and harmonious Bulguksa Buddhist temple in Kyongju. This collection of buildings still stands today, and is so important to Korean cultural history that it's been designated as "Historic and Scenic Site No. 1" by the South Korean government. It was also declared a UNESCO World Heritage Site in 1995. Built in 751 on the slopes of beautiful Mount Tohamsan, the names of the various features give us some idea of the ethereal and refined nature of this complex: there's the Cloud Bridge Stairway, the Mauve Mist Gate, the Floating Shadow Pavilion, and, of course, the Pagoda That Casts No Shadow. The nearby Seokguram Grotto is a manmade grotto of stone within which a massive statue of the Buddha was worshipped then and still is to this day. This enormous Buddha was surrounded by Bodhisattvas and other disciples of the Buddha, by four Deva kings, and was accompanied by the 11-headed Goddess of Mercy.

Silla craftsmen also brought the art of bronze bell making, which as we've seen first emerged way back in the Shang dynasty in China, to an extraordinary level of sophistication. The oldest Silla bell that's survived through to the present day dates to 725; but the most famous surviving bell of all is the so-called Emile Bell, which was cast in 771 and resides today in the glorious National Museum of Korea in Kyongju. The Emile Bell, superbly decorated with flying angels and lotus flowers, is nearly 8 feet in diameter and 11 feet high, making it also the largest surviving Korean bell. Some ancient sources do refer to a much larger bell, unfortunately now lost; a bell that was once housed in a Silla temple and was purported to weigh more than 300 tons. Silla bronze bells were able to blend the Chinese technique of casting the striker and clapper bells with their own technological innovations, which accounts for the particularly sonorous sound in these Silla bells compared even to the great Chinese bells. The result was that with their exquisite shape, design, and sound, the bells of Silla are simply unequalled by even the finest cast bronze bells of ancient China or ancient Japan.

As we noted earlier, throughout this entire period of Silla unified rule in the south, the northern regions of the Korean peninsula remained under the control of the Parhae state. Where the Silla left many traditional Three Kingdoms aristocratic administrative structures in place, the Parhae created a new system of government that was a lot more closely modeled on that of the Chinese Tang dynasty. With thousands of Parhae students studying in Changan and returning home, of course, Parhae culture flourished as it attempted to emulate the highest achievements of the Tang. In fact, the Chinese were so impressed by Parhae that some Tang official histories describe Parhae as "the flourishing land in the East." The Parhae capital of Sanggyong was carefully modeled on the design of the Tang capital Changan. The city was surrounded by a Tang-style rectangular outer wall, with an inner wall constructed around the palace and government buildings. A broad thoroughfare was constructed linking the south gate of this inner citadel with the great southern gate of the outer wall. As was the case in Tang Changan, great residential buildings were erected on either side of the thoroughfare.

I think we should return now to political matters as we begin to bring this lecture to its conclusion. Silla civilization reached its zenith during the reign of King Kyongdok, who ruled from 742–765. Yet even this powerful king faced renewed pressure from members of the true-bone aristocracy who were determined to break the power of the throne and the power of the ruling families that had dominated it for a century by this stage. Kyongdok tried to appease his rivals; he introduced some political reforms based also on the Tang dynastic model. But this was to no avail, and rebellion broke out, which lasted on and off for the next 20 years until in the end the hereditary line of Silla's royal ruling family had been destroyed.

The immediate consequence of this was that with the authority of the throne now undermined, aristocratic families turned upon each other. In their competition for wealth and power, nobles assembled their own personal armies and also armed the slaves and the landless peasants who began to roam and menace the countryside almost at will. Records show that the Late Silla period was dominated by shifting alliances of aristocratic families who seized the throne, only to become the target for new rebellions and new revenge. Twenty kings ruled during this 150-year-long period of Silla decline, and every single reign was marked by instability and conflict.

As we noted earlier, in contrast to Tang government, the Silla version of the Confucian exam system had permitted only the sons of the aristocracy to vie for positions in the administration. Men of other ranks, no matter how well qualified, were excluded, which meant that capable intellectuals of the head-rank six social class, for example, were blocked from applying for positions of real political power in the Silla. Unrest grew amongst the intellectuals. It came to a head late in the ninth century after a Silla candidate, one Choe Chiwon, passed the very difficult Tang dynasty exam—remember the exam that only 30 men passed each year—and was appointed to an important administrative position in China. This leading intellectual Confucian scholar, highly respected in Tang China, later submitted detailed proposals to the Silla court for political reform, but he was ignored and rebuffed, and so he retired in disgust to the countryside. After this snub, head-rank six scholars began to actively work against the Silla government.

At the same time, the intense struggle between the aristocratic clans began to abate somewhat in the mid-ninth century as a number of these powerful families actually gave up their aspirations for the throne and began to focus on getting rich through trade instead. These families came to dominate the maritime shipping lanes of the region and established themselves at the center of a flourishing trade system that now connected Japan, Korea, and Tang China. This in turn led to outbreaks of piracy, and military garrisons were established at a number of strategic locations around the coast, particularly Wando Island, which is a major island just off the southwest coast of Korea, where garrisons were set up to combat the pirate fleets. The commandant of the Wando Island, one Jang Bogo, created a very powerful military force indeed—up to 10,000 men, we read—that controlled the coastal waters and put an end to Chinese piracy. Jang Bogo effectively became the master of the Yellow Sea, and he used his power to actively interfere in Silla political affairs by supporting particular allies in their attempts to become king and also trying to personally marry members of his family into the royal family. But by 846, Jang Bogo was dead, the victim of assassination.

Political rivalry flared up again late in the ninth century. Powerful families now abandoned the capital and set themselves up in a series of fortified compounds near the major population centers. They became known as the "castle lords," and they exercised authority over their own private armies, and also the regions and the peasants around their castles in a manner quite similar to the nobles who'd later operate in feudal Europe. Of course, this further weakened the central authority of the Silla kings; this made it impossible for them to collect taxes, for example. Peasants abandoned their farms in large numbers and wandered the land as rebels.

Large-scale peasant revolts broke out in 889, and the government forces found it very difficult to put down these huge peasant armies, particularly the Red Trousered Bandits, who seized control of the region southwest of the capital. Three powerful castle lords emerged to take control of competing rebel forces, setting in motion a three-cornered contest for mastery of the Korean peninsula. One castle lord, Kyonhwon, sacked the Silla capital in 927 and killed the king; but the other two, Wang Kon and Kungye, prevented him from toppling the Silla state. Kungye was later killed by his own people, which meant that there were now two powerful lords competing for control of the land. Wang Kon, who came from a noble family in the northern Kaesong region, considered himself to be a successor of the old Koguryo kingdom from the Three Kingdoms period, and he came up with a new name for the state he wanted to construct to replace Silla: the Koryo state. Wang Kon built strong alliances with other northern nobility and also shrewdly pursued a policy of friendship with the Silla king, partly to forge an alliance that would allow him to defeat his rival Kyonhwon.

In the end, the army of Wang Kon crushed the army of Kyonhwon in 934 C.E. At about the same stage, the same period, the Parhae kingdom in the north was defeated by militarized nomads who came in out of Manchuria, and members of the Parhae ruling class fled to the new state of Koryo where they received a warm welcome from Wang Kon. One year later, actually in 935 C.E., the last Silla king abdicated, allowing Wang Kon to quickly achieve complete reunification of the Korean peninsula under his rule, really for the first time in the history of Korea. Wang Kon was careful to placate the Silla aristocracy. He gave the former king the highest post in his new government; he personally married a woman of the Silla royal family. Wang Kon, who's now known today as King Taejo, now officially named this new era the Koryo dynasty.

The Koryo, which gave its name to the modern nation of Korea, would go on to rule for nearly 500 years. The Koryo and its epic conflict with the Mongols will be the subject of our next lecture, and this will be the last in this series of four on the history and culture of ancient Korea. See you shortly.

Korea—The Koryo
Lecture 26

As we saw in our last lecture, after the victory of Wang Kon over his rival Kyonhwon, the tide of battle turned in Koryo's favor, and in the year 935 C.E., the last king of Silla abdicated in favor of Wang Kon. At about the same time, the Parhae kingdom in the north was overrun by nomads, and Wang Kon welcomed the evicted Parhae nobility into his court, bringing about the complete unification of the Korean Peninsula under one government for the first time in its history. The Koryo would go on to rule unified Korea for the next 500 years. In this lecture, we'll look at the Koryo, its government, culture, society, and bitter struggle with the Mongols.

Consolidation of Koryo Power
- After the abdication of the last king of Silla, King Taejo (Wang Kon's posthumous reign name) attempted to unite the disparate nobles whose fragmentation had so blighted the late Silla period. He treated the Silla nobility with great generosity and invited many nobles into the Koryo bureaucracy. Despite these overtures, many of the regional castle lords maintained their independent status and rejected attempts by the Koryo government to control them.

- The king attempted to placate and control these lords by establishing marriage ties with more than 20 noble families and bestowing on them the royal family name. But by the time Taejo died from disease in 943, political consolidation was far from complete.

- In the end, it was the reforms of Kwangjong, the fourth king of the Koryo (r. 949–975), that finally consolidated Koryo central rule and crushed the power of the landed nobility. The elite military and political figures who had helped in the founding of the Koryo state were incensed by these reforms and resisted strongly. In response, Kwangjong instituted a brutal purge of dissenters. The opposition was crushed, and the Koryo were able to assert their royal authority over the entire peninsula.

Political Ideologies

- In the age of authoritarian rule that followed the purges, Confucianism became even more widely accepted as the best system to ensure ethical government. Confucian scholars provided the new political orthodoxy of the Koryo as they deepened their control of the state.

- At the same time that Confucianism was becoming more entrenched in government, a new trend in Buddhism was also gaining popularity: Son or Zen Buddhism, which emphasized enlightenment through meditation rather than the written word.

- Another intriguing ideology that emerged early in the Koryo period was a particular form of geomancy first introduced in Korea by a monk called Toson. Toson argued that the natural features of a land area influenced whether the family living in that area would enjoy prosperity or decay. Because of Toson's influence, it became critically important for Koryo families to select propitious sites for building, particularly for family dwellings and tombs.

- After King Kwangjong's death, many of his reforms lapsed, and Confucian scholars of the Silla's old head-rank six lineages became increasingly powerful. Members of this class detested strong central monarchy and were determined to create a genuine Confucian-style society that would control the political process.

- Rather than opposing this powerful group, King Songjong (r. 981–997) worked closely with the Confucian scholars and, by doing so, helped to reestablish the foundations for Koryo's social order.

Koryo Political Structures

- Aristocratic Koryo government was reorganized around three ministries, two responsible for making policy decisions and one for carrying out directives and handling day-to-day administration. The highest officials in the land met in joint sessions of the privy council, and a powerful censorate was installed to scrutinize officials for wrongdoing.

- The state of Koryo was initially divided into 12 provinces, but by 1018, the provincial system was more sophisticated. The entire country was divided into a capital region, several large circuits, and border regions. Administration of this complex structure was handled by a mix of local officials and powerful government ministers in the capital. To establish a pool of educated and ethical men for government service, Koryo established the Kukchagam, a national university, in 992.

- The Koryo administration also focused on land reform, articulating an underlying premise that all land in the country essentially belonged to the king. However, the government distinguished between public land (managed directly by the state) and private land (held by individuals and families, often in perpetuity), which meant in theory that the wealth of both the government and the aristocracy grew.

- In a social land structure very different from that pursued by Chinese dynasties, freeborn peasant farmers were not eligible to receive land allocations from the state but could farm public land if they paid 25 percent of their output in taxes. Farmers working on private land had to pay 50 percent of their yield to the noble families that "owned" the land. Below the freeborn farmers in this hierarchical society were low-born peasants, slaves, and outcasts.

Koryo Foreign Relations

- Before his death, the Koryo founder, Taejo, had sought to extend the northern borders into the territories that had once been controlled by the Koguryo kingdom. His successors continued this effort, establishing forts across the north and pushing toward the Yalu River.

- These efforts brought Koryo into conflict with the militarized Khitan nomads, the same people who had conquered the Parhae state. Koryo's other great northern foe was the Jurchen nomads, who dwelt further east in Manchuria. Weary of constant harassing attacks from these fierce nomadic peoples, the Koryo decided to build their own "Great Wall" across the northern frontier.

Official records state that more than 300,000 laborers were employed for 11 years to build Korea's "Great Wall," a massive rampart across the northern frontier.

- The Jurchen then entered into a trade relationship with the Koryo, supplying horses and furs for Koryo salt and iron weapons. But under new leadership, the Jurchen began raiding the Koryo again; their nomadic horsemen easily surmounted the wall and defeated the Koryo standing armies.

- The Koryo responded by creating a new military force—the Extraordinary Military Corps—which, in 1107, drove the Jurchen back to the steppes and built nine new forts in the northeast to contain them.

Koryo Cultural Achievements
- Throughout all these tribulations, the Koryo state remained committed to rule by ethical civilian officials, which meant that Confucianism was the orthodox philosophy of the Koryo. Because of the aristocratic nature of Koryo society, however, it was the sons of the aristocracy who were groomed to pass the Confucian exams and rule the state.

- The individual spiritual philosophy of Buddhism also thrived in elite circles. Koryo Buddhism was focused on using the technology of woodblock printing to create translations of the Buddhist canon. Buddhist temples and monasteries proliferated, and enormous state Buddhist festivals were held throughout the year.

- The crowning glory of Koryo artistic achievement was celadon ceramics. Koryo celadon was particularly notable for its gorgeous jade-green colors and for the variety of extraordinary shapes produced.

Cultural Disruption
- Inevitably, this refined, aristocratic world of privilege and aesthetic appreciation was severely disrupted, first by power struggles in the great hereditary houses and then by a revolt led by a Buddhist monk.
  - The third and most serious disruption came in 1170, when a military revolt broke out against high-handed civilian officials. After the massacre of countless government officials, the rule of the state passed into the hands of the military, but its attempt to govern through a supreme council quickly broke down, leaving political and social chaos in its wake.

  - A powerful general put an end to the chaos by establishing a personal dictatorship, leaving the Wang family on the throne but deposing any kings who would not obey him.

  - Then peasant revolts broke out across the country, the worst in 1193, when 7,000 rebels were slaughtered in battle with the military, and again in 1198, when the entire slave population of the capital was in turmoil.

- In the midst of this chaos, with the foundations of Koryo society having been shaken to the core, the Mongols appeared! The Mongols were pastoral nomadic peoples who dwelt in the steppes of Central Asia. In the early 13th century, under the leader Chinggis Khan, they began a series of expansionary campaigns into China and much of Inner Asia.

- The first contact between Mongols and Koryo took place when they formed an alliance to destroy a Khitan army that had crossed the Yalu to escape the Mongols. The Mongols then demanded tribute from Koryo, but the Koreans refused, and after a Mongol envoy was killed returning from Koryo in 1225, the Mongols prepared to invade.

- In 1231, the Mongols overcame stubborn Koryo resistance and pressed toward the capital. When the Koryo sued for peace, the Mongols left military commanders in charge and agreed to withdraw their troops. But a Koryo military dictator then decided to resist the Mongols; he withdrew his forces and government to Kanghwa Island in 1232 to exploit the Mongols' only real weakness: an irrational fear of the sea.

- Frustrated, the Mongols instituted a scorched-earth policy on the mainland, burning the grain fields and capturing mountain fortresses. In one invasion alone in 1254, the Mongols took 200,000 captives, left countless dead, and reduced huge areas of Korea to ashes.

- Over the next decade, peace overtures to the Mongols were gradually accepted. The Mongols, who in the meantime had subdued China and declared the Yuan dynasty in 1271, then sought Koryo assistance for their attempted invasions of Japan.

- The Mongol rulers of China, who respected the resistance of the Koryo military, placed some regions of Korea under their direct control but left others under the rule of Koryo officials. But Mongol levies of gold, silver, cloth, grain, falcons, and young women devastated a nation already weakened by 30 years of resistance.

- In the mid-14th century, the tide turned against the Mongols. As the Ming dynasty arose in China and began to drive the Mongols back to the steppes, the Koryo king Kongmin decided to oppose the Mongols and to destroy the power of the families who had worked with them.

- The last years of the Koryo were chaotic. The king was assassinated, peasant revolts broke out again, and Japanese pirates raided the Koryo coast at will. In 1392, the last Koryo king was overthrown, and the Choson dynasty was established. The Choson would rule Korea down to 1910, when Korea was annexed by the rising power of Japan.

Suggested Reading

Eckert et al., *Korea Old and New*, chapter 1.

Lee, *A New History of Korea*, chapters 5–6.

Questions to Consider

1. What was the philosophy of geomancy, and why did it become so widespread in Korea during the Koryo period?

2. What were some of the most significant political and cultural achievements during the mature period of the Koryo, and how do these still resonate in Korean society today?

Korea—The Koryo
Lecture 26—Transcript

As we saw in our last lecture, after the victory of Wang Kon over the forces of his rival Kyonhwon, the tide of battle turned in Koryo's favor, and in 935 C.E. the last king of Silla abdicated in favor of Wang Kon. At about the same time, the Parhae kingdom in the north was overrun by nomads and Wang Kon welcomed the evicted Parhae nobility into his court. This not only gave Wang Kon and his forces complete victory over all rivals, but also allowed for the complete unification of the Korean peninsula under one government for the first time in its history.

The Koryo would go on to rule unified Korea for the next 500 years, and it's remembered today as one of the most important and successful of all Korea's dynasties. The Koryo, its government, culture, society, and bitter struggle with the Mongols are the subject of this lecture, the last in this series of four on the history and culture of ancient Korea.

King Taejo, which is Wang Kon's posthumous reign name, now attempted to unite the disparate nobles whose fragmentation had so blighted the Late Silla period. First, he paid due homage to his predecessors the Silla by treating the Silla nobility with great generosity and by taking as his queen a woman from the Silla royal house. He also invited many Silla nobles into the Koryo bureaucracy, establishing a tradition of continuity amongst the ancient and elite Korean clan families that would continue, despite changes in the ruling house, to resonate in Korean politics right through to the 20th century, as we'll see. But despite these overtures, many of the regional castle lords continued to maintain their independent status in the countryside and rejected attempts by the Koryo government to control them. Even many members of the nobility who'd actually supported Taejo in his campaigns of conquest refused to give up their private armies. The king attempted to placate and control them by establishing marriage ties with more than 20 noble families, and even by bestowing the royal family name on some of these lords; but by the time Taejo died from some sort of disease in 943, political consolidation was far from complete.

In the end, it was the reforms of Kwangjong, the fourth king of the Koryo—one of Taejo's sons, who ruled from 949–975—which finally consolidated Koryo central rule and crushed the power, at least for a while, of the landed nobility. He did this in a series of thoughtful, related steps. First, he enacted a Slave Review Act that was designed to restore to freedom many of the peasants who'd been enslaved during the Later Three Kingdoms period. He knew this would be resented by the nobles, because by depriving them of their slaves it reduced their economic and military power. Next, the king attempted to put in place a genuine Confucian civil service exam system that was open to men of intelligence and ability, not just to the sons of the nobility. These elite military and political figures who'd helped in the founding of the Koryo state were obviously incensed by these reforms and resisted strongly. In response, King Kwangjong instituted a brutal purge of the dissenters. He spared no one, even imprisoning or executing those military commanders who'd fought side by side with his father to help found the Koryo dynasty. As a result of these steps, opposition was crushed and the Koryo were able to assert their royal authority over the entire peninsula.

In the age of authoritarian strong central rule that followed the purges, Confucianism became even more widely accepted as the best system to ensure good ethical government. It was Confucian scholars who now provided the new political orthodoxy of the Koryo as they deepened their control of the state. Interestingly, at the same time that Confucianism was becoming more entrenched in government, a new trend in Buddhism was also becoming increasingly popular, Son—or you'll know it better by its Japanese name Zen Buddhism—which emphasized enlightenment through meditation rather than the written word. Son was particularly well received by the landed gentry, and the monks of the so-called Nine Mountain Sects of Son gained wide respect amongst the government and other elites.

Another intriguing ideology that emerged early in the Koryo period was a particular form of geomancy, first introduced into Korea by a monk called Toson. Toson began to argue that the natural features of a land area—essentially the geographical and environmental configuration of a particular place, a particular property—influenced whether the family living in that area would enjoy prosperity or decay. These arguments were, of course, very similar to the Chinese principles of feng shui, which had first emerged in the pre-dynastic cultures of China's history, and were eventually codified under the Zhou. All the Chinese capitals followed rules of feng shui for their design and location, which meant trying to orient the buildings in the most propitious manner to achieve the best spiritual balance with nature and the cosmos. Because of Toson's influence, it soon became critically important for Koryo families to also select a propitious site for a building, particularly for a family dwelling or a family tomb. At the same time, inauspicious sites could be improved by placing a temple right on top of them. Toson is reported to have wandered all over Korea assessing topographical features as auspicious or inauspicious, gaining widespread influence amongst the elite families of Koryo.

After King Kwangjong's death, many of his reforms lapsed, and Confucian scholars of the Silla's old head-rank six lineages became increasingly powerful. Members of this class detested strong central monarchy and were determined instead to create a genuine Confucian-style society that would control the political process. Rather than opposing this powerful group, King Songjong, who ruled from 981–997, decided to work closely with the Confucian scholars, and by doing this he helped reestablish the foundations for Koryo's social order. The elite lineages now used marriage to expand the power of their families, gaining greater political influence by bringing two already powerful families together. The two most exalted lineages during this period were the Ansan Kim and Inju Yi families, who between them managed to control the throne for the next 130 years. All the powerful families now lived in the Koryo capital at Kaesong, constructing their palaces according to the principles of geomancy, and dwelling in opulent splendor in a city of broad streets and great buildings, full of monasteries, temples, and mansions.

Aristocratic Koryo government was reorganized now around three specific ministries. Two of these were responsible for making high policy decisions, while the other, the so-called "Secretariat for State Affairs," carried out these policy directives and handled day to day administration. The highest officials in the land met in joint sessions of the Privy Council—is there an echo here, by the way, of those ancient gatherings of elite families from the Neolithic past in Korea?—and a powerful censorate was also installed now to scrutinize officials for any wrongdoing, and this became a strong disincentive against corrupt behavior.

In terms of provincial administration, the state of Koryo was in the beginning divided into 12 provinces, and officials were dispatched from the capital to administer each of them. But by 1018, the provincial system became even more sophisticated, similar to some of the extraordinarily complex provincial systems we've seen installed by various Chinese dynasties like the Han and the Tang. The entire country was now divided into a capital region, several large provincial circuits, and also border regions. Four capital cities and five regional military commands were established to rule eight provinces, which were further subdivided into districts, counties, and garrisons.

Needless to say, administration of this complex state structure was handled by a mix of local officials and powerful government ministers in the capital; and as all the Chinese dynasties had realized, effective administration required the ongoing availability of a pool of educated and ethical men. To help achieve this, Koryo established the Kukchagam national university in 992, which was organized very much like a modern university, very much like my university. It was divided into a number of different colleges; each college specialized in different subjects and disciplines. The colleges focused on the sources of Chinese tradition, another on law, the art of calligraphy, a college of medicine, a college of accounting. King Songjong was particularly focused on spreading education throughout his country, and he brought young men from local areas to study at the university. During the reign of Injong, between 1122 and 1146, state schools were set up in rural areas to educate local youth.

The Koryo administration also focused on land reform during this period, and articulated an underlying and actually quite startling premise I think that all land in the country essentially belonged to the king. The government did, however, distinguish between public land that would be managed directly by the state and private land that would be held by individuals and families, often in perpetuity. This meant in theory that the wealth of both the government and the landowning aristocracy grew. But in a social land structure very different to that pursued by Chinese dynasties, freeborn peasant farmers weren't eligible to receive land allocations from the state;

so there's no equal field system in Koryo Korea. Instead, freeborn farmers could farm public land if they paid 25 percent of their output in taxes to the government. Frankly, farmers working on private land were much worse off because they had to pay 50 percent of their yield to the noble families that owned the land in perpetuity.

Below the freeborn farmers in this rigidly hierarchical society—much more so than in contemporary China—were the lowborn peasants who had to live in special districts and do whatever work was assigned to them: farm labor, mining, producing silk, or making paper. At the very bottom of the heap—almost the very bottom of the heap—were the slaves. Government-owned slaves performed duties in the palace and government buildings, of course; privately-owned slaves did whatever duties were assigned to them by members of the aristocratic families. Slave status was hereditary, and slaves could certainly be bought and sold. There was even an outcast group something like the untouchables in India made up of butchers, wicker workers, and female entertainers and comfort women known as the *kaiseng*, all of whom were despised by the freeborn population and whose status was almost worse than that of the slaves.

Turning from Koryo ideas about government and social structure to foreign relations: Even before his death, the found of the Koryo King Taejo had sought to extend the northern borders deep into the ancient territories that had once been controlled by the Koguryo kingdom. His successors continued this effort, establishing garrison forts across the north and pushing towards the Yalu River. This brought Koryo into conflict with a group of militarized nomads, the Khitan nomads. This was the same people who'd conquered the Parhae state, as we discussed in our last lecture. In the winter of 1010, we read in the Koryo annals that a Khitan army of 400,000 troops crossed the frozen Yalu River and drove south for the Koryo capital, which they sacked and pillaged. Eventually, with their supply lines stretched thin, the Khitan were forced to fight a bloody retreat back to the Yalu, at the cost of perhaps 40,000 men.

Koryo's other great northern foe was the Jurchen nomads, who dwelt further east again in Manchuria. Sick and tired of this constant harassment, these fierce attacks, from these well-armed nomadic peoples, archer-warriors, the

Koryo decided to build their own "Great Wall" clear across the northern frontier. The official records tell us that over 300,000 laborers were employed for 11 years between 1033 and 1044 to build this massive rampart, which was obviously modeled on China's Great Northern Wall. The rampart linked 14 walled towns in a line that stretched northwards from the mouth of the Yalu, through the mountains near the headwaters of the Chongchon and Taedong rivers, all the way out to the east coast. With the wall in place, the Jurchen decided to enter into a trade relationship with the Koryo, at least for a while, supplying horses and furs from the steppes in exchange for Koryo salt and iron weapons. But under new leadership, the Jurchen again began raiding the Koryo, and their nomadic horsemen easily found a way over or around the wall and defeated several Koryo standing armies. This time the Koryo responded by creating a new elite military force—it was called the "Extraordinary Military Corps"—which in 1107 drove the Jurchen back to the steppes and then built nine new forts in the northeast to try and keep them out; to try and contain them.

As we'll see later in the course, while all this was going on, China was under the control of the powerful Song dynasty; but by 1125, the Jurchen, the same nomads, succeeded in defeating first the Khitan and then the Song themselves, capturing the northern Chinese capital at Kaifeng. The Song were forced to retreat south, and China was divided again between the Jurchen-controlled north and the Southern Song, who ruled all of southern China now from a border roughly halfway between the Huang He and the Yangtze; but again, more about that in a later lecture.

Throughout all these tribulations, the Koryo state remained committed to rule by ethical civilian officials, which meant that Confucianism was the orthodox philosophy of the Koryo; although because of the aristocratic nature of Koryo society, it was essentially the sons of the aristocracy that were mostly groomed to pass the Confucian exams and to rule the state. But, as well as this somewhat modified form of collective Confucianism, the individual spiritual philosophy of Buddhism continued to thrive within elite circles. Koryo Buddhism was focused on using the technology of woodblock printing to create vast woodblock translations of the Buddhist canon. The first massive carving of the *Tripitaka*, a major collection of Buddhist scriptures, was undertaken in 1087 as a sort of ritual observance seeking the Buddha's assistance against the Khitan threat. This was destroyed by the Mongols, and a new version, the famous *Tripitaka Koreana* that can still be seen today at the Haein-sa Temple, was completed in 1251.

This amazing woodblock is renowned for the accuracy of the translation; indeed, it's regarded as the most accurate translation of core Buddhist texts in the world today, also of treatises and laws ever made. But also it's renowned for the beauty of the exquisite carving in wood of the Chinese characters in which this text is translated. The blocks are made of a birch wood that was specially treated to prevent them from decaying. These blocks were soaked in sea water for three years, then they were cut into the Chinese characters, then boiled in saltwater, then exposed to the wind for three years, after which they were finally ready to be carved properly. After each block was superbly carved, it was painted in a poisonous lacquer to keep the insects away, and then each block was framed with metal to prevent warping.

As this sort of extraordinary care indicates, Buddhism was integral to everyday life in Koryo and was the major force shaping its cultural achievements. Temples now proliferated—there were as many as 70 Buddhist temples in the capital city alone—and enormous state Buddhist festivals were held throughout the year; one, we read about a vegetarian feast prepared for 100,000 monks. As well as temples, Buddhist monasteries proliferated throughout the land; and because they were tax exempt, the Buddhist establishment became increasingly wealthy and powerful.

The crowning glory of Koryo artistic achievement was a particular type of ceramics called celadon. This technique developed under Chinese Song dynasty influence, but even the Chinese came to acknowledge in the end that Koryo celadon was the world's finest example of ceramic art. Koryo celadon was particularly notable for its gorgeous jade-green colors, and also for the variety of beautiful shapes: cups, jars, and wine pitchers of course; but also water droppers, delicate teapots engraved with flowers, along with an amazing range of animal figures. The distinctive decorative elements of Koryo celadon were created by overlaying different glazes on contrasting types of clay bodies. In one particular design, the Sanggam design, small pieces of different colored clays were inlaid into the base clay, and when these layers were later carved away they revealed a range of varying, beautiful colors. So extraordinary was Koryo celadon that modern potters with modern materials and modern tools struggle to recreate the complex Koryo celadon techniques to this day. I hope you get a chance to see Koryo celadon; you'll find them in most of the great art museums of the United States and indeed the world.

Inevitably, this refined aristocratic world of privilege and the aesthetic appreciation for Buddhism, art, and culture was severely disrupted. The first disruption came as the balance of power between the great hereditary houses was broken through the ambition of certain families. In 1122, a leader of the Yi lineage had become so powerful, so ambitious, that he desired the crown. He imprisoned the king and was about to assume the throne himself when he was driven into exile. The next disturbance was led by a Buddhist monk, who in 1136 raised an army against the king; but this revolt, too, was suppressed. The third and most serious disruption came from the military, which had traditionally been looked down upon by the Koryo; we'll see something very similar, by the way, in early medieval Japan. Officers who'd served the state well in defending it against the Khitan and Jurchen nomads were poorly rewarded; common soldiers were viewed as menial servants. In the year 1170, a military revolt broke out against the high-handed civilian officials. The cry of soldiers and officers alike became: "Death to all who wear the civil official headdress!"

After the massacre of countless government officials, the rule of the state passed into the hands of the military; but its attempt to govern through a supreme council quickly broke down, leaving political and social chaos in its wake. A powerful general put an end to the chaos by establishing a personal dictatorship and by leaving the ruling Wang family on the throne, but deposing any kings who wouldn't obey him. But peasant revolts broke out across the country, the worst in 1193 when 7,000 rebels were slaughtered in battle with the military; and again in 1198, when the entire slave population of the capital was in turmoil. In the midst of all this chaos, with the foundations of Koryo society having been shaken to the core, the Mongols turned up.

The Mongols had such an impact on Eastern civilization that we'll be devoting two complete lectures to them later in the course. All we need to say here, I think, is that the Mongols were another group of pastoral nomadic peoples who dwelt in the steppes of Central Asia, part of this great heritage of militarized nomads we've considered so many times in this course already, like the mighty Xiongnu, the Yuezhi, the Scythians, and the Jurchen. In the early 13th century, under their quite extraordinary charismatic leader Chinggis Khan, the Mongols began a series of expansionary campaigns into China and indeed much of Inner Asia. The first contact between Mongols and the Koryo took place when they formed an alliance together to destroy a Khitan army that had crossed the Yalu River to escape the Mongols. The Mongols then demanded tribute from Koryo but the Koreans refused, and after a Mongol envoy was killed returning from Koryo in 1225, the Mongols prepared to invade. In 1231, the Mongols overcame stubborn Koryo resistance and pressed on towards the capital. At that point, the Koryo sued for peace, so the Mongols left military commanders in charge and agreed to withdraw their troops.

But a Koryo military dictator then decided to resist the Mongols and came up with the idea of withdrawing his forces and the government to Kanghwa Island in 1232 to exploit the Mongols' only real weakness, which is a somewhat irrational fear of the sea. Because of this fear of the sea and the fear of crossing the sea, the Mongols could only glare across the strip of ocean that separated the mainland from the island, where the ruling class continued to govern and to enjoy luxurious lives based on the grain tax revenues that were now being shipped from the peasant farmers of the mainland to the island by boat. Frustrated, the Mongols instituted a scorched earth policy on the mainland. They burnt the grain fields; they captured the mountain fortresses, the defenders of which were then massacred. In one invasion alone in 1254, the Mongols took back with them 200,000 captives, they left countless dead, and they reduced huge areas of Koryo Korea to ashes.

The peasants lost heart, of course, for resistance with all this. As this happened, the government tried to seek divine assistance by having that magnificent Koryo *Tripitaka* that we just discussed carved; and for the next decade, peace overtures to the Mongols were gradually accepted. The Mongols, who in the meantime had subdued all of China and declared the Yuan dynasty in 1271—events we'll, of course, be pursuing later in the course—then sought Koryo assistance for their attempted invasion of Japan. As we'll also see in a later lecture, both attempts failed because of the intervention of fierce storms, of mighty winds that blew up; winds the Japanese later called the *kamikaze*, the "divine winds."

The Mongol rulers of China, who actually grudgingly respected the resistance of the Koryo military, placed some regions of Korea under their direct control but left many other regions under the rule of Koryo officials. But regular Mongol levies of gold, silver, cloth, grain, falcons, and also of young women devastated a nation already weakened at this stage by 30 years of resistance. Naturally, these burdens fell most heavily on the peasants, who had to meet the Mongol levies plus the taxes still being demanded by their own government. At the same time, many leading Koryo families began to work closely with the Mongols for their mutual enrichment.

But all this changed in the mid-14th century when the tide started to turn all across Eurasia against the Mongols. In China, as the mighty Ming dynasty arose and began to drive the Mongols back to the steppes, so a new Koryo king Kongmin decided to oppose the Mongols also and to destroy the power of the families who'd worked with them. When the Ming dynasty was declared in 1368, Kongmin adopted a pro-Ming policy and appointed a monk, Sin Ton, as his Prime Minister. Together, they worked to oust officials from the powerful families and to redistribute some land to the peasants.

The last years of the Koryo were chaotic. The king was assassinated, peasant revolts broke out again, and Japanese pirates raided the Koryo coast at will, devastating trade and the villages. The upshot of all this was the overthrow of the last Koryo king and the establishment of the next great dynasty of Korean history, the Choson, which, as we'll see in a later lecture, would rule Korea for 512 years, from 1392 until August 22, 1910, when Korea was annexed by the rising power of Japan.

Next time (my segue there), we're going to turn our focus towards Japan, and in a series of four lectures we're going to trace the emergence of Japanese civilization from its mysterious beginnings through to their transformation into a feudal society late in the 12th century. But we haven't finished with our consideration of the Korean contribution to Eastern civilization; a contribution based on a beautiful environment that bestowed the name "land of morning calm" on the first dynasty. But as we've seen, I think, despite a dedication of rich and poor alike to Buddhism and the production of magnificent architecture, woodblock carvings, and delicate celadon pottery, the history of Korea from the bloody Three Kingdoms period through the Silla and Koryo dynasties was anything but calm.

Next time, folks, we're heading to ancient Japan; I'll see you then.

Japan—Geography and Early Cultures
Lecture 27

In the next four lectures, we will discuss early Japanese culture and history, beginning with the environmental context in which Paleolithic humans first settled the islands, then moving through the Neolithic, Yamatai, Nara, and Heian periods, up to the transformation of Japan from an imperial to a feudal society late in the 12th century. We will explore the interplay of local and imported cultural influences in early Japanese societies. As was the case with Korea, Japanese culture was deeply influenced by Chinese cultural prototypes, but Japan, too, became much more than just a carbon copy of China. Instead, sealed off from the East Asian mainland by geographical barriers, the inhabitants of the Japanese archipelago developed their own unique traditions.

Geography and Climate of Japan

- Modern Japan consists of four large islands (from north to south, Hokkaido, Honshu, Shikoku, and Kyushu) and hundreds of smaller ones. This archipelago is some 1,500 miles long, and stretches from the cool northern latitudes off the coast of Russia to warmer southern latitudes off the coast of South Korea.

- The climate varies considerably throughout the archipelago, but most of the major cities, including Tokyo, have climates ranging from temperate to subtropical, with four distinct seasons.

- The fact that the many islands of Japan are separated from the mainland by several hundred miles of sea water has fostered a sense of security and isolation that helps explain the emergence of a distinct Japanese culture. This isolation also helps explain why, unlike Korea, the Chinese never invaded Japan and why the Mongols were unsuccessful in their invasions.

- Japan is actually part of a huge chain of islands located along the northwest edge of the Pacific that stretches from the Aleutian

Islands in the north to the Philippines in the south. This extensive island chain is the product of, and still heavily influenced by, tectonic forces.

- o Because Japan sits at the intersection of four tectonic plates, it has undergone regular and violent geological shaping and upheaval.

- o Most of Japan consists of geologically young mountains, driven up by plate collisions. These mountains are steep, jagged, and rugged, producing fast-moving streams and regular landslides.

- o The tectonic forces have also produced volcanoes, the highest and most famous of which is Mount Fuji at 12,388 feet.

Japan's steep, rugged mountains are the result of its location at the intersection of four tectonic plates.

- These rugged and unstable mountain ranges are unsuitable for farming, limit settlement patterns, and are difficult to climb or cross. They have been serious barriers for internal transportation and communication from the beginning of Japanese history. This situation, in turn, led to the emergence of regionally autonomous states in early Japanese history and to an increased reliance on water transport systems.

- The sediment regularly washed from the mountains joins with rich volcanic soil to create narrow but fertile coastal plains. These plains are where the first farmers settled and where the first towns and cities were built.

- Japan's location between the great mainland continent of Asia and the Pacific also creates a distinctive and challenging weather environment, with large quantities of snow in some areas in the winter and high temperatures and torrential rains in the summer. These wind and weather systems powerfully influenced settlement patterns.

- The combination of plentiful fresh water and a long growing season created a paradise for plants and herbivores in some regions. These conditions also meant that when foraging humans first arrived on the archipelago, they found a rich variety of potential foodstuffs awaiting them.

The Paleolithic Era in Japan

- The archipelago was linked to the mainland by land bridges during long periods of the geological past, and across these land bridges, the first human migrants came to Japan, beginning at least 35,000 years ago. The Paleolithic lifeways these early communities pursued mark the beginning of the development of Japanese history and culture.

- Two Japanese archaeological sites—Hoshino and Sozudai—have yielded the oldest manufactured implements found, including choppers, picks, and basic hand axes. Dating of volcanic ash and other materials found at the sites indicates that they were occupied perhaps 400,000 to 200,000 years ago.

- A much more recent Japanese site is Zazaragi, which has yielded stone tools that have been dated to roughly 40,000 years ago; these stone points and scrapers must have been manufactured by modern humans.

- These dates for the colonization of Japan correspond with key developments during the last ice age.
  - As we discussed earlier, conditions across East Asia at the height of the last ice age were bitterly cold, and sea levels were much lower. The Yellow Sea was a dry plain, and even

the Sea of Japan was just a large lake that drained through the present Korea Strait. These larger areas of dry land facilitated the movement of plants, animals, and humans between parts of East Asia that are now underwater.

○ The arrival of humans perhaps 35,000 years ago in what is now the Japanese archipelago probably corresponded to the migrations of megafauna.

• Hanaizumi, at the northern tip of Honshu Island, is one of the few sites to provide us with a glimpse of Paleolithic lifeways. Stone and bone tools, along with animal bones found here, have led researchers to believe that it was probably a kill site or bone dump, rather than a residential camp.

• Archaeologists divide the Late Paleolithic era in Japan (beginning 30,000 years ago) into four phases, each characterized by different stone technologies. In phase I, humans used long flakes for tools; in phase II, true blades; in phase III (after 17,000 B.P.), microblades; and in phase IV, arrowheads and spearheads.

• It is also during the Late Paleolithic that we start to find evidence of humans using art as a form of self and communal expression. Stones shaped like humans have been found in Japan dating to the Late Paleolithic, and at the Iwato site, a face sculpture pecked into the hilt of a stone tool was found, dated to somewhere between 20,000 and 10,000 years ago.

The Jomon Era

• At the very end of the Paleolithic, human communities in Japan began to make some of the world's earliest known ceramics, the so-called Jomon pottery, which gave rise to a new era in Japanese history, called the Jomon era.

○ Initial evidence of this extraordinary pottery came from the Fukui and Kamikuroiwa cave sites, where pottery shards dating to around 12,000 years ago were discovered. More recent discoveries have pushed these dates back by another 2,000 years.

- As was the case with new ceramic developments in Korea, archaeologists are uncertain whether this technological innovation was indigenous or influenced by new arrivals from northeast Asia.

- The appearance of this pottery might also be linked to global climate change, specifically, the availability of more plentiful foodstuffs at the end of the last ice age. Humans invented new technologies and strategies to exploit these resources, including arrows, pit traps, fishing hooks and nets with sinkers, harpoons, and canoes; of course, they needed pottery vessels to store and carry food.

- Although the term "Jomon culture" is used to describe most of the 10,000 years that preceded the B.C.E./C.E. divide, because of environmental differences, Japanese Neolithic lifeways were far from uniform. Even the pottery shows considerable variation, and considerable trading of pottery and other valuable objects took place within and between individual islands.

- Although the original impetus for this technological innovation was probably the need for vessels to store foods, many of the more elaborate pieces of Jomon pottery appear to have been manufactured for use in religious or shamanistic rituals, probably related to fertility and seasonal regeneration, as well as human reproduction. Once agriculture was introduced and communities became dependent on successful harvests, the earlier interest in the magical qualities of seasonal regeneration and human reproduction became even more important.

- With so many resources available to these "affluent foragers," there was no rush to adopt farming; it was eventually forced on sedentary foraging communities through population increases.
  - By the late Jomon period (from roughly 5000 B.C.E.), evidence of agriculture begins to appear in the archaeological record in the form of farming tools and the remains of major grain crops found in ancient pottery.

- o From around the same period, we also have evidence that full-scale villages were starting to appear, consisting mostly of pit dwellings with roofs made of wood, thatch, or earth.

- o All these processes of lifeway and technological evolution led to periods of enhanced cultural activity, particularly in central Honshu, after 3000 B.C.E.

The Yayoi Culture

- During the 1st millennium B.C.E., strikingly new technologies begin to appear in the Japanese archaeological record: new pottery, technologies, and lifeways known collectively today as the Yayoi culture.

- The Yayoi people are associated with complex technologies, such as bronze and iron metallurgy; glassmaking; weaving; and advanced agricultural techniques, including horticulture, slash-and-burn, and wet-rice farming.

- The transition from Jomon to Yayoi was gradual but nonetheless dramatic. It has been described by archaeologist Gina Barnes as "not just a change in subsistence pattern but an entire restructuring of the material economy of the Japanese islands."

- Most Yayoi evidence comes from Kyushu and corresponds to similar complex changes that were occurring in the Korean Peninsula at the same time; the direction of cultural influence is from Korea to Japan.

- Excavations in western Japan have suggested that the Jomon and Yayoi people were, in fact, two distinctly different groups of humans. Jomon people were shorter, more robust, and round-faced; Yayoi were taller, gracile, and long-faced—strong evidence that the Yayoi people were most probably immigrants from Korea.

- The Yayoi brought with them new pottery styles and wet-rice agriculture, which led to a population boom on the plains of northern

Kyushu. Both the Yayoi people and their lifeways then expanded explosively throughout the western lowlands of the archipelago.

- As far as we can tell, there was little conflict between the Yayoi newcomers and the Jomon people, who seem to have been receptive to new ideas about farming. The one area of resistance to Yayoi agriculture appears to have been in the northeast of the country, where Jomon peoples retained their commitment to a marine-based lifeway.

- Rice farming spread through the rest of the islands in two stages: through Honshu by around 100 B.C.E. and throughout the rest of the islands by 700 C.E., bringing with it new tools, architectural styles, and cultural ideas.

- With the advent of full-blown agriculture, more complex technologies, larger villages, and metallurgy, Japanese culture had clearly entered a new stage, one that would be marked by the emergence of surpluses, social complexity, elites, and powerful individuals, such as chiefs.

Suggested Reading

Barnes, *China, Korea and Japan.*

Pearson, *Ancient Japan.*

Questions to Consider

1. What are some of the advantages and disadvantages of Japan's geographical isolation as an island state?

2. What is the meaning of the use of Jomon pottery, arguably the first pottery ever produced in world history?

Japan—Geography and Early Cultures
Lecture 27—Transcript

Hello everyone, and welcome to this first lecture in our course on the *Foundations of Eastern Civilization* that's focused on the island nation of Japan. I plan to spend the next four lectures talking about early Japanese culture and history, beginning with the environmental context in which Paleolithic humans first settled the islands, then taking us through the Neolithic, the Yamatai, the Nara and the Heian Periods, up to the moment of transformation of Japan from an imperial to a feudal society late in the 12th century. The major theme that we'll continue to explore in this series of four lectures is the degree to which early Japanese societies were able to balance the interplay of local and imported cultural influences. What I think we'll see here again I think is, just as was the case with Korea, Japanese culture was undoubtedly deeply influenced by Chinese cultural prototypes and was particularly welcoming to Tang dynasty civilization.

But again, like Korea, Japanese society and culture became much more than just a carbon copy of China. Instead, sealed off from the East Asian mainland by geographical barriers, the inhabitants of the Japanese archipelago were able to develop their own unique traditions. This reminds us, of course, of another central theme that's been running right through our course: the role of the environment in shaping society and culture. You've already heard me say this several times by now, so I might as well say it again in the Japanese context: There's only one place to start an investigation of the history and culture of Japan, and that's with the environmental context in which it flourished.

Let's take a look now at the rich and challenging geography of the island nation called Japan today. Modern Japan consists of four large islands—from north to south, Hokkaido, Honshu, Shikoku, and Kyushu—and hundreds, actually thousands, of smaller ones. This archipelago of islands is some 1,500 miles long and stretches from cool northern latitudes off the coast of Russia (latitudes equivalent to Montreal in Canada) to warmer southern latitudes off the coast of South Korea (on more or less the same parallel as the Bahamas). As you'd imagine, due to this long north-south extension of the country, the climate varies considerably throughout the archipelago. But most of the major cities, including Tokyo, have climates ranging from temperate to subtropical, and each has four distinct seasons. The thousands of islands that make up Japan have a combined area of roughly 146,000 square miles, which means it's just a little larger than Italy and a little smaller than California.

Because these many islands of Japan are separated from the mainland by several hundred miles of seawater—although actually only about 120 miles at the closest point—this has fostered a sense of security, even isolation, which helps explain the emergence of a distinct Japanese culture. This isolation also helps explain why, unlike Korea, the Chinese never invaded Japan, and also why the Mongols were unsuccessful in their two attempts at invasion. But although this freedom from invasion has contributed to the distinctiveness of Japanese culture, Japan has never really been isolated from the influence of powerful neighboring cultures.

If you'll allow me to take a big picture geographical perspective for a moment, the geographical chain of islands to which Japan belongs is much more extensive than just the Japanese archipelago. Japan is part of the same huge chain located along the northwestern edge of the Pacific that stretches all the way from the Aleutian Islands in the north to the Philippines in the far south. All these islands share lifeways that are inevitably dependent on the ocean for food, for transport, and for defense; but they also share something else, something geological, and something actually very dangerous. This extensive island chain is the product of, and of course still heavily influenced by, the tectonic forces that shape the surface of the earth. Geologists have understood the principles of plate tectonics for only about 50 years now, and they're constantly learning more all the time about this the great paradigm of earth science. We do know that heat in the center of the earth is constantly melting sections of the planet's mantle, moving it upwards on internal convection currents. In other places, cooler, denser slabs of lithosphere—that is, oceanic crust; the crust found mostly underneath the oceans—are being dragged back down into the mantle. It's these thermal movements that cause the great crustal plates of the earth's surface to move, generating earthquakes, volcanic activity, and mountain building.

The internal heat deep inside our planet that drives great continents across the surface of the planet comes from a combination of different forces. It comes from the meteoric collisions that pounded the surface of the early earth during the Hadean eon; it comes from radioactivity; and it comes from pressure caused by the forces of accretion and gravity that were active when our planet was being formed. If you think about this for a moment, the heat inside our planet that drives plate movements and causes places like Japan to suffer devastating earthquakes is actually a result of the way stars and solar systems are formed, and of the effects of gravity on these objects. In other words, the heat that created the environmental niche in which the future nation of Japan would flourish is a direct product of the origin and evolution of the entire universe, starting with the Big Bang. How's that for a big history perspective?

Japan sits at the intersection of no less than four different tectonic plates, so has undergone regular violent geological shaping and upheaval. The devastating earthquake we all remember of 2011, which generated that massive tsunami and nearly triggered a nuclear catastrophe, was just one of up to 1,000 earthquakes that rattle Japan every single year. Another product of Japan's tectonic location is that most of the country consists of geologically young mountains driven up by these same plate collisions. These mountains aren't old and eroded, but steep, jagged, and very rugged; they produce fast-moving streams and regular landslides. The tectonic forces have also produced volcanoes, the highest and most famous of which is Mount Fuji, of course, at 12,388 feet above sea level. These rugged and unstable mountain ranges are unsuitable for farming, they obviously limit settlement patterns, and they're very difficult to climb or cross, so have been serious barriers for internal transportation and communication from the beginning of Japanese history.

This geological context in turn led to the emergence of regionally autonomous, even isolated, states early in Japanese history, and, of course, to an increased reliance on water transport systems. The sediment that's regularly being washed from these young mountains joins with rich volcanic soil to create narrow but very fertile coastal plains. Although these plains make up only about 13 percent of Japan's total area, the fertility of these plains has meant that here's where the first farmers settled; here's where the first towns and eventually cities were built. One of the most important of these plains in early Japanese history is the Tsukushi Plain in northern Kyushu; this is the southernmost of Japan's four major islands. Because this is close to Korea and China, the region became an early center of emerging Japanese culture, and as we'll see was strongly influenced by the more sophisticated culture of the neighbors.

Japan's location between the great mainland continent of Asia and the wide Pacific Ocean also creates a distinctive and quite challenging weather environment. In winter, cold winds blow out of Asia and dump large quantities of snow on the mountain ranges of Japan, although the Pacific coast remains relatively mild and dry. But in the summer, warm moist air blows in from the south, bringing high temperatures and often torrential monsoonal-type rains. These wind and weather systems have also powerfully influenced settlement patterns in Japan. For example, the Pacific coastal plains are much more conducive to intensive farming than the coasts along the Sea of Japan. Because of its long north/south stretch and varied terrain, Japan also contains a wide variety of plants and animals; but because the archipelago was linked to the mainland by land bridges during long periods of the geological past, these same plants and animals are also found in many other parts of East Asia, so there's nothing particularly unique about them. But the combination of plentiful fresh water and a long growing season has created a paradise for plants, and for the herbivores that feed off them. These conditions also meant that when foraging humans first arrived on the archipelago, they found a rich variety of potential foodstuffs awaiting them: obviously forest and seafood, along with plentiful boar, deer, and many smaller animals that had crossed these land bridges from the mainland. It's across these same land bridges that the first human migrants came to Japan, beginning at least 35,000 years ago and maybe even earlier.

The Paleolithic lifeways these early human communities pursued mark the beginning of the development of Japanese history and culture. To be honest with you, as was the case in Korea, there's much we don't yet know about Paleolithic lifeways in Japan because the evidence is so scarce and so ambiguous. Indeed, the field of paleo-archaeology (ancient archaeology) is still relatively new in Japan; actually much newer again in Korea. One example of this, the first discoveries of stone tools in Japan weren't made until as recently as 1949. But evidence from two Japanese archaeological sites, Hoshino and Sozudai, has yielded the oldest manufactured implements including different choppers, picks, and very basic hand axes. The dating of volcanic ash and other materials found at these sites shows us that that they were occupied a very long time ago, perhaps between 400,000 and 200,000 years ago, which means these sites were almost undoubtedly occupied by our hominid ancestors *Homo habilis* perhaps, more likely and *Homo erectus*. A much more recent Japanese site, both in terms of its discovery and also the dates of its artifacts, is at Zazaragi, and this has yielded stone tools that have been dated to roughly 40,000 years ago, which means that these stone points and scrapers were most probably manufactured by modern humans. This suggests that Paleolithic *Homo sapiens*, after migrating through China and down through Korea, or perhaps across that great Yellow Sea plain, might've crossed land bridges to Japan as early as 50,000 years ago, although this date is still very controversial.

But I think after 35,000 years ago, we're on firmer chronological ground; and all sites dated since 35,000 B.P. are definitely assumed to have been populated by modern humans. These dates for the colonization of Japan correspond with key developments during the last ice age, of course. As we discussed in our first lecture on Korea, despite some fluctuations in climate, conditions all over East Asia at the height of the last ice age were bitterly cold and sea levels were much lower. Not only was the Yellow Sea a dry plain, but even the deeper Sea of Japan to the north was just a large lake that drained through the present Korea Strait. These increased dry land areas facilitated the movement of plants, certainly of animals, and of humans between parts of East Asia that are now under water. Ice Age humans considered the large animals of the period their primary food source, which meant that where the great herds of bison or mammoth went, so too did hunter-gatherer bands. This not only explains why some human groups migrated, for example, into frigid Siberia during the coldest part of the Ice Age (quite extraordinary), but it also the migration of East Asian hunters across that great Bering Strait land bridge that opened up at this period and that took them into the Americas a least 15,000 years ago, perhaps much earlier.

The arrival of humans perhaps 35,000 years ago in what's now the Japanese archipelago probably corresponded to the migrations of different herds of megafauna. To reinforce this, ancient megafaunal bones have actually been dredged up from the bottom of the Sea of Japan, proving that large game once roamed this region. But, of course, this also means that many early human sites are now deep underwater, although one important site from the Paleolithic is an exception. The Hanaizumi site lies at the northern tip of Honshu Island, and it's one of the few sites to provide us with a glimpse of lifeways during the long Paleolithic period. At this site, paleontologists have found the bones of bison, for example, also of elk, of ancient elephants preserved in a peat bog and dated to between 35,000 and 15,000 B.P. Both stone tools but also bone tools have also been discovered here; and this combination of animal bones and tools leads researchers to believe that Hanaizumi was probably a kill site or even a bone dump rather than a residential camp. This reminds us, of course, that one of the main reasons for the scarcity of Paleolithic evidence in Japan, and indeed all over the world, is that humans were nomadic throughout this long era; they rarely settled in any one place long enough to leave a substantial record. Indeed, very few Paleolithic-era human skeletons have been discovered in Japan, although the limestone fissure at the Minatogawa site near Okinawa has yielded valuable evidence about human colonization and lifeways during the period.

Archaeologists divide the Late Paleolithic Era in Japan, which begins about 30,000 years ago, into four phases, each characterized by different types of stone tools, different stone technologies, which are found in the layers they're excavating. In Phase I, for example, the deeper layer, we find that humans used long flakes for tools; these aren't really very workable shapes. But by Phase II as we move up, humans had learned to manufacture true blades, which archaeologists define as flakes more than twice as long as they are wide, and with regular parallel sides. After about 17,000 B.P., in Phase III, humans began to manufacture micro blades; so these are a range of tiny little bladelets for all sorts of specialized cutting uses. By Phase IV, both the front and back surfaces of these blades were being shaped, so now we start seeing arrowheads, we see spearheads; these are clear signs of advanced hunting lifeways.

As is the case across much of Afro-Eurasia, it's also during the Late or Upper Paleolithic period that we start to find evidence of humans using art as a form of self and communal expression. Stones shaped like humans have been found in Japan dating to this Upper Paleolithic; and at the Iwato site, a face sculpture pecked into the hilt of a stone tool was found, dated very broadly at this stage somewhere between 20,000 and 10,000 years ago.

Archaeologists have also excavated some quite extraordinary river stones at the Kamikuroiwa site, and these date to about 10,000 years ago. These stones appear to be decorated with images of females with long, heavy breasts wearing what looks like grass skirts.

With improved tool technology, a greater awareness clearly of art and perhaps magic and symbolic thinking, and the waning of the last ice age, human history in Japan marked the beginning of the Neolithic or New Stone Age by manufacturing what's probably the world's first pottery. At the very end of the Paleolithic, human communities in Japan began to make some of the world's earliest-known ceramics, the so-called Jomon Pottery, which gave rise to a new era in Japanese history: the Jomon Era. Initial evidence of this extraordinary pottery came from the Fukui and Kamikuroiwa cave sites where pottery shards dating to around 12,000 years ago were discovered; this is very early for pottery. But more recent discoveries have pushed these dates back by perhaps another 2,000 years; and if this is true, it means that the world's first vessels made of baked clay weren't manufactured in Sumeria or West Asia, but were manufactured in the Japanese archipelago.

As was the case with new ceramic developments in Korea that we discussed earlier, archaeologists are uncertain whether this technological innovation was an indigenous product or was influenced by new arrivals from northeast Asia. Certainly the appearance of this pottery might also be linked to global climate change. As we've discussed several times in this course already, from about 14,000 years ago the earth began to slowly warm. It's not a smooth process—there are cooling periods returning as well—but it's a general warming trend. As a result, tundra and conifer forests began to retreat northwards, to be replaced by broadleaf and deciduous trees like beeches and oaks. By 12,000 years ago, global sea levels had risen substantially as the great glacial ice sheets that had covered much of the world now melted, and this meant that Japan was now cut off from the Asian mainland.

The new forests provided plentiful foodstuffs for Neolithic Jomon Era foragers: nuts and acorns, for examples, and the animals that grazed in the forests, particularly various species of deer. Along the coasts, fishing and the exploitation of other marine resources provided a new and viable lifeway. As was the case with coastal gatherers in Korea, we actually have plenty of evidence of just what these coastal lifeways were like in the form of huge midden mounds of discarded shells and other types of debris. Humans also invented a whole range of new technologies and strategies to exploit these resources: We find arrows now; we find pit-traps for animals, we find fishing hooks and nets with sinkers; harpoons, canoes; even dogs have been domesticated, surely as an aid to hunting; and, of course, humans now needed pottery vessels to store and carry these resources. Although the term "Jomon Culture" is used to describe most of the 10,000 years that preceded the B.C.E./C.E. divide, because of these different environmental lifeways that Japanese Neolithic humans pursued these lifeways were far from uniform. Even the pottery shows considerable variation. In central Honshu itself, just one island, we find three distinctly different types of textured-surface pottery being produced during the Middle Jomon period. There was also a lot of trading of pottery and other valuable objects going on within the islands and between individual islands.

Although the original impetus for this technological innovation was probably the need for vessels to store foods, many of the more elaborate pieces of Jomon pottery appear to have been manufactured for use in early religious or shamanistic rituals. Indeed, we can say that Neolithic Japanese communities invented some quite extraordinary rituals to help ensure a continuing food supply and to ask for protection from the gods from environmental disaster. The Katsusaka mountain people are a great example of this. This was a Neolithic community that lived in semi-permanent villages, and outside and surrounding their pit houses they put up large phallic standing stones. These clearly indicate an interest in fertility and in the seasonal regeneration of crops, but also in linking this somehow to human reproduction. At other sites, pottery doll-like human figures with great bulging eyes have been found, often with their arms snapped off. Again, archaeologists speculate whether this procedure might've been part of some sort of a fertility rite.

Once agriculture was introduced and these communities became utterly dependent on successful harvests, this earlier interest in the magical qualities of seasonal regeneration, of fertility, and of human reproduction became even more important. Some of the ancient sexual fertility rituals that were performed by early farmers continue to resonate in parts of rural Japan to this very day. One example of this: In Tochigi Prefecture, after the seedlings have been transplanted into paddies, replicas of male and female genitalia are made of straw—although increasingly today they're made of plastic—and they're suspended from great bamboo frames. This may sound bizarre, but when the wind blows in a certain direction, the male organ appears to penetrate the female in an obvious attempt to use ritual human sexual activity and the power of nature to ensure crop fertility.

But with so many resources available to these "affluent foragers," there was no rush to adopt farming until it was eventually I guess we could say forced on these sedentary foraging communities through population increases. By the late Jomon period—that is, from roughly 5000 B.C.E. on—evidence of agriculture does indeed begin to appear in the archaeological record in the form of farming tools and the remains of major grain crops found inside these ancient pottery shards. From around the same period, we also have evidence that full-scale villages were starting to appear, consisting mostly of pit dwellings with roofs made of wood, thatch, or earth. Large communal storehouses also begin to be constructed in the millennia that followed. All these processes of lifeway and technological evolution led to periods of enhanced cultural activity, particularly in central Honshu, after about 3000 B.C.E. During the first millennium B.C.E., strikingly new technologies begin to appear in the Japanese archaeological record: new pottery, new technologies, and new lifeways known collectively today as the Yayoi culture.

The Yayoi people are associated with complex technologies like bronze, for example, and later iron metallurgy; like glassmaking, weaving, and advanced agricultural techniques, including horticulture obviously, but now also slash and burn farming and wet rice farming. The transition from Jomon to Yayoi was gradual, but it was nonetheless dramatic. It's been described by archaeologist Gina Barnes, and let me quote Professor Barnes, as "not just a change in subsistence pattern but an entire restructuring of the material economy of the Japanese islands." Most Yayoi evidence comes from Kyushu—remember, this is the southernmost of the four large islands and is thus the closest part of Japan to Korea—and it corresponds to similar complex changes that were occurring in the Korean peninsula at more or less the same time. This really means that the direction of cultural influence seems pretty clear: from Korea into Japan.

Excavations in western Japan have suggested that the Jomon and Yayoi people were in fact two distinctly different groups of humans. Jomon people, the older group, were shorter, more robust, rounder in face; the Yayoi were taller, gracile, long-faced, strong evidence, we think, that the Yayoi people were most probably immigrants from Korea. The Yayoi brought with them new pottery styles and I mentioned wet rice agriculture, and this was so successful it led to a population boom on the plains of northern Kyushu. Both the Yayoi people and their lifeways then expanded explosively throughout the western lowlands of the archipelago. As far as we can tell, there was little conflict between the Yayoi newcomers and the Jomon people, who seem to have been actually quite receptive, even welcoming, to new ideas about farming. The one area of possible resistance to Yayoi agriculture appears to have been in the northeast of the country where Jomon people retained their commitment to a marine-based lifeway, which was already incredibly efficient and productive.

Rice farming spread through the rest of the islands in two stages: through Honshu by around 100 B.C.E., and throughout the rest of the islands by 700 C.E., bringing with it new tools, new architectural styles, and new cultural ideas. With the advent of full blown agriculture, of more complex technologies, much larger villages now, and the arrival of metallurgy, Japanese culture had clearly entered a new stage; one that, as we'll see, would be marked by the emergence of surpluses, of social complexity, of elites, and powerful individuals like chiefs.

In our next two lectures we have much fascinating cultural history to investigate: the Bronze Age in Japan first; the extraordinary Tomb Period; the powerful Yamato kings; ongoing interaction with Korea; the arrival of Buddhism and the Buddhist-dominated Nara period that followed. Then we'll conclude this four lecture mini-series on early Japan by discussing the glories of the Heian, a period of magnificent and sophisticated cultural flowering that still resonates throughout Eastern civilization to this day. I'll see you next time.

Japan—Treasures of the Tomb Period
Lecture 28

With the arrival in Japan of the Yayoi people during the 1st millennium B.C.E., Japanese history and culture entered a new stage. This next phase would be marked by the creation of resource surpluses, social complexity, the emergence of elites, and the appearance of powerful individuals, culminating in a full-fledged imperial state. In this lecture and the next, we will investigate these important stages in the cultural development of Japan: the Bronze Age of the Yayoi; the Tomb Period; the reigns of the powerful Yamato kings; interaction among Japan, Korea, and China; the arrival of Buddhism; the development of the first law codes; and the culmination of all this in the glorious Nara period.

Jomon and Yayoi Lifeways

- Jomon communities appear to have been relatively egalitarian, communal in structure, and peaceful. Yayoi communities, in contrast, were often located on hilltops surrounded by defensive stockades and moats. Archaeologists have found numerous caches of weapons in these sites and many human skeletons that show clear evidence of violent attack.

- Yayoi burials are also clearly distinguished from Jomon by the value of grave goods found in the more lavish funerary structures and by the fact that elite graves are located in special cemetery sections. This is evidence of the emergence of sharp hierarchies in Yayoi communities based on wealth and status, something that is not found in the archaeological record left by Jomon communities.

- We find marked regional differences in Yayoi communities throughout the archipelago. For example, most Yayoi communities had access to bronze metallurgy, but the tools and weapons they made were quite different. Some communities specialized in bronze weapons, possibly owned by individuals, while others used bronze to make bells that seem to have been owned by the entire community.

- Along with archaeological evidence of Yayoi elites, we also have literary evidence from the 1st century C.E. on, in the form of Han and Wei dynasty annals. Third-century sources describe the Wa people (the Chinese name for the residents of the Japanese archipelago) as having divided into more than 100 small states, with several under the hegemonic control of a country called Yamatai.
    o The Chinese sources also contain several references to a powerful woman who ruled the Yamatai state as queen, the extraordinary and enigmatic Himiko, who is described as having employed shamanistic skills to secure and control the throne.

    o The Wei dynasty annals inform us that Himiko was one of at least two (and perhaps more) female rulers of Yamatai.

    o When Queen Himiko died in perhaps the year 258 C.E., the Wei sources note, "a great mound was raised, more than a hundred paces in diameter." The so-far fruitless search for this burial mound has occupied Japanese scholars for generations.

Yamatai Tombs
- By the 6th century C.E., the tombs of elite Yamatai dead were massive. The largest were surrounded by moats and faced with stone paving, and each could contain from one to several coffins. Grave goods discovered in these tombs include mirrors, swords, tools, ritual utensils, pieces of armor, and saddles, all presumably for protection in the afterlife.

- Archaeologists believe that these tombs were strongly influenced by the burial methods used in the Korean Peninsula during the contemporaneous Three Kingdoms period.

- Many of the tombs were decorated with paintings and engravings on the stone antechamber walls.
    o Some of these illustrations show groups of humans and animals apparently engaged in some sort of ritual to offer magical protection for the dead. Others depict what might be

mythological subjects: shields, quivers, a bird on the prow of a boat, and a man about to seize an extraordinary animal.

o Intriguingly, many of these same symbols and images would continue to resonate in later Japanese art and were often incorporated into Buddhist art following the arrival of that spiritual ideology from Korea.

- Today, these great tomb mounds, which are the most visible archaeological feature in all of Japan, are covered in grass and trees and resemble tranquil parks, but such was not their original appearance.

  o When first raised, the mounds were surrounded by rings of fired-clay statues—*haniwa* figures.

  o The carefully arranged *haniwa* seem to capture in stone the sort of ritual ceremonies that must have accompanied the burials of kings and other elites.

- Representations and artifacts of armor abound in all East Asian tombs of this period, and in the Japanese tombs in particular, we see the antecedents of the powerful warrior class that later came to dominate Japanese society— the samurai. Also common to the tombs of ancient Chinese, Korean, and Japanese elite warriors is the horse.

Many of the *haniwa* are sufficiently detailed to give us some idea of how elite men and women dressed during the Tomb Period.

- The source of the power of the kings and other elites buried in these Chinese, Korean, and Japanese tombs was wealth from successful farming and trade. Strong archaeological evidence indicates that agricultural productivity in Japan grew enormously in the 5th century C.E. because of new tools and techniques that arrived from Korea, including the first iron tools and plows and improved irrigation techniques.

- The more powerful kings, buried in the largest, keyhole-shaped tombs, also entered into a complex network of allegiances with other, less powerful chieftains in various regions of Japan.
  - Archaeologists can determine both the status of the interred and the allegiance network to which he or she belonged by calculating the number and quality of polished bronze mirrors found in the tombs.

  - The picture archaeologists describe is of a handful of central, powerful kings distributing mirrors to allies and subordinates as part of the allegiance network, similar to the tributary system successfully used by various Chinese dynasties.

  - By the 6th century, however, many of the regional Yamatai chiefs seem to have become less autonomous, probably because they were being incorporated into new and more powerful kinship groups that were emerging.

  - Later written sources suggest that the 5th and 6th centuries also witnessed the development of a court system, which was serviced by specialized social groups called *be*, who supplied the elites with food, tools, weapons, clothing, and perhaps scribes. These courts were dominated by hereditary kinship or clan groups, although these were probably political rather than family groups at this stage.

The Emergence of States
- By the mid-6th century, the Yamato kingdoms and their allied cultures were on the verge of the next major development in Japanese culture: the appearance of a genuine complex state.

- Many of the criteria that archaeologists use to define states were in place: elites supported by agricultural surpluses, tributary systems, trade, monumental architecture, craft specialization, kings, and courts. What was missing was any sort of formal administrative system, nor were writing, bureaucracy, laws, taxation, or any mechanism for directly controlling outlying territories in place.

- The appearance of a clear-cut state in Japan can be attributed partly to the arrival of Buddhism, which had a powerful effect on cultural and political development.
  - The arrival of Buddhism, probably around 400 C.E., sparked violent clashes between those clans that supported the "foreign" ideology and those that opposed it because it clashed with vested interests they had in local ritual systems.

  - In the end, the pro-Buddhist factions won, and the Buddhist hierarchy that arose as a result came to compete with the political rulership of the Yamato, strongly influencing state development.

  - As we have seen in India, the Kushan Empire, the Northern Wei and Sui dynasties, and elsewhere, Buddhists relied on state tolerance and patronage in Japan. In return for this, Buddhist hierarchies supported rulers and imperial administrations; state building often went hand in hand with religion building.

- After the arrival of Buddhism and a temple hierarchy, the next major influence on state building in Japan came at the end of the 6th century. A kinship clan known as the Soga, who may also have been immigrants from Korea, seized power in the Yamato court.

- The powerful leader of the Soga in the late 6th and early 7th centuries was Soga no Umako, who maintained his power by manipulating the kingship through marriage. State histories of the 8th century make much of the enlightened reigns of Umako's niece Queen Suiko and her famous nephew and regent Prince Shotoku. He is said to have centralized Soga power, issued the first constitution in Japanese history, and launched a program of cultural investigation.

- The ambitious programs of Umako and Shotoku provoked a backlash against the Soga by other clans. In 645, two princes from rival clans staged a coup d'état, assassinating the leading Soga and their supporters. These princes then introduced a new formal taxation and administrative structure, aimed at more strongly centralizing power.

- The next major influence on state formation in Japan occurred 18 years later; this was the victory in 663 C.E. of the Tang and Silla alliance over the Paekche kingdom in Korea, which created a foreign-affairs crisis in Japan.
  - Fearing imminent attack by combined Tang/Silla forces, those Japanese islands and coasts closest to Korea were heavily fortified.

  - The need to pay for these expensive fortifications led to the introduction of a more sophisticated government bureaucracy based on written communication and formal taxation. It also allowed the court to establish even firmer central control of the outlying regions of Japan.

- The final stage in the process of creating a powerful and formal state in Japan occurred during the reigns of Temmu and his consort Jito in the second half of the 7th century.
  - First, a census of the population was taken to extract more taxes, conscripted labor, and military service. Then, the power of local nobles was further weakened, the first complete legal codes were promulgated, and Buddhism was brought more firmly under state control.

  - But perhaps the most important innovation of all carried out by Temmu and Jito was the adoption of the official title *tenno* for the ruler of Japan and the name Nihon or Nippon for the Japanese state. Both these terms have survived for more than 1,300 years; to this day, Japan is referred to as Nippon-koku— literally, the "State of Japan," and the emperor as the *tenno*, or "heavenly sovereign."

o   Another of the great projects of Temmu and Jito was the construction of a new and permanent capital city, Heijo (modern Nara), as the symbol of their new state. The construction of this city, strongly influenced by Chinese urban planning and the great Tang capital of Changan, marks the beginning of another new era in Japanese history, the Nara period.

Suggested Reading

Schirokauer et al., *A Brief History of Chinese and Japanese Civilizations*, chapter 6.

Totman, *A History of Japan*.

Questions to Consider

1. Why did the relative egalitarianism of the Jomon period give way to the appearance of sharp hierarchies and powerful leaders during the Yayoi period?

2. Is it reasonable to suggest that the emergence of the mounted warrior aristocrat in China, Korea, and Japan is a reflection of the power of the mounted armies of the steppe nomadic people?

Japan—Treasures of the Tomb Period
Lecture 28—Transcript

We concluded our last lecture by noting that with the arrival in Japan of the Yayoi people during the first millennium B.C.E., who brought with them from Korea wet rice agriculture, more complex technologies, larger villages, and also bronze metallurgy, Japanese history and culture entered a new stage. This next phase would be marked by the creation of resource surpluses, by increasing social complexity, by the emergence of elites, and the appearance of powerful individuals like chiefs, until eventually a fully-fledged imperial state was in place in Japan, or the land of Nippon as it would now be called.

In this lecture and the next, we'll investigate these important stages in the cultural development of Japan: the Bronze Age of the Yayoi; the Tomb Period that followed; the rules of the powerful Yamato kings; ongoing interaction between Japan, Korea, and China, of course; the almost inevitable arrival of Buddhism in the islands; the development of the first law codes in Japan; and the culmination of all this in the glorious Nara period. Let's begin this next lecture on our journey through the foundations of Eastern civilization by picking up the story of the Yayoi people and the sophisticated cultural and technological innovations that they introduced to the Japanese archipelago.

As was the case wherever agriculture appeared in various regions of the world, the intensive rice farming techniques introduced to Japan by the Yayoi quite quickly led to a greater availability of food, increasing population densities, and the associated problems of organizing these larger concentrations of people. This in turn led to a clear division of labor and to the appearance of distinct social hierarchies, of power, and of increased competition for resources between different communities. So inevitable are all these processes, is it any wonder that the transition from foraging to farming is often called the most important revolution in all of world history?

As I mentioned last time, there's little evidence of actual conflict between the Jomon and Yayoi communities, but there are certainly stark differences between their lifeways. Jomon communities appear to have been relatively egalitarian, communal in structure and nature, and peaceful. Yayoi communities, on the other hand, were often located on hilltops surrounded by defensive stockades and moats. Archaeologists have found numerous caches of weapons in these sites and many human skeletons that show clear evidence of violent attack. Yayoi burials are also clearly distinguished from Jomon by the value of grave goods found in the much more lavish funerary structures that appear, and also by the fact that elite graves are located in special cemetery sections. All this is clear evidence to archaeologists of the emergence of sharp hierarchies in Yayoi communities; hierarchies based on wealth and therefore on status, something that's frankly not found in any of the archaeological record left behind by Jomon communities.

But I don't want to give the impression that Yayoi culture was homogenous or uniform throughout the archipelago; there are, in fact, marked regional differences. Most Yayoi communities had access to bronze metallurgy, for example, but the tools and weapons they made are quite different. Many bronze weapons were imported, presumably from Korea, but for some reason these were often melted down and recast. Differences in bronze usage might also reflect the fact that there was a wide range of cultural influences now coming in from China as well as from Korea. Some communities specialized in bronze weapons, most of which have been found inside the elite tombs, suggesting individual ownership by these powerful elites. Because of this, other Yayoi communities used their bronze not for weapons, but to make bells that appear to have been the possession of the entire community and were probably employed in agricultural rituals; so distinct differences in bronze usage there.

Along with all this archaeological evidence of powerful Yayoi elites emerging, we also have literary evidence from the first century C.E. onwards in the form of Han dynasty Chinese records. I should note that early Japanese and Korean cultures left very little in the way of official histories or other literary records behind. The oldest book actually written in Japan, in fact, wasn't written until the eighth century C.E. But in China, of course, where the writing of literature and history already had a long tradition by this stage—thousands of years of writing—we have superb records of the observations of Chinese government officials and Chinese historians on events occurring all over East Asia, which is most fortunate for us students of Eastern civilization. So we're able to read in the Chinese *Hou Hanshu*; this is the *Annals of the Later Han Dynasty*. We're able to read that kings of the Wa people, which was the Chinese name for the residents of the Japanese archipelago, had entered into a tributary relationship with the Han and first sent envoys to the Han court through their Korean commandery, you remember, of Lelang in 57 C.E., and then again, we read, 50 years later in 107 C.E. These envoys brought tribute to the Han in the form of cloth, pearls, bows and arrows, and also slaves, and in return they received silk, gold, swords, and jade from the Chinese Han court.

But even more striking evidence of political developments in Japan comes from references in the Wei dynasty annals composed during the third century C.E., during China's Age of Disunity. The sources describe the Wa people as having divided now into more than a hundred small states, with several under the hegemonic control of a country called Yamatai. Despite centuries of investigation, it seems impossible to know where exactly in Japan this Yamatai kingdom was located; scholars are divided between Kyushu or other regions including the Kinai region. The Chinese sources also contain several references to a powerful woman who ruled the Yamatai state as queen. This is the extraordinary and enigmatic Himiko, who's described as having employed shamanistic, almost magical, skills to secure and control the throne.

We read in the Chinese sources that Himiko lived in a stockade protected by guard towers, and that she had 1,000 servants, all of whom were female, although the only person that ever saw her in person was her brother. In 238, the Wei sources tell us that Himiko sent tribute to the Wei court in northern China seeking a tributary relationship. The request was accepted and Himiko was named as "Ruler of the Wa, friendly to the Wei." This was a powerful validation of her claims to leadership in the Yamatai. Part of her tribute from the Wei included a gold seal and 100 bronze mirrors. These important Wei dynasty *Annals* also inform us that Himiko was one of at least two—perhaps more; the sources are ambiguous—female rulers of Yamatai. There is, for example, another reference to a young woman, perhaps a niece of Himiko, named Ichiyo, who was also chosen to be leader of the Yamatai. A reference to a tribute mission from Ichiyo to the Wei court is pretty well the last reference we have to the kingdom of Yamatai; the last that there is in the Wei sources, sadly for us.

One interpretation of this, of these references to the reigns of these powerful women in the Yamatai kingdom, is that perhaps Yamatai was essentially a matriarchal society; but, of course, with so little evidence this is really impossible to substantiate. When Queen Himiko died in perhaps 258 C.E., the Wei sources note that "a great mound was raised, more than a hundred paces in diameter." The so-far fruitless search for this burial mound has occupied Japanese scholars for generations; but they've had plenty of other massive tombs to investigate. Indeed, by the sixth century C.E., the tombs of elite Yamatai dead were massive. The largest were surrounded by moats and faced with stone paving, and each could contain from one to several coffins. The grave goods discovered in these elaborate tombs include bronze mirrors obviously, swords, different tools, ritual utensils, pieces of armor, and saddles for horses, all presumably for protection in the afterlife. Archaeologists believe that these tombs were strongly influenced by the burial methods being used in the Korean peninsula during the contemporaneous Three Kingdoms period that we investigated in an earlier lecture. Many of the tombs were decorated with paintings and engravings on the stone antechamber walls. Some of these illustrations show groups of humans and animals apparently engaged in some sort of ritual to offer magical protection for the dead. Others depict what might be mythological subjects: there are shields, quivers for arrows, a bird perched on the prow of a boat, a man about to seize an extraordinary animal, giant toads. We really have no idea of the mythical stories in which these figures must've played a role. Intriguingly, many of these same symbols and images continue to resonate in much later Japanese art, long after the Yamatai had gone; and they were often even incorporated into Buddhist art following the arrival of that spiritual ideology from Korea.

Today these great tomb mounds, which are certainly the most visible archaeological feature in all of Japan, are covered in grass and trees and resemble tranquil parks; but such wasn't their original appearance. When first raised, the mounds were surrounded by rings of low-fired clay statues, which many of you may well have seen because they're housed in many of the great art museums of the world: the enigmatic *haniwa* figures. The tombs and the carefully arranged *haniwa* seem to capture in stone, frozen in stone really, the sort of ritual ceremonies that must've accompanied the burials of the kings and these other elites. The clay *haniwa* figures include a variety of humans (we find warriors, shamans, we find dancers in all sorts of poses, farmers, servants), also animals (there are fish, pigs, monkey statues, and horses, of course), and all sorts of artifacts (weapons, musical instruments, even boats), all lined up in this frozen ritual procession of clay. Many of the *haniwa* are sufficiently detailed to give us a pretty good idea of how men and women even dressed during this Tomb period, particularly men and women of the elite class. Both men and women appear to wear some kind of robe on the upper parts of their bodies; on the lower half, women wore skirts and the men wore baggy trousers that actually looked something like a skirt. There's some suggestion that the common people may have worn a kind of poncho made of a single sheet of cloth with a central hole for the head. The two-piece costume worn by both sexes suggests that the famous one-piece kimono, which eventually became a trademark of the Japanese way of life, must've been a later historical development.

Like the great terracotta tomb of Qin Shi Huangdi just outside of Xiang today, like the tombs of the Han emperors, and like the tombs of Koguryo kingdom in Korea, the mound tombs of Japan during this period clearly reflect the fact that these elite leaders weren't only aristocrats, they were warriors. Representations and artifacts of armor abound in all these East Asian tombs from this period; and in the Japanese tombs in particular, we see the antecedents of the powerful warrior class that later came to dominate Japanese society, the samurai. I'll have much more to say about the samurai in a later lecture. In China, the Wei dynasty aristocrats were clad in full body armor and were well trained in the horse riding traditions of the steppes just to the north of their kingdom. In Korea, the tombs there depict men in suits of armor made of bone and iron. The Yamato tombs have yielded iron body armor and iron helmets, and many of the *haniwa*, these clay figures outside the tombs, are dressed as fully armed warriors. Also common to the tombs of ancient Chinese, Korean, and Japanese elite warriors is the horse. Sixth-century *haniwa* depict horses lavishly fitted out with gild bronze harnesses, with ornaments, and saddle decorations. Silla tombs in Korea contain effigies of horses made of iron; in Yamato tombs, horse effigies are made of clay. There's also evidence that that some type of horse sacrifice must've been carried out in Yamatai Japan at the death of the horse's owner, because this act is specifically prohibited in a later law code, the *Nihon Shoki*. The emergence of the mounted warrior aristocrat in China, Korea, and Japan is a reflection of the power of the mounted armies of the steppe nomadic people who, as we've seen many times in this course and as we'll see again, had such a devastating but also galvanizing impact on all these ancient East Asian sedentary civilizations.

The source of the power of the kings and the other elites buried in all these Chinese, Korean, and Japanese tombs was wealth, and must in turn have been a product of successful farming and successful trade, which allowed the elites to accumulate such massive resources. It's not surprising that there's strong archaeological evidence that agricultural productivity in Japan grew enormously through the fifth century C.E., probably because of new tools and new farming techniques that arrived again from Korea, including the first iron tools, the first iron plows, and also improved irrigation techniques.

Trade was also expanding, if the remains of large ancient storehouses found at Osaka Bay and also evidence of increased commercial interaction with Korea are any indication. It's the surpluses of food and other goods that accumulated because of these developments that clearly explain the source of Yamato royal power. The more powerful kings buried in the largest keyhole-shaped tombs also entered into a complex network of allegiances with other less powerful chieftains in various regions of Japan. Archaeologists can determine both the status of the interred but also the allegiance network to which he or she belonged by calculating the number and quality of polished bronze mirrors, which were expensive and thus a valued form of tribute in all East Asian societies, and they can calculate how many of these are found in the individual tombs. The picture archaeologists describe, then, is of a handful of central, powerful kings distributing mirrors to allies and subordinates as part of this allegiance network, similar to the tributary system so successfully employed by various Chinese dynasties, as we've seen.

By the sixth century, however, many of the regional Yamatai chiefs seem to have become less autonomous, probably because they were being incorporated into new and more powerful kinship groups that were emerging. Later written sources reflecting back suggest that the fifth and sixth centuries also witnessed the development of a court system with kings and queens serviced by specialized social groups called *be*, who supplied the elites with their food, their tools, their weapon, their clothing, and perhaps their scribes. These courts were dominated now by hereditary kinship or clan groups, although these clan groups were probably political rather than family groups by this stage. In fact, there appears to have been no dominant single family line amongst these Yamato kings until the sixth century, when a dominant lineage did indeed emerge.

All these developments meant that by the mid-sixth century, the Yamato kingdoms and their allied cultures were on the verge of the next major development in Japanese culture: the appearance of a genuine complex state. Many of the criteria that archaeologists use to define states were certainly in place: We have elites supported by agricultural surpluses, by tributary systems, by quite extensive trade, certainly by monumental architecture in the form of these tombs, a lot of craft specializations going on, and now we have kings, and queens, and courts. But what was missing was any sort of formal administrative system; there's no writing yet, there's no bureaucracy, there's no written laws, no system of taxation, nor any mechanism for directly controlling the outlying territories. We've already seen that all these developments occurred in Korea during the Three Kingdoms era. In the final part of this lecture, we need to trace the appearance of the first genuine state in Japan and follow this through to the beginning of the sophisticated Nara period early in the eighth century.

The appearance of a clear-cut state in Japan can be attributed, perhaps ironically, partly to the arrival of Buddhism, which had a powerful effect on cultural development certainly, but also political. As we saw in a previous lecture, Buddhism was introduced into Korea by proselytizing monks during the Three Kingdoms era. It's more than likely that these same monks also introduced the first writing system into Korea in order to translate the important sutras of the Buddhist faith. Tradition then ascribes the transmission of writing into Japan in 405 C.E. to the work of two Korean Paekche kingdom scribes who served as Yamato treasury accountants. But it's not until 150 years later in the mid-sixth century that intricately written Buddhist sutras also start to turn up in the Yamato kingdom, evidence that the Buddhist faith had arrived in Japan a little earlier.

Initially, the arrival of Buddhism sparked violent clashes between those clans that supported this imported and thus foreign ideology and those that opposed it because it clashed with vested interests they had in local ritual systems. In the end, the pro-Buddhist factions won and the Buddhist hierarchy that arose as a result came to compete with the political rulership of the Yamato, strongly influencing state development. As we've already seen many times in this course, Buddhists have always relied on state tolerance and state patronage, whether from the great emperor Asoka in India, King Kanishka of the Kushan empire, the rulers of the Northern Wei and later the Sui dynasties in China, or the leaders of Paekche, Silla, and Koguryo kingdoms in Korea. In return for this royal patronage, Buddhist hierarchies supported the rulers and their imperial administrations, so that state building often went hand in hand with religious building. This was just as true, of course, in the relationship that developed between the Christian church and various secular rulers in Europe, and between the Islamic faith and the various caliphates that came to support it and that were in turn supported by the religious hierarchy.

After the arrival of Buddhism and the appearance of a temple hierarchy, the next major influence on state building in Japan came at the end of the sixth century. Influenced by events in Korea and in China, a kinship clan known as the Soga, who may have also been immigrants from Korea by the way, seized power in the Yamato court. The Soga were skilled in arts and crafts, they were great patrons of Buddhism, and they married their daughters into the Yamato court to secure their own power. The powerful leader of the Soga in the late sixth and early seventh centuries was Soga no Umako, which literally translates to "Umako of the Soga." He maintained his power and prestige by manipulating kingship through marriage.

State histories of the eighth century make much of the enlightened reigns of Umako's niece, Queen Suiko, who lived a pretty long life for those times between 554 and 628 C.E., and her famous nephew and regent, Prince Shotoku, who lived between 574 and 622. Shotoku is said to have centralized Soga power by founding a twelve-rank court system that led to the reorganization of officials very much in a sort of legalistic, bureaucratic Chinese fashion. The system also seems to have been partly inspired by Confucianism because in a radical departure from the earlier hereditary system, appointment to the ranks was now based on merit, not birth. Shotoku is also credited with issuing in 604 C.E. the first constitution in Japanese history, the so-called "Constitution of Seventeen Articles." This was a set of moral and political principles that outlined the power of the Yamato lord. Finally, Shotoku launched a program of cultural investigation and enrichment by sending students and envoys to various courts and China and Korea to learn as much as possible about the continental way of life.

But the ambitious programs of Umako and Shotoku provoked a backlash against the Soga by other clans. In 645, an important year in Japanese history, two princes from rival clans staged a coup d'état, assassinating the leading Soga and their supporters. These princes then introduced a new formal taxation and administrative structure in a series of reforms later historians celebrate now as the Taika Reforms of 645 C.E., reforms that were aimed at more strongly centralizing power. Ironically, they were able to do this because of the expertise in Chinese statecraft and astronomy that students sent to China by Shotoku had amassed.

The next major influence on state formation in Japan occurred 18 years later, and this was because the victory in 663 of the Tang and Silla alliance, you remember, over the Paekche kingdom in Korea actually created a grave foreign affairs crisis in Japan. The Japanese now feared imminent attack by combined Tang and Silla forces, so the Japanese islands and coasts closest to Korea in the south were heavily fortified. The Yamato needed to pay for these expensive fortifications, and this led to the introduction of a much more sophisticated government bureaucracy based on written communications and on formal taxation. It also allowed the court to establish even firmer central control of those outlying semiautonomous regions of Japan. These changes occurred quickly and are a clear example of a foreign threat strongly influencing domestic reform.

The final stage in the process of creating a powerful and formal state in Japan occurred during the reigns of Temmu between 631 and 686 and his consort Jito from 645 into the eight century; so essentially the second half of the seventh century into the early eight. First, a census of the population was taken in order to extract more taxes, more conscripted labor, and more military service from the people. This is the first census in Japanese history, obviously incredibly important for historians. Then, second, the power of local nobles was further weakened, the first complete legal codes were promulgated, and Buddhism was brought more firmly under state control. But perhaps the most important innovation of all carried out by Temmu and Jito was the adoption of the official title *tenno* for the ruler of Japan and the name of Nihon or Nippon for the Japanese state. These were the intentional final steps in legitimizing and strengthening the power of the throne and in creating a modern, well-organized central government to rule the state. *Tenno* means "heavenly sovereign," and was actually a Chinese term to describe an emperor who sits at the center of his realm while everything else revolves around him. Nihon or Nippon means "the base or the origin of the sun," which now came to be the official name for the country. Both these terms have survived for more than 1,300 years; to this day, Japan is referred to as "Nippon-koku," literally the "State of Japan," and the emperor as the "Tenno," or "Heavenly Sovereign."

Another of the great projects carried out by Temmu and Jito was the construction of a new and permanent capital city as the symbol of their new powerful state. In 710, the capital was moved from Fujiwara to a new city, Heijo, known today by its modern name as Nara. The construction of this city, strongly influenced by Chinese urban planning and obviously by the great Tang capital of Changan, marks the beginning of another new era in Japanese history: the Nara period. Although the Nara period lasted for less than 80 years, it had a profound influence on the development of Japanese religion, literature, law, government, and certainly on the visual arts. This glorious Nara period will be the subject of our next lecture as we continue our journey through the rich foundations of Eastern civilization.

Japan—Nara and the Great Eastern Temple
Lecture 29

In perhaps the most important innovation introduced into Japanese culture by the rulers Temmu and Jito, the official title *tenno* was adopted for the ruler of Japan and the name Nihon or Nippon for the Japanese state. The adoption of these terms constituted the intentional final steps in legitimizing and strengthening the power of the throne and transforming Japan into a full-fledged state. At the end of the last lecture, we also saw another of the great projects of Temmu and Jito: the construction of a new capital city, Heijo, as the symbol of the new state. The founding of this city marks the beginning of a new era in Japanese history, the Nara Period.

The City of Heijo
- The Taika reforms of the year 645 C.E. are recognized by many historians as the moment that the Yamato began to transform itself from a kingdom to a legitimate state. These efforts to create a state based on Tang administrative models took place over a period of about 100 years, from the end of the 6th century to the beginning of the 8th.
  - In both Japan and Korea during this same period, the reforms involved a complete restructuring of the administration, taxation, and legal systems of the two countries along Tang dynasty lines.

  - It is no surprise that both countries also decided to build planned capital cities as the symbols for their new states, cities that might mirror the glorious Tang capital of Changan.

- The capital city of Heijo (modern Nara) was completed in 710, during the reign of Empress Jito, and gives its name to the Nara period. By the mid-8th century, Nara was home to about 100,000 people.

- Like Changan, Heijo had a central avenue that ran from the southern gate to the palace in the north. The avenue bisected a grid of streets, and within the grid, land plots were allocated according to rank, with the elites and their mansions located closest to the palace.

- The palace itself had a huge main gate manned by armed guards. Stretching away from the gate in both directions was a wall 30 feet high, protecting a palace complex that measured 1,300 by 1,100 yards.

- At the heart of the palace was the Great Supreme Hall, where the emperor oversaw state ceremonies and greeted foreign dignitaries. The hall was also the center of court life and was surrounded by pleasure gardens, offices, kitchens, and storehouses.

- Some idea of the wealth and aesthetic sensibilities of the imperial and other elite families who lived in Nara can be gained from the valuable goods preserved in the Shosoin, a storehouse still standing in the compound of the Todaiji Temple today. The Shosoin contained books, weapons, silk, bronze mirrors, musical instruments, medicines, and magnificent art objects of gold, glass, mother of pearl, and lacquer.

The Todaiji Temple and Japanese Buddhism

- The magnificent Todaiji Temple in Nara reminds us that this was also a great age of Buddhism in Japan, as it was in contemporary China and Korea. The temple was constructed just to the east of the palace and contained a gigantic bronze Buddha cast partly from thousands of bronze mirrors that the ladies of the court had donated.
  - The temple complex also featured two pagodas more than 330 feet high. The original function of the pagoda structure was to house sacred relics of the Buddha.

  - In the year 752 C.E., the Great Buddha and temple complex were officially dedicated by the emperor. Early Japanese sources tell us that the ceremony involved 10,000 monks, 4,000 musicians and dancers, and 7,000 state officials. As the ceremony reached its climax, a visiting Indian Buddhist monk painted in the colored eyes of the Great Buddha.

- When Buddhism was first introduced into Japan, the Buddha was regarded by the people as a *kami*, a generic term used to describe any of the supposedly innumerable divinities in the world.
  - In the 6th and 7th centuries, the new religion came to be seen as a kind of magic, similar to the magical religion that developed into Shintoism.

  - In both cases, people believed that supernatural entities could be accessed through prayer and ritual to cure illness, avert disaster, and obtain the good things in life. Thus, it was natural for them to pray for such blessings simultaneously at Shinto shrines and Buddhist temples.

  - The survival of Shintoism, whose origins can probably be traced back to the Jomon period, is thus another example of the Japanese retention of indigenous beliefs and characteristics, despite the overwhelming cultural influence from China.

  - Japan adopted Buddhism and Confucianism from China, but the Japanese continued to observe the rites of Shintoism, which revolves around the worship of ancestors and a host of nature spirits and deities.

- For the first century or so following its arrival in Japan from Korea during the Three Kingdoms era, Buddhism remained a largely private religion for powerful families, such as the Soga.

- Around the time of the Taika reforms in 645, Buddhism started to reach a larger audience, partly because of state patronage. King Jomei had the Great Temple of Paekche constructed near his palace, and King Temmu then built what was called the Daikan Daiji, or Great Official Temple. For various political reasons, the government decided to invest great amounts of treasure and labor in supporting the Buddhist religion and building its infrastructure.

- This support reached a climax during the Nara period, particularly during the reign of Emperor Shomu (r. 724–749). It was Shomu who had the Todaiji Temple constructed and presided over the ceremony to dedicate the massive Buddha in the Great Buddha Hall.

- By this stage in Japan's history, Buddhism had become the religion of the state, and large state prayer rituals were conducted, not so much for personal salvation but for the protection of the nation as a whole. Indeed, the rulers of Nara used fairly strict legal codes and government authority to control the version of Buddhism that was taught to the people.

- Socially, the Buddhist hierarchy was now on the same level as elite government officials and was materially supported by state resources. But Buddhist affairs also increasingly came under the control of bureaucrats. For example, those entering the priesthood now needed government permission, and the legal codes contained lists of prohibitions and restrictions on the behavior of monks.
  o On the one hand, this control meant that Japanese Buddhism was unable to produce any original religious philosophy because it might transgress the state-sponsored orthodox version.

  o On the other hand, the religious community, supported by the wealth and resources of the state, was able to create glorious art.

Nara Period Art and Literature
- The temples around Nara, many of which survive today, were masterpieces of architectural planning. Much of the art inside the temples was created by visiting or resident Chinese and Korean artists.

- Horyuji Temple contains a superb elongated sculpture known as the *Kudara Kannon*. Some of the oldest paintings in Japan are found on the cabinet-sized Jewel-Beetle Shrine in the same temple, which is decorated with iridescent beetle wings set into metal edging.

Nara temple complexes were carefully planned, with buildings placed in a particular vertical order based on the perspective from the main gate toward the back hall.

- The Toshodaiji Temple of Nara was founded by a Chinese monk named Ganjin. Shipwrecked and delayed by storms and government opposition, Ganjin finally reached Japan after six attempts, but by then, he had gone blind!
  - The sculpted portrait of Ganjin in the Toshodaiji Temple reminds us that the Buddhist culture of Nara was very cosmopolitan, with important practitioners coming from India, Korea, and China.

  - This was one of the great periods of Silk Roads exchanges, and we know that priests, merchants, and ambassadors from Tang China, the Silla court, India, and Persia regularly visited Nara.

  - Partly this was a reflection of the "internationalism" of Buddhism, and partly it was a product of the hunger for transcultural exchange that so characterized this extraordinary era of Eastern civilization. Japan would not experience this level of contact with the outside world again for more than 1,000 years, until after the Meiji Restoration of the 19th century.

- In literature, too, the Nara period was a golden age. Sacred texts from China and Korea were copied and commented on in flowing calligraphy; we actually know of some 100,000 volumes of sacred text that have survived from the 8th century!
  o Japan's first history texts were also produced at Nara, including the *Kojiki* (*Record of Ancient Matters*), published in 712 C.E., and the *Nihon shoki* (*Chronicles of Japan*), published in 720.

  o One of the greatest anthologies of Japanese poetry was also produced during the Nara period: the *Manyoshu* (*Collection of Ten Thousand Leaves*), which contains more than 4,500 poems.

From Nara to Heian
- Although the Nara court had to face no foreign crises or full-blown civil wars, it did have its share of problems, including periodic famines and a two-year smallpox epidemic. But the biggest challenges came from bitterly disputed succession problems and power struggles. At the center of many of these struggles was the Fujiwara clan, whose ancestors had helped stage the anti-Soga coup in 645.

- The emperor Shomu (r. 724–756) was from the Fujiwara clan. His clan used intermarriage into the royal blood line to advance their claims and managed to dominate many of the leading positions on the Council of State Affairs. But after the death of Shomu, his Fujiwara consort left no male heirs; thus, their daughter was eventually placed on the throne.

- Empress Koken/Shotoku left no successor, and her reign was punctuated by the increasing power and independence of the Buddhist hierarchy and the unbridled ambition of the Fujiwara. These problems would provide instability in Japan for centuries to come.

- In 781, the great-grandson of Tenji, Kanmu, acceded to the throne. He was already middle aged and was determined to move quickly to reduce the power of the Buddhist temples and the ambitious noble kinship groups. To meet these goals, he moved the court from Nara to a new capital at Nagaoka.

- A decade later, the capital was moved again to a new site at Heian (modern Kyoto). This capital would remain the royal seat for the next 1,100 years.

Suggested Reading

Saburo Ienagi, *Japanese Art.*

Schirokauer et al., *A Brief History of Chinese and Japanese Civilizations,* chapter 6.

Tsunoda and Carrington, *Japan in the Chinese Dynastic Histories.*

Questions to Consider

1. Why do some scholars regard the Japanese city of Nara as the ultimate terminus of the Silk Roads?

2. Why is the Nara period seen as a cultural golden age in Japanese history?

Japan—Nara and the Great Eastern Temple
Lecture 29—Transcript

Welcome to this third lecture in our mini-series on ancient Japan. Last time we saw that in perhaps the most important innovation of all introduced into Japanese culture by the rulers Temmu and Jito, the official title *tenno* was adopted for the ruler of Japan and the name Nihon or Nippon for the Japanese state. These were their intentional final steps in legitimizing and strengthening the power of throne and transforming Japan into a fully-fledged state. You remember that *tenno* means the "heavenly sovereign" and Nihon or Nippon means the "base or the origin of the sun," which now came to be the official name for the entire country. Both these terms survive to this very day, of course: Japan referred to as Nippon-koku, the "State of Japan," and the emperor as the Tenno, or the "Heavenly Sovereign."

I also mentioned briefly that another of the great projects of Tenmu and Jito was the construction of a new capital city to be the symbol of their new centralized state. In 710, the capital was moved from Fujiwara to a new city, Heijo, or modern Nara. It's hardly surprising that the design and construction of this city would be strongly influenced by Chinese urban planning in general and by the great and magnificent Tang capital of Changan in particular. The construction of Nara marks the beginning of a new era in Japanese history, the Nara Period, and that, of course, is the subject of this, our next lecture, in our exploration of the foundations of Eastern civilization.

You might remember that for many historians the Taika reforms of 645 C.E. are recognized as the moment that the Yamato began to transform itself from a kingdom to a legitimate state. But as we saw in our last lecture, the crucial reforms to create a state based on Tang administrative models actually took place over a much longer period of about a hundred years, from the end of the sixth to the beginning of the eighth centuries. This began with the rise to power of Soga no Umako, continued with the reign of Prince Shotoku, certainly the coup of Kamatari and Tenjo, and it concluded then with this reformist agenda promoted by Temmu and Jito. During this same period in Korea, the Silla kingdom was also in the process of transforming itself into a Tang-style state, as I'm sure you remember. In both Korea and Japan, the reforms involved a complete restructuring of the administration, taxation, and legal systems of the two countries along Chinese Tang dynastic lines. It's no surprise that both countries also decided to the build their own great planned capital cities as the symbol for these new states, cities that might mirror in some way the glorious Tang capital of Changan. In Korea, you remember, the Silla built Kyongju as their capital, while in the north, the Parhae state built their capital Sanggyong, both of which were closely modeled on the grid plan of Changan. In Japan, too, rulers Tenmu and Jito decided to construct a new permanent city at Nara.

Before this, different Yamato kings had ruled from what were called different "shifting" palaces, but now it was time for something permanent, something splendid. Nine of the shifting palaces of the Yamato kings had been located in the small confines of the Asuka Valley in the southern Nara Basin. The first gridded city of the Yamato was Fujiwara, built in 694 just north of the Asuka Valley. This impressive palace and its administrative buildings were linked to the northern Nara Basin and to Osaka Bay by government roads, which were also laid out on a grid pattern that corresponded to the land division system that was in place at the time. Temmu and Jito decided to also construct their new and permanent capital in the northern Nara Basin, where so much transport infrastructure was already in place. The capital city of Heijo, again it's known today by the name of the modern city of Nara, was completed in 710 towards the end of the reign of Jito, and it gives its name to the Nara period.

By the mid-eighth century, Nara was home to about 100,000 people at a time when demographers estimate the total population of the Japanese archipelago was probably around 6 million. I guess this seems tiny compared to the 1 million people who lived inside the city walls at Changan with another million living just outside, of course, out of a Tang dynasty population of some 80 million; but this was by far the most impressive city and actually most impressive population density ever seen in ancient Japan; and because it was modeled on Changan, the city's dimensions were also impressive. Like Changan, a great central avenue, in this case 80 yards wide, the Suzaku Avenue, ran from the southern gate through to the palace in the north. The avenue bisected a grid of streets that measured three miles from north to south and three-and-a-half miles from east to west. The land plots within the grid were then allocated according to rank, with the elites and their mansions located closest to the palace. After processing up Suzaku Avenue, dignitaries and envoys would've entered the palace through the huge Main Gate that had a tiled roof and was painted in brilliant red, green, and white. All the gates were manned by armed guards, and with the exception of very high ranking government bureaucrats, written passes were required for entry into the palace complex. Stretching away from the gate in both directions was a wall 30 feet high, protecting a palace complex that measured 1,300 by 1,100 yards. At the heart of the palace was the Great Supreme Hall, inside which the emperor oversaw state ceremonies and rituals or greeted foreign dignitaries. The Great Hall was also the center of court life and was surrounded by pleasure gardens, offices, kitchens, and storehouses.

Some idea of the wealth and aesthetic sensibilities of the imperial and the other elite families who lived in Nara can be gained from the valuable goods collected in the Shosoin, a log cabin-like storehouse still standing in the compound of the Todaiji Temple today. This is frankly one of the greatest collections of early Eurasian art ever assembled. The Shosoin contained ancient books, weapons, silk, bronze mirrors, wonderful musical instruments, medicines, and magnificent art objects of gold, glass, mother of pearl, and lacquer. Many of these objects had traveled along the Silk Roads, which you might remember were flourishing again during the Tang dynasty; so these objects came in from Korea certainly, but also India, Persia, Greece, even the Mediterranean basin. The collection includes Persian glass, Sasanian silver vessels, an extraordinary ivory ruler from India, Tang dynasty ceramic pagoda models, and musical instruments from deep in the heart of Central Asia. For many Silk Roads scholars, Nara is regarded as literally the eastern terminus of these great Trans-Eurasian trade routes. The possession of these objects by the Nara court also reminds us that the elites of Tang China, of Silla Korea, and of Nara Japan shared much in common; and these shared beliefs, these shared aesthetics if you like, also help us understand why even today these nations with this shared heritage of Eastern civilization still adhere to many certain common philosophical, legal, and administrative models and ideals.

I mentioned the magnificent Todaiji Temple in Nara; this also reminds us that this was a great age for Buddhism in Japan, as it was frankly in contemporary China and Korea. The Todaiji Temple was constructed just to the east of the palace—in fact, Todaiji means the "Great Eastern Temple"—and it contained a gigantic bronze Buddha cast partly from thousands of bronze mirrors that the ladies of the court had donated for this very purpose. This Buddha was over 50 feet tall and weighed, so we read, one million pounds; this was undoubtedly the largest bronze statue ever cast to that point in world history. The Buddha was housed in the Great Buddha Hall, which with dimensions of 280 by 150 feet was also undoubtedly the largest wooden building constructed anywhere in the world to this point in time. The temple complex also featured two towering pagodas more than 330 feet high, amongst the highest buildings ever constructed anywhere in East Asia; this really was a temple that set several new global records.

The original function of the pagoda structure, which appeared all over Buddhist East Asia—as we've seen, certainly in China and Korea also—was to house sacred relics of the Buddha, pieces of bone or teeth like the finger bone I mentioned that I've personally seen that's housed at the enormous Famen Temple complex just outside of Xian in China to this day, purported to be the finger bone of the Buddha. The Todaiji pagodas weren't only impressively high, but also visually stunning and quite brilliantly engineered. The central pole in each was largely unconnected to the surrounding wooden bracketing, which allowed the building to shake during earthquakes without falling down. But alas these wooden pagodas were very vulnerable to fire and so the originals have been lost, although we can say that the world's oldest wooden building can still be found in Nara today, having survived since the eighth century. On the ninth day of the fourth month of 752 C.E., the Great Buddha and temple complex was officially dedicated by the emperor. Early Japanese sources tell us that this ceremony involved 10,000 monks, 4,000 musicians and dancers, and perhaps 7,000 state officials; and as the ceremony reached its climax of music and dancing, a visiting Indian Buddhist monk named Bodhisena painted in the colored eyes of the Great Buddha. This is still regarded as one of the most magnificent spectacles ever staged in all of Japan's long history.

When Buddhism was first introduced into Japan, the Buddha was regarded by the people as a *kami*, a generic term commonly used to describe any of the supposedly innumerable divinities and spirits in the world. In the sixth and seventh centuries, the new religion came to be seen as a kind of magic, similar to the attitude the common people felt towards their own indigenous and also quite magical religion, particularly that which developed into Shintoism. In both cases, the people believed that these supernatural entities could be accessed through prayer and ritual to cure illnesses, to avert disasters, and to obtain the good things in life. It was only natural for them to pray for such blessings simultaneously at Shinto shrines and now at the Buddhist temples. The survival of Shintoism, whose origins can probably be traced right back to as early as the Jomon period, is thus another example of how, despite the overwhelming cultural influence coming from China, Japan was nonetheless able to retain its own distinctive indigenous beliefs and indigenous characteristics. Japan most definitely did adopt Buddhism and Confucianism from China, but the Japanese continued to observe the rites of Shintoism, which revolve around the worship of ancestors and a host of nature spirits and deities. As we'll see later in the course, in 1868—so the Early Modern period—in an attempt to create a new and much more modern Japan while not losing sight of the traditions of the past, the Meiji government tried to turn Japan into an "official Shinto state," and even make Shintoism the basis for government. But by then, more than 2,000 years after Buddhism had first came to Japan, there was no way to purify Shinto and eradicate this pervasive influence of Buddhism, despite the best efforts of the Department of Shinto.

For the first century or so following its arrival in Japan from Korea during the Korean Three Kingdoms period, Buddhism remained a largely private religion for the powerful families like the Soga. Prince Shotoku of the Soga was deeply interested in Buddhism. He had temples built and devoted much of his private time to studying the Buddhist sutras. In a nunnery attached to the temple of Horyuji just outside of Nara, there's actually a piece of embroidered cloth with an inscription that legend has it was something the Prince had once said to his wife: "The world is folly; only the Buddha is true." Around the time of the Taika reforms in 645, Buddhism started to reach a larger public audience, partly because of state patronage. King Jomei had the Great Temple of Paekche constructed near his palace, and King Temmu then built what's called the Daikan Daiji, or the Great Official Temple. What was clearly going on here with this official recognition is that for various political reasons, the government had decided to invest great amounts of treasure and labor into supporting the Buddhist establishment and the religion and building its infrastructure. All this reached a climax during the Nara period, particularly during the reign of Emperor Shomu between 724 and 749. It's actually Shomu who had the great Todaiji Temple constructed close to the palace and who presided over the extraordinary ceremony to dedicate the massive Buddha housed in the Great Buddha Hall.

By this stage in Japan's history, Buddhism had now become the religion of the state; and large state prayer rituals were conducted not so much for personal salvation now, but really for the protection of the nation as a whole. Indeed, the rulers of Nara used fairly strict legal codes and government authority to now try and control the version of Buddhism that was being taught to the people. Socially, the Buddhist hierarchy was now on the same level as the elite government officials and was also materially supported by state resources; but Buddhist affairs were also increasingly coming under the control of bureaucrats. One example of this is that those entering the priesthood now needed government permission, and the legal codes contained lists of prohibitions and restrictions on the behavior of monks. Monks and nuns were now forbidden to hold ceremonies outside of the temples; there were new laws now against people congregating for religious purposes. On the one hand, this meant that in this increasingly legalistic age, Japanese Buddhism was unable to produce any original religious philosophy because in some way it might transgress the new state-sponsored orthodox version, which was now exclusively focused on using Buddhism to protect the authority of the state. But having said that, on the other hand this did mean that the religious community, supported by the wealth and resources of the state, was able to create brilliant material culture in the form of glorious religious art. This trend was helped by the fact that the ruling class believed the more splendid the temples and statues were, the greater would be the spiritual return for the state. So the Nara period is regarded today as a glorious age in the history of art and culture in Japan, frankly in Eastern civilization more widely. I'd like to briefly explore some of this with you now in the final part of this lecture.

It's no surprise that most of the visual art that survives from the Nara period is Buddhist, given what we've just been discussing. We're talking here about sculptures, ritual objects, silk tapestries, and, of course, copies of the sutras that are masterpieces of calligraphy. The temples around Nara, many of which survive to this day, were and are veritable treasure troves. Architecturally, the temples were masterpieces of planning in which the buildings were placed in a particular vertical order based on careful sight perspective from the front main gate all the way back towards the main hall. We can almost imagine the feelings of visitors as they entered these complexes: the soaring pagodas, the carved roofs somehow suspended between heaven and earth, and the brilliant contrast between bright red-painted structures and whitewashed walls. Imagine the awe of the common people in particular, long accustomed to humble dwellings and small villages, as they entered the great halls full of massive pillars, huge Buddhist statues, and monks in these flowing saffron-colored robes with their serene faces. To the people, the statues must've seemed like actual realizations of the eternal Buddha himself. This aesthetic, visually splendid sense of the meaning of Buddhism explains the rich artistic treasures that were produced during the Nara period. It also reminds us, of course, that all religions have used magnificent architecture and art to create a similar sense of awe and wonder amongst the faithful, as any visitor to the great cathedrals of Europe or the magnificent mosques of the Islamic world can testify.

Although brilliant Japanese painters and sculptors of the Nara period are known, much of the art inside these temples was actually created by visiting or resident Chinese and Korean artists. Horyuji Temple, for example, contains a superb elongated sculpture known as the *Kudara Kannon*. Some of the oldest paintings in Japan are found on the cabinet-sized Jewel-Beetle Shrine in this same temple, which is decorated with iridescent beetle wings set into metal edging. The Toshodaiji Temple of Nara was founded by a Chinese monk named Ganjin who, after being shipwrecked, delayed by storms, and also by government opposition, actually needed six attempts before he finally reached Japan; but by then, he'd gone blind. The sculpted portrait of Ganjin in the Toshodaiji Temple brilliantly captures his blindness, but it also reminds us that the Buddhist culture of Nara was very cosmopolitan, with many important practitioners having come from Korea, China, even from India.

Let's remember again that this was one of the great periods of Silk Roads exchanges. We know that priests, merchants, and ambassadors from Tang China, from the Silla court, from India, even from Persia regularly visited

Nara, Japan. Partly this was a reflection of the internationalism of Buddhism, but partly it was a product of the hunger for transcultural exchange that so characterizes this extraordinary era of Eastern civilization. But we should note something very important here: We should note that Japan would rarely experience this level of contact with the outside world, this sense of cosmopolitanism again, not for more than a thousand years until after the Meiji Restoration of the 19th century.

In literature, too, the Nara period was a golden age. Sacred texts from China and Korea were copied and commented upon in flowing calligraphy. We actually know of some 100,000 volumes of sacred text that have survived from the eighth century through to today. Japan's first history texts, indeed some of the very first texts of any genre produced in Japan, were also written during this Nara period, including the *Kojiki*, or the *Records of Ancient Matters*, published in 712 C.E., and the *Nihon shoki*, or the *Chronicles of Japan*, in 720; needless to say, two very important books for historians. The books abound with songs, prose passages, and poetry about magic battles and fascinating stories from the past. One of the greatest anthologies of Japanese poetry was also produced during the Nara period: the *Manyoshu*, or the *Collection of Ten Thousand Leaves*, which actually contains more than 4,500 superb, poignant poems. The *Manyoshu* reminds me that before we leave the rich and glittering Nara period, we need to remember that we've largely been describing the world of the super secular and spiritual elites thus far in this lecture. But one of the poems in the *Manyoshu*, written by the poet Yamanoue no Okura, describes the impoverished lives of the peasants who labored to supply the resources that sustained these very elites. Let me just read a little for you:

> By my pillowside my father and mother crouch,
> And at my feet my wife and children;
> Thus am I surrounded by grief and hungry piteous cries.
> But on the hearth no kettle sends up clouds of steam
> And in our pot a spider spins its web
> We have forgotten the very way of cooking rice.

Let me begin to conclude this lecture now by noting that although the Nara court had to face no foreign crises and no fullblown civil wars, it did have its share of problems, including periodic famines and also a smallpox epidemic that lasted for two years between 735 and 737. But the biggest challenges to the Nara court came from bitterly disputed succession problems and power struggles. At the center of many of these struggles was the Fujiwara clan, whose ancestors had actually helped stage the anti-Soga clan coup right back in 645. The great Emperor Shomu, who reigned from 724–756 and who presided over the dedication of the Great Buddha, was of the Fujiwara clan. The Fujiwara used intermarriage into the royal bloodlines to advance their claims, but also managed to dominate many of the leading positions on the Council of State Affairs. But after the death of Shomu, his Fujiwara consort left no male heirs, so their daughter was eventually placed on the throne. Empress Koken/Shotoku actually reigned twice: After the initial reign she was forced to abdicate, but she overthrew her successor and came back to reign again. But she left no successor, however, and her reign was punctuated by the increasing power and the increasing independence of both the Buddhist hierarchy and also the unbridled ambition of the Fujiwara.

As we'll see in our next lecture, these problems would provide instability in Japan frankly for centuries to come. Eventually the great grandson of Tenji, Kanmu, acceded to the throne in 781. He was already middle aged and was determined to move quickly to try and reduce the power of the Buddhist temples and also of the ambitious noble kinship groups. In order to do this, he decided that the court simply had be moved again, moved from Nara, which was too closely associated with the powerful court families and the Buddhist hierarchy. The site the emperor selected for his new capital at Nagaoka had other advantages, too, including much better access to water transport, which would then link the capital to the port at Naniwa and on to the Sea of Japan. So the capital was moved, but there were problems with construction at the first site; and a decade later, the capital was moved again to a new site at Heian, or the modern city of Kyoto. This proved a much better choice because the capital at Heian would go on to remain the royal seat of power for the next 1,100 years, until the 19th century.

The Heian period up until 1185 will be the subject of our next lecture; this will be our last on Japan for a while. But I certainly promise to return to Japan in future lectures to explore how the warrior class gradually gained enough power to replace the imperial system with a feudal shogunate.

Let me begin to conclude here, though, by noting that with the emulation of the government and culture of the Chinese Tang dynasty during the seventh and eighth centuries by various other regional societies—by kingdoms in Korea and now in Japan—East Asia became a coherent regional entity based, as I suggested earlier, on common aesthetic values; certainly on common philosophies; certainly we see with Buddhism on common religion; a common literary tradition; and very similar state structures. But again, Korea and Japan never became carbon copies of the Tang, and neither did their common values ensure peaceful relations nor parallel development thereafter. Indeed, I think we can say the history of the region for the next 1,300 years was to be dominated just as much by violent struggles between these East Asian neighbors as it was by shared values or shared fortunes. Thank you.

Japan—The World of the Heian
Lecture 30

lthough the Heian period began with a strong assertion of imperial power by Emperor Kanmu, this was not to last. Under the influence of the aristocracy, the Heian introduced a new political and social system—part imperial, part feudal—that would dominate Japan for almost 1,000 years. After 1185 C.E., real power moved from the capital at Kyoto to the countryside, where it resided in the hands of shoguns and their armies of samurai warriors. The Heian period saw two centuries of relative peace, dominated by the powerful Fujiwara house. But the emperor increasingly became only a figurehead, and it was the Fujiwara regents who were the power behind the throne.

Heian System of Government

- For the first 50 years of the Heian, Emperor Kanmu and his successors successfully maintained the preexisting framework of the imperial state system. But after that first half century, the house of Fujiwara began to assert its authority and eventually came to dominate the state without ever actually displacing the imperial house.

- This structure, which has continued to a certain extent to the present day, allowed the emperor to continue to function as the titular head of the government and to remain an object of veneration, although he possessed no real political power. Ever since the 9th century, the Japanese political order has been based on a split between a publicly recognized imperial figure and a separate agent of effective rule.

- This profound change in the Japanese system of government can be traced to the rise of the Fujiwara hereditary house, which in turn can be explained by changes in the principles of land ownership.

Land Ownership in Japan

- Under the pre- and early-Heian legal system, all land essentially belonged to the crown. The government had the right to allocate land for farming and for aristocratic and Buddhist estates and to decide which land was taxable and which was tax free. The noble estates were augmented by land from local peasant farmers who could not meet their tax burdens.

- Eventually, in many of the outlying districts of Japan, powerful noble houses were able to increase their land holdings so significantly that the officials of the central government lost authority and control over them. These great estates (*shoen*) became hereditary possessions of aristocratic families, who were often granted tax-exempt status in return for supporting the central government and were often also immune from bureaucratic interference.

- Because the elite landowners were often away in court, the estates were managed by administrators, who also received rights of income from the lands. These rights (*shiki*) entitled individuals to a percentage of income from the estates and could be further subdivided or sublet and even passed on to heirs. Over the centuries, the system became extraordinarily complicated; eventually, four levels of rights holders were recognized even in a single estate!

- The government attempted to regulate the process, but the great estates continued to grow, as did the power of the families that controlled them. Government officials dispatched to rural areas to collect taxes on the remaining public-owned land also became increasingly autonomous and wealthy. In the capital, the great families competed for status and power; the most important public offices came to be dominated by the nobility.

- With wealth, power, and even the bureaucracy now essentially under private control, the Heian government became very different from the government of the Nara period. For most of the 9th and 10th centuries, it was controlled by the house of Fujiwara.

- Using intermarriage with the imperial family to amass power, by 857, the northern branch of the Fujiwara clan had one of its members in a powerful position to influence the throne: the statesman Fujiwara no Yoshifusa.

  o When a grandson of Yoshifusa was placed on the imperial throne as Emperor Seiwa, Yoshifusa became regent to the young emperor.

  o This new regent position (*kanpaku*) was institutionalized and became the mechanism whereby the Fujiwara could wield real power.

  o Although there were some attempts to oppose the power of the Fujiwara, the clan used the regent system to effectively dominate and control Heian government for centuries.

Heian Literature

- Over time, the elite society of the Heian period grew more aloof from the common people and began to ridicule rural lifeways. Day-to-day administration of government and private estates was now handled by underling officials, leaving the aristocrats free to devote themselves to their refined lifestyle in court and to pursue their aesthetic interests.

- A famous literary work from the period is the *Genji Monogatari* (the *Tale of Genji*), written by a lady-in-waiting at court, Lady Murasaki Shikibu. With extraordinary insight, Lady Murasaki describes the romantic intrigues of her time, offers intricate and subtle psychological portraits of her characters, and gives us rich insight into the world of the Heian elite.

- Another great literary work of the period, the *Tale of Konjaku*, describes a harsh and miserable peasant lifestyle very different from the refined world of the capital.

Heian Warrior Class

- Before conscription had been introduced during the Tomb Period, trained warriors had been associated with particular hereditary houses far back into early Japanese history. Even after conscription was introduced, this class of "private" fighters never disappeared.

The *Tale of Genji* demonstrates the author's great store of knowledge about relations between men and women and the refined interests of the Heian elites.

- With the abandonment of the conscription system just before the Heian period, the central government lost the ability to raise state armies. Military power and responsibility passed into the hands of provincial officials and the great hereditary houses. The warrior class that arose did not live in the capital but in the provincial regions—and it was these fighters who evolved into the famed samurai.

- Samurai warriors were members of a rural elite, living on their own lands. In certain regions, large local warrior organizations developed, in which the samurai honed their skills through repeated clashes. These organizations kept order in the provinces, fighting for various wealthy patrons and jockeying for power.

- Two of the greatest warrior associations coalesced around the powerful Minamoto and Taira clans; members of both were involved in rebellions in the 10th century. By the 11th century, some of these clashes had developed into full-scale wars, including one that lasted between 1028 and 1087.

Heian Cultural Achievements

- Undoubtedly, Heian culture deeply reflected Chinese traditions; most literature copied Chinese models and was written in Chinese, and young men received their formal education by learning to read and write in the Chinese language and studying the classics of Chinese philosophy. The Japanese writing system also reflected Chinese influence.

- The other overwhelming influence that came to Japan filtered through China was Buddhism. In the Heian period, different and distinctly Japanese variants of Buddhism began to emerge, which went on to also influence the further development of Shinto.

  - Emperor Kanmu supported the ideals of a Buddhist monk, Saicho, who spread the broad and accommodating Tendai version of Buddhism.

  - Tendai Buddhism holds that everyone can gain enlightenment through meditation. It became so popular in Japan that Saicho's temple at Mount Hiei grew into a vast complex of 3,000 buildings.

  - In the late 9th century, a bitter split developed between the followers of another Tendai monk, Ennin, and those of his successor. This led to the introduction of a new force in Japanese Buddhism: well-armed temple militias, whose *akuso* ("evil monks") engaged in violence and learned the skills of combat.

  - The other major school of Buddhism during the Heian was Shingon, founded by the monk Kukai (774–835). This version was focused on mystic spoken formulae and on the secret oral transmission of knowledge from master to student. The teachings were esoteric and difficult to understand, yet because Shingon used mystical rites, incantations, and exorcism, it also became popular in the Heian.

  - The great majority of Japanese people during the Heian lived in a world permeated by religion and magic. In this strange mix, various versions of Buddhism and Shintoism blended with Confucianism, yin and yang philosophy, geomancy, and exorcism.

- As we have already seen, the Heian was a rich era for literature. Superb Chinese-style poetry and prose was written, along with Japanese vernacular poetry. Many of the Heian classic poems were collected and published in the *Kokinshu* (*Collection of Ancient and Modern Poetry*).

- Japanese architecture was also transformed in the Heian, particularly the layout of new temples. When Saicho and Kukai built their temples, they abandoned the formal symmetrical plans of the Nara and accommodated construction to the natural environment. Trees, rock outcrops, and streams became an integral part of the spiritual experience in a way that has remained distinctly Japanese ever since.

- Painting thrived in the Heian period, notably on the screens of sliding doors that were decorated with landscapes. Late in the Heian, glorious picture scrolls also appeared, which combined text and images to illustrate scenes from fictional tales.

The End of the Heian

- Despite the sumptuousness of cultural life in the court, late in the Heian period, the countryside was transformed as the equal-field system fell apart and aristocratic clans accumulated most of the land for themselves and their private armies.

- By the 12th century, the two most powerful clans—the Taira and Minamoto—were engaged in open war. In 1185, the Minamoto emerged victorious, a victory that brought to an end the Heian period.

- The Minamoto claimed the right to rule in the name of the figurehead emperor and installed a shogun (military governor), who now ruled the imperial structure. The Minamoto established the new seat for their government at Kamakura, and as we will see later in the course, they went on to rule Japan for the next four centuries in an era known as the Kamakura shogunate.

Suggested Reading

Hurst Jr., "The Structure of the Heian Court."

Saburo Ienagi, *Japanese Art.*

Tyler, "Introduction" to *The Tale of Genji.*

Questions to Consider

1. How did the house of Fujiwara manage to dominate the Japanese state during the Heian without actually displacing the imperial house?

2. What is *The Tale of Genji*, and what insights does it give us into the refined lifestyle of the elites during the Heian?

Japan—The World of the Heian
Lecture 30—Transcript

Although the Heian Period, which followed the Nara, began with a strong assertion of imperial power by Emperor Kanmu, this wasn't to last. Under the influence of a powerful aristocracy, the Heian introduced a new Japanese political and social system—part imperial, part feudal—that would go on to dominate Japan for almost a thousand years. The Heian capital built at Kyoto in 794 was also destined to remain the Japanese capital for more than a thousand years, until 1868. But as we'll see, after 1185 C.E., real power moved to the countryside where it now resided in the hands of military governors called shoguns and their personal armies of samurai warriors. As we'll see in this lecture, the founding of the new Heian capital was followed by two centuries of relative peace dominated by the powerful Fujiwara house. But the emperor increasingly became only a figurehead, and it was the Fujiwara regents who literally became the power behind the throne.

The Heian remains one of the most fascinating periods in this long history of Japan, politically and certainly also culturally. It began with a political structure closely modeled on that of Tang China, but it ended as something quite different again; something that was distinctly and recognizably Japanese. The Heian period is the subject of this lecture, our last in this series of four on the early history and culture of Japan.

One of the major reasons Emperor Kanmu decided to move his court to a new capital at Heian was to reduce the power of two groups who'd constantly threatened to undermine the authority of the emperor during the Nara period: the Buddhist hierarchy, and also the ambitious noble kinship groups. Now by having temples built on the outskirts of his new capital, unlike at Nara where they'd actually been central to his palace, Kanmu was able to reduce the influence of the Buddhist monks on his secular government. By increasing the authority of the bureaucracy, he also helped keep the hereditary kinship families at bay, at least for a while. For the first 50 years of the Heian, Kanmu and his successors successfully maintained the preexisting framework of the imperial state system.

But after that first half century, the house of Fujiwara began to assert its authority and eventually came to dominate the state without ever actually displacing the imperial house. This system of government, which to a certain extent has continued right through to the present day, allowed the emperor to continue to function as the titular head of the government and to remain an object of veneration. But despite the continuing aura and mystique surrounding the many emperors of Japan that have followed Kanmu, they've actually possessed no real political power. Ever since the ninth century, in fact, the Japanese political order has been based on this split between a publicly recognized imperial figure and a separate agent of effective rule. This arrangement helps account for the exceptional longevity of the Japanese imperial house, of course. Because emperors haven't actually ruled, they haven't been subject to deposition during times of turmoil. That is, ruling parties, ruling houses, and ruling factions have come and gone, but the imperial house has survived through to today.

This profound change in the Japanese system of government can be traced squarely to the rise of the Fujiwara hereditary house, and this in turn can be explained by changes in the principles of land ownership in Japan. These are messy, but we need to explore them; they're very complicated. Under the pre- and early-Heian legal systems, all land essentially belonged to the crown. The government had the right to allocate land for farming, and for aristocratic and Buddhist estates, of course, and also to decide which land was taxable and which was tax free. The noble estates were augmented by local peasant farmers who could often not meet their tax burdens, and so allowed their plots to be swallowed up by the large estates. Eventually this meant that in many of the outlying districts of Japan, powerful noble houses were able to increase their land holdings, and obviously thus their wealth and power, so significantly that the officials of the central government effectively lost authority and control over them. These great estates, called *shoen* in Japanese, became hereditary possessions of aristocratic families, who were often granted tax exempt status in return for supporting the central government, and who were often also immune from bureaucratic interference. This was actually a further incentive for small landowners to place their fields under the control of these large estates, because they could now share in the tax free status. Because the elite landowners were often far away in court, the estates were managed by administrators who also received rights of income from the lands. These rights, they're called the *shiki*, entitled individuals to a percentage of income from the estates, and these rights could be further subdivided or even sublet and passed on to one's heirs.

Over the centuries, this system became extraordinarily complicated—men and women might hold different kinds of rights on different estates—until eventually four levels of rights holders were recognized even in a single estate. From the bottom up, these were the farmers, the *shomin*; then the managers, the *ryoshu*; then the influential families or the officials of the estate, *shokan*; and finally the patrons of the estates who lived far away in the capital, the *ryoke*. The government did attempt to regulate this process, but the great estates continued to grow, and so did the power of the families that controlled them. Government officials dispatched to the rural areas to try and collect taxes on the remaining public-owned land also became increasingly autonomous and wealthy. In the capital meanwhile, the great families competed for status and power, and for the most important public offices that had come to be dominated now by the nobility. With wealth, power, and even the bureaucracy now essentially under private control, the Heian government became something very different to the government of the Nara period. As imperial government declined, so de facto government had become essentially privatized.

For most of the 9th and 10th centuries, this privatized government was controlled by the house of Fujiwara, a name, by the way, which literally translates as "wisteria plain." The Fujiwara clan eventually grew so large that it divided into four main branches or groups of families; it's the Hokke or Northern Fujiwara branch that came to dominate the Heian court. Using intermarriage with the imperial family to amass power, by 857 the Northern Fujiwara had a member of their clan in a powerful position to influence the throne, the statesman Fujiwara no Yoshifusa. When a grandson of Yoshifusa was placed on the imperial throne as Emperor Seiwa, Yoshifusa became regent to the young emperor. Yoshifusa was the first man not of imperial rank to assume the title of regent; he was also the first in what would be a long line of Fujiwara clan regents. This new regent position, called the *kanpaku*, was institutionalized, and so became the mechanism whereby the Fujiwara could wield real power; the regent was now literally the power behind the throne, and all the regents were Fujiwara men.

Although there were some attempts to oppose the power of the Fujiwara, they used the regent system so effectively to dominate and control Heian government for centuries. Under the old system, the aristocrats had acted as officials, similar in a way to the role of Confucian bureaucrats in China. During the Yamatai and Nara periods, officials and peasants had certain views in common; poems in the *Manyoshu* reflect empathy for the shared experiences of life amongst the two classes. But the elite society of the Heian period grew more and more aloof from the people, and came to ridicule the rural lifeways upon which their privileged lives depended. Day to day administration of government and private estates was now handled by underling officials, leaving these aristocrats free to devote themselves wholly to their super-refined lifestyle in court. Shut off from the real world, unburdened by any genuine political responsibility, these elites lived a life of luxury and pursued their aesthetic interests. As a result, Heian elite society was responsible for quite extraordinary achievements in literature, visual arts, ideas about beauty, and the subtle refinements of courtly life. The perfect Heian gentleman now took great care over his appearance, wearing a magnificently-colored court cloak, grape-colored trousers embroidered with wisteria designs, and a glossy crimson under robe The women were even more splendidly attired; indeed, in many ways this was a quite magnificent age for the elite women of Japan. We have startling evidence of this in a famous literary work from the period, the *Genji monogatari*, the famous *Tale of Genji.*

Although certain Shinto sects actively marginalized women, as we've already seen in this short series on Japan, the history of early Japan features many powerful and successful women rulers. Now in this super-refined world of the Heian, a lady in waiting at court, Lady Murasaki Shikibu, had the talent and opportunity to write what many consider to be one of the world's first, indeed one of the world's finest, novels. The book isn't structured in a modern sense like a novel, not in a technical sense; rather it strings together a series of tales centered on the figure of the fictional Prince Genji, the "shining prince," and on the people of the generation that follow his. With extraordinary insight, Lady Murasaki describes the romantic intrigues of her time and offers intricate and subtle psychological portraits of her characters. No doubt the ladies and gentlemen of the Heian court would've recognized themselves in the book because it so brilliantly brings to life its particular place and time. But like the Buddhist art of the Nara, the *Tale of Genji* transcends the Heian because the protagonists it portrays are such universal characters. This book demonstrates the author's great store of knowledge about relations between men and women, about ways of living, about poetry, music, painting, and all the refined interests of the elites.

Lady Murasaki, who lived between 978 and 1031, wrote the book when the Fujiwara house was at the height of its power. Fujiwara Michinaga was the outstanding aristocrat of the time, and many believe that the character of Genji was modeled on him. The prince and his friends live amongst the gardens and palaces of the Heian court, cultivating their super-refined lifestyle. They pass their time mixing subtle perfumes, composing fine poetry, and wooing cultivated women. But Heian men had no real idea of what the women they were wooing actually looked like, because the women were hidden behind screens with only their sleeves showing. Beautiful women were valued for round, white faces and extraordinarily long hair; but what men really fell in love with was a woman's sense of the aesthetic, as revealed through her talents at poetry and calligraphy. Calligraphy was seen as the key to a woman's soul, so the Heian version of love at first sight was a man falling in love with a woman after glimpsing a few beautifully drawn brush strokes.

But the *Tale of Genji* is more even than a brilliantly realized evocation of an era; it also offers a profound meditation on the passing of time and the sorrows that time can bring to sensitive humans. As Genji and his friends age, they realize that past joys and past relationships have gone forever; their thoughts suffuse the tale with a melancholy spirit that presents a subtle contrast to the elegant atmosphere of the Heian court. Lady Murasaki Shikibu created one of the great literary works of the Japanese language, a rich insight into the world of Heian elite and a universal tale of the passing of time and the inevitability of ageing and death.

By way of contrast, another great literary work of the period, the *Tale of Konjaku*, describes a harsh and miserable peasant lifestyle very different to the refined world of the capital. Despite the fact that aristocratic wealth in the capital was based on the agricultural resources produced on the great estates in the country by these farmers, during the Heian there existed a wide gap between the elite way of life and that of the common people. This is also reflected in the clothing worn by members of the different classes. Members of the peasantry wore simple and practical dress because their work demanded freedom to move. This was in stark contrast to the physically limiting and inconvenient clothing of the court, particularly the 12-layered garment of elite women.

But there was another increasingly powerful group that emerged during the Heian, the warrior class. They also preferred the simple and practical clothing of the common people to facilitate their art of fighting. Heian refined elites also looked with disdain upon the military, but realized they couldn't do without them. Before conscription had been introduced right back during the Tomb period, trained warriors had been associated with particular hereditary houses far back into early Japanese history. Even after conscription was introduced, this class of private fighter never really disappeared. With the abandonment of the conscription system just before the Heian period, the central government lost the ability to raise state armies. Military power and responsibility now passed into the hands of the provincial officials and the great hereditary houses. The warrior class that arose didn't live in the capital but in the provincial regions, and it's these fighters who evolved into the famed samurai. These warriors actually lived on their own lands and were well-versed in practical agriculture. Frankly, fighting equipment was expensive—horse, armor, weapons, specialized training—something that the rural elite could afford only through successful farming.

In certain regions in the countryside, large local warrior organizations developed, notably along the eastern frontier regions of Kanto, where they honed their skills by repeatedly clashing with each other. It's these fighting organizations that kept order in the provinces, fighting for various wealthy patrons and jockeying for power. Local lords who claimed descent from the powerful hereditary families proved particularly adept at constructing and maintaining the loyalty of what were increasingly becoming private armies. Two of the greatest warrior associations coalesced around the powerful Minamoto and Taira clans, and members of both were involved in rebellions in the 10th century. By the 11th century, some of these clashes had developed into full-scale wars, including one that lasted for about 60 years between 1028 and 1087. The Minamoto and Taira continued to amass power; and as we'll see a bit later in the course, it's the ongoing conflict between them that effectively ended the Heian.

But before concluding this initial series of four lectures on early Japan, we must now take a brief look at some of the other rich cultural achievements of the Heian. This will also help us consider again, I think, the degree to which these societies were able to escape (or not) the pervasive cultural influence coming from China.

There's no doubt that Heian culture deeply reflected Chinese traditions. Most literature, for example, copied Chinese models and was written in Chinese classical script. Young men received their formal education by learning to read and write in the Chinese language, and through studying the great classics of Chinese philosophy and Chinese literature. Actually, as an interesting side note to this, because girls rarely received formal Chinese education, Lady Murasaki Shikibu had to write the *Tale of Genji* in vernacular Japanese because her Chinese was so basic; how ironic. The Japanese writing system also reflected Chinese influence. Scholars borrowed many characters from Chinese, for example, and they used them to represent Japanese words. They also directly adopted some Chinese characters straight into the Japanese syllabic script, in which, by the way, symbols represent now whole syllables rather than just a single sound as in the alphabetic script. The other overwhelming influence that came to Japan filtered through China was Buddhism, which, as you remember, was flourishing during the preceding Nara period. Now, in the Heian, different and distinctly Japanese variants of Buddhism began to emerge, which went on to also influence the further development, by the way, of Shinto religion.

Although Emperor Kanmu had originally moved the court from Nara to Heian to curtail the power of the Buddhist hierarchy, Buddhism continued to flourish under the Heian. Emperor Kanmu supported the ideals of one monk in particular, Saicho, who lived from 767–822. In 804, he traveled to Tang China to seek sanction there from the Buddhist hierarchy. Upon his return, he turned away from the worldliness of the Nara temples and adopted the broad and accommodating Tendai version of Buddhism, which he then promoted despite bitter opposition from the Nara religious establishment, as you'd imagine. Tendai Buddhism believes that everyone can gain enlightenment through meditation. It became so popular in Japan that Saicho's little temple at Mount Hei grew into a vast complex eventually of some 3,000 buildings. A later follower of Saicho named Ennin also traveled to China, but in the late ninth century a bitter split developed between the followers of Ennin and those of his successor. This led to the introduction of a new force in Japanese Buddhism, well-armed temple militias. These *akuso*, the so-called "evil monks," engaged in violence, they learned the skills of combat, and by the 11th century all of the leading temples were maintaining what we'd have to call large standing armies of *akuso*. Mount Hei itself had several thousand troops that regularly descended on the capital to terrorize the residents and to demand titles, administrative positions, and more land.

The other major school of Buddhism during the Heian was Shingon, founded by the monk Kukai, who lived 774–835. Like Saicho, Kukai also traveled to China, he gained imperial patronage, and he founded his own monastery on a mountain, Mount Koya. Shingon Buddhism was focused on mystic spoken formulae and on the secret oral transmission of knowledge from master to student. The teachings were esoteric, they were difficult to understand, yet because Shingon used mystical rites, incantations, and even exorcism it also became deeply popular in the Heian period, appealing to the common people who'd always been attracted to the magic possibilities of Buddhism.

This reminds us that, like their ancient predecessors, the great majority of Japanese people during the Heian lived in a world permeated by religion and magic. In this strange syncretic mix, various versions of Buddhism and Shintoism blended with Confucianism, with yin and yang philosophy, with geomancy or feng shui, and also with exorcism. Residents of the capital would purify themselves regularly; they'd avoid travel to different places or even in different directions on inauspicious days; and they sought exorcism from priests when they were sick. As well as the powerful Buddha, people continued to worship their local spirits; and all of this, as we'll see in a later lecture, fed back into the development of Shintoism.

But our focus is on the arts here for the last part of this lecture. We've already seen that the Heian was a rich era for literature. Men wrote superb Chinese-style poetry, Tang-style poetry, and prose; and writing in the Japanese vernacular, often by women, also thrived, as the *Tale of Genji* so inestimably demonstrates. Japanese vernacular poetry also reached superb heights of expression, and many of the Heian classic poems were collected and published in the *Kokinshu*, the *Collection of Ancient and Modern Poetry*. All this further influenced Japanese writing itself: As the syllabic use of characters evolved, they were gradually abbreviated and simplified, leading to the appearance of new symbols that were distinctly different from the Chinese characters. Japanese architecture was also transformed in the Heian, particularly the layout of new temples.

When Saicho and Kukai decided to build their temples on mountains, they abandoned the formal symmetrical plans we discussed of Nara and they accommodated the construction of their temples to the natural environment. Now trees, rock outcrops, and streams became an integral part of the spiritual experience in a way that's remained distinctly Japanese ever since. The design of private dwellings was also influenced by this new esthetic. Heian mansions all featured a garden now; artificial hills were created; carefully placed bamboo and trees; a pond was always crossed by a bridge. Like all Japanese buildings of the period, the structures, with their beautiful polished wood floors, were now raised a few feet off the ground to allow a stream to pass underneath.

Painting also thrived, notably on the screens of sliding doors that were decorated with landscapes. Heian artists took Japanese painting away from the Chinese-inspired art of the Nara period. Late in the Heian, glorious picture scrolls started to appear that combined text and images to illustrate scenes from the tales. The scrolls painted to illustrate the *Tale of Genji* are particularly gorgeous, illustrating the superb story with richly colored pictures of the luxurious apparel and refined lifeway of the aristocrats, also with elegant cursive script and on handsome colored paper on which all the elements were combined and expressed. These early combination scrolls later evolved into picture-only scrolls that featured a continuous horizontal strip of painted images unfolding a story in chronological order, not unlike the embroidered Bayeux Tapestry in France, which richly illustrates William of Normandy's 1066 conquest of England.

But despite of, or even perhaps because of, the sumptuousness of cultural life in the court, late in the Heian period the countryside was transformed as the equal-field system fell apart and aristocratic clans accumulated most of the land for themselves and for their private armies. By the 12th century the two most powerful clans, Taira and Minamoto, were engaged in open war until in 1185, the Minamoto emerged victorious, a victory that brought to an end this extraordinary, glorious, cultural Heian period. The Minamoto now claimed the right to rule in the name of the figurehead emperor and they installed a shogun, a new title for a military governor, who now ruled the imperial structure. The Minamoto established the new seat for their government at the town of Kamakura, and as we'll see later in the course, they went on to rule Japan for the next four centuries in an era known as firstly the Kamakura and then the Muromachi shogunates.

But for now I think we need to take leave of Korea certainly and also of Japan just for a while, because I think we need to take a brief visit to some other regions that fell within the powerful Chinese cultural zone: the fascinating states of Southeast Asia. In these lectures on Korea and Japan, I've tried to show that although both these states took their inspiration from Chinese culture, their political and cultural structures developed along lines that I think we can say were distinctly different from those of the powerful Middle Kingdom. Yet Japan and Korea clearly had a place in the larger Eastern cultural zone, influenced by Chinese religion, philosophy, law, and imperial administration. I look forward to joining you again next time as we further widen our investigation of the foundations of Eastern civilization by journeying to Southeast Asia to see if we can discern similar, but also different, cultural developments there.

Southeast Asia—Vietnam
Lecture 31

In this lecture and the next, we'll look at the history and culture of the Southeast Asia region. Inevitably, Vietnam, Cambodia, Thailand, Malaya, and various other states in the region became members of the vast cultural zone dominated by China. We will investigate the impact of many of the foundational elements of Eastern civilization we have looked at earlier on the states and peoples of Southeast Asia, and we'll explore the impact that political, economic, and cultural developments in Southeast Asian states had on China and Eastern civilization more generally. In this lecture, we begin with the history and culture of Vietnam, from its earliest interactions with ancient China through its colonization by the French in the 18th century.

Ancient Viet History

- The first recorded mention of the Viets appears in Han dynasty annals, where they are described as "southern barbarians" who resisted Qin dynasty raids into south China in the 220s B.C.E. At that time, the Viet kingdom extended quite a way along the southern coast of what is Chinese territory today.

- The Qin raids had little political impact, but they boosted the small-scale trade that had existed between the Viets and Chinese for centuries. In exchange for Chinese silk, the Viets sent to China ivory, tortoiseshell, pearls, peacock feathers, and aromatic woods.

- In the decades that followed the Qin raids, expansionist Viet rulers defeated the warlords who controlled the Red River valley (which today is in China) and brought their lands under Viet control.

- The Viets intermarried with many of their neighbors, including the residents of the Red River valley and the Khmer (Cambodian) and Thai people, all of which contributed to the formation of the Vietnamese people as a distinct ethnic identity. This willingness of the Vietnamese to intermarry suggests that, before Vietnam was conquered by the Han, Vietnamese culture had much in common with the other peoples of Southeast Asia and was distinctly different from Chinese culture.

o   For example, none of the Southeast Asian spoken languages had any linguistic relationship with Chinese. The Viets also had a strong tradition of village autonomy and favored the nuclear family over the larger extended family preferred by the Chinese.

o   Even after the Chinese conquered Vietnam politically and after the introduction of Buddhism from China, many of these distinct cultural practices were preserved.

Chinese Conquest of Vietnam

- As the Western Han began to consolidate power throughout China and East Asia in the 3rd century B.C.E., they soon came into contact with the Viets. Initially, the Han accepted an acknowledgement of vassal status from the Viets, along with periodic payments of tribute, but in 111 B.C.E., the Han decided to conquer the Viets outright and govern them directly as a Han province.

- The Red River area was garrisoned with Han troops, and Chinese administrators who were dispatched to the region encouraged local lords to learn the Chinese language and culture. Realizing that they had much to learn from the Han state, the Viet elites decided to cooperate with the Chinese. The Chinese government saw the Viets as another "barbarian" people, ripe for assimilation, and thus, worked hard to introduce the essential elements of their civilization into their new southern province.

- Over the centuries of Han rule that followed, the Viet elites were drawn into the superb government structure administered by the Han Confucian bureaucracy. In the rural areas, the Han introduced sophisticated Chinese agricultural techniques and irrigation technology, which quickly made Vietnam the most productive rice-growing region in all of East Asia.

- As a result, the Viet population grew, particularly along the Red River valley and coastal regions to the south. The Viet elites then used the lessons of Chinese statecraft to extend their own military control over regions further west and south, which helped spread elements of Chinese culture more widely throughout Southeast Asia. The Chinese must have assumed that the Vietnamese barbarians were well on their way to becoming civilized.

- But as many later invaders were to learn, the roots of Vietnamese resistance to conquest and colonization ran deep. Ultimately, the Chinese were frustrated by a series of revolts against their hegemony by Vietnamese elites and even more so by the failure of Viet peasants to adopt Chinese culture.

Opposition to Chinese Rule

- As the decades of colonialism passed, the elites increasingly chaffed against Chinese hegemony. Viet lords galvanized the common people to join them in revolt.

- One of the most famous revolts was instigated by women—the Trung sisters—who led an uprising against the Han in 39 C.E. The actions of the Trung sisters further demonstrate the profound difference that existed in the status of women in Vietnamese and Chinese societies, a major contributing factor to the failure of the Chinese to assimilate the Viets.

- Along with cultural incentives to resist the Chinese, the Vietnamese struggle was assisted by the fragile links that bound Chinese administrators to their colonies. Vietnam was a long way from the Chinese capitals in the north, separated by daunting environmental obstacles. These problems meant that Chinese administrators charged with supplying military expeditions and garrisons in the south faced logistical nightmares.

- The well-informed Viet elites were also quick to seize on periods of political turmoil and nomadic invasion in China to assert their independence. They tried several times to free themselves at these

The opposition of Vietnamese women to the repressive Confucian family system was evidenced by the revolt against the Han led by the Trung sisters.

opportune moments—for example, in the interregnum between the early and later Han and during the Age of Disunity.

- Finally, the Viets staged a massive rebellion after the fall of the Tang dynasty in 907 C.E., and by 939, the people had won political independence from their giant northern neighbor. Both the Mongols and the Ming dynasty later tried to reassert control over Vietnam, but both efforts ended in humiliating defeats for the invaders.

Independent Vietnam
- From the late 10th century on, a succession of local dynasties ruled a politically independent Vietnam, beginning with the Le dynasty, which governed for almost three decades between 980 and 1009 C.E.

- Although the Vietnamese were now free from direct Chinese control, Chinese cultural exports, particularly ideas about government, continued to play a critical role in Vietnam and even helped legitimize claims to authority among the various local dynasties.

- Still, the Vietnamese scholar-bureaucrats never enjoyed the prestige of their Chinese counterparts, partly because the control of the central government at the village level was much less secure. Local officials tended to identify more with the peasantry than with their government masters in the capital and, on some occasions, even led uprisings against the ruling dynasties.

- Government scholar-bureaucrats also had to contend with competition from well-educated Buddhist monks. And unlike the situation in China, Korea, or Japan, these Vietnamese Buddhist monks had much stronger links with the villages and peasants than they did with the state hierarchy, which made them more resistant to the bureaucrats.

- In sum, the fact that independent Vietnam had so many competing centers of power prevented the dynastic rulers and their bureaucrats from achieving the sort of authority over the people that their counterparts in other East Asian states enjoyed.

Vietnamese Expansion

- The main adversaries of the Vietnamese were the Cham and Khmer peoples, who occupied lowland areas to the south that the Vietnamese sought to settle themselves. With their well-organized bureaucracy and larger military, the Vietnamese fought a series of generally successful expansionary wars between the 11th and 18th centuries against the Chams, driving them into the highlands.

- Once settled on the Chams' former farmlands, the Viets turned their attention to the Khmer people, who occupied the Mekong Delta. Once again, Indian-style Khmer armies were no match for well-trained Chinese-style Vietnamese troops. By the time French missionaries began to arrive in the 18th century, the Vietnamese had already occupied much of the Mekong Delta and were pushing into territory that today is part of Cambodia.

- As Vietnamese armies, farmers, and administrators moved further away from the capital in Hanoi, however, the ruling dynasties found it more difficult to maintain control of the provinces. And as the southern Viets intermarried with Chams and Khmers, differences in culture between north and south also began to emerge.

o Although both groups still identified themselves as Vietnamese, the northerners came to view the southerners as less intelligent and less sophisticated.

o This meant that as Hanoi's hold on the south weakened, regional military commanders became more independent.

- By the 16th century, the Nguyen family had emerged in the south to challenge the legitimacy of the Trinh dynasty in the north. For the next two centuries, the Nguyen (who ruled from Hue on the northern Mekong Delta) fought the Hanoi-based Trinh, and Vietnam was essentially divided into a north-and-south political structure.

French Colonization
- The struggle between the Nguyen and Trinh dynasties so absorbed the energies of the Vietnamese people that it distracted them from recognizing a growing external menace: France!

- When French missionaries first appeared on the shores of Vietnam in the 17th century, the Vietnamese people were welcoming, and many converted to Catholicism. But by the late 18th century, French interest in Vietnam had become less spiritual and decidedly more political.

- A rebellion staged by the Tay Son dynasty in the late 1770s resulted in the overthrow of the Trinh and Nguyen dynasties. The French decided to throw their support behind a surviving Nguyen prince in the south, Nguyen Anh, who used French resources to attack and eventually destroy the Tay Son rulers in the north. Nguyen Anh then proclaimed a united Vietnam and ruled from the old Trinh capital at Hue, rewarding his French allies with a special place in court.

- Nguyen Anh proclaimed himself Emperor Gia Long, launching the first dynasty in centuries to rule a united Vietnam. But the French were to be bitterly disappointed by their backing of Gia Long, because he and his successors proved to be arch conservatives who were deeply committed to strengthening Confucian values.

- Gia Long's successor came to view the French Catholics as a danger to the dynasty and began a campaign of persecution against the missionaries. Outraged, church authorities in France demanded action from the government, and Napoleon III approved a naval expedition in 1858 to punish the Vietnamese. By 1862, the court at Hue had been forced to cede several provinces in the Mekong Delta to France, and by 1890, the whole of the country was under French control.

- In the 20th century, failed attempts by the French to reassert control over their Southeast Asian colonial empire eventually got caught up with the Cold War, and tens of thousands of young American soldiers learned just how deeply the roots of Vietnamese resistance against foreign control grew, just as countless thousands of Chinese and even Mongol soldiers had learned centuries and millennia before.

Suggested Reading

Chapuis, *A History of Vietnam*.

Tarling, ed., *The Cambridge History of Southeast Asia*, volume 1.

Questions to Consider

1. How was Vietnamese culture both strongly influenced by but also able to resist the powerful cultural influence coming from the Chinese?

2. How have ethnic and cultural differences within Vietnam contributed to a historical north-south divide?

Southeast Asia—Vietnam
Lecture 31—Transcript

Hello folks and welcome. Following our two series of lectures on ancient Korea and ancient Japan, and before we return to events in China following the fall of the Tang dynasty, I thought it might be a good idea if we devoted the next two lectures to the history and culture of the Southeast Asian region. Partly we should do this because the history and culture of Vietnam, Cambodia, Thailand, Malaya, and the various states and islands of the region is so fascinating in its own right; and partly we need to do this because these states also inevitably found themselves members of the vast Eastern cultural zone dominated by China, although as I hope to show you, Southeast Asia was also heavily influenced by both Indian and Islamic culture. But it makes sense, I think, to widen our lens even further now and investigate the impact of many of the foundational elements of Eastern civilization that we've so far considered in this course on the states and peoples of Southeast Asia. At the same time, we'll also try and tease out what impact political, economic, and cultural developments that occurred in these Southeast Asian states had on China and on Eastern civilization more generally.

In this first lecture, we focus exclusively on the history and culture of Vietnam, from its earliest interactions with ancient China through to its colonization by the French in the 19th century. As many of you are aware, of course, Vietnam played a critical and costly role in the Cold War during the 20th century, so it might be interesting if we try and trace these more recent events right back to their ancient historical origins. In our second lecture in this mini-series, we'll briefly consider the history, the culture, and the fortunes of other states of Southeast Asia, including Cambodia, Thailand, Malaya, parts of Indonesia, even the Philippines over roughly the same chronological period.

In this first lecture, what we'll see, I think, is that Chinese relations with Vietnam were almost always tense, at least until the 20th century. From the moment Chinese armies began venturing into the region as early as the 3rd century B.C.E., they met with spirited resistance from the Viet people. Sometimes the Chinese were successful in gaining political control of Vietnamese towns and rural areas, and because of this the Viet people absorbed many Chinese cultural elements. Often the Viet elites were able to cleverly use many of these Chinese ideas and techniques about governance in particular to build their own strong, independent kingdom. Later, they expanded this kingdom further to the south until they had constructed a powerful state that managed to remain independent until the arrival of European colonists. In a nutshell, that's the story of Vietnam that I'd like to unfold for you in this lecture; a story of Vietnamese absorption, resistance, and ultimately the use of many of the key cultural inventions of Eastern civilization, which allowed the Viet people to carve out their own place in world history.

The first recorded mention of the Viets appears, not surprisingly to us, in Han dynasty annals, where they're described as "southern barbarians" who resisted Qin dynasty raids into south China in the 220s B.C.E. At that time, their kingdom—which the Chinese called "Nam Viet," or "people in the south," hence the modern name of Vietnam, of course—extended quite a way along the southern coast of what's actually Chinese territory today. The Qin raids had little political impact, but they did give a boost to the small-scale trade that had existed between the Viets and the Chinese for centuries before this. In exchange for Chinese silk, the Viets sent to China ivory, tortoiseshell, pearls, peacock feathers, and also many aromatic woods from the extensive coastlands and tropical forests of the region.

In the decades that followed the Qin raids, expansionist Viet rulers defeated the warlords who at that time controlled the Red River Valley, which today is actually in southern China, and brought their lands under Viet control. The Viets then intermarried with many of their neighbors, including the residents of the Red River Valley, and the Khmer and Thai peoples, all of which contributed to the formation of the Vietnamese people as a distinct ethnic identity. The willingness of the Vietnamese to intermarry with Khmers, today's Cambodian people, and the Thais suggests that before Vietnam was conquered by the Han, Vietnamese culture had much in common with the other peoples of Southeast Asia and was, in fact, distinctly different to Chinese culture. One example of this: None of the Southeast Asian spoken languages had any linguistic relationship with Chinese.

The Viets also had a strong tradition of village autonomy, often physically symbolized by the bamboo hedges that still surround many Vietnamese villages to the present day. The Viets and other peoples of Southeast Asia also favored the smaller nuclear family over the much larger extended family preferred by the Chinese, and, of course, explicitly sanctioned by Confucianism as being critical for the exercise of filial piety. Nor did the Viet people develop the same strong clan associations that characterized Chinese, Korean, and particularly Japanese society, as we've so recently seen.

Another significant difference, I think, is that Vietnamese women had much greater freedom and influence on public life than women in China ever enjoyed. The Viet people also dressed differently to the Chinese; for example, the women preferred long skirts, where Chinese peasant women wore long black pants. The Viets enjoyed cockfighting as a popular pastime; the Chinese didn't. The Viets chewed betel nuts and blackened their teeth; practices the Chinese found, frankly, disgusting.

Even after the Chinese conquered Nam Viet politically and after the introduction of Buddhism from China, many of these distinct cultural practices were preserved by the Viet people. Indeed, partly in response and resistance to Chinese domination, the Viet people clung on to these cultural differences ever more tightly, particularly at the grassroots level, and this preserved a certain cultural distinctiveness that once again ensured that Vietnam never became a carbon copy of its giant neighbor to the north, even after Chinese armies came marching in during the Early Han dynasty.

As the mighty Early or Western Han began to consolidate its power throughout China, East Asia, and Central Asia in the third century B.C.E., they soon came into contact with the Viets. Initially, the Han were happy to accept an acknowledgement of vassal status from the Viets, along with periodic payments of tribute, so that Nam Viet became part of the vast Han tributary empire. But in 111 B.C.E.—no surprise, again, during the reign of the emperor Wu Di, the marshal emperor—the Han decided it was time to conquer the feisty Viets outright and to govern them directly as a Han province; the same, of course, as the Han were doing in Korea at precisely this same time, as I'm sure you remember. The Red River area was quickly garrisoned with Han troops and Chinese administrators who were dispatched to the region now worked closely with local lords and officials, encouraging them to learn Chinese language and culture. Indeed, realizing they had much to learn from the sophisticated and, of course, incredibly well-organized Han state to the north, the Viet elites decided to cooperate with the Chinese. The Chinese government, on the other hand, saw the Viets as another barbarian people ripe for assimilation; and so they worked hard to introduce the essential elements of their civilization into their new southern province.

Over the centuries of Han rule that followed, the Viet elites, very much like the Korean elites, were drawn into the superb government structure administered by the Han Confucian bureaucracy. They attended Chinese schools, they learned to read and write Chinese language, they studied Confucius and all the other great classics, and they took the Confucian exams. In the rural areas, the village areas, the Han introduced sophisticated Chinese agricultural techniques and also irrigation technology, which quickly made the warm and moist environment of Nam Viet the most productive rice growing region in all of East Asia. As a result, the Viet population grew, and high population densities were soon in place all along the Red River Valley, and also along the coastal regions to the south. The Viet elites then used the lessons of Chinese statecraft to begin to extend their own military control over regions further west and south, which helped spread elements of Chinese culture more even widely throughout Southeast Asia. The Chinese must've assumed that the Vietnamese barbarians were well on their way to becoming civilized; that is, Sinotized. But as many later powerful invaders were to learn, the roots of Vietnamese resistance to conquest and cultural colonization ran very deep indeed. Ultimately the Chinese were to be frustrated by a series of revolts against their hegemony by Vietnamese elites, and even more so by the failure of Viet peasants to adopt Chinese culture.

The elites had learned much from the Chinese; but as the decades of colonialism passed, this made them chaff even more against Chinese hegemony, particularly as provincial Chinese administrators could barely conceal their disdain for barbaric Vietnamese practices. In the end, what emerged was an intense determination to drive the Chinese out, as Viet lords galvanized the common people to join them in revolt. One of the most famous of these revolts was instigated by women, the Trung sisters, who in 39 C.E., riding their war elephants at the head of a powerful guerilla force, led a dangerous uprising against the Han. The actions of the Trung sisters further demonstrate the profound difference that existed in the status of women in Vietnamese and Chinese societies, which was a major contributing factor to the failure of the Chinese to assimilate the Viets. Vietnamese women were bitterly opposed to the Confucian family system, which wanted to confine them to their homes and subject them to male authority. Women in Vietnam had long demanded and achieved a much higher status and more dominant role in society than women in China, or in Korea or Japan, for that matter. This was equally true through Southeast Asia more generally, where women had dominated the markets for centuries and had been heavily involved in all sorts of business ventures.

Along with these powerful cultural incentives to resist the Chinese, which crossed all class and gender barriers as we've seen, the Vietnamese struggle was assisted by the fragile links that bound Chinese administrators to their colonies; so here again, the environment plays a critical role in the way that history unfolds. Nam Viet was an awful long way from the great Chinese capitals in the north, separated by wide rivers, rugged mountain ranges, and very thick jungles. These environmental problems or barriers if you like and the tyranny of distance meant that Chinese administrators charged with supplying military expeditions and garrisons in the south faced logistical nightmares. Very few Chinese actually lived in the Red River Valley—small regiments of bureaucrats certainly, soldiers of course, and merchants, but that was all—and few of them lived there permanently.

The well-informed Viet elites were also very quick to seize upon periods of political turmoil and nomadic invasion in China to advance their cause and assert their independence. They tried several times to free themselves at these opportune moments: in the interregnum between the Early and Later Han, for example, and again during the long Age of Disunity. Finally, they were able to stage a massive rebellion after the fall of the Tang dynasty in 907 C.E. After 30 years of struggle, by 939 the people of Nam Viet had won political independence from their giant northern neighbor after 1,000 years of colonization. Both the formidable Mongols and the powerful Ming dynasty later tried to reassert control over Vietnam, but both efforts ended in humiliating defeats for the invaders. From 939 until the conquests of the French in the 19th century then, the Vietnamese were masters of their own fate.

From the late 10th century on, a succession of local dynasties ruled a politically independent Vietnam, beginning with the Le dynasty that governed for about three decades between 980 and 1009. Although the Vietnamese were now free from direct Chinese control, Chinese cultural exports, particularly ideas about government, continued to play a critical role in Vietnam and even helped legitimize claims to authority amongst the various local dynasties. The kings of Nam Viet ruled from Chinese-style palaces in the midst of Forbidden City-type complexes modeled on those in Changan and later Beijing. The bureaucracy was also Confucian; there were secretariats, ministries, and a bureau of censorship to control corruption. Potential bureaucrats still had to master the Confucian classics and take the civil service exams, just as we've seen so recently was the case in Korea and Japan.

But the Vietnamese scholar-bureaucrat never enjoyed the sort of prestige that their Chinese counterparts enjoyed, partly because the control of central government at the village level was much less secure in Vietnam. Local officials tended to identify more with the peasantry than with their government masters in the capital, and so they looked out for local above national interests. Often it was these same local officials, ostensibly representatives of the central government, who led uprisings against the ruling dynasty when its demands on the common people became too oppressive. Government scholar-bureaucrats also had to contend with competition from well-educated Buddhist monks; but unlike the situation in China, Korea, or Japan, these Vietnamese Buddhist monks had much stronger links with the villages and with the peasants than they did with the state hierarchy, which made them more resistant to the bureaucrats. Buddhism had proven itself remarkably adaptable to local cultural traditions wherever it spread, of course, we've seen this several times; so it's no surprise that the Vietnamese version of Buddhism held women in very high esteem. In a region where women had relative equality and even public power, this, of course, further endeared the monks to the community.

If I can sum all this up, independent Vietnam had so many competing centers of power that this prevented the dynastic rulers and their bureaucrats from achieving the sort of authority over the people that their counterparts in the other East Asian states enjoyed. Not that this situation prevented the central government from constantly trying to expand the size of their state and the power of their control. Despite the watering down of Chinese-style authority, the well-organized Vietnamese central state still enjoyed significant advantages over its neighbors to the south and to the west.

The main adversaries of the Vietnamese during this period were the Cham and Khmer peoples, who occupied both lowland areas to the south that the Vietnamese sought to settle themselves. The Vietnamese launched periodic raids into the region, but they also traded with the hill peoples who dwelt above the lowlands for various forest products. But these contacts were limited to commerce only, because the Vietnamese regarded the hill dwellers as "naked savages," and so tried to keep cultural exchange to a minimum. With the steep, malarial, jungle-covered hills above the Red River Valley occupied by these "nude savages," the only expansionary route open to the south was along the narrow coastal plain; and so with their well-organized bureaucracy and their much larger military, the Vietnamese fought a series of long and generally successful expansionary wars between the 11th and 18th centuries against the Chams, an Indianized people who lived along these southern coasts. As a result, the Chams were driven back into the highlands, where their descendants live to this day.

Once settled on the Chams' former farmlands along the coat, the Viets turned their attention to the Khmer people, who'd quietly occupied the delta of the mighty Mekong River while the Viets had been preoccupied with the Chams. Once again, Indian-style Khmer armies were no match for these well-trained Chinese-style Vietnamese troops. By the time French missionaries and colonialists began to turn up in the Mekong Delta in the 18th century, the Vietnamese had already occupied much of the delta of the river and were pushing into territory that today is actually part of Cambodia.

As Vietnamese armies, farmers, and administrators moved further and further away from the capital in Hanoi, the ruling dynasties found it more and more difficult to maintain control of the provinces in the south, just as the Chinese had done centuries earlier in their attempts to colonize the Red River Valley. As the southern Viets intermarried with Cham peoples and with Khmers, so differences in culture between north and south also began to emerge. Although both groups still identified themselves as Vietnamese, the northerners came to view the southerners as less energetic, less intelligent even; as slower in speech and slower in movement; as generally less sophisticated. This meant that as Hanoi's hold on the south weakened, regional military commanders became more independent.

By the 16th century, the Nguyen family had emerged in the south to challenge the legitimacy of the Trinh dynasty ruling from Hanoi in the north. For the next two centuries, the Nguyen, who ruled from their capital Hue on the northern Mekong Delta, fought the Hanoi-based Trinh, and Vietnam was essentially divided into a north and south political structure. This is a situation that no doubt sounds very familiar to many of you; isn't it extraordinary how far back the roots of north/south divisions often extend in world history, particularly in places like Korea and now in Vietnam? Yet neither the Nguyen nor the Trinh dynasties accepted this division as permanent, and each sought to reunite all of Vietnam under a single king. This epic struggle so absorbed the energies of the Vietnamese people that frankly it distracted them from recognizing a new, growing external menace. This time, for the first time in its history, the threat to Vietnam came not from China in the north, but from a distant land that the Vietnamese knew almost nothing about: It came from France.

As we'll see in future lectures, European colonizing powers were destined to have a dramatic impact on much of East and Southeast Asia, and also on the core elements of Eastern civilization. But perhaps we need to pause here just for a moment and take stock of where we are chronologically in this course to help minimize the confusion I'm probably causing you all by sort of jumping backwards and forwards in time like this as we explore these different regions and their histories.

In China, you might remember, we've taken our story up to the end of the Tang dynasty at the very beginning of the 10th century C.E. We'll return to China very shortly to trace in a series of eight lectures Chinese fortunes under the Song dynasty, followed by the Yuan, and the Ming, and finally the Qing dynasties, which will bring us through to the early 20th century. As we'll see, Europeans first turn up in China in the form of Jesuit missionaries during the Ming dynasty; and under the succeeding Qing dynasty, Europeans came to utterly dominate Chinese fortunes. In Korea, we've brought our story through to the end of the Mongol occupation late in the 14th century. When we return to Korea to bring that part of the story up to the 20th century, we'll see far less interaction between the European powers and an increasingly reclusive Korea, which instead was destined to lose its independence to a colonizing Japan in the 19th century. We've taken our series on Japan through to the dissolution of the Heian period in 1185, and the replacement of an imperial political structure with a quasi-feudal one. When we return to follow the story of Japan from its so-called medieval period through to the Meiji Restoration and into the 20th century, we'll see far more substantial interaction with the Europeans. But because Japan was successfully able to reinvent itself as a modern industrial power under the Meiji, the archipelago never became a European colony.

Having taken stock of our chronological situation, let me begin to conclude this lecture on Vietnam now by saying something about the impact of French colonization. French missionaries first turned up on the shores of Vietnam during the 17th century, having been rebuffed by the shoguns in Japan—the warlords, the military rulers of Japan—as we'll see later in the course. Initially the Vietnamese were very welcoming; they gave the missionaries ample opportunity to try and convert the people of Vietnam to Catholicism. Many did convert—thousands, in fact—and French merchants soon followed the missionaries to begin to establish trade relations between Southeast Asia and France.

But by the late 18th century, French interest in Vietnam had become less spiritual and decidedly more political, even imperialistic. After the Tay Son dynasty staged a major rebellion in the late 1770s, the dynasty gained control of most of the country, virtually eliminating both the Trinh and Nguyen dynasties in the process. But the French for various reasons decided to throw their support behind a surviving Nguyen prince in the south, Nguyen Anh, who used French resources and French weapons to attack and eventually destroy the Tay Son rulers in the north. Nguyen Anh then proclaimed a united Vietnam and ruled from the old Trinh capital at Hue in the south, rewarding his French allies with a special place in the court. The Nguyen dynasty was the first in centuries to rule a united Vietnam, and Nguyen Anh proclaimed himself the Gia Long Emperor of Vietnam.

But the French were to be bitterly disappointed by their backing of Gia Long, because he and his successors proved to be arch conservatives who were deeply committed to strengthening Confucian values, this great ancient tradition of Eastern civilization. Gia Long's successor came to view the French Catholics actually as a danger to the dynasty, and began a campaign of persecution against the missionaries. Outraged by this, church authorities in France demanded action from the government, and Napoleon III approved a naval expedition in 1858 to punish the Vietnamese. By 1862, the court at Hue had been forced to cede several provinces in the Mekong delta to France; and by 1890, the whole of the country was under the control of the French. This was the start of their great colonial empire in Southeast Asia.

With the French in control on the cusp of the 20th century, we take leave now of Vietnam. We'll return to events in the region before this course is concluded; but as many of you know, failed attempts by the French to reassert colonial control over their Southeast Asian colonial empire after the Second World War eventually got caught up with the Cold War, and tens of thousands of young American soldiers learned again just how deeply the roots of Vietnamese resistance against foreign control were, just as countless thousands of Chinese and even Mongol soldiers had learned centuries and millennia before this.

We'll stay in Southeast Asia for one more lecture; so please join me next time as we discuss the history and the culture of other states of this fascinating region, states that were more powerfully influenced by Indian and Islamic culture than they were by the Chinese.

Southeast Asia—Indian and Islamic Influences
Lecture 32

In the first of two lectures on Southeast Asia, we traced the history of Vietnam from its earliest interactions with China through to its colonization by the French in the 18th and 19th centuries, bringing it to the cusp of the 20th century. In addition to history, however, this course is also about the origins and evolution of the core philosophical, political, religious, artistic, and cultural practices and beliefs that distinguish Eastern civilization. Thus, in this second lecture on Southeast Asia, we will return to religion and trace the spread of Buddhism, Hinduism, and Islam to see what impact these "foreign" belief systems had in the region and on Eastern civilization more generally.

The Spread of Religion from India

- At the same time that Buddhism was spreading north from India into Central and East Asia, it was also beginning to attract a following in Southeast Asia. As we've seen earlier, the Silk Roads played a critical role here, although this time, it was the maritime Silk Roads. Buddhist ideas and beliefs were carried by sailors who traveled from India across the Indian Ocean to Southeast Asia.

- As a result, by the 1st century C.E., clear signs of Indian cultural influence appeared across the Southeast Asian region.
  - o In Java; Sumatra; other islands of modern Indonesia; and the mainland regions of the Malay Peninsula, Cambodia, and Vietnam, rulers of states began to adopt the Indian model of kingship and to call themselves *raja* ("king") in the manner of Indian rulers.

  - o As we saw in the last lecture on Vietnam, many rulers also converted to Buddhism and appointed Buddhist advisers to their courts.

- But Buddhism was not the only Indian religion to make its way across the maritime trade routes to Southeast Asia; Hinduism also left an indelible mark on the region.
  - In addition to reading the great Buddhist treatises, many Southeast Asian rulers also embraced the classics of Indian literature, such as the epic poems the *Mahabharata* and *Ramayana*, which promoted Hindu values.
  - These rulers did not show any enthusiasm for the caste system, and they continued to acknowledge the nature spirits that their people had worshiped for millennia, but they did find Hinduism attractive because the faith supported the principle of monarchical rule.

Origins and Ideas of Hinduism

- Hinduism emerged in India at more or less the same time as Buddhism as a syncretic faith incorporating Vedic texts, pre-Aryan practices, and many gods of different origins. Ultimately, Hinduism triumphed in India because it addressed the needs of the Indian people more effectively than Buddhism did.

- Hindu values are most clearly represented in the *Bhagavad Gita* (*Song of the Lord*), a short poetic work that illustrates the obligations and rewards of Hinduism. The overall message of the work is that salvation is not achieved through meditative detachment and renunciation of ordinary life, as in Buddhism, but through actively participating in the world and meeting the responsibilities of one's caste.

- The message of the *Gita* led to the four essential aims of human life that are still at the heart of Hinduism today.
  - One must be obedient to religious and moral laws (*dharma*).
  - One should pursue economic well-being and honest prosperity (*artha*).
  - One should enjoy social, physical, and sexual pleasures (*kama*).

- One must work for the salvation of the soul (*moksha*).

- By articulating these realistic and less demanding aims for life, Hinduism eventually replaced Buddhism as the most prominent religion in India.

Indian Influence in Southeast Asia

- The first Southeast Asian state to reflect strong Indian and Hindu influence was Funan, located on the lower reaches of the Mekong River. The wealthy rulers of Funan controlled the bulk of trade between India and China.
  - These rulers took to calling themselves *raja* and claimed divine sanction for their rule, as Indian kings did; they also introduced ceremonies and rituals worshiping Hindu gods.

  - As these traditions became more entrenched at court, they spread among the common people, helping embed Hindu ethics and practices deeply into Southeast Asian culture.

  - During the 6th century C.E., Funan was wracked by a bitter internal power struggle, and by the end of the century, the once-powerful state had passed into oblivion.

- After the fall of Funan, political leadership of Southeast Asia passed into the hands of the rulers of the kingdom of Srivijaya, based on the island of Sumatra.
  - Between 670 and 1025, Srivijaya elites built a powerful navy and controlled commerce throughout the region.

  - Unlike Funan, however, the rulers and trade officials of Srivijaya were devout Buddhists, and that faith prospered under their patronage.

  - Srivijaya remained a wealthy and powerful trading state for almost 400 years, until the south Indian state of Chola eclipsed it in the 11th century.

The magnificent buildings at Angkor Wat and Angkor Thom, built by the Khmers, are a testament to the powerful influence of Indian religion on Southeast Asian culture.

- With the decline of Srivijaya, three kingdoms—Angkor, Singosari, and Majapahit—dominated Southeast Asian affairs until the 16th century. The most famous of these kingdoms is Angkor, based in modern Cambodia and ruled by the Khmers from 889 to 1431.

  o In the 9th century, kings of the Khmers built their capital at Angkor Thom; the city was designed as a microscopic reflection of the Hindu world.

  o During the 12th century, the Khmers turned from Hinduism to Buddhism and added Buddhist temples to the complex at their capital without removing earlier Hindu structures.

- From the 8th century on, much of the coastal trade of India came to be controlled by Muslim merchant communities. Thus, in addition to Chinese and Indian cultural elements, Islamic culture also began to filter into Southeast Asia.

Origins and Beliefs of Islam

- The word *Islam* actually means "submission," signifying obedience to the will of Allah. From the moment the religion of Islam appeared, it quickly attracted followers and took on political and social significance; it also soon reached far beyond its Arabian homeland. By the 8th century, the world of Islam was matched only by Tang China as the great political, cultural, and social giant of Eurasia.

- The prophet Muhammad was born into a world of nomadic Bedouin pastoralists and merchants in about 570 C.E. By the age of 30, he was a successful merchant living in Mecca, where the people recognized many gods and where many Jewish and Christian communities existed.
  - Sometime around the year 610, the 40-year-old Muhammad underwent a profound spiritual transformation. He became convinced that there was only one true deity—Allah ("God")—and that recognition of any other gods was wicked.

  - Muhammad experienced visions that he interpreted as revelations being delivered to him by the archangel Gabriel, a messenger from God. Without necessarily meaning to found a new religion, he told his family and friends about these revelations, and by 620, a zealous minority of Meccans had joined Muhammad's circle.

  - As Muhammad spoke about the revelations he had received, some of his followers prepared written texts of his teachings. During the early 620s, devout followers compiled these texts and issued them as the Quran ("recitation"), the holy book of Islam.

- The new faith of Muhammad was based on five simple obligations:
  - Acknowledgment of Allah as the only god and Muhammad as the last prophet

  - Daily prayer to Allah while facing Mecca

- o Fasting during the daylight hours of the month of Ramadan

- o Contribution of alms for the relief of the poor

- o Undertaking of the *hajj* (the pilgrimage to Mecca) at least once, if possible.

- Because Islamic monotheism offended the polytheistic Arabs, the growing popularity of Muhammad's preaching brought him into religious conflict with the rulers of Mecca. In 622, Muhammad fled to the rival trading city of Yathrib, which Muslims soon started calling Medina ("the city of the prophet").

- Muhammad and his followers eventually grew strong enough to return to Mecca, defeat the authorities there, and launch a series of campaigns against other towns and clans; by the time of the prophet's death in 632, much of Arabia was under Islamic control.

The Spread of Islam
- After Muhammad's death, his advisers selected one of his closest friends and disciples to serve as caliph (or deputy), Abu Bakr. Under his leadership, Islamic armies began to carry their message into the world beyond Arabia. Eventually, the Muslims conquered Palestine, Mesopotamia, Egypt, North Africa, the Sasanian Empire, Persia, Afghanistan, northern India, and most of Spain.

- In the islands and coastal ports of Southeast Asia, trading contacts facilitated the spread of Islam. Beginning with small port towns on the northern coast of Sumatra, the religion eventually spread across the Straits of Malacca to Malaya, on to Java, then to the Celebes Islands and Mindanao in the southern Philippines.

- The version of Islam that was eventually embraced by many Southeast Asian communities was suffused with mystical strains and was able to accommodate itself to earlier animist, Hindu, and Buddhist beliefs and rituals.

- The huge Islamic caliphates that appeared throughout Afro-Eurasia following the spread of Islam functioned as a political, commercial, and cultural bridge that connected much of that area into a single zone of exchanges, including many areas beyond direct Islamic political control.

- By the 9th century, extensive Muslim merchant communities were in residence in Spain, in North Africa, all over the Middle East, in India, in Central Asia, and in the southern port cities of Tang dynasty China. Over the centuries that followed, conversions throughout Southeast Asia also brought the sailors and merchants of that extensive region into the Muslim cultural orbit.

Suggested Reading

Church, *A Short History of Southeast Asia.*

Tarling, ed., *The Cambridge History of Southeast Asia*, volume 1.

Questions to Consider

1. How did developing trade contacts between certain Southeast Asian states and India lead to the introduction of Hinduism and other Indian cultural influences into the region?

2. How did Southeast Asia's role as "middle man" lead to the spread of Islam into the region, an event of world historical significance?

Southeast Asia—Indian and Islamic Influences
Lecture 32—Transcript

In our last lecture, the first of this two-lecture series on Southeast Asia, we looked at the culture of Vietnam and traced the history of that nation from its earliest interactions with ancient China through to its colonization by the French in the 19th century. We concluded with Vietnam on the cusp of the 20th century; a century in which, as I'm sure many of you remember, failed attempts by the French to reassert colonial control over their Southeast Asian empire eventually fed into Cold War tensions and dragged the United States military into a long and costly war.

As well as being interested in history, however, at its heart this course is about the origins and evolution of the core philosophical, political, religious, artistic, and cultural practices and beliefs that distinguish Eastern civilization; so in this second lecture, I want to return to religion specifically, and trace the spread and impact of Buddhism, of course, but now also Hinduism and even Islam on Southeast Asia to see what transformational impact these foreign belief systems had on Southeast Asia in particular, and on Eastern civilization more generally.

Of course, we've already had much to say about the impact of Buddhism on Eastern civilization. In previous lectures, we examined its origins in India back in the sixth century B.C.E., then its spread along the Silk Roads into China during the First Silk Roads Era, partly facilitated at least by the tolerant attitude of the great Kanishka and other Kushan kings. We then observed the impact of Buddhism on China during the Age of Disunity, and its extraordinary growth amongst both elites and common people during the Sui and Tang dynasties. More recently in the course, we've discussed the extraordinary impact Buddhism had on early Korean and Japanese culture, where it utterly transformed not only religious practices and art in those two regions but, as we've seen, also politics. At the same time Buddhism was spreading north from India into Central and East Asia, it was also beginning to attract a following in Southeast Asia. Again, the Silk Roads played a critical role here, although this time it was the maritime Silk Roads. Buddhist ideas and beliefs were carried by sailors who traveled from India eastwards across the Indian Ocean to Southeast Asia.

Merchant mariners began to trade across the waters between India and Southeast Asia from at least as early as 500 B.C.E., perhaps much earlier, and these exchanges intensified during the First Silk Roads Era between roughly 100 B.C.E. and 200 C.E. As a result, by the first century C.E., clear signs of Indian cultural influence were appearing all over the Southeast Asian region. In Java, Sumatra, other islands of modern Indonesia, and also the mainland regions of the Malay Peninsula, Cambodia, and Vietnam, rulers of states began to adopt the Indian model of kingship and to call themselves *raja*, or "kings," in the manner of Indian rulers. Many of these states also adopted the Indian classical language of Sanskrit as the means for written communication. As we saw in our previous lecture about Vietnam, many rulers also converted to Buddhism and appointed Buddhist advisors to their courts. By associating themselves with an honored and ancient religion like Buddhism and by patronizing the Buddhist establishment, this enhanced the legitimacy of rulers and gave them valuable allies in the monastic hierarchies.

But Buddhism wasn't the only Indian religion to makes its way across these maritime trade routes to Southeast Asia; Hinduism also left an indelible mark on the region. In addition to reading the great Buddhist treatises, many Southeast Asian rulers also began to embrace the classics of Indian literature, like the great epic poems the *Mahabharata* and the *Ramayana*, which promoted Hindu values. These rulers didn't show any enthusiasm for the caste system, however, which is interesting; and they also continued to acknowledge the many nature spirits that their people had worshipped for thousands of years before this. But they did find Hinduism, like Buddhism, attractive because the faith supported the principal of monarchical rule, particularly the idea that some were born into a particular class whose destiny it was to rule over others. You can imagine how attractive this idea was to kings and other elites.

I think I need to say a few words here about the origins and ideas of Hinduism as we further investigate the influence of outside belief systems on Eastern civilization. You might remember from an earlier lecture that Buddhism, which emerged as an alternative to the sort of classical Vedic religion of India, attracted widespread popularity in India in the centuries either side of the Common Era divide. Hinduism emerged in India at more or less the same time as a very syncretic faith that incorporated some of the classical Vedic texts, many pre-Aryan practices (that is, dating right back to the ancient Indus civilization), and also many gods of different origin. In response to the success of Buddhism, Hinduism was able to transform itself into an immensely popular religion of salvation, and ultimately Hinduism triumphed because it became a faith that addressed the needs of the Indian people frankly more effectively than Buddhism was able to.

Hindu values are most clearly represented in the famous *Bhagavad Gita*, the *Song of the Lord*. This is a short poetic work that illustrates both the obligations of Hinduism and also its rewards. The *Gita* was composed by many poets between 300 B.C.E. and 300 C.E., and probably took its final revised form sometime around 400 C.E. *The Bhagavad Gita* illustrates an episode from the *Mahabharata* and it takes the form of a dialogue between Arjuna, who's a war-weary warrior from the elite *Kshatriya* and his charioteer Krishna, who was actually the powerful Hindu god Vishnu disguised as a lowly human. Vishnu convinces Arjuna, who's sick of killing and doesn't want to fight anymore, that only by active engagement in the world of caste obligations is it possible to attain salvation. In other words, salvation isn't achieved through the sort of meditative detachment, the renunciation of ordinary life that Buddhism demands but rather through active participation in the world and through the meeting the responsibilities of one's caste. Again, we can see here why kings would be particularly attracted to Hinduism because it explicitly validates the notion that there must be leaders, there must be those who are led, and there must be kings and their subjects, each with their specific roles and duties in life.

This led to the articulation of the idea that there are four essential aims of human life, aims that are still at the heart of Hinduism today: One must be obedient to religious and moral laws; this is the first law, this is called *dharma*. One should pursue economic wellbeing and honest prosperity; this is *artha*. One should enjoy social, physical, and sexual pleasures; this is *kama*. One must work for the salvation of one's soul; this is *moksha*. A proper balance of the first three aims would help individuals attain the salvation articulated in the fourth, *moksha*.

By articulating these supremely realistic and frankly much less demanding aims for life, Hinduism eventually replaced Buddhism as the most prominent religion in India, where Buddhism was perceived to have grown more remote from the masses. Later Buddhist monks didn't communicate their message to larger society as zealously as their predecessors had, so Hinduism attracted increasing popular support and also patronage from the wealthy. The powerful Gupta emperors, who eventually reunited India and ruled a great empire in the fifth and sixth centuries C.E., and many of their successors patronized Hinduism in the same way Ashoka and Kanishka had done for Buddhism 700 years earlier by this stage. Over the centuries that followed, Hinduism, and even the more recent faith of Islam, has completely eclipsed Buddhism in India, where it's now very much a minority faith.

The first Southeast Asian state to reflect strong Indian and Hindu influence was Funan. This was located in the very lower reaches of the Mekong River valley, and was thus beyond the control of the Vietnamese rulers that we discussed last time. Funan grew very wealthy indeed because it also controlled the Isthmus of Kra. This is a narrow portion of the Malay Peninsula only some 25–30 miles wide, across which merchants were able to transport their trade goods because this allowed them to avoid a much longer ocean voyage around the tip of the Malay Peninsula. Because of this, the rulers of Funan were able to control the bulk of the trade between India and China. No surprise, they grew very wealthy indeed; they used this wealth to construct elaborate systems of water storage and irrigation that are still visible to aerial archaeologists today. The rulers of Funan also took to calling themselves *raja*, and they claimed divine sanction for their rule the same way kings in India were doing. They also introduced ceremonies and rituals worshipping Shiva, Vishnu, and other Hindu gods like the great elephant god Ganesh. As these traditions became more entrenched at court, they spread amongst the common people as well, helping embed Hindu ethics and Hindu practices deeply into Southeast Asian culture.

During the sixth century C.E., Funan was wracked by a bitter internal power struggle; and this allowed their state to be overwhelmed by Chams, who then settled in Vietnam, and Khmers, who settled in the modern day state of Cambodia. By the late sixth century, the once-powerful Funan state had passed into oblivion.

After the fall of Funan, political leadership of Southeast Asia passed into the hands of the rulers of the kingdom of Srivijaya, which was based on the island of Sumatra. Between 670 and 1025, Srivijaya elites built a powerful navy and controlled commerce throughout the region. Their navy was so strong that many port cities all over the region were forced to accede to their authority. They also kept open an all-sea route between China and India, eliminating now the need for this overland portage across the Isthmus of Kra. Unlike Funan, however, the rulers and trade officials of Srivijaya were devout Buddhists, and that faith prospered under their patronage. We have a real sense here, I think, of these powerful ideologies in a state of almost constant competition throughout the region. Srivijaya remained a wealthy and powerful trading state for almost 400 years, until the expansive South Indian state of Chola eclipsed them in the 11th century.

With the decline of Srivijaya, three new kingdoms—Angkor, Singosari, and Majapahit—dominated Southeast Asian affairs until the 16th century. The most famous of these kingdoms is Angkor, based in modern Cambodia and ruled by the Khmers for a long period, from 889 through to 1431 C.E. The magnificent buildings at Angkor Thom and Angkor Wat built by the Khmers are further testament to the powerful influence of Indian culture on the region. The kings of the Khmers in the 9th century built their capital at Angkor Thom, and with the help of Brahmin advisors designed the city as a microscopic reflection of the Hindu world.

At the heart of this great complex was a temple representing the Himalayan Mount Meru, the sacred abode of Shiva. But during the 12th century, the Khmers turned from Hinduism to Buddhism, and so began to add Buddhist temples to the complex without removing the earlier Hindu structures, further evidence of this extraordinary syncretic mixing of these two very different faiths in the region of Southeast Asia. The complex was vast; it formed a square with each side two miles long, surrounded by a moat filled by a nearby river. During the 12th century, the Khmer kings also constructed a smaller but much more elaborate temple center at nearby Angkor Wat. In 1431, Angkor was abandoned by the Khmers after it was invaded by the Thai people. The magnificent temples were overgrown by the jungle and completely forgotten for 400 years until French missionaries and colonists rediscovered the sites in the 19th century. Today, the temple complexes,

UNESCO World Heritage sites obviously, stand as a magnificent example of the influence of Indian cultural traditions on Southeast Asia.

I've tried to show you in this lecture and the first one that Southeast Asia functioned for a very long time as a sort of commercial and cultural middle ground between Arabia, India, East Africa, and, of course, East Asia. For centuries in the great ports of the region, Chinese and East Asian traders met their Indian counterparts; high value export goods from Tang China were transferred to Arabian or Indian ships; and imports from as far away as the Mediterranean were loaded into the emptied Chinese vessels to be carried back to China, Korea, and Japan. But now we need to add something else to this already very intriguing mix, because from the eighth century on, much of the coastal trade of India came to be dominated by Muslim merchant communities who'd settled in western Indian regions like Gujarat following the spread of Islam into the subcontinent. This meant that, as well as classical Chinese and classical Indian cultural elements, Islamic culture also now began to filter into Southeast Asia to add to the already extraordinary rich syncretism that was already going on.

It was after the collapse of the Srivijaya kingdom in the 11th century that a way was opened up for the widespread introduction of Islam. Although the rulers of Srivijaya had opened their ports to Indian traders, because they were devout Buddhists there had been little incentive for the traders and sailors of Southeast Asian ports to convert to Islam. But with the collapse of Srivijaya, Muslim missionary activity in the region increased dramatically. Before I comment upon the success of these missionary efforts, perhaps I should pause here for a moment and also say something briefly about the origins and beliefs of Islam.

The word *Islam*, as I'm sure you know, means "submission," signifying obedience to the will of Allah, the only god in this monotheistic religion. One who accepts the Islamic faith is a *Muslim*; that is "one who has submitted." From the moment the religion of Islam appeared, it quickly attracted followers and also quickly took on political and social significance as well, and it soon reached far beyond its Arabian homeland. By the eighth century, the world of Islam, the realm of Islam, was matched only by Tang China as the great political, cultural, and social giant of all of Afro-Eurasia.

The prophet Muhammad was born into a world of nomadic Bedouin pastoralists and merchants in about 570 C.E. His parents died before he was six, and he was raised by his uncle and grandfather. He was then employed by a wealthy woman, a widow named Khadija, who he married in or about 595. By the age of 30, Muhammad was a successful merchant living in Mecca, where the people recognized many gods and where there were many Jewish and Christian communities. But sometime around the year 610, the 40-year-old Muhammad underwent a profound spiritual transformation. He became convinced that there was only one true deity, Allah, which means "God," and that recognition of any other gods was wicked. Muhammad experienced visions that he interpreted as revelations that were being delivered to him by the archangel Gabriel, a messenger from God. Without necessarily meaning to found a new religion, he started to tell his family and friends about these revelations, and by 620 a zealous minority of Meccans had joined Muhammad's circle.

As Muhammad spoke about the revelations he'd received, some of his followers prepared written texts of his teachings. During the early 620s, devout followers compiled these written versions and issued them as the Quran, the "recitation," the holy book of Islam. Muhammad's new faith was based on five simple obligations; isn't it extraordinary how the great global religions of the world are based on fairly simple obligations (actually it isn't so extraordinary; it makes a lot of sense)? Muslims must acknowledge Allah as the only god, and Muhammad as the last prophet; Muslims must pray to Allah daily while facing Mecca; they must fast during the daylight hours of the month of Ramadan; they must contribute alms for the relief of the poor; and they must try and undertake the *hajj*, the pilgrimage to Mecca, at least once in their lives.

Because Islamic monotheism offended the polytheistic Arabs, the growing popularity of Muhammad's preaching brought him into religious conflict with the rulers of Mecca. Eventually, the pressure mounted until in 622 Muhammad was forced to flee to the rival trading city of Yathrib, which the Muslims soon started calling Medina, "the city of the prophet." Known as the *hijra*, or "migration," the year of Muhammad's move to Medina, 622 C.E., serves as the official starting date for the Islamic calendar. Muhammad and his followers eventually grew strong enough to return to Mecca, to defeat the authorities there, and then launch a series of campaigns against other towns and other clans. By the time of the Prophet's death in 632, much of Arabia was under their control.

After Muhammad's death, his advisors selected one of his closest friends and disciples to serve as caliph, which means "deputy." Abu Bakr thus became head of the Islamic state, as well as chief judge, and chief religious and military leader; and under his exceptional leadership, Islamic armies began to carry their message into the Byzantine worlds, into the Sasanian Empire, well beyond Arabia. They attacked at precisely the moment that these great civilizations were exhausted and soon conquered Palestine and Mesopotamia. During the 640s, Muslim troops also conquered Egypt right across North Africa. By 651, they'd toppled the Sasanians and incorporated much of Persia into their realm. By 711, they were in Afghanistan, Northern India, and then they crossed the Straits of Gibraltar, conquering most of Spain. The speed and scale of the expansion of Islam is frankly one of the most extraordinary phenomena in all of world history.

Despite the reputation for *jihad* or holy war, in most areas where Islam spread, it was peaceful contacts and voluntary conversion that were much more important than force; and in the islands and coastal ports of Southeast Asia, it was trading contacts that facilitated the spread of the religion there. The first areas to be won over to Islam were small port towns on the northern coast of the island of Sumatra. From there the religion spread across the Straits of Malacca to the north into Malaya; then on to Java where, after a long and bitter struggle with Hindu-Buddhist kings in the interior, the whole island was eventually converted. From here, Islam was carried by merchants and missionaries on to the Celebes Islands, then on to Mindanao in the southern Philippines. This pattern of the spread of the Islamic faith shows that the port cities and merchants throughout Southeast Asia were the most receptive to the new faith; and this clearly demonstrates the power of trade as an instrument of conversion: Once one of the key cities in a trading network converted, it was in the best interest of the other cities to follow suit to enhance personal relationships with other merchants and to provide a common basis in Muslim law now to regulate business deals. Conversion also tied more tightly these port cities to the great trade networks already established by Muslim merchants, thus linking the Mediterranean, the Middle East, Arabia, and India with Southeast and East Asia.

The version of Islam that was eventually embraced by many Southeast Asian communities was suffused with mystical strains and was able to accommodate itself to much earlier animist, and also Hindu and Buddhist beliefs and rituals. Active amongst those spreading the faith were the Sufis, a radical and mystical sect of Islam that many believed possessed magical powers. As Sufis established mosques and schools in the region, they allowed their converts to retain some of their pre-Islamic beliefs, similar to the way, as we've seen, in which earlier Buddhist missionaries to China had attempted to fuse Buddhism with Daoist and Confucian ideas. Because of this approach, and the long tradition of relative gender equality in Southeast Asia that we discussed last time, women were allowed to have much greater power and even equality within the family and in public society than in more traditional Muslim states. As in Vietnam, trading in local and regional markets continued to be dominated by small-scale female entrepreneurs; and in western Sumatra and some other regions, lineage continued to be traced through the female line, even after the arrival of Islam and its tendency to promote male domination, certainly male descent.

Looking at all these developments from a world historian's perspective, we can say that the huge Islamic caliphates that appeared throughout Afro-Eurasia following the spread of Islam functioned as a political, commercial, and cultural bridge that connected much of that vast world zone into a single zone of exchanges, including many areas beyond direct Islamic political control. By the ninth century, extensive Muslim merchant communities were in residence in Spain, all across North Africa, all over the Middle East, in India now, in Central Asia, and, of course, in the southern port cities of Tang dynasty China. Over the centuries that followed, conversions throughout Southeast Asia also bought the sailors and merchants of that extensive region into the Muslim cultural orbit. Some conversions also took place within China. The oldest mosque in China, remember, was built in the great Tan imperial capital of Changan; and still today, as I've mentioned to you a couple of times, this is a place of extraordinary serenity in the midst of the bustle and the noise and the excitement of the great modern city of Xian, as I've personally experienced and as I'm sure many of you have.

But it's also worth making the point again here that most foreign religions, with the obvious exception of Buddhism, were unable to make much headway against the ancient and deeply ingrained foundational ideas of Eastern civilization, ideas like Confucianism and Daoism. As we return to China for our next series of lectures, we'll continue to explore the fate of foreign religions in China, including Christianity, which, despite the best efforts of brilliant Jesuit missionaries in the 16th century, was similarly unable to win many converts amongst the Chinese.

But while there's no denying the roots of Eastern civilization very run deep indeed, that's not to say that these external cultural ideas we've been discussing haven't played a role in moderating and influencing these roots, and this has been particularly the case in Southeast Asia.

In the next group of lectures, we'll return to China where we have much to explore: economic growth under the Song dynasty; subjugation again under the Mongols; the return of indigenous rule under the Ming; and the Qing dynasty, which, despite the fact that China was controlled again by foreign Manchu rulers in this case, was a period of deeply conservative rule that had major ramifications not just for Eastern civilization, but frankly for the making of the modern world. Please join me next time as we attempt to answer a very intriguing question: Was there really almost an industrial revolution in Song China in the 11th century, 700 years before the Industrial Revolution took place in Europe? See you then.

The Industrial Revolution of the Song
Lecture 33

In the next 12 lectures, we will bring our consideration of the foundations of Eastern civilization up to the early 20th century by exploring the last four dynasties of Chinese history, the Song, Yuan (or Mongol), Ming, and Qing, as well as the Choson dynasty in Korea and the Tokugawa shogunate and Meiji era in Japan. We will have a pair of lectures on each of the Chinese dynasties first, focused on developments in the foundational ideas that we've explored earlier. In this lecture, we'll see the remarkable agricultural and industrial revolution staged by the Southern Song dynasty in China that turned the Song into the economic powerhouse of the world.

Emergence of the Song
- Following the collapse of the Tang dynasty in the year 907 C.E., China entered two short-lived and tumultuous periods known as the Five Dynasties and Ten Kingdoms.
  - In the north, dynasties succeeded each other in quick succession, none lasting longer than 16 years.

  - Irrigation systems fell apart, floods devastated the countryside, and famine was widespread.

  - Refugees fled to southern China, where the political situation was more stable, but warfare between warlords was endemic.

- This chaotic half century was brought to an end by the Northern Song dynasty, which was proclaimed in 960 C.E. and, by 978, had reimposed imperial rule over most of China.

- The Song dynasty is divided into two periods: the Northern Song (960–1126 C.E.), which ruled from Kaifeng in northern China, and the Southern Song (1126–1279), which ruled from the southern capital in modern-day Hangzhou.

o   Although a combined reign duration of more than three centuries looks like evidence of successful dynastic rule, in fact, the Song never built a powerful state like that of the Han or Tang.

o   Part of the reason for this is that Song rulers generally mistrusted military leaders and preferred to keep the military under the control of bureaucrats. The Song elites placed greater emphasis on civil administration, industry, education, and the arts.

History of the Song

- It was the first Song emperor, Zhao Kuangyin (reign name: Song Taizu), who inaugurated the policy of subordinating the military to the bureaucracy. Zhao Kuangyin began his career as a junior military leader for one of the small dynasties of northern China and rose through the ranks to the position of general. He then led a mutiny against the ruling emperor of the later Zhou dynasty. In 960, his troops proclaimed him emperor, a position he held until his death in 976.

- In the years after he came to power, Taizu and his army consolidated Song rule throughout northern China. Taizu was aware of the importance of having a powerful army, but he was also fearful of the potential for regional commanders to become autonomous warlords; thus, he enacted various measures to keep the military under bureaucratic control.

- Taizu regarded all state officials as servants of the imperial government, and he set about reforming the political administration of the state to increase the power of the emperor. For example, to reduce the control of high-ranking officials, assistants were also appointed to these positions, which led to a further division of duties and, thus, of individual power.

- The early Song emperors also greatly expanded the size of bureaucracy and made sure it was based on merit, not rank. They reintroduced the highly competitive Confucian civil service exam, and they rewarded loyal bureaucratic officials handsomely. These measures resulted in perhaps the most centralized form of imperial government yet seen in world history.

- But these reforms also caused two problems that weakened the dynasty and eventually led to the fall of the Northern Song: (1) The vast administration put the imperial treasury under enormous pressure, and (2) tactical military decisions were left to scholar-bureaucrats, who had little military education or talent.

- It is hardly a coincidence, then, that nomadic peoples flourished along China's northern borders throughout the entire Northern Song period.
  o The Khitan, a semi-nomadic people from Mongolia, constantly threatened the Song and demanded and received large tribute payments of silk and silver.

  o In the early 12th century, another nomadic group, the Jurchen, attacked and conquered the Khitan and, in 1123, invaded northern China.

  o The Jurchen captured the Song capital of Kaifeng, declared the establishment of their own Jin dynasty, and immediately pushed further south, intent on conquering all of China.

  o The Song court fled south to the Yangtze Valley, where a son of the last Northern Song emperor stemmed the Jurchen tide and declared himself first emperor of the Southern Song dynasty in 1127.

  o A treaty signed in 1141 established the border between the Southern Song and Jurchen Jin dynasties about halfway between the Yellow and Yangtze rivers. This division of China remained the situation until 1279, when the Mongols ended the rule of both dynasties!

Song Agricultural Developments

- Generally in world history before the modern era, the prerequisite for economic growth has always been an increase in agricultural production, the largest sector of the premodern economy.

- During the attempted invasions of Vietnam by the Tang dynasty that we discussed earlier, the Chinese had encountered new strains of fast-ripening rice, which allowed cultivators to harvest two or even three crops a year instead of one. This strain of Champa rice was introduced into the fertile fields of southern China, leading to a greatly expanded supply of food.

- Of course, this increased agricultural impact had dramatic demographic consequences: In the year 600 C.E., the population of China was about 45 million, but by 1200 C.E., it had increased to roughly 115 million! This rapid growth was also a result of the well-organized food-distribution transport networks put in place by the Tang and Song.

- Increased food supplies and populations naturally encouraged the growth of cities; during the Southern Song, China was the most urbanized state in the world. The capital of Hangzhou had close to 2 million residents, and several other cities were home to 1 million each. City dwellers supported hundreds of restaurants, taverns, teahouses, brothels, music halls, theaters, shops, and more.

- Another result of increased food production was the emergence of a commercial agricultural sector.
  - Because of the large harvests produced by fast-growing rice, farmers could now buy cheap rice and devote their time to growing other crops, such as vegetables and fruits, to sell on the commercial market.

  - This led to an explosion of regional specialization as farmers began to grow profitable crops well suited to the environment of their provinces and export these over great distances.

Song Technological and Industrial Developments

- The enormous success of the agricultural sector led inevitably to spectacular developments in technological and industrial production. One striking example was the expansion of the porcelain industry. Song porcelain became a work of art, and vast quantities of it were exported across Eurasia.

- Production of iron and steel also surged under the Song, the result of techniques that made these metals stronger and of increased demands from commercial farmers and the military.
  - Between the 9th and 12th centuries, Song iron production increased almost tenfold, to levels that would not be seen anywhere in the world again until the 19th century.

  - Most of this increased supply of iron and steel went into weapons and agricultural implements; for example, imperial armaments manufacturers produced about 16.5 million iron arrowheads per year. Iron was also used for large-scale construction of bridges and pagodas.

- Song inventors are also justly famous for their innovations with gunpowder, a dangerous mixture of charcoal, saltpeter, and sulfur discovered during the Tang dynasty. By the 11th century, the Song military was using primitive bombs. Over time, gunpowder chemistry diffused throughout Eurasia; by the 13th century, various Islamic and European states were experimenting with iron-barreled cannons.

- Although some form of basic printing was known as early as the Sui dynasty in the 7th century, printing also reached a high standard of quality and production under the Song. Printers experimented with reusable, movable type, which sped up production. The ability to produce texts quickly and cheaply contributed to a wider dissemination of knowledge.

- During the Song era, to feed a voracious appetite for spices, Chinese mariners began to build the best ships in the world and to sail them across the deep oceans. Within China, merchants designed human-powered paddlewheel boats to ply the rivers and canals.

o Oceangoing vessels were constructed with iron nails, waterproofed with oils, and included bulkheads made waterproof with oil-based caulking. They used canvas and bamboo sails, were steered using a stern-post rudder, and were navigated with the aid of the "south-pointing needle"—the magnetic compass.

o Chinese ships mostly plied the waters between Japan and Malaya, but some of them ventured into the Indian Ocean and called in at ports in India, Ceylon, Persia, and East Africa. These long-distance sailors helped to diffuse Chinese naval innovations.

Song Economic Developments

- Increased agricultural production, improved transportation, population growth, urbanization, and large-scale industrial production hugely stimulated the Chinese economy, making it by far the most advanced in the world at the time.

- In southern China, various regions traded their specialized crops or manufactured goods with one another, creating a thriving market economy. Millions of cultivators produced fruits and vegetables for sale on the open market, and manufacturers of silk, porcelain, and other goods supplied both domestic and foreign markets. With a fully integrated economy, foreign demand for Chinese goods fueled further economic growth.

- Trade grew so rapidly that China experienced a shortage of copper coins under the Song. To alleviate the shortage, merchants developed alternatives to cash that resulted in even more growth and the emergence of what could be described as the world's first modern banking system. Letters of credit came into common use; later developments included promissory notes, checks, and the world's first paper money!

- The Song presided over a land of enormous prosperity, and this economic surge had implications well beyond China. In the next lecture, we will explore some of the ramifications of this transformation, both for Chinese society and many of the core ideas of Eastern civilization and for world history.

Suggested Reading

McKnight, *Law and Order in Sung China*.

Tanner, *China: A History*, chapter 7.

Questions to Consider

1. How was the Song dynasty able to restore order following the collapse of the Tang but then lose control of northern China to the nomads?

2. Is it an exaggeration to suggest that an "industrial revolution" almost took place in southern China several centuries before it ultimately did in Europe?

The Industrial Revolution of the Song
Lecture 33—Transcript

Welcome back to China. After our recent excursions into the fascinating early history and culture of Korea, of Japan, and most recently of Southeast Asia, it's time to return to China now and pick up our story there in about 900 C.E. In the next 12 lectures, I intend to bring our consideration of the foundations and evolution of Eastern civilization up to the early 20th century by exploring the last four dynasties of Chinese history—the Song, the Yuan or Mongol, the Ming, and the Qing dynasties—and also the Choson dynasty in Korea and the Tokugawa shogunate and the Meiji eras in Japan. We'll have a pair of lectures on each of the Chinese dynasties first, focused on developments in the foundational ideas that we've explored much earlier in the course: ideas about political organization; about how to manage a vast economy; ideas about philosophy, religion, social relations, and, of course, attitudes about gender relationships.

But the critical idea I want you to take away from this first lecture on the Song dynasty is this: Under the Southern Song, China staged a remarkable agricultural and then industrial revolution that turned it into the economic powerhouse of the world. As we'll see, the Song dynasty was founded when a military leader of one of the small states that formed in the wake of Tang dynasty collapse staged a palace coup in 960. Although this leader became an effective emperor, the Song faced continuous threats from the militarized nomads in the north—no surprise to us there—who they placated through diplomacy and through the payment of tributes in silk and silver. But all this was to no avail, because in the end the nomads overran northern China again and the Song were driven south, where they ruled southern China only from their new capital of Hangzhou. This was the moment when the Southern Song government began to lead China into a 150-year-long period of unprecedented economic growth. The Southern Song state was smaller, more like the small, commercial states of Europe that emerged at the end of the Middle Ages, and particularly into the Renaissance. Defense was a constant problem, and to defend itself Song rulers had to find new sources of revenue. Because of this need, the Song became intensely interested in commerce and in other forms of economic innovation, and this explains why there was a burst of astonishing new inventions in China. These economic developments are the main subject for this first lecture on the Song dynasty, a lecture that could be subtitled "Nearly an Industrial Revolution in China half a millennium before the Industrial Revolution occurred in Europe." Let's pick up the story early in the 10th century.

Following the collapse of the Tang dynasty in 907 C.E., China entered two shortlived and tumultuous periods known as the Five Dynasties and then the Ten Kingdoms. In the north, dynasties succeeded each other in quick succession, the longest I think lasting longer only for 16 years. The irrigation systems fell apart, floods devastated the countryside, and famine was widespread. Refugees fled to southern China where, although the political situation was more stable, warfare between warlords was endemic. This chaotic half century was brought to an end by the Northern Song dynasty, which was proclaimed in 960 and that by 978 had re-imposed imperial rule over most of China.

The Song dynasty is divided into two periods: The Northern Song is dated from 960–1126, which ruled from Kaifeng in northern China as their capital; and the Southern Song dynasty, dated 1126–1279, which ruled from their great southern capital in modern day Hangzhou. Although a combined reign duration of more than three centuries looks like evidence of pretty successful dynastic rule, in fact, the Song never built a powerful state like that of the Han or the Tang. Part of the reason for this is that Song rulers generally mistrusted military leaders and preferred to keep the military under the firm control of bureaucrats. This meant that Song elites placed much greater emphasis on civil administration, certainly industry, on education, and the arts, as we'll see, so they were never as militarily strong as their predecessors.

It was the first Song emperor himself who inaugurated this policy. Zhao Kuangyin, who adopted the reign name Song Taizu, began his career as a junior military leader for one of these small dynasties of northern China, and he rose steadily through the ranks to the position of general. He then led a mutiny against the ruling emperor of the so-called Later Zhou dynasty, justifying this breach of trust by claiming that there was urgent need for competent rule in the face of dangerous threats from the Khitan nomads in the north. Zhao Kuangyin had a reputation for honesty and for effective leadership, and in 960 his troops proclaimed him emperor, a position he then held until his death 16 years later in 976. Over the centuries since, historians have also proclaimed their trust in him, sanctioning his mutiny by arguing that, like a good Confucian ruler, this was done for the good of the country.

The usurper general was, of course, keenly aware that he too could be overthrown at any time, hence this desire I mentioned to try and bring the military under effective civilian administration. Over the next several years, he and his army consolidated Song rule throughout northern China. As a military commander, Taizu was naturally aware of the importance of having a powerful army, and specialists estimate that the Song may have spent maybe 75 percent of its annual revenue during this early period on military expenditures. But again, Taizu was also fearful of the potential for regional commanders to become autonomous warlords, so he enacted a series of various measures to keep the military under bureaucratic control. These were very thoughtful, very clever. They included dividing the army into three balanced units; rotating troops and officers regularly throughout these units; separating financial control from military control; and also establishing a strongly centralized command structure. He even persuaded some of his more independent generals to retire to a life of luxury. Ultimately, the Song completely subordinated the control of the entire military apparatus to high-ranking civilian government officials who constituted the Privy Council.

In fact, Song Taizu regarded all state officials—from the lowest to the highest—as servants of the imperial government, so he set about also reforming the political administration of the state to increase the power of the emperor. To reduce the control of the highest ranking officials, assistants were also appointed to these positions, which led to a further division of duties and thus also a diminution of individual power. The early emperors also greatly expanded the size of the bureaucracy and made sure that it was based on merit, not just on rank. This, of course, meant the reintroduction of the highly competitive Confucian civil service exam, which you'll remember was first introduced right back in the second century B.C.E. under the Han and then further entrenched as one of the pillars of good government by both the Sui and the Tang dynasties. Those who made it all the way through and passed the highest level "palace exam" were awarded the title of *jinshi*, or "advanced scholar." This is the highest degree that could be attained, and these officials were eligible to serve as the highest officials in the land. But there were also other routes, much easier exams for example, into the lower levels of administration; and this meant that ultimately the Song accepted many more candidates into the bureaucracy than the Sui or the Tang had done. They also paid these bureaucrats very well indeed. That is, in exchange for their loyalty, the Song rewarded their officials handsomely. These measures resulted in perhaps the most centralized form of imperial government ever seen in world history to that point.

But these reforms also caused two big problems that weakened the dynasty and eventually led to the fall of the Northern Song. The first problem, no surprise here, was financial: This vast administration cost a fortune to maintain. As the size of the bureaucracy and the employees' wages grew, the imperial treasury came under enormous pressure. Conservative officials, in a manner that actually sounds particularly modern I think, began to argue that they needed budget cutting reforms; they argued against any military action taken against the restive Jurchen nomads in the north, for example, because these military endeavors were seen as just too expensive. Efforts by the administration to meet debt by raising taxes obviously upset the peasants, who staged two major rebellions early in the 12th century. But by that point, well-paid bureaucrats so dominated the Song administration that it was impossible to seriously reform the system.

The second major problem the Northern Song faced was military. Partly this problem was caused by the fact that scholar-bureaucrats had little military education or perhaps even little talent for military affairs, yet it was they who were now making the tactical decisions to send Song armies into the field or not. It's hardly a coincidence, then, that nomadic peoples flourished again along China's northern borders throughout the entire Northern Song period. As we saw in our lectures on Korea, from the early 10th through to the early 12th century, the Khitan, a seminomadic people from Mongolia, created a vast steppe empire stretching from northern Korea back up into Mongolia. The Khitan people constantly threatened the Song and demanded and received large tribute payments of silk and silver. Then in the early 12th century, another even more formidable nomadic group, the Jurchen, who we also met in one of our Korea lectures, attacked and conquered the Khitan, and in 1123 invaded northern China, sweeping across the Great Walls and down to the Yellow River. The Jurchen captured the Song capital of Kaifeng, they declared the establishment of a new dynasty—their own dynasty, the Jin dynasty—and then immediately pushed further south, intent upon conquering all of China. Hard pressed by the Jurchen, the Song court fled south to the Yangtze valley, where a son of the last Northern Song emperor stemmed the Jurchen tide and declared himself first emperor of the Southern Song dynasty in 1127.

From then on, the Song dynasty survived and ruled in Southern China only. A treaty was signed in 1141 that established the border between the Southern Song and the Jurchen Jin dynasties roughly halfway between the great river systems of the Yellow and Yangtze. The Song had no option other than to acknowledge the Jin now as their symbolic overlords and pay them tribute, but this worked to secure the state because although the Jin tried a couple more times to conquer southern China, they were never successful. For about 150 years, China was divided again right across the middle, and this remained the situation until 1279, when the Mongols turned up and ended the rule of both of these dynasties for good.

Let's turn now to the main focus of this lecture: the revolutionary economic developments that essentially modernized China under the Southern Song. The Southern Song was responsible for a remarkable series of agricultural, technological, industrial, and commercial and financial developments that transformed China, as I said at the start of the lecture, into the economic powerhouse of the world. The Southern Song presided over this land of enormous prosperity; and this economic surge had implications well beyond China, because this stimulated trade and production throughout much of the Eastern hemisphere, including the Indian Ocean.

These impacts can best be explored, I think, if we look at three aspects of Song economic growth. The first of these developments was in the agricultural sector, particularly the impact of new strains of fast-growing rice. It's interesting that generally in world history, until the very modern era at least, the prerequisite for economic growth has always been an increase in agricultural production, which is, of course, the largest sector of the pre-modern economy. This was just as true of the Industrial Revolution in Britain in the 18th century as it was of the situation in Song China in the 12th. Indeed, it's doubtful that there would've been an industrial revolution in Britain if there hadn't first been a complete revolution of the agricultural sector, and then also a social revolution that fed into an industrial revolution.

During the attempted invasions of Vietnam by the Tang dynasty that we discussed in an earlier lecture, the Chinese had encountered new strains of fast-ripening rice, and these allowed cultivators to harvest two, sometimes even three crops of rice in a single year instead of just one. This strain of Champa rice was introduced into the fertile fields of Southern China, leading to a greatly expanded supply of food. Of course, this increased agricultural impact had dramatic demographic consequences: In 600 C.E., the population of China, as best as we can estimate, was about 45 million; but by 1200 C.E., the population of China had increased to roughly 115 million. This rapid population growth was a result of greater agricultural productivity certainly, but also of the well-organized food distribution transport networks that had been put in place by the Sui, by the Tang, and also by the Northern Song. Increased food supplies and increased populations naturally encouraged the growth of cities so that during the Southern Song, China was by far the most urbanized state or region in the world. The great capital of Hangzhou had close to two million residents, but several other cities of the Southern Song were home to a million people each, and scores of other cities had populations of 100,000-plus. By way of comparison, we can estimate the population of Paris in about 1200 to have been around 250,000; London only about 80,000.

City dwellers supported hundreds of restaurants, as we can imagine; taverns flourished; there were teahouses, brothels, music halls, theaters, clubhouses, gardens, markets everywhere; all sorts of specialized shops dealing in silk and gems, porcelain, expensive lacquer ware. Hangzhou residents had some particular and very interesting local customs. The many taverns each had several floors, and the sophisticated urban patrons would move to higher or lower floors according to their drinking plans for the night. Those who only wanted a quick cup or two of wine would sit down at the street level; but those planning a long evening of drinking and dining looked for tables on higher floors. Of course, something very similar to this still takes place in great Chinese restaurants and taverns to this very day.

Another result of increased food production was the emergence of a commercial agricultural sector. Because of the large harvests being produced by the fast-growing rice in the south, farmers could now actually buy cheap rice for their own food and instead devote their time and their fields to growing other crops like vegetables and fruits to sell at great profit on the commercial market. This led to an explosion of regional specialization as farmers began to grow profitable crops well-suited to the environment of their particular province and then export these over large distances. The wealthy southern province of Fujian, for example, imported rice for their own food and devoted its land instead to the production of lychees, of oranges, of tea, and of sugarcane, which fetched very high prices in the great urban markets that operated 24/7 in the many cities of Southern Song China. Market-oriented cultivation went so far that the Song authorities were worried. They tried to force the Fujianese farmers to grow their own rice so as to avoid the buildup of an excessive dependence on imports, but frankly with little success.

Indeed, the enormous success of the agricultural sector led inevitably to spectacular developments in technological and then industrial production. Abundant food supplies like this allowed many people to abandon farming and pursue technological and industrial interests instead, leading to a truly remarkable series of innovations. The first striking example of this was the expansion of the porcelain industry. During the Tang era, potters had discovered the technique of producing porcelain. This is lighter, thinner, and much more adaptable than pottery, and when it's fired with glorious glazes, Song porcelain soon became a work of art. Once again, you'll see this in many of the great art museums of the world. The technique gradually diffused westwards, so that Abbasid craftsmen in the Islamic realm also began to produce their own large quantities of porcelain. But despite that, demand for the frankly superb Chinese porcelain remained high, and vast quantities were exported all over Eurasia under the Song. Archaeologists have discovered Song porcelain at sites in Southeast Asia obviously, the coast of India, Persia, even the port cities of East Africa. Chinese porcelain plates, bowls, and cups gained such a high reputation that the fine tableware of the world ever since has been known as "chinaware."

Production of iron and steel also surged under the Song due to techniques that made these metals stronger, and also because of increased demands from the military and commercial farmers. By using coke instead of coal in their furnaces, Song manufacturers produced a superior grade of metal. This might remind some of you of the work of the famous English inventor Abraham Darby, who also used coke smelting techniques to produce superior iron; except that the Song were doing this 500 years before Darby was even born. Between the 9th and 12th centuries, Song iron production increased almost tenfold to levels that wouldn't be seen anywhere in the world until the 19th century. To give you a quick statistical example of this: As early as 1078, China was producing around 125,000 tons of iron. By way of comparison, the British iron industry produced only 76,000 tons of iron in 1788, more than 700 years later. Most of this increased supply of iron and steel went into weapons and also agricultural implements; imperial armaments manufacturers produced about 16.5 million iron arrowheads per year, for example. But iron was also used for large-scale construction of bridges and pagodas, certainly the first iron bridges built anywhere in the world. These Song metallurgical innovations soon diffused out of China, initially, ironically, to the north to the Jurchen and other militarized nomads who copied Chinese techniques to produce their own iron weapons to use against the Song.

Song inventors are also justly famous for their innovations with gunpowder. Daoist alchemists had discovered how to make gunpowder back during the Tang dynasty as they tested various concoctions seeking elixirs to prolong life. After several accidents, they realized that it was actually pretty dangerous to mix charcoal, saltpeter, and sulfur; this is more designed to shorten rather than prolong life. But, of course, military officials were quick to recognize the potential, and were soon using gunpowder in bamboo "fire-lances," a kind of flamethrower that spurted sheets of explosive fire out of one end of the lance. By the 11th century, the Song military were also using primitive bombs, although often these early weapons were so unreliable and difficult to control that they ended up going off accidentally and caused more confusion than actual damage. But over time, gunpowder chemistry became more refined; and, of course, such a useful technique quickly diffused throughout Eurasia, until by the 13th century various Islamic and European states were experimenting with iron-barreled cannons.

Although some form of basic printing—and we've discussed this—was known as early as the Sui dynasty in the seventh century, printing also reached a very high standard of quality and production under the Song. Tang dynasty printers, remember, had used fixed block-printing techniques: They'd carved a reverse image of an entire page into a wooden block, ink the block, and press the page upon it. But Song printers began to experiment with reusable, moveable type, including, by the way, characters that were made out of baked clay. They fashioned dyes in the shape of Chinese characters, they then arranged them in a frame, and, of course, they inked them and pressed the page on top. Reusable type like this sped up production and allowed printers to make revisions, making it possible to produce texts quickly, cheaply, and in large quantities. All this contributed to the dissemination of knowledge as large numbers of printed books were produced on all sorts of subjects: Buddhist and Confucian texts obviously, but also calendars, better agricultural almanacs, medical manuals, and even popular literature appeared and spread in large quantities all over China. A handful of these Song texts printed using movable type have survived through to the present, including Zhou Bida's *Notes on the Jade Hall*, first printed using movable type in 1193. Song officials were themselves responsible for the widespread dissemination of printed works throughout China because they plastered the countryside with pamphlets on government initiatives and on improved agricultural techniques.

While all this was going on, Song inventors also made stunning advances in naval technology. Before the Tang, Chinese sailors tended to stay close to the coast, and actually relied on Persian, Arab, Indian, and Malay mariners for long-distance maritime trade. But during the Song era, to feed a voracious appetite for spices, Chinese mariners began to build the best ships in the world and to sail them across the deep oceans. Within China, merchants designed human-powered paddlewheel boats to ply the rivers and canals. The much larger oceangoing vessels were now constructed with iron nails that were waterproofed with special oils; they included bulkheads made waterproof with a sort of oil-based caulking. These large ships used canvas and bamboo sails; they perfected a stern-post rudder to steer with; and they navigated with the aid of what the Song called the "south-pointing needle," the magnetic compass. Chinese ships mostly plied the waters between Japan and Malaya, but some of them ventured into the Indian Ocean and called in at ports in India, Ceylon, Persia, and even the East African coast. Needless to say, these long-distance sailors helped to diffuse Chinese naval innovations more widely; most importantly the compass, which was soon being used by mariners all over the Indian Ocean basin.

All these developments led to the emergence of a genuine and very modern market economy in China, by far the most advanced in the world at the time. Increased agricultural production, improved transportation, this surging population growth, urbanization, and now large-scale industrial production hugely stimulated the Chinese economy. Within Southern China, the various regions traded their specialized crops or their manufactured goods now with each other, creating a thriving internal market economy. Millions of cultivators produced fruits and vegetables for sale on the open market, and manufacturers of silk, porcelain, and other goods supplied both the domestic and, of course, also the foreign markets. With a fully integrated economy, foreign demand for Chinese goods fueled further rapid economic growth. In fact, trade grew so rapidly that China experienced a shortage of copper coins under the Southern Song. To alleviate the shortage, merchants developed alternatives to cash that resulted in even more growth and the emergence of what I think we must describe as the world's first modern banking system. Letters of credit soon came into common use; they were known as "flying cash." They allowed merchants to deposit goods or cash at one location and draw the equivalent in cash or goods somewhere else. Later developments included the use of promissory notes, which pledged payment of a given sum at a later date, and also of checks, which allowed bearers to draw funds against cash deposited with bankers.

Eventually, these developments resulted in the world's first paper money. In return for cash deposits from their clients, wealthy merchants started to issue printed receipts that the bearers could then redeem for merchandise. In a society short of coins, these notes greatly facilitated commercial exchange; but, of course, if the merchants weren't able to honor their notes, disorder and riots sometimes followed. By the 11th century, the Southern Song Chinese economy was absolutely dependent on paper money; so to avoid disturbances, the Song government began prohibiting private parties from issuing paper money and reserved the right for the state. The first notes printed by the government appeared in 1024; and by the end of the century, the government was issuing notes throughout Song China complete with serial numbers.

Let me conclude this lecture now by stating the obvious: Much of the southern regions of China experienced this unprecedented economic growth during the Southern Song era. Under the Song, China unleashed this remarkable series of innovations in agriculture, technological innovations, industry, commerce, and finance that turned their state into the great economic powerhouse not just of Afro-Eurasia but of the entire world. The Song presided over this land of enormous prosperity, and this economic surge had implications well beyond China.

In the next lecture, we're going to explore some of these ramifications of this transformation, both for Chinese society and, of course, for many of the core ideas of Eastern Civilization; but also for world history. I look forward to joining you soon.

Intellectual and Cultural Life of the Song
Lecture 34

As we saw in the last lecture, with the commercially minded Southern Song administration in charge, China unleashed a remarkable series of agricultural, technological, industrial, and commercial developments that transformed the state into the economic powerhouse of the world and had implications well beyond China. In this lecture, we'll see the impact of this era of heightened economic activity on the core foundational ideas of Eastern civilization, particularly in everyday life, intellectual life, and attitudes toward women. We will then conclude this two-lecture series on the Song dynasty by widening our focus to look at its impact on the world economy of the 13th century.

Everyday Life in the Southern Song

- Visual art, particularly painted scrolls, provides us with some insights into the daily lives of city dwellers in the Song. The 18-foot-long *Qingming* scroll, for example, shows fields and villages, donkeys bringing produce to market, and wealthy women being carried in sedan chairs toward the city while poorer women walk. We also see boats laden with passengers and goods, streets lined with shops, and hawkers selling food, tools, and clothes in a market stretched out along a bridge. The scene looks remarkably similar to life in China today!

- Court records from the Southern Song show all manner of claims being brought to the magistrates by men and women: arguments over land, houses, inheritances, fraud, gambling, violence, and so on. There is sharp evidence of an increasing gap between rich and poor, particularly between the wealthy merchant class in the cities and the still relatively impoverished rural peasant class.

- Song art and documents also reveal that better transport technology and infrastructure, along with the widespread dissemination of printed materials, meant that for the first time, ordinary people

The *Qingming* scroll shows a commercial world that is familiar to most citizens of the global village of the 21st century.

in both town and country gained access to knowledge and ideas that had been restricted to the elites for the previous several thousand years.

- With so much domestic and foreign trade, along with the explosion of urbanization, Southern Song China was transformed into a prosperous, cosmopolitan, and strikingly modern society. Residents of major cities grew accustomed to seeing merchants from foreign lands. Foreign faiths and philosophies also became increasingly entrenched in premodern China.

Debates over Core Values
- With so many foreign faiths and ideologies—Buddhism, Nestorian Christianity, Zoroastrianism, Islam—competing with the core beliefs of Chinese and Eastern civilization, intense discussion and debate took place among scholars over the issue of whether Chinese values should be preserved or foreign faiths and ideologies should be permitted and even promoted.

- At the heart of these debates was the fact that the Song had been unable to achieve the sort of military dominance over their neighbors that the Han and Tang had done; this profoundly disturbed Song intellectuals.

- Those who felt the ever-present military threat from the nomadic north, along with the powerful cultural influences emanating from the large numbers of foreigners now living in Song China, became less open to foreign ideas and more intent on preserving core Chinese cultural identity.

- One immediate ramification of this was a turn against Buddhism, despite the fact that this ancient Indian philosophy had been a core Chinese and Eastern spiritual ideology for more than 1,000 years.
    - o The scholar Sun Fu argued that "allowing the teachings of the barbarians" to bring disorder to "the teachings of our sages" was a humiliation to Chinese scholarship.

    - o Another scholar, Shijie, wrote that it was unforgiveable for Chinese to "forget their ancestors and abandon sacrifices to them, serving instead barbarian ghosts."

- The fact that many of the nomadic confederations in the north had all zealously adopted Buddhism seemed to further underline Buddhism's foreignness, even danger.

- Yet another cause of the increasing antagonism among Daoists, Confucians, and Buddhists was the wealth and power of the Buddhist hierarchy. Buddhist monasteries often owned high-value, tax-free land, allowing them to accumulate grain and rice, which they then distributed during times of famine. This charitable act was a powerful conversion mechanism.

- For centuries, Buddhist monasteries had been important elements in local Chinese economies, but Buddhism still posed challenges to traditional Chinese and Eastern beliefs. For example, Buddhism's call for individuals to seek perfection by observing an ascetic ideal conflicted with traditional Chinese morality centered on the family and obligations of filial piety.

- Buddhism responded to these objections by trying to tailor its message to Chinese audiences and by offering its ideology as a faith that reinforced family values. Buddhists argued that sending just one son into a Buddhist monastery would bring salvation for 10 generations of his kin!

- The result of all these compromises and adaptations was the emergence of a syncretic version of Buddhist faith. But many Song scholars actively advocated for native Chinese beliefs—primarily Confucianism—in the hope of limiting the attraction of all foreign religions.

Neo-Confucianism

- In the midst of these debates, Song Confucians were becoming increasingly well read in Buddhist scripture. As they read more, they could not help but admire the systematic way in which Buddhist scripture tried to deal with complex issues, such as the nature of the soul and the relationship of the individual with the cosmos—topics not generally explored by Confucianism.

- These intense intellectual investigations of Buddhism eventually led to the emergence of a form of Neo-Confucianism, which became so prevalent that it has gone on to dominate much of Chinese intellectual thinking to the present day.

- Southern Song scholars discussed how to improve the Confucian civil service exam service and make it more relevant to contemporary life. Others worked on developing philosophical frameworks for Confucianism that could stand up to the sophisticated metaphysical challenges of Buddhism.

- Increasing attention was also paid to building a more ideal society by starting at the bottom—by reforming families and local communities along Confucian lines. This led to a general call for the reestablishment of "family values."

- One result of this was a tightening of patriarchal structures as a means of enhancing family solidarity and promoting idealized "traditional values."

- Another result was that the veneration of family ancestors became much more elaborate during the Southern Song.

• The most important Song Neo-Confucian scholar was Zhu Xi (1130–1200). Immensely learned, Zhu Xi managed to hold down several important government jobs while writing about 100 books of sophisticated philosophy. He attempted to synthesize faith and reason by arguing that real self-knowledge could be attained only through an investigation of the natural world.

- Not surprisingly, this Aristotelian argument led to a spectacular growth in the physical and practical sciences in Song China. Song scientists made tremendous advances in medicine, astronomy, chemistry, and so on.

- Zhu Xi's insistence on the correctness of his own interpretations offended many other scholars as pretentious. Toward the end of his life, the Southern Song government condemned his work as "spurious learning." Within a few decades of his death, the government reversed its condemnation and gave Zhu Xi's ideas unprecedented political support.

Women in the Song Dynasty

• Because of the development of printing during the Southern Song and the subsequent widespread dissemination of various forms of literature, we have more written evidence about women's lives during this period than at any previous stage in the history of Eastern civilization.

• All kinds of women are found in Song sources: wives and widows, maids, midwives, nuns, singers, courtesans, spirit mediums, farmers' daughters, poets, and more. The impression we get from the sources is that within the home, women were influential and important, but outside of the home—in commerce or government—they had far less power.

- Increased wealth in society meant that women were purchased in large numbers by families to become servants, concubines, and prostitutes. Upper-class families could "sell" their daughters to prospective husbands by offering large dowries. As the legal status of women gradually improved, it was the wives and widows who increasingly gained control of those dowries, rather than the husbands and their families.

- All this seems to indicate that gender developments during the Song were generally favorable to women, but other practices paint a much harsher view of the lives of women under the Song, particularly the appearance of foot-binding.
  - During the Tang dynasty, such powerful women as Empress Wu and Yang Guifei had promoted an ideal in which it was fashionable for women to engage in physical activity, such as riding horses and playing polo.

  - Under the Song, notions of beauty shifted to promote a more delicate and restrained version of the "ideal woman." Women began to veil their faces and ride in curtained sedan chairs; the feet of young girls were tightly wrapped in cloth to prevent natural bone growth.

  - The practice of foot-binding was largely confined to wealthy families. It was not common among peasants and other classes, where women were needed for their physical skills around the farms and factories.

Global Economic Impact of the Song
- By the 12th century, China was undoubtedly the wealthiest and most powerful state on earth, a situation that continued for several centuries, including under the Mongols and the Ming. At the same time, Europe was barely emerging from what historians once called the Dark Ages.

- The Song economy was so dynamic that it could not be contained by China's borders. A huge global demand developed for Chinese exports; at the same time, wealthy Chinese consumers developed a taste for exotic goods that further stimulated trade throughout much of Afro-Eurasia.

- If the levels of production, innovation, and export of the Song had spread and been sustained, the industrialization of the world might have been led by China rather than Europe. Why did innovation not spread from China? Ironically, the reunification of China was at least partly to blame.
  - As we will see in a future lecture, after 1279, China was united again under the Mongols and then by the Ming and Qing dynasties. Each of these governments had less need for revenues from commerce, and indeed, the Ming eventually attempted to ban all foreign trade.

  - At the same time, global communications were still slow in the 12th and 13th centuries. Thus, Chinese inventions, including gunpowder, printing, and the compass, spread very slowly by today's standards.

  - The bottom line is that the world was not yet united enough, commercial enough, or interconnected enough for an industrial revolution to take place.

- By the 13th century, China was the largest, wealthiest, and most powerful state that had ever existed in the history of the world. It was, thus, a glittering prize for the new and formidable power that was emerging in the Central Asian steppes during that same century: the Mongols!

Suggested Reading

Ebrey, *The Cambridge Illustrated History of China*, chapter 6.

————, *The Inner Quarters*.

Fung Yulan, *A History of Chinese Philosophy*.

Questions to Consider

1. How did Confucians respond to the challenges of Buddhism during the intellectual ferment of the Song dynasty?

2. What was the status of women in Song China, and why did foot-binding become so prevalent?

Intellectual and Cultural Life of the Song
Lecture 34—Transcript

Welcome to this second lecture on the remarkable Song dynasty of China. I concluded our last lecture by stating the obvious: that much of China, particularly the south, experienced unprecedented economic growth during the 12th and early 13th centuries during the Southern Song era. With the commercially-minded Southern Song administration in charge, China unleashed a remarkable series of agricultural, technological, industrial, and commercial developments that transformed their state into the economic powerhouse of the world. The Song presided over a land of enormous prosperity, and as I mentioned last time, this economic surge inevitably had implications well beyond China. In this lecture, we're going to explore some of these ramifications, both for Chinese society and for Eastern civilization, but more generally for world history.

But the first big question I want to consider today is: What impact did this era of heightened economic activity have on the core foundational ideas of Eastern civilization, particularly everyday life, intellectual life, and, a perennial theme of this course, attitudes towards women. After addressing that question, I'd like to conclude this two-lecture series on the Song dynasty by widening our focus to look at the impact of all this on the world economy of the 13th century.

First, then, what do we know about everyday life in the Southern Song dynasty? How did all this economic growth and technological innovation influence the way people lived? We should start, I think, with the insights provided by visual art here, particularly the glorious painted scrolls that Song artists produced, which provide us with a lavishly illustrated glimpse at the daily lives of city dwellers in particular. The famous 18-foot-long *Qingming* scroll, for example, shows fields and villages outside of the city; it shows donkeys bringing produce to market; wealthy women are being carried in sedan chairs towards the city, while poorer women are all walking in towards the markets. Of course, there's another reason for this: a new practice that came to dominate the lives of elite women during the Song, and that's foot binding; more about that shortly. As the city comes into view on the scroll, we see boats laden with passengers and goods, we see streets lined with shops, there are hawkers selling food, tools, and clothes in a market stretched out along a bridge. In the streets we see Buddhist monks, Daoist priests, Confucian scholars, merchants, artists, storytellers, dancers, children, barking dogs. It all looks very modern and also remarkably similar to life in China today. In fact, this was a commercial world that would be familiar to most citizens of the global village of the 21st century. Everyone is using money; everyone is involved in the orderly flow of commerce; everyone is subject to the rule of law.

Actually, thinking of law, in another nod to modernity, court records from the Southern Song show all manner of claims being brought to the magistrates by men and women; everybody's suing everybody. There are arguments over land; over house ownership; over inheritances; over fraud, gambling, violence, disputes over money, and so on. There's also sharp evidence of an increasing gap between rich and poor, particularly between the wealthy merchant class in the cities and the still relatively impoverished rural peasant class. But what also becomes clear from Song art and Song documents is that the construction of better transport technology and infrastructure, along with the widespread dissemination of printed materials that we discussed last time, meant that for the first time ordinary people in both town and country gained access to knowledge and ideas that had been the restricted knowledge, the restricted property, of the elites for the previous several thousand years; these ideas that were at the heart of Eastern civilization.

With so much domestic and foreign trade going on, and the explosion of urbanization that we also discussed last time, Southern Song China was transformed into a prosperous, cosmopolitan, and very modern society. Trade goods and foreign ideas now poured into China again by land and sea. Muslim merchants from the Abbasid Empire joined subjects of Byzantium and traders from India and Central Asia in making their way to China along the Silk Roads land routes. Residents of all the major Chinese cities now grew accustomed again to seeing merchants from foreign lands in the same way that residents of Changan had gotten so used to foreigners in their midst during the Tang dynasty. Musicians and dancers from Persia became particularly popular entertainers in these great cosmopolitan cities of Southern China. With the flourishing of maritime trade, Arab, Persian, Indian, and Malay mariners arrived frequently from the Indian Ocean and

South China Sea to establish large merchant communities in the bustling southern seaports of Guangzhou and Quanzhou. Even under the Tang, of course, huge numbers of foreign merchants had been dwelling in these southern port cities. We know this because of accounts from the Late Tang period that describe a campaign of brutal terror unleashed by a rebel general named Huang Chao, which resulted, so we read, in the massacre of 120,000 foreigners when he sacked Guangzhou in 879. But these numbers were replaced and then some under the Southern Song.

Because of these widespread cosmopolitan interactions, foreign faiths and philosophies also became increasingly entrenched in pre-modern China. As we well know, the establishment of trade and exchange contacts with much of Eurasia during the first Silk Roads era had first opened Chinese and Eastern civilization to outside influence by as early as the first century B.C.E. We've also seen that during the Han and the centuries following, particularly in the Age of Disunity, a number foreign religions established themselves in China. The first of these, as you well know, was Buddhism, which started to arrive during the Early Han dynasty. By the late sixth century, communities of Nestorian Christians were also established in China; and Manichaeism, this mysterious Central Asian religion, had trickled in from Central Asia along the same trade routes. In the early seventh century, we have evidence that the Iranian pre-Islamic faith of Zoroastrianism was also being practiced in China; and later that same century, Islam was also being established in the heartlands of China as the construction of the Great Mosque in the heart of the Tang capital Changan demonstrates.

With so many foreign faiths and ideologies beginning of compete with the core beliefs of Chinese and Eastern civilization, one result of all this cultural exchange was intense discussion and debate amongst scholars over the issue of whether core Chinese values needed to be preserved, or whether foreign faiths and ideologies should be permitted and indeed even promoted. These debates are fascinating. They enriched but also complicated intellectual life in Song China. At the heart of these debates was the fact that the Song had been unable to achieve the sort of military dominance over their neighbors that the Han and Tang had done, and this profoundly disturbed Song intellectuals. Those who felt acutely the ever-present military threat from the nomadic north, and also the powerful cultural influences emanating from the huge numbers of foreigners now living in Song China, became less open to foreign ideas and more intent upon preserving core Chinese cultural identity. We have plenty of examples of writers rejecting all things foreign simply because they were foreign.

One immediate ramification of this was a turn against Buddhism, despite the fact that this ancient Indian philosophy had now been a core Chinese and Eastern spiritual ideology for more than a thousand years by this stage. Scholar Sun Fu argued that, and I quote, "allowing the teachings of the barbarians" to bring disorder to "the teachings of our sages" was a humiliation to Chinese scholarship. Another scholar, Shi Jie, wrote that it was unforgiveable for Chinese to, and again I quote, "forget their ancestors and abandon sacrifices to them, serving instead barbarian ghosts." The fact that many of the nomadic confederations in the north—the bitter enemies, remember, of the Southern Song—had all zealously adopted Buddhism seemed only to further underline Buddhism's foreignness, even its danger. Another cause of the increasing antagonism between Daoists, Confucians, and Buddhists was the wealth and power of the Buddhist hierarchy. As we've seen several times in this course already, monasteries owned a lot of high value, often tax-free land. They used these advantages as powerful conversion mechanisms because they were able to accumulate and store grain and rice, and then distribute this amongst locals during times of famine. So Buddhist monasteries had for centuries been important elements in local Chinese economies and they were well supported by local communities because of this.

But Buddhism posed additional challenges to traditional Chinese and Eastern beliefs. Buddhism continued to place great emphasis on written texts as the point of departure for speculation about the nature of the human soul, for example. We know that Confucianism also valued written texts; but Daoists had little or no interest in written texts. Buddhists continued to call for individuals to seek perfection by observing an ascetic ideal; whereas Chinese morality was centered on the family, on the obligations of filial piety, and thus rejected the self -focus of the Buddhists. We have clear evidence that many Chinese intellectuals resented the fact that the Buddhist monasteries paid no taxes. Not only did this mean that they weren't contributing to state revenues, but they used this advantage to proselytize and convert.

Buddhism responded to these objections as it had always done: by trying to tailor its message to Chinese audiences. We've already seen, of course, that Buddhists had become adept at translating the concept of *dharma* to the original meaning of the Dao or "the way," and also translating the Buddhist notion of nirvana as being the same as the Daoist notion of *wuwei*, or "noncompetition," or "disengagement," or "inaction." Buddhists also offered their ideology as a faith that would reinforce family values. One particularly powerful argument they promoted was that if a family sent just one son into a Buddhist monastery to become a monk, this would bring salvation for 10 generations of his kin. The result of all these compromises and adaptations was, as we've seen in several earlier lectures, the emergence of a syncretic version of Buddhist faith. We've looked at Chan Buddhism before, known as Son Buddhism in Korea or Zen Buddhism in Japan; versions of the faith that emphasized intuition and insight over written texts in the search for enlightenment.

For all these reasons, these complaints against Buddhism's foreignness and syncretic adaptations, many Song scholars actively advocated for native Chinese beliefs, mostly Confucianism, in the hope of limiting the attraction of all foreign religions, but particularly Buddhism. Yet to me there's something ambiguous about all this, because at the same time Song Confucians were also becoming increasingly well-read in Buddhist scripture. As they read more, they couldn't help but admire the systematic way in which Buddhist scripture tried to deal with complex issues such as the nature of the soul and the relationship of the individual with the cosmos. These are topics that weren't generally explored by Confucianism. These intense intellectual investigations of Buddhism led eventually to the emergence of a form of Neo or New Confucianism, which became so prevalent that it's gone on to dominate much Chinese intellectual thinking through to the present day. Indeed, you might remember from a lecture very early in this course that many intellectuals and even government officials in the People's Republic of China today are strongly advocating for more Neo-Confucian values in modern Chinese society.

Much of this stems from the Song dynasty, when revitalizing Confucianism was seen by many as the best way of strengthening core Chinese and thus core Eastern culture. Thus Southern Song scholars discussed how to improve the Confucian civil service exam system, for example; how to make it more relevant to contemporary life. Other Song intellectuals worked on developing philosophical frameworks for Confucianism that might stand up to the sophisticated metaphysical challenges of Buddhism. Increasing attention was also paid to building a more ideal society by starting at the bottom: by reforming families and local communities along Confucian lines. This led to a general call for the reestablishment of "family values"; isn't this a phrase that sounds strangely modern, the sort of appeal that's consistently made by conservative politicians all over the world in the 21st century? "We need to get back to family values." One result of this, as we'll see in a moment, was a tightening of patriarchal structures as a means of enhancing family solidarity and promoting these idealized traditional values. But another result was that the veneration of family ancestors became much more elaborate during the Southern Song, with descendants diligently seeking out the graves of their earliest traceable ancestors. Before long, whole extended families were traveling great distances all over Southern China to attend elaborate graveside rituals of filial worship.

The most important Song Neo-Confucian scholar of all was Zhu Xi, who lived quite a long life, from 1130–1200. His reputation today is of a brilliant intellectual who sincerely attempted to reconcile both Buddhism and Daoism with Confucian values. He was immensely learned in all the classics and the commentaries, all the great histories of China, and all the teachings of his predecessors. Zhu Xi managed to hold down several important government jobs while writing about 100 books of sophisticated philosophy. He wrote extensively on metaphysical themes such as the nature of reality. Like his near contemporary Thomas Aquinas in Europe—who was faced with a different but similar dilemma of having to reconcile the compelling logic that he found in his reading of Classical Greek philosophy, particularly of Plato and Aristotle, with the Christian scriptures—in that same sort of vein, Zhu Xi attempted to synthesize faith and reason by arguing that real self-knowledge could only be attained through an investigation of the natural world. Not surprisingly, this essentially Aristotelian argument led to a spectacular growth in the physical and practical sciences in Song China. Song doctors discovered and used inoculations against small pox, for example; they had hospitals far in advance of anything in Europe in the 12th century. Song scientists also made tremendous advances in astronomy, chemistry, zoology, botany, mapmaking; and their algebra was the most sophisticated anywhere in the world.

However, Zhu Xi's insistence on the correctness of his own interpretations offended many other scholars as pretentious, and towards the end of his life even the Southern Song government had condemned his work as "spurious learning." But within a few decades of his death, the government reversed its condemnation and gave Zhu Xi's ideas unprecedented political support. In 1241, the emperor himself credited Zhu Xi with "illuminating the true way," and students for the Confucian exams were now ordered to study his commentaries on the great Confucian texts as preparation for the test.

But this support reflected a new political reality rather more than an ideological shift. By this stage in the Song dynasty, the Mongols had already overrun the Jin in the north, and the Song state was in grave, indeed mortal, jeopardy. By promoting these conservative Confucian values, the hope was that this would stiffen citizens' resolve against yet another group of foreign invaders. Subsequent dynasties also found it expedient to promote Zhu Xi's Neo-Confucian school as orthodox, often for political reasons; and this, I think, explains its long influence on East Asian intellectual life.

Let's turn now to the next topic in this lecture and return to a foundational theme that we've pursued throughout this entire course: the role of women, this time during the Song dynasty. Because of the development of printing during the Southern Song and, as I mentioned, the subsequent widespread dissemination of various forms of literature, we actually have more written evidence about women's lives during this period than at any other stage in the long history of Eastern civilization. All kinds of women are found in these fascinating Song sources: widows managing inns, maids running away from abusive masters, midwives delivering babies, nuns, singers, courtesans, spirit mediums, farmers' daughters skilled at weaving silk, we read about women poets, happily married wives, elderly widows; the list is quite extraordinary. The impression we get from all these sources is that within the home women appear powerful and important, but outside of the home—in commerce and government, for example—women had far less power. With the explosion of printed materials, many women did become better educated than ever before and learned to read and write. Increased wealth in society also meant that women were now purchased in large numbers by families to become, for example, servants, concubines, even prostitutes. Upper class families could "sell" their daughters to prospective husbands now by offering large dowries; and as the legal status of women gradually improved, it was the wives and widows that increasingly gained control of these dowries rather than the husbands and their families.

All this seems to indicate that gender developments during the Song were positive, were generally favorable to women. But other practices paint a much harsher view of the lives of women under the Song, particularly the appearance of the practice of foot binding. During the Tang, powerful women like Empress Wu and Yang Guifei had promoted an ideal in which it was fashionable for women to engage in physical activity like riding horses, even playing polo. Now, under the Song, notions of beauty shifted to promote a more delicate and restrained version of the ideal woman. Women began to veil their faces and ride in curtained sedan chairs. The only examination a doctor was permitted of his female patient was to take the pulse of a delicate wrist extended through a curtain.

These changed notions of beauty help explain, I think, the emergence of this practice of foot binding during the Song dynasty. It actually began with dancers in the Northern Song period, and soon spread to elite families. By the Southern Song period, wealthy mothers everywhere were tightly wrapping the feet of six and seven year old girls with cloth, which prevented natural bone growth and resulted in tiny, malformed, curved feet. Women with bound feet couldn't walk easily; they needed canes or servants to carry them around in litters. The practice was largely confined to wealthy families where it was thought that a girl with bound feet would be more attractive to potential suitors because her movements would be more dainty and more ladylike. It wasn't at all common amongst the peasants and other classes where women were needed for their physical skills around the farms and weaving in the factories. We have to say, I think, that foot binding was clearly used as a mechanism for controlling the behavior of elite girls. Like the practice of veiling in the Islamic world, it placed women of privileged classes under tight male control, both emotionally certainly but now also physically. Neo-Confucianism, with its conservative insistence that women should have no desire to own property or to feel any jealousy if their husband took a concubine, profoundly influenced and supported this mechanism of physical control. With the appearance of foot binding, a practice that would continue until the Communist government banned it in the mid-20th century, we must conclude that, on balance, the Southern Song era was a harsh one for Chinese women.

Let me quickly begin to conclude this lecture now by returning to the larger question: the impact of the Southern Song on the global economy. Remember, by the 12th century, China was the wealthiest, most surging, most powerful economic state on earth; a situation that continued for several centuries following the Song, including under the Mongols as we'll see and under the Ming dynasty. At the same time, Europe was barely emerging from what historians used to call the Dark Ages; we call that, I guess, the High Middle Ages today. As we'll see in a lecture fairly soon, when Marco Polo visited China late in the 13th century, he and his colleagues were utterly astonished at the wealth, the complexity, and the sophistication of Chinese civilization, and at the standard of living being enjoyed by this huge population, so far in excess of anything in Europe.

The Song economy was so dynamic that it couldn't be contained by China's borders; as I mentioned last time, a huge global demand developed now for Chinese exports. At the same time, wealthy Chinese consumers also developed a taste for exotic goods that further stimulated trade throughout much of Afro-Eurasia. Spices from Indonesia, kingfisher feathers and tortoiseshell from Vietnam, pearls and incense from India, and horses, of course, and melons from Central Asia were in huge demand in China. But having said that, it was Chinese exports that were driving global trade; they were so valuable that they became status symbols of success everywhere. Over much of Asia and East Africa, wealthy merchants wore Chinese silk now and set their tables with chinaware as a sign of their success and their refinement. All this wealth, increased productivity, and commercial activity had a significant interregional impact; so Song economic success stimulated trade and production throughout much of the Eastern Hemisphere until late in the 13th century.

I think a really important, really interesting historical question we could ask is: What if all those Song technological and financial innovations had spread? Is it conceivable that an industrial revolution could've started in East Asia 800 years ago? If so, if these levels of production, of innovation, of export had been sustained, the industrialization of the world would've been led by China, not by Europe; which means we'd all be speaking Chinese today and certainly wearing East Asian clothing.

Fascinating question: Why did innovation not spread from China, given that the Chinese economy was interacting so much with the wider Afro-Eurasian economy? Ironically, I think, the reunification of China was at least partly to blame. As we'll see in a future lecture, after 1279 China was unified again under the Mongols, and then the by Ming and Qing dynasties. Each of these governments had less need now for revenues from commerce, and indeed the Ming and the Qing eventually attempted to ban all foreign trade. At the same time, global communications were still very slow in the 12th and 13th centuries; so Chinese innovations, even extraordinarily useful ones—like gunpowder, like printing, like the compass—actually spread very slowly by today's standards. The bottom line is that the world wasn't yet united enough, or commercial enough, or interconnected enough for an industrial revolution to take place. When an industrial revolution did eventually happen, it occurred, as you know, in Europe rather than China; and this in turn meant that Europe eventually acquired the economic, the technological, and the military strength to use these extraordinary East Asian inventions like gunpowder to utterly dominate and colonize all of East Asia.

With that thought in mind, we conclude our brief examination of this fascinating Song dynasty period and its impact on Chinese society, Eastern civilization, and world history. I might as well say it one more time: By the 13th century, China was the largest, wealthiest, and most powerful state that had ever existed in the history of the world. That, of course, is why it was such a glittering prize for the new and formidable power that was emerging in the steppes of Central Asia: the Mongols. The Mongol invasions wouldn't only profoundly influence Chinese and Eastern civilization, but would also change the course of world history. Please join me next time as we begin a two lecture series on the extraordinary Mongols.

The Mongols Conquer the World
Lecture 35

Early in the 13th century, the Mongols moved out of their homeland to eventually conquer Central Asia, China, Korea, parts of India and Russia, much of the Middle East, and regions of Eastern Europe, establishing the largest contiguous empire ever seen. Although history tends to remember the Mongols as mass murderers and destroyers of cities, a more nuanced view reminds us that the Mongols also fostered trade, patronized the arts, promoted religious tolerance, and provided security and cultural unity across Eurasia. In this lecture and the next, we will look at the precedent for the Mongol invasions, the conquests themselves, and the process by which the Mongols ultimately became victims of their own success.

The Turkic Peoples

- The precedent for the Mongol invasions came from the Turkic peoples, who originated in the Altai Mountains of Central Asia. The Turks are renowned for several reasons, not the least of which is that they established an enormous Turkic Empire in Central Asia. Indeed, between the 6th and 8th centuries B.C.E., the Turks were powerful enough to compete with the Chinese for control of Central Asia.

- In 542 C.E., Chinese annals refer to a nomadic people who were in the process of building a great steppe empire, which eventually stretched from Mongolia all the way to the Black Sea. This first Turkic empire lasted from 552 to 581 C.E.

- But with the rise of the Tang dynasty in China, the Turks were forced to accept Tang hegemony for the next century. In 683, Turkic forces under the leadership of Khan Kutlugh defeated Tang forces and recaptured much of their original realm. This second Turkic empire lasted until 734 C.E.

- In the mid-8th century, the Turks entered a period of decline. As the Turks lost control of their empire to other Central Asian peoples, such as the Uygurs, they began to migrate away from their homeland; moving to the southwest, they settled in Sogdia, to the north of modern-day Afghanistan.

- The steppe empires established by different Turkic-speaking peoples were well organized and were administered through a combination of tribal government traditions, centralized bureaucracies, and provincial governors. The Turks borrowed many of these ideas from the Chinese, particularly from the Tang, and many Turks also adopted Chinese-style Buddhism.

- Late in the 8th century, the religion of Islam came roaring into the steppes through a series of vigorous military campaigns that plunged deep into Central Asia, proffering an alternative to Chinese and Eastern civilizational influences. The Turks responded aggressively, launching invasions of the Middle East and India that lasted well into the 15th century, but at the same time, the Turks eventually converted to the religion of those they were attacking: Islam.

- Under a series of powerful leaders, the Turks defeated almost all who came up against them and ultimately established Islamic Turkish regimes from India to Turkey. The ability of the Turkic people to create and effectively administer vast regions of Inner Eurasia acted as an inspiration to Chinggis Khan and spurred the Mongols to try to emulate their achievements.

  o Early in the 13th century, the Mongols began their own campaign of conquest, and during the following century, they subdued much of Eurasia from Korea to the Danube River.

  o After building their enormous empire, the Mongols established what historians have come to recognize as the Pax Mongolica— the "Mongol Peace"—which facilitated trade and exchange across Eurasia for centuries after the Mongols had disappeared.

  o At roughly the same size as the former Soviet Union, the Mongol Empire was by far the largest empire the world had known to that point, and it is still recognized today as the largest contiguous empire in all of world history.

Chinggis Khan (c. 1162–1227)

- Mongol success owed much to the guiding genius who launched his people into history: Chinggis Khan. The son of a minor Mongol chief, he was born around 1162 and named Temujin ("Man of Iron").

- When his father was killed by enemies, Temujin spent years in exile on the steppes, gathering followers and

The human and infrastructure devastation wrought by Chinggis Khan and his Mongol forces was felt for centuries.

using tribal war and diplomacy to patch together a new Mongol confederacy. In 1206, he was recognized as Chinggis Khan, a title that can be interpreted as "Great Ruler" or "Universal Ruler."

- Chinggis began the era of unified Mongol imperial rule by launching his first campaigns of conquest against the Uyghrs and Tanguts in Central Asia and then against the Jin dynasty in northern China. By 1215, the Mongols had forced the Jin court to relocate and renamed their capital Khanbaliq ("city of the khan"). This became the capital of Mongol China.

- Leaving part of his army to control northern China, Chinggis Khan led Mongol forces west into parts of Afghanistan and eastern Persia. At the time, these Central Asian regions were still being ruled by Turks, specifically, the Khwarazm Turks.
  - o The Mongols offered the Khwarazm shah the chance to avoid conquest and establish trade relations with the Mongols, but

when the shah tried to have Chinggis Khan murdered, the Mongols sought revenge.

o In the end, the Khwarazm shah was killed and his armies were shattered. To make sure the Khwarazm state could never again challenge his own empire, Chinggis Khan then wreaked violent destruction on the region.

- By the time Chinggis Khan died in 1227, he had laid the foundations for a vast Mongol empire. Through his charisma and military skill, he had united the Mongols into a new confederation and established Mongol supremacy in northern China, Central Asia, and parts of Persia.
  o But Chinggis was content to rule through his control of the army and never attempted to establish any form of central government or provincial administration for his empire.

  o His heirs would continue the campaigns of expansion the great khan had started, but the burden now also fell on them to design a more durable imperial structure.

- Before his death, Chinggis divided the empire into four sections, or khanates, each to be administered by a son or grandson. He was succeeded as Great Khan by his third son, Ogedei, who was proclaimed supreme leader of the Mongols in 1229.

- Under Ogedei's leadership, Mongol expansion continued in all directions: deep into western Afghanistan and Persia, into China, far east into Korea, northwest into Armenia and Georgia, and deep into Eastern Europe. Only Ogedei's death may have prevented the complete conquest of Europe.

- After Ogedei's death, virtual civil war broke out among the other khans, and the four-khanate structure Chinggis had original planned resulted in the division of the vast Mongol realm into four regional empires. For as long as the Mongol Empire existed, ambition fueled constant tensions among the four khans that controlled these regions.

The Four Khanates

- In the 1230s, under Ogedei, the Mongols of the Golden Horde launched invasions of Russia and Eastern Europe; these invasions continued after Ogedei's death in the 1240s. The Mongols raided small Russian states in the north but chose never to occupy the region, although they maintained hegemony over Russia until the mid-15th century.

- Further south, Chinggis's grandson Mongke led armies into Tibet between 1251 and 1259 and continued to harass Korea.

- At about the same time, Mongke's brother Hulegu defeated the Islamic Abbasid caliphate that controlled Persia, Palestine, and Syria. But in 1260, Hulegu's attempts to conquer all of the Middle East and Egypt were confounded when the Mongol tide in West Asia was stopped in Syria by the Egyptian Mamluk army.

- When it came to governing their vast realm, the Mongols adopted different tactics in the different lands they controlled. In Persia, they made major concessions to local interests; Mongols occupied all the highest positions, but Persians served as ministers, provincial governors, and high-ranking state officials. In essence, the Mongols allowed the Persians to administer the ilkhanate so long as they delivered tax receipts to the Mongol rulers and maintained order.
  - Initially, the Mongol rulers observed their native shamanism, but they were remarkably tolerant of all faiths. In Persia, the Mongol elites gradually converted to Islam.

  - In 1295, Ilkhan Ghazan publicly embraced Islam, and most of the Mongols in Persia followed his lead.

  - The tide of Mongol religious tolerance turned at this point; Ghazan's conversion led to large-scale massacres of Christians and Jews and the restoration of Islam to its formerly privileged position in Persia.

o   The conversion to Islam posed a problem for independent Mongol women, who agreed to adopt some aspects of Islamic women's culture but by no means all.

The Mongol Military
- The Mongol military force numbered, at best, perhaps 130,000 mounted warriors. How was it that this relatively small army was able to carve out the largest empire the world had seen?

- First, the Mongol military organization was incredibly effective because of its simplicity. Its structure was based on an ancient tradition of militarized steppe nomads and used the decimal system.
    o   The smallest unit of the army was a squad of 10 men, called an *arban*.

    o   Ten *arbans* constituted a company of 100, called a *jaghun*.

    o   Ten *jaghuns* made up the equivalent of a regiment of 1,000—a *mingghan*.

    o   Ten *mingghans* constituted a force of 10,000 mounted warriors—a *tumen*, the equivalent of a modern division.

- Military discipline also distinguished Mongol soldiers from their peers. All males from ages 15 to 60 and capable of undergoing rigorous training were eligible for conscription into the army.

- These forces were then exquisitely tailored for mobility and speed. To facilitate mobility, soldiers were lightly armored, and because they were adept at living off the land, Mongol units functioned independently of supply lines, dramatically speeding up their movement.

- Mongol campaigns were preceded by careful planning, reconnaissance, and the gathering of information on enemy territories and military strength. These advantages of organization, mobility, and discipline also allowed the Mongol forces to fight on several fronts at once.

- In the cities they plundered, the Mongols were careful to recruit skilled military professionals. The experienced Chinese engineers Hulegu conscripted provided the Mongol forces with experts at building and operating a variety of siege machines.

- Another advantage the Mongols possessed was their ability to traverse great distances quickly, even in appallingly cold winters. Frozen rivers were like interstate highways to them, providing rapid passage into the heart of large urban settlements on the banks.

- Finally, we can't ignore the fact that the Mongols were also brutally skilled in their use of terror tactics to control conquered peoples, particularly in the early stages of expansion. Mongol commanders practiced mass murder, torture, and forced the resettlement of hundreds of thousands of conquered peoples.

Suggested Reading

Buell, *The A to Z of the Mongol World Empire*.

Morgan, *The Mongols*.

Schirokauer et al., *A Brief History of Chinese and Japanese Civilizations*, chapter 9.

Questions to Consider

1. How were the Mongols, with relatively small military forces, able to create the largest contiguous empire ever seen in world history?

2. Were the Mongols terrorists or unifiers?

The Mongols Conquer the World
Lecture 35—Transcript

Hello and welcome to the first of two lectures in which we take a look at the mighty Mongols and how their campaigns of conquest altered the course not just of Eastern civilization, but of all world history. The Mongol invasions are a quintessential example, I think, of the processes of cultural evolution and cultural syncretism that so characterize the history of the vast Afro-Eurasian world zone during the first and second millenniums of the Common Era. Early in the 13th century, the Mongol hordes moved out of their homeland to eventually conquer Central Asia, all of China, Korea, parts of India, parts of Russia, much of the Middle East, and even regions of Eastern Europe, establishing the largest contiguous empire ever seen. It was the Mongol leader Chinggis Khan, who lived from 1162–1227 and who claimed to have a Chinese-style mandate from heaven to rule the world, who was responsible for creating the Mongol Empire.

Although history still tends to remember the Mongols as mass murderers and destroyers of cities, a more nuanced view reminds us that the Mongols also fostered trade and exchange between East and West, they patronized the arts, they promoted religious tolerance, and they provided security and cultural unity across much of Eurasia. Because of this, some historians even go so far as to claim the Mongols as one of the principal architects of the modern world. The Mongols were Central Asian nomads, of course, like so many others we've met in this course; the great unsung heroes, frankly, of history who'd been interacting with the agrarian sedentary communities since at least the second millennium B.C.E. Like most of these great nomadic confederations, within the Mongol world decisions were made by a council of warriors; and this meant that although the chiefs or khans had great power, they were still regarded as the first among equals. Mongol women had considerable freedom, respect, and influence, particularly when compared with the status of women in most sedentary civilizations, as we've seen throughout this course; and there are several examples known to us of Mongol women who gained great political power. As we'll see, like all militarized nomads, the Mongols held a distinct military advantage over sedentary military forces through their advanced cavalry tactics and, of course, their supreme horse riding skills; also their mobility and field craft, and their extraordinary prowess with the composite bow and arrow. But eventually, as I intend to show you in these two lectures, the Mongols became sedentized and acquired the languages, the religions, the cultural patterns, even the administrative structures of many of the peoples they'd conquered.

The precedent and perhaps even the inspiration for the Mongol invasions came from the Turkic peoples, who didn't originate in modern Turkey but thousands of miles to the east in the Altai Mountains of Central Asia. Because their impact upon the Mongols and Eurasia was so profound, I think we need to spend a few minutes considering the Turks here first. The Turks are justifiably renowned for several reasons, of course, not the least of which is that they established an enormous Turkic Empire in Central Asia. Indeed, between the sixth and eight centuries B.C.E., the Turks were powerful enough to compete with the Chinese for control of Central Asia. The word *Turk* actually appears for the first time in Chinese annals in 542 C.E., where it's used to refer to a nomadic people who were in the process of building this a great steppe empire, which eventually stretched from Mongolia all the way to the Black Sea. This first Turkic Empire lasted for almost 30 years, from 552 until 581. But with the rise of the powerful Tang dynasty in China, the Turks were forced to accept Tang hegemony for the next century, until 683 when Turkic forces under the leadership of Khan Kutlugh defeated Tang forces and recaptured much of the original realm. This Second Turkic Empire then lasted right through until 734, and it's during this era that the oldest known Turkic inscriptions appeared.

Dated to the 720s, the inscriptions were carved into stone by the ruling elites, who used them to record the creation myths and the history of the Turkic peoples. These marvelous accounts are written in a series of inscriptions on funerary stele—which are inscribed upright stone slabs—that were discovered near the River Orkhon in northwestern Mongolia. Here's the inscription of one great and powerful leader Turk leader, Bilga Qaghan:

> When the blue sky above and the dark earth below were made, human beings were created between the two. My ancestors Bumin Qaghan and Istami Qaghan rose above the sons of men. Having become their masters, they governed and established the empire and the institutions of the Turkic people. They had many enemies in

the four corners of the world, but waging military campaigns, they subjugated and pacified them, making them bow their heads and bend their knees.

In the mid-eighth century, the Turks entered a period of decline, perhaps, some scholars suggest, because of their conversion to the Central Asian religion of Manichaeism that we've mentioned several times in the course already. As the Turks lost control of their empire to other Central Asian peoples such as the Uygurs, they began to migrate away from their homeland; moving to the southwest initially, they settled in Sogdia, to the north of modern day Afghanistan. The Uygurs, who took the Turks' place in their former homeland, then settled themselves in the modern Chinese province of Xinjiang, the great western province of China, where they remain to this very day. The Uygurs later converted to Islam, and to this day the relationship between the ethnic Han migrants who moved into Xinjiang and the Muslim Uygurs remains tense and often quite violent. Another group of Central Asian peoples that displaced the Turks were the Kyrgyz; the modern country of Kyrgyzstan is, of course, named after the Kyrgyz peoples. All this just demonstrates just how relevant these events of 1,200 years ago remain in the 21st century.

The steppe empires established by different Turkic-speaking peoples were very well organized and were administered through a combination of old tribal government traditions, centralized bureaucracies, and also provincial governors. Needless to say, the Turks borrowed many of these ideas from the Chinese, particularly from the Tang; and many Turks also adopted Chinese-style Buddhism, further evidence of the widening influence of Eastern civilization as it continued to spread throughout Central Asia, a process that had commenced with the establishment of the first Silk Roads by the Early Han dynasty almost a thousand years before.

Late in the 8th century, the religion of Islam came roaring into the steppes through a series of vigorous military campaigns that plunged deep into Central Asia, proffering an alternative to Chinese and Eastern civilizational influences. The Turks responded aggressively: They launched invasions of the Middle East and invasions into India that lasted well into the 15th century.

But at the same time, the Turks eventually and inevitably converted to the religion of those they were attacking: Islam.

It's beyond our scope here to follow the history of the Turks into the pre-modern and modern world; but suffice to say that under a series of powerful leaders they defeated almost all who came up against them, and ultimately established formidable Islamic Turkish regimes from India into Turkey. What's relevant to us today is that it was the ability of the Turkic people to create and effectively administer vast regions of Inner Eurasia that acted as an inspiration to Chinggis Khan and spurred the Mongols to try and emulate their achievements.

Early in the 13th century, the Mongols began their own campaign of conquest; and during the following century, they subdued much of Eurasia, all the way from Korea to the Danube River. After building their enormous empire, the Mongols established what historians have come to recognize as the Pax Mongolica, a Latin term for "the Mongol Peace." This facilitated trade and exchange across Eurasia for centuries after the Mongols had disappeared. At roughly the same size as the former Soviet Union, the Mongol Empire was by far the largest empire the world had ever known to that point, and it's still recognized today as the largest contiguous empire in all of world history.

But if I can sort of jump ahead and give you a brief preview of the end of their story: In the end, the Mongols became victims of their own success. When their empire expanded far beyond its administrative centers it began to weaken, because it inevitably became so dependent on provincial governors who, of course, used their positions to amass their own autonomous power and wealth. Haven't we seen that story unfold often in the history of China? It's also become something of a historian's rule of thumb ever since, I think, at least until the empires of the industrial age, that empires become more and more difficult to hold together once they expand beyond the distance that the ruler's army can march in a single season.

But I'm getting ahead of myself here. Let's return to the beginning of this story; let's point out again that Mongol success owed much to the guiding genius who launched his people into history: Chinggis Khan. Son of a minor Mongol chief, he was born in we think 1162 and named Temujin, which means "Man of Iron." When his father was killed by enemies, Temujin spent years in exile on the steppes, gathering followers and using tribal war and tribal diplomacy to patch together a new Mongol confederacy. His efforts were crowned in 1206 when he was recognized by the entire Mongol confederation as Chinggis Khan, a title that can be interpreted as "Great Ruler" or "Universal Ruler," both of which hint at the aspirations to world power held by the Mongols. Chinggis began the era now of unified Mongol imperial rule by launching his first campaigns of conquest against the Uyghr people and also the Tanguts in Central Asia, and then turned south against the Jin dynasty, which was ruling in the northern regions of China; so it was Chinggis Khan himself who first attempted to bring Mongol rule into China.

As you'll remember from our previous pair of lectures, since 1127 the nomadic Jurchen people had been in control of the north ruling as the Jin dynasty, while the Southern Song dynasty, of course, continued ethnic Han rule in the south of China. Mongol armies first began to raid Jin dynasty China in 1211, and four years later, by 1215, they'd captured the Jurchen capital, which was near modern Beijing, forcing the Jin court to relocate elsewhere. This capital city was renamed Khanbaliq, or "City of the Khan," and this became the capital of Mongol China. If you've visited Beijing, you'll know that Mongol influence in architecture and urban design can still be seen today in parts of old Beijing. By the time of Chinggis Khan's death, the Mongols had control over large regions of northern China; but as we'll see in the next lecture, it would be up to Chinggis's sons and grandsons to complete the conquest of the Jin and then press on against the powerful Song in the south.

Leaving part of his army to control Northern China, Chinggis Khan then led Mongol forces west into parts of Afghanistan and eastern Persia. At the time, these Central Asian regions were still being ruled by the Turks, specifically a group called the Khwarazm Turks. The Mongols offered the Khwarazm shah the chance to avoid conquest and to establish trade relations with the Mongols; but when the Shah tried to have Chinggis Khan murdered, the Mongols sought bloody revenge. In the end, the Khwarazm shah was trapped and killed on an island in the Caspian Sea and his armies were shattered. To make sure the Khwarazm state could never again be a challenge to his own empire, Chinggis Khan then wreaked violent destruction on the region.

Mongol forces ravaged dozens of cities, demolishing buildings and killing hundreds of thousands of people; frankly, it's impossible to ever know exactly how many. The Mongols also destroyed the delicate *qanat* irrigation systems, which severely reduced agricultural production. This human and infrastructure devastation wrought by the Mongols in this region was felt for centuries afterwards.

By the time Chinggis Khan died in 1227, he had laid the foundations for a vast Mongol empire. Through his own charisma and obvious military skill, he'd united the Mongols into a new confederation and had established Mongol supremacy in Northern China, much of Central Asia, and even parts of Persia. But Chinggis was content to rule through his control of the army and never attempted to establish any form of central government or serious provincial administration for his empire. His heirs would continue the campaigns of expansion the great Khan had started, but the burden now also fell on them to take up the task of somehow designing a more durable imperial structure.

Before his death, acutely aware of the potential for dangerous power struggles amongst his sons and grandsons, Chinggis had divided the empire into four sections or khanates, each to be administered by a son or grandson. He was then succeeded as great khan by his third son Ogedei, who was proclaimed supreme leader of the Mongols in 1229. Under Ogedei's leadership, Mongol expansion continued in all directions: deep into western Afghanistan, further into Persia; deeper into China to finally subdue the Jin dynasty; then far east into Korea, events we discussed in an earlier lecture; and also northwest into Armenia and Georgia; and eventually deep into Eastern Europe. Indeed, only Ogedei's death may have prevented the complete conquest of Europe by the Mongols. The great khan had given his permission to conquer all of Europe as far as the "Great Sea," which means the Atlantic Ocean; and when Ogedei died on December 11, 1241, formidable Mongols forces were actually on the outskirts of Vienna, about to launch a winter campaign into Austria and Germany.

Ogedei was a powerful and unifying leader who through sheer force of character was able to control the sort of internal power struggles that Chinggis Khan had feared. But after his death, virtual civil war broke out between the other khans, and the four-khanate structure Chinggis had original planned resulted in the very real division now of the vast Mongol realm into four regional empires. From 1241 on, then, a group of khans known as the Great Khans would rule China, which always remained the wealthiest part of the empire. Descendants of Chaghatai, another of the sons of Chinggis Khan, took control now of these Central Asian realms. Persia was ruled by a group of Mongols known as the Ilkhans; and the khans of the Golden Horde dominated much of Russia for the next two centuries. But despite this mutually agreed upon four khanate system, for as long as the Mongol Empire existed, ambition fueled constant tension between the four khans that controlled their various regions.

In the rest of this lecture and also part of the next, we're going to follow the messy and confusing fortunes of these khanates through to the end of the Mongol Empire. It was Mongols of the Golden Horde under Ogedei that launched the invasions of Russia and Eastern Europe in the 1230s, which continued after his death into the 1240s. When Ogedei died in 1241, by the way, his widow took over as ruler; and there was a second period of female rule in 1248 when Guyuk Khan died. This reminds us of the relative gender equality that was a feature of Mongol society, indeed a feature of all Central Asian militarized nomadic confederations. The Mongols of the Golden Horde prized the steppes north of the Black Sea as prime pastureland for their horses; so they raided the small Russian states to the north of these steppes frequently but they chose never to occupy the region, mostly because they saw Russia as an unattractive land of deep forests that made the steppe-dwelling Mongols who lived in these wide open spaces of grassland most uncomfortable. Despite this, the Golden Horde did maintain hegemony over Russia right through until the mid-15th century, when the princes of Moscow finally rejected Mongol domination and began to build their own powerful and eventually formidable and expansionary state. But even after that, Mongols descended from the Golden Horde continued to rule the Crimea until the late 18th century, where they played a significant role in many a military campaign of the pre- and early modern period.

Further south, Chinggis's grandson Mongke led armies into Tibet between 1251 and 1259, and continued to harass Korea, as we've seen. At about the same time, Mongke's brother Hulegu defeated the Islamic Abbasid caliphate that controlled much of Persia, much of Palestine, and Syria. This was a monumental victory that brought to an end the great Classical Age of Islam that we've discussed so many times in this course. But in 1260, Hulegu's attempts to conquer all of the Middle East and on into Egypt were confounded when the Mongol tide in West Asia was stopped in Syria by the powerful Egyptian Mamaluk army. Hulegu's army was amazingly cosmopolitan. It included groups of specialists from all different peoples the Mongols had conquered, but particularly brilliant Chinese catapult operators who could build and then use siege machinery right on the spot. Hulegu proved remarkably effective at integrating these various soldiers, but also the artists and professional administrators of all the peoples that he'd conquered to create a very effective and a very syncretic military force.

When it came to governing their vast realm, the Mongols adopted different tactics in the different lands that they controlled. In Persia, they made major concessions to local interests. The Mongols themselves occupied all the highest positions, but Persians served as ministers, as provincial governors, and as high-ranking state officials. In essence, the Mongols allowed the Persians to administer the ilkhanate so long as they delivered tax receipts to the Mongol rulers and maintained order. Over time, the Mongols themselves assimilated to the ancient and sophisticated Persian Islamic traditions. Initially, all the Mongol rulers observed their native shamanistic, sort of spiritual beliefs; but they were remarkably tolerant of all faiths, including Islam, Nestorian Christianity, Catholic Christianity, Buddhism certainly, even Judaism. But in Muslim Persia, the Mongol elites gradually converted to Islam. This culminated in 1295 when Ilkhan Ghazan publicly embraced Islam, and most of the Mongols in Persia followed his lead.

The tide of Mongol religious tolerance turned at this point; Ghazan's conversion led to large scale massacres of Christians and Jews in the ilkhanate, and the restoration of Islam to its formerly privileged position throughout Persia. The conversion to Islam posed a problem for the independent Mongol women, however; they agreed to adopt some aspects of Islamic women's culture, but by no means all. In Persian miniature paintings from the mid-14th century that I've seen, we can sometimes see Mongol elite women on horseback promenade. The Persian women in the background of these scenes have their faces veiled, but the Mongol women have refused to veil their faces.

Let me turn to another question now as we begin to conclude this lecture: How was it that a relatively small Mongol military force, numbering perhaps 130,000 mounted archer warriors at best, was able to carve out the largest empire the world had ever seen? The first reason obviously has to do with Mongol military organization, which was incredibly effective I think because of its simplicity. This structure was based on the ancient tradition of militarized steppe nomads and utilized the decimal system. The smallest unit of the army was a squad of 10 men, called an *arban*; 10 *arbans* then constituted a company of a hundred men, called a *jaghun*; 10 *jaghuns* made up the equivalent of a regiment of a thousand, a *mingghan*; and 10 *mingghans* constituted a huge force of 10,000 mounted warriors called a *tumen*, the equivalent I guess of a modern division.

Military discipline also distinguished Mongol soldiers from all their peers. All males who were aged from 15–60 and who were physically capable of undergoing rigorous training were eligible for conscription into the army. These forces were then exquisitely tailored for mobility and speed. To facilitate this mobility, the soldiers were lightly armored when compared to the heavy armor used by many of the armies they faced. Because they were so adept at living off the land, Mongol units functioned independently of supply lines, which, of course, dramatically sped up the movement of their forces. Discipline was also brought to a very high level, inculcated in the traditional hunts that all the cavalry participated in, even in times of peace. Nor were Mongol military campaigns slapdash, ill-considered affairs; far from it. All their campaigns were preceded by very careful planning, careful reconnaissance, and by the gathering of information on enemy territories and military strength. These advantages, then, of organization, mobility, and discipline also allowed the Mongol forces to fight on several fronts at once.

Unlike many other mobile fighters in history—such as the Xiongnu, the Huns, or even the Vikings—the Mongols were also very comfortable in the art of the siege. As I noted earlier, they were careful to recruit skilled military professionals from the cities they plundered. The experienced Chinese engineers that Hulegu conscripted provided the Mongol forces with experts at building and operating a wide variety of siege machines, which, as I said, were mostly built on the spot using local trees.

Another advantage the Mongols possessed was their ability to traverse large distances quickly, even in appallingly cold winters. Frozen rivers were actually like interstate highways to the Mongols, providing rapid passage into the heart of large urban settlements on the banks. In addition to standard siege engineering, the Mongols also became very adept at river work and river engineering. A couple of examples: In April, 1241, Mongol forces crossed the Eastern European river Sajo in spring flood conditions with 30,000 cavalry during one night before the Battle of Mohi, which allowed them to easily defeat the Hungarian king Bela IV and lay waste to half of Hungary. Similarly, another example, in the attack against the Khwarezm shah during the first phase of Mongol expansion, a flotilla of barges was constructed across the river to prevent the escape of their enemies.

I don't want to forget, gloss over, or ignore the fact that the Mongols were also brutally skilled in their use of terror tactics to control conquered peoples, particularly in the early stages of expansion. Mongol commanders certainly practiced what we'd call mass murder today, torture, and the forced resettlement of hundreds of thousands of conquered peoples. In Baghdad, Hulegu, wishing to make an example of the city that had refused to surrender, massacred close to a hundred thousand men, women, and children. So foul was the stench from the ruined city that Hulegu was forced to move his camp upwind. He also destroyed the ancient irrigation systems in a region that had constructed some of the first large-scale irrigation structures in all of world history thousands of years earlier, and this seriously damaged and set back Mesopotamian agriculture for decades, perhaps centuries.

But when Mongke came to power, he moderated Mongol policies. He restored economic productivity to the regions; he provided security for trade. In the next lecture, we'll certainly explore the impact of this restoration of economic productivity and commercial activity on the empire in general, and also focus in on the 150-year-long rule of the Mongols in China. Join me next time please as we look at the influence of the Mongol Yuan dynasty on Chinese and Eastern civilization and also try to critically evaluate the legacy of the Mongols to subsequent world history. Thank you.

Shaking the Foundation—Mongols in the East
Lecture 36

I n the last lecture, we considered the origins of the Mongols and followed their conquests through two major expansionary phases. In previous lectures, we have also considered the impact of the Mongols on Korea and the good fortune the Japanese enjoyed in avoiding Mongol invasion. In this lecture, we will focus more closely on the impact of the Mongols on Chinese history and culture—the heartland of Eastern civilization. We will then conclude by taking a world historian's perspective again, to consider the ramifications of the Mongol conquests on subsequent Eurasian and global history.

Government under the Mongols

- Although Chinggis Khan did not give any serious thought to imperial administration, the Mongols eventually learned to govern their empire. Under Khan Mongke, Mongol terror tactics were moderated, cultural differences of conquered peoples were accommodated, and thought was given to the skills required for competent imperial rule.

- During the reign of Mongke and his successors, the Mongols learned to mint coins, collect taxes in an orderly way, take censuses of the cities and states they controlled, and establish a courier system that connected the vast reaches of Eurasia. For commercial exchange, they regularized trade tolls, improved roads, and guaranteed merchant security.

- After centuries of fragmentation, the Silk Roads began to operate again, and much of Eurasia was effectively unified under Mongol rule. Government within the empire was often conducted by tributary vassal rulers who were rewarded with lavish gifts, and Mongol law was enforced by the constant threat of military retribution.

The Conquest of China

- As we have seen, the Mongols were not always the victors in their campaigns of conquest, but they were successful in China.
  - Chinggis Khan's early campaigns against the Jin dynasty were only the first step in a process that eventually resulted in the incorporation of all of China into the Mongol Empire.

  - In a series of violent and bloody campaigns between 1213 and 1220, Chinggis succeeded in bringing most of China north of the Huang He under Mongol control.

  - After the Great Khan died in 1227, his son Ogedei continued the attacks against the Jin, until the dynasty fell in 1234.

- Ogedei's younger brother, Tolui, had four sons, whose mother, Beki, ensured that they learned the arts of warfare, as well as reading and writing. Beki's oldest son, Mongke, became Great Khan of the Mongols, a position he held for only eight years before his death in 1259. Mongke was effectively the last khan to have supreme control over the Mongol world, which was then divided into the four khanates.

- Another son of Beki, Kublai Khan, was initially granted control of wealthy landed estates in northern China. Kublai worked hard to secure allies among the Jin and Han Chinese elites as he prepared to launch raids against the Song dynasty in the south.

- Kublai and Beki were effective and efficient administrators in northern China; they encouraged and supported farming, for example, to build a strong and reliable population of tax-paying farmers. For much of this period, Kublai was something of an absentee landlord, but gradually, he became more involved in the government of northern China.

- The first military campaigns against the Song began in 1258, led by Mongke Khan. After Mongke's death, civil war broke out among the Mongols; Kublai Khan claimed the title of Grand Khan in 1264, but not all the hordes recognized his authority. Nonetheless, with his power secure in China, Kublai turned his full attention to the enormous riches and resources of the Southern Song.

- Through a series of bloody and hard-won campaigns beginning in 1267, Kublai eventually defeated the well-armed Song forces. In 1271, he declared himself emperor of a reunited China, although the Southern Song capital of Hangzhou did not fall to Mongol forces until February 1276. Kublai chose the name Yuan for his new dynasty.

Mongol Rule in China

- Ruling a vast agricultural and commercial state was a new challenge for the Mongols. Never really trusting local Chinese administrators, Kublai and the later Yuan emperors tried to maintain political control and social stability by creating a balance of ethnic power in government and by combining Mongol and Chinese techniques of administration.

- The emperor and court centered their administration on the capital and ruled the provinces through subordinate officials, who were supervised by still other officials. To guard against the building of local power bases and regional autonomy, provincial administrators needed the permission of these imperial supervisors before any major decisions could be made.

- Kublai Khan dismantled the Confucian exam system that had provided China with high-quality bureaucrats for 1,500 years and brought many Persian and other West Asian Muslims to China, where they were given high administrative posts in the Yuan dynasty government.

- Despite the best efforts of Persian and Central Asian officials, history has judged the Yuan administration of China as inefficient. Although corruption was punished, the provinces were ruled with a considerable degree of independence and self-serving authority. Eventually, Mongol government became so lackadaisical that

Chinese Han officials employed to work with the Mongols openly criticized the government for its decentralization and inefficiency.

- Much of our knowledge of Chinese society under the Yuan comes from the famous Venetian traveler Marco Polo.
  - In 1271, accompanied by his father and uncle, the 17-year-old Marco set out on an epic journey across Asia, arriving at the court of Kublai Khan in 1275. According to Marco's later account, his skills and knowledge were so impressive to the great emperor that Kublai Khan employed him for the next 17 years as a trusted adviser, which allowed Marco to observe a great deal about Chinese society and government.

  - The descriptions of the Chinese court and way of life provided later in the *Travels of Marco Polo* seemed so absurd to 13th-century European readers that they were dismissed as lies. But Polo's accounts of the great canals, granaries, social services, advanced technology, and even regular bathing of the Chinese were so astonishing that his book became a bestseller.

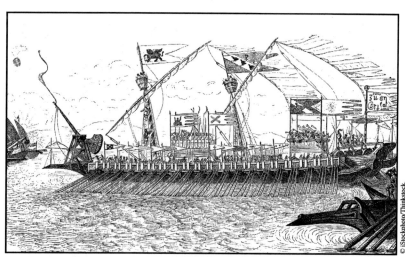

Scholars estimate that Marco Polo probably traveled a total of 15,000 miles on his journeys to and from Asia.

The Decline of the Mongols

- By the late 13th century, economic problems beset several parts of the Mongol Empire. In Persia, excessive spending gradually drained the treasury, and tax revenues began to dry up.
  - In the early 1290s the ilkhans tried to resolve these financial difficulties by introducing paper money, but merchants closed their shops rather than accept the currency, and commerce ground to a halt.

  - After the death of Ilkhan Ghazan in 1304, the dynasty went into a steep decline, blighted by intense factional disputes.

  - When the last Mongol ruler of Persia died without an heir in 1335, the ilkhanate collapsed, and local governors then ruled Persia until the arrival of the Turks late in the 14th century.

- Similar financial problems beset the Yuan administration in China at about the same time. Paper money was also used in China, but the Yuan did not maintain adequate reserves of bullion to back the currency. People quickly began to lose confidence in the economy as prices rose sharply.
  - From the 1320s on, power struggles, assassinations, and civil wars blighted Mongol China.

  - In the midst of this chaos, a nationalist rebellion broke out in the south in 1352, led by a young Buddhist ruler named Hongwu. As we will see, Hongwu went on to establish the powerful Ming dynasty, which would rule China until 1644.

  - In 1368, Hongwu's forces captured the Yuan capital, and the Mongols departed China for good. Under the Ming, government was stabilized and China was defended from further invasion for three centuries.

Impact of the Mongols

- From the early days of their empire, the Mongols prized commercial and trade relationships with neighboring economies, and they continued this policy during the cycles of expansion and consolidation that followed.

- o The well-traveled and well-maintained roads through the Mongol Empire linked lands from the Mediterranean basin to China, just as in the heyday of the first great Silk Roads era.

- o But we should also note that the Mongol Empire had a negligible influence on seaborne trade. Because maritime trade was much greater, both in value and volume, than overland trade, historians now intensely debate whether the century of Mongol rule really did have a profound impact on trans-Eurasian cultural exchange.

- It is indisputable, however, that during the century-long Pax Mongolica, East and West Eurasia were closer than ever before. This was mostly attributable to the encouragement of travel and communication by Mongol rulers, who established a courier network across Eurasia and maintained diplomatic relationships among themselves and with rulers of other states.

- Just as in the earlier Silk Roads eras, trans-Eurasian trade routes during the Mongol era also served as highways for the transmission of religions through missionaries.

- Although the Mongols are justifiably renowned for the slaughter and havoc wrought by their invasions, historians today tend to focus more on the stability and connections established by Mongol control of their vast empire.

- The Mongols encouraged trade and borrowed from established civilizations, helping to spread the technological knowledge of Eastern civilization from China to Europe, with dramatic implications for subsequent world history.

- The Pax Mongolica also gave Europeans a new awareness of the wider world, which acted as a powerful spur to European exploration, expansion, and, ultimately, colonization.

- Several times in this course, we have considered the critical role of militarized steppe nomadic peoples in diffusing Eastern culture and technology to the West and Western religions and beliefs to the East. In the 13th and 14th centuries, it was the Mongols who facilitated an intensive exchange of goods and ideas that helped lead directly to the emergence of a premodern "world system." This system was the forerunner to the emergence of capitalism, enhanced global connections, and the subsequent age of European hegemony.

- But the largest empire ever seen was fleeting and could not endure because of logistical problems and difficulties of imperial administration; thus, the mighty Mongols slipped quietly from the great stage of world history.

- Despite all the negatives associated with the rule of pastoral nomads and other outsiders, Chinese civilization actually gained something during its period of Mongol domination: a confidence in its ability to survive, to bend just enough to ward off the worst blows and defeats that these alien "barbarians" could inflict.
  o Far from the court of Kublai Khan, Confucian and Daoist teachings continued, and circles of artists and poets found ways to maintain confidence in the core foundational ideas of Eastern civilization.

  o In the next lecture, we'll see how this hidden repository of distinctive culture would resurface to guide China's fortunes during 300 years of Ming dynasty rule.

Suggested Reading

Buell, *The A to Z of the Mongol World Empire*.

Moule and Pelliot, *Marco Polo*.

Tanner, *China: A History*, chapter 8.

1. What were some of the impacts of Mongol rule on Chinese society and culture?

2. Why did the Silk Roads revive under the Mongols, and what was the impact of this revival on Eastern (and Western) civilization?

Shaking the Foundation—Mongols in the East
Lecture 36—Transcript

Hello and welcome to this second lecture on the Mongols and on their impact on Eastern civilization.

Last time, we looked at the origins of the Mongols and the conquests and migrations of their Turkic predecessors, who centuries before the Mongols had created their own formidable Turkic Empire throughout much of Inner Eurasia. We also followed the Mongol conquests through various expansionary phases, and the military organization and skills they used to construct and administer the largest empire the world had ever seen to that point in history. But as fascinating as all this is, particularly to a historian like me, in a course primarily focused on Eastern civilization we need in this lecture I think to sort of zoom in more closely on the impact of the Mongols on Chinese history and culture in particular, and thus on the very heartland of Eastern civilization. We've already seen in previous lectures the impact of the Mongols on Korea, and I've mentioned the good fortune the Japanese enjoyed in avoiding Mongol invasion through the intervention of the divine kamikaze wind; I'll return to that attempted invasion a little later in the course. But let's return to China now for the bulk of this lecture, and then conclude by panning back out again and taking a world historian's perspective again to consider the ramifications of the Mongol conquests for subsequent Eurasian and indeed global history.

As we saw last time, although Chinggis Khan didn't give any serious thought to imperial administration, the Mongols did eventually learn to administer, to govern, the largest empire ever seen. This required so many languages, of course, and also considerable intercultural knowledge; and it was under Khan Mongke that Mongol terror tactics were moderated, that cultural differences were accommodated, and that serious thought was given to the skills required for competent imperial rule. So during the reign of Mongke and his successors, the Mongols learned to mint coins, for example; to collect taxes in an orderly way; to have censuses taken of the huge number of cities and states they now controlled; and also to establish a Mongol courier system that connected the vast reaches of Eurasia. Even more importantly for commercial and transcultural exchange, the Mongols regularized all trade tolls, they improved roads, and they guaranteed merchant security, all of which gave a tremendous boost to trade and commercial and diplomatic travel. After centuries of fragmentation, the Silk Roads began to operate again, and much of Eurasia was effectively unified under Mongol rule and Mongol law. In fact, the period of Mongol rule is regarded as the third great Silk Roads era.

Government within the empire was generally conducted now by tributary vassal rulers who were rewarded with lavish gifts; and Mongol law was enforced, naturally, by the constant threat of brutal military retribution. Throughout this period, the nucleus of the military remained the cavalry of some 130,000 highly-skilled Mongol horsemen augmented, as we saw last time, by infantry and also siege troops from captured states. Of course, the Mongols weren't always successful in their campaigns of imperial conquest; as we've seen in earlier lectures, they failed dismally in their attempted invasions of both Japan and Vietnam. But they were far more successful in China, where Chinggis Khan's early campaigns against the Jin dynasty that I mentioned last time were only the first step in a process that eventually resulted in the incorporation of all of China into the Mongol Empire.

In a series of violent and bloody campaigns between 1213 and 1220, Chinggis succeeded in bringing most of the region of China north of the Huang He, north of the Yellow River, under Mongol control. After the Great Khan died in 1227, his son Ogedei continued the attacks against the Jin, until the Jin dynasty finally fell in 1234. Ogedei's younger brother Tolui had four sons, all grandsons of Chinggis Khan. Each of these boys was raised by their extraordinary, formidable mother Beki to be skilled in the arts of warfare, but she also made sure they learned to read and write the Mongol script. As a daughter in law of Chinggis Khan and as mother of four grown, powerful sons, Beki held enormous prestige in the Mongol world. She was also a skilled politician who used tribal politics and clever diplomacy to ensure that her oldest son Mongke became Great Khan of the Mongols, a position that he held for only eight years before his death in 1259. Mongke was effectively the last khan to have supreme control over the Mongol world, which now divided into the four khanates that we discussed last time. Another of the sons of the extraordinary Beki was Hulegu, who, as we saw, was responsible for the destruction of Baghdad and the end of the Islamic Abbasid caliphate in Persia.

But a third son of Beki is probably the most famous khan of all after Chinggis. This is Kublai Khan, who was initially granted control of some wealthy landed estates in northern China. Kublai then worked hard to secure allies amongst the Jin and Han Chinese elites as he prepared to launch raids against the formidable Song dynasty that was still in power in the south. He was so successful at building this sort of series of alliances that several generals eventually defected from the Song and came over to the Mongols, and this played a key role in the total conquest of China. Kublai and Beki were effective and efficient administrators in Northern China. They encouraged and supported farming, for example; they tried to build a strong and reliable population of taxpaying farmers. Although a Nestorian Christian by faith, Beki also exemplified the tolerant Mongol attitude towards other religions; she supported Daoism, she supported Buddhism, and she supported Islam. For much of this period, Kublai was something of an absentee landlord; but gradually he became more involved in the government of Northern China.

The first military campaigns against the Song began in 1258 and were led by Mongke Khan personally. After Mongke's death, civil war broke out amongst the Mongols. Kublai Khan was proclaimed the title of Grand Khan in 1264, but not all the hordes recognized his authority. Nonetheless, with his power secure in China, Kublai now turned his full attention to the enormous riches and resources of the Southern Song. In a series of bloody and hard-won campaigns beginning in 1267, Kublai used huge forces and actually thousands of ships, as well as skilled Persian and Uygur engineers, to eventually defeat the well-armed Song forces. In 1271, Kublai Khan declared himself emperor of a reunified China; although the Great Southern Song capital of Hangzhou didn't finally fall to his Mongol forces until five years later, in February, 1276. He constructed a new capital in the north now where modern Beijing is today, and apart from a very brief period early in the Ming, Beijing has remained the capital of China from that moment until today; the capital of the Yuan, of most of the Ming, and all of the Qing dynasties, and, of course, the capital of the People's Republic of China.

The design of the capital was carefully and intentionally based on descriptions in the *Book of Rites*, one of the classics of Zhou dynasty literature that had been around for about 2,000 years by this point and, of course, one of the books that we met very early in our course. In fact, Kublai intentionally used the Zhou classics to validate his reign; the name he chose for his new Yuan dynasty was also drawn from ancient Chinese tradition. The word *Yuan* is found in the Zhou *Book of Changes* and means "the origins of the universe."

Ruling a vast and complex agricultural and commercial state like China was a new challenge for the Mongols. Never really trusting local Chinese administrators, Kublai and the later Yuan dynasty emperors tried to maintain political order, social stability, and regular tax revenue by creating a balance of ethnic power in government and by combining Mongol and Chinese techniques of administration. To help facilitate this, the people of the Yuan dynasty were now divided into four categories or classes based on their ethnicity: Mongols on the top, of course; a group known as diverse peoples second; then the vast Han Chinese population; and at the bottom the Southern Chinese. With the Mongols as the elite group in this hierarchy, the categorization was clearly designed to keep them at the top of the social and political pecking order.

To further emphasize this, all Mongols living in China enjoyed substantial legal and tax advantages. The emperor and the court centered their administration on the capital, and they ruled the provinces through subordinate officials who were supervised by other specially appointed imperial officials. To guard against the building of local power bases and regional autonomy, provincial administrators needed the permission of these imperial supervisors before any major decisions could be made. Many of these supervisors were actually Persian, because from the moment that the Mongols had encountered the Persian officials of the Abbasid Caliphate, they'd been deeply impressed with their skills in government. Kublai Khan dismantled the Confucian exam system that had provided China with high-quality bureaucrats for 1,500 years, and instead brought many Persian and other West Asian Muslims to China where they were given high administrative posts in Yuan Dynasty government. From Chinese sources, we actually know something about one of these Muslim administrators in particular: a Muslim from Tashkent in Central Asia who became a high Yuan government official. Ahmed was able to maximize tax revenues through a series of reforms that greatly enriched the government and, of course, also enriched Ahmed and his family.

Yet despite the best efforts of Ahmed and other Persian and Central Asian officials, history has judged the Yuan administration of China as inefficient. The Mongols certainly did their best to root out corruption and corrupt officials were flogged by the Mongols; this is in stark contrast to the much more civil atmosphere that had characterized the Song dynasty court. But despite their efforts to oversee provincial administrators, the provinces were ruled with a considerable degree of independence and self-governing, self-serving authority. The only important function of regional officials was to keep the tax revenues and other goods and services flowing into the imperial government, and frankly the Mongols didn't really care how this was done. The Yuan dynasty did introduce some laws, but these were so ineffectual that even Han Chinese officials claimed that they were too lenient. In fact, Mongol government eventually become so lackadaisical that even those Chinese Han officials employed to work with the Mongols openly criticized the Yuan government for its decentralization and its inefficiency.

But other than government, what do we know about how Chinese society functioned under Mongol hegemony; and what, if any, were the long term impacts of Mongol rule on the foundational ideas of Chinese culture? Much of our knowledge of Yuan China actually comes from the famous Venetian traveler Marco Polo. Polo was born in or about 1254. He was a member of a very 0successful family of merchants who operated in the Venetian Republic during the 13th century. In 1271, accompanied by his father and uncle, the then 17-year-old Marco set out on an epic journey across Asia, arriving three-and-a-half years later at the court of Kublai Khan in 1275. Upon meeting the Khan, the Polo's presented him with sacred oils from Jerusalem and a letter from the Pope. Marco Polo knew several languages and he'd acquired a great deal of political and geographical knowledge in his travels. According to Marco's own account, these credentials and skills were so impressive that he was employed by the great emperor Kublai Khan for the next 17 years as the emperor's trusted advisor, which allowed him, of course, to observe a great deal about Chinese society and Chinese government. Marco did eventually return to Venice in 1295 after another epic journey; in fact, scholars estimate that in all Marco Polo probably traveled a total of 15,000 miles on these twin journeys. But upon returning home, Marco found himself caught up in a bitter war between Genoa and Venice, and he was imprisoned for several years before being released in 1299. It was while he was in prison that he dictated to his cellmate the famous account of his travels and his many years in China, known ever since as the *Travels of Marco Polo*.

Marco Polo's detailed descriptions of the sophisticated Chinese court and way of life seemed so absurd to 13th-century Europeans that they were dismissed as a pack of lies. But his accounts of the great canals of China, the granaries, social services, advanced technology, even regular bathing of all Chinese—all of which were completely unknown in Europe—were so astonishing that his book became a bestseller and it's remained one to this very day. Polo reported, for example, that China's social welfare system took care of sick, aged, and orphaned citizens; he also noted that the great emperor had 12,000 personal retainers. But Polo also noted that ethnic animosity was intense in Yuan China. He wrote, and let me quote Marco Polo here: "All the Han detested the rule of the Great Khan because he set over them Mongols, or still more frequently Muslims, whom they could not endure for they treated them just as slaves." Those ethnic Chinese who did work with the Han often prospered, but many others had their lands confiscated or were forced into serfdom, even slavery, and often transported far from home. In fact, I mentioned this briefly last time, modern historians have been pointing out and tracing more recently the fact that the Mongols substantially redrew the ethnic map not just of China but of much of Eurasia by forcing literally millions of people of different ethnicities to leave their native lands and resettle far away.

Before we leave our important guide Marco Polo, let me tell you that after being released from prison, Marco did eventually become a successful and wealthy merchant; but although he sponsored many other successful expeditions into Asia, he himself never left Venice again until his death in 1324.

By the late 13th century, economic problems were beginning to beset several parts of the Mongol Empire. In Persia, excessive spending gradually drained the treasury and tax revenues began to dry up. In the early 1290s, the ilkhans tried to resolve these financial difficulties by introducing paper money in the hope that this would drive precious metals back into the hand of the government. But merchants closed their shops rather than accept the worthless paper and commerce quickly ground to a halt. After the death of Ilkhan Ghazan in 1304, the dynasty went into a steep decline blighted by intense factional disputes. When the last Mongol ruler of Persia died without an heir in 1335, the ilkhanate collapsed and local governors then ruled Persia until the arrival of the Turks late in the 14th century. Similar financial problems beset the Yuan administration in China at about the same time. The Mongols also used paper money in China—as we've seen, so did the Tang and Song dynasties before them—but unlike the Chinese dynasties, the Yuan didn't maintain adequate reserves of bullion to back up the paper currency; so the people quickly began to lose confidence in the economy as the prices rose sharply. At the same time, as was the case in the Persian Ilkhanate, political infighting in the Yuan Court also hastened Mongol decline in China.

From the 1320s on, power struggles, assassinations, even civil wars blighted Mongol China. In the midst of this chaos, a nationalist rebellion broke out in the south in 1352 led by a young Buddhist ruler named Hong Wu. As we'll see next time, Hong Wu went on to establish the powerful Ming Dynasty, which would rule China for almost 300 years until 1644. In 1368 Hong Wu's forces captured the Yuan capital, and the Mongols departed China for good to return to the steppes from whence they'd come. Under the Ming, government was stabilized and China was defended from further invasion—including, as we'll see, from the occasionally still restive and aggressive Mongols—for three centuries. We'll explore this in the next two lectures of the course; and as we'll see, under Ming China, China prospered and its indigenous culture was fostered in an era that strongly supported and promoted again the core values of Eastern civilization and also attempted to block out any unwholesome, and increasingly unwelcomed, foreign influence.

But first, of course, I need to try and wrap up these two lectures on the Mongols by assessing again their impact on Eastern civilization and their impact indeed on all of world history. From the early days of their empire, the Mongols prized commercial and trade relationships with neighboring economies, and they continued this policy during the cycles of expansion and consolidation that followed. This meant that all merchants and foreign ambassadors traveling anywhere in the Mongol realm who carried proper documentation (passports really) and proper authorization from the Mongols were protected; this greatly increased overland trade. During the 13th and 14th centuries, thousands of European and Islamic merchants made their way from Europe and West Asia to the distant lands of China. Marco Polo was only one of the best known of these; his account of his travels certainly inspired many others to follow in his footsteps. The well-traveled and well-maintained roads throughout the vast Mongol Empire thus linked lands from the Mediterranean Basin to China, just like during the heyday of the first Great Silk Roads era.

But we must also note that the Mongol Empire had a negligible influence on seaborne trade because they didn't control the sea lanes, and it's because of this fact that some world historians part company now on the question of Mongol global influence. Because maritime trade was much larger both in value and volume than the overland trade that passed through the territories directly under the control of the Mongol Empire, historians now intensely debate whether the century of Mongol rule really did have such a profound impact on trans-Eurasian cultural exchange. But it is indisputable that during the century-long Pax Mongolica, the Mongol Peace, East and West Eurasia were closer perhaps than ever before. Mostly this was because Mongol rulers positively encouraged travel and communication; I mentioned they established this courier network that rapidly relayed news, information, and government orders across Eurasia. With this sort of direct encouragement from the khans, missionaries, traders, and adventurers like Marco Polo now began to journey with ease to and fro all over Africa, Arabia, Central Asia certainly, and even Europe. Despite periodic outbreaks of civil war, throughout the Mongol Era the great khans of China, the ilkhans of Persia, and the khans of all the other regions under Mongol control maintained close communication with each other by means of diplomatic embassies.

But at the same time, the khanates also had diplomatic relationships with rulers and states much further afield: in Korea, way to the south in Vietnam, in China, of course, in India, Russia, and even Western Europe. We know of several European ambassadors who traveled all the way to the Mongol realm and into China to deliver messages from authorities in Europe seeking to form alliances with the Mongols. We also know that diplomats traveled westwards, including Rabban Sauma, a Nestorian Christian monk born who was born in the Mongol capital of Khanbaliq and who then went on to visit Italy and France as a representative of the Persian ilkhan.

Just like the earlier Silk Roads eras, trans-Eurasian trade routes during the Mongol Era also served as highways for the transmission of religions through missionaries. Several Christian missionaries journeyed to the Mongols. One of the most famous is John of Plano Carpini who was sent by Pope Innocent IV to visit the great khan in 1246; I'll have something more to say about John, or Giovanni, in the next two lectures from now. Later, the famous Flemish Franciscan William of Rubruck visited Mongke's court in 1254, and John of Monte Corvino made thousands of converts during his extensive visits to China between 1289 and 1322. This was the beginning, by the way, of a sustained attempt to spread Christianity into China that continued under the Ming and the Qing, as we'll shortly see. Between 1325 and 1354, the famous Muslim traveler Ibn Battuta, perhaps one of the greatest travelers who ever lived, also traveled extensively through Afro-Eurasia, benefitting from the Pax Mongolica, the Mongol Peace. Ibn Battuta visited Constantinople and every Middle Eastern Islamic state; also India, Sri Lanka, Indonesia, and even China. He several times noted in his journals that the merchants of Eurasia benefited enormously from lower tariffs under the Mongols, and that silk and spices were flowing from east to west along the old Silk Roads, both by land and by sea.

So, although justifiably renowned, notoriously really, for the slaughter and the havoc wrought by their invasions, historians today tend to focus more on the stability and the connections established by Mongol control of their vast empire. Undoubtedly, the Mongols encouraged trade, they borrowed from old established civilizations, and they helped spread the technological knowledge of Eastern civilization—knowledge of gunpowder, for example, ship building techniques, medicine, printing—all the way from China to Europe, with dramatic implications for subsequent world history. In the Middle East, the Mongols patronized art, superb architecture, and the writing of important histories; to China, the Mongols introduced new crops, and Islamic ideas about astronomy and ceramics. The Pax Mongolica also gave Europeans a new awareness of the wider world, which certainly acted as a powerful spur or incentive to European exploration, European expansion, and ultimately European colonization of much of the world.

Time and again in this course we've considered the critical role of militarized steppe nomadic peoples in diffusing Eastern culture and Eastern technology to the West, and also diffusing Western religions and Western beliefs into the East; people like the Xiongnu, the Yuezhi, the Scythians, and the Huns. In the 13th and 14th centuries, it was the Mongols who facilitated an intensive exchange of goods and ideas that helped lead directly to the emergence of a sort of pre-modern, interconnected "world system." This system, many world historians now argue, was the forerunner to the emergence of capitalism, of enhanced global connections, and the forerunner to the subsequent age of European hegemony.

But the largest empire ever seen was fleeting, and it couldn't endure because of logistical problems and difficulties of imperial administration; and so the mighty Mongols slipped quietly from the stage of world history. The ultimate impact of all this on Eastern civilization is intriguing and equally significant, I think. Despite all the negatives associated with the rule of pastoral nomads and other outsiders, Chinese civilization actually gained something during its period of Mongol domination. This was a confidence in its ability to survive; to bend just enough to ward off the worst blows and defeats that these alien barbarians could throw at them. Chinese civilization survived by strengthening those core facets of cultural identity independent of who was wearing the mantle of the Son of Heaven. Far from the court of Kublai Khan, Confucian and Daoist teachings continued, and circles of artists and poets found ways to maintain confidence in the core foundational ideas of Eastern civilization. Next time, we'll see how this hidden repository of distinctive culture would resurface to guide China's fortunes during 300 years of Ming dynasty rule.

The Rise of the Ming
Lecture 37

The Ming dynasty is perhaps best known for its famous porcelain and other artistic achievements, but it should also be recognized for the remarkable job it did in stabilizing Chinese fortunes and preserving many of the foundational elements and ideas of Eastern civilization when they threatened to unravel. However, as we will see in this lecture and the next, this stabilization and preservation came at an enormous cost and ultimately resulted in the surrendering of Chinese power, innovation, and global leadership to the new and rising power of world history: the Europeans.

The Early Ming Period
- After the Yuan dynasty collapsed in the mid-14th century because of internal dissent and pressure from peasant uprisings, the Ming dynasty moved quickly to restore native rule to China.

- Hongwu, the leader of the uprising against the Yuan, ruled as the first Ming emperor, from 1368 to 1398. Hongwu chose the name Ming ("brilliant") for the new dynasty, and after driving the Mongols out, he set to work to build a tightly centralized Chinese-run state.

- As emperor, Hongwu made extensive use of a new class of bureaucrat called mandarins. These were imperial government officials whose job was to travel throughout the land and supervise the implementation of government policies. Hongwu also placed great trust in eunuchs; indeed, three of the most famous eunuchs in China's long history served the imperial court during the Ming dynasty.
  o One of these was the great Muslim admiral Zheng He; another was Liu Jin, who served Prince Zhu Houzhao and whose corrupt behavior is blamed by historians for seriously undermining the credibility of the Ming dynasty.

○ The third famous eunuch of the Ming was Wei Zhongxian, an illiterate former hoodlum who used the art of flattery to get close to Emperor Wanli.

- One of Hongwu's finest successors was Emperor Yongle (r. 1403–1424). He is renowned for launching a series of naval expeditions that sailed throughout the Indian Ocean basin and showed Chinese colors as far away as East Africa. These expeditions were led by the eunuch admiral Zheng He.

- Yongle's successors discontinued these expensive maritime expeditions but maintained the tightly centralized state that Hongwu had established. One of the reasons the expeditions were stopped is that the Ming emperors were determined to prevent new invasions of China. In particular, they were concerned about the Mongols, who remained active and dangerous to the north of the Great Wall. Because of this concern, in 1421, Yongle decided to move the early Ming capital from Nanjing back to Beijing.

- The early Ming emperors commanded powerful armies that were able to keep the Mongols under control militarily, but later emperors were far less able and efficient, and by the mid-15th century, Ming military forces

In their desperation to keep out the Mongols and with an increasingly less effective military, the Ming administration made the reconstruction of the Great Wall a major defensive priority.

had lost much of their effectiveness. Later Ming emperors, in their desperation to protect their realm from Mongols and other militarized nomads, rebuilt and extended the Great Wall system.

- The defensive policies pursued by the Ming rulers were part of a larger determination to eradicate Mongol—and, indeed, any foreign—cultural influence from China and to create a stable society in the image of the classical Chinese past.
  - o With Ming government encouragement, individuals gave up the Mongol names and dress they had adopted under the Yuan.

  - o The government sponsored the study of Chinese cultural traditions that the Mongols had suppressed or ignored, especially Confucianism. Imperial academies and regional colleges were established throughout China to teach the foundational ideas and philosophies of Eastern civilization.

  - o Most importantly, the Ming restored the civil service exam system that the Mongols had dismantled.

Weakening of the Ming

- The vigor of the early Ming emperors, such as Hongwu and Yongle, did not survive beyond the mid-16th century, after a series of problems combined to weaken the dynasty.

- One of the most difficult challenges the government had to deal with was an outbreak of vicious piracy in the Yellow and South China seas.
  - o For several decades between the 1520s and 1560s, pirates and smugglers, mostly based in Japan, operated almost at will along the east coast of China.

  - o The Ming navy and coastal defenses proved woefully ineffective in dealing with the outbreak; conflicts with pirate gangs severely disrupted coastal regions and, sometimes, well into the interior.

- We can see further evidence of ineptitude in the fact that the later Ming emperors lived more and more extravagantly in the Forbidden City, a vast imperial enclave built in the heart of Beijing.

- The Forbidden City was built between 1406 and 1420; engineers estimate it probably required 1 million conscripted laborers to construct. When completed, the complex contained 980 separate buildings and covered an area of close to 8 million square feet!

- Walking through the Forbidden City, it is easy to imagine the Ming emperors living their sheltered lives deep inside this vast complex, receiving news about the outside world only through eunuchs and servant administrators, news that was heavily filtered and censored.

- Most later Ming emperors adapted to the situation by ignoring government affairs while satisfying their various appetites for wine, women, and other pleasures.

- When a series of famines struck China in the early 17th century, the government proved itself incapable of organizing relief efforts. As the famine worsened and no aid was forthcoming from Beijing, the desperate peasants resorted to eating grass roots and tree bark. By the 1630s, angry peasants were organizing revolts; as they gathered momentum, city after city withdrew its loyalty from the Ming.

- At the same time, Manchu invaders in north seized the opportunity to invade China by joining forces with the peasants in a concerted attack on the Ming. By the early 1640s, the combined rebel and Manchu forces controlled much of China, and they turned in a calculated pincer movement toward Beijing. The last emperor of the Ming was so sheltered by court eunuchs and mandarins that he had no idea of the seriousness of the situation until it was far too late.

- In April 1644, with the forces of rebel leader Li Zicheng about to capture Beijing, the last Ming emperor, Chongzhen, organized a feast and invited all the members of the imperial household except his sons to attend. Using his sword, he killed all of them to prevent them from falling into rebel hands. Then, still wearing his glorious imperial costume, he ran outside and hanged himself from a Japanese pagoda tree. The forces of Li Zicheng captured the inner city.

Imperial Administration under the Ming

- Both the Ming and later Qing dynasties attempted, at least in their early days, to preside over a well-organized and tightly centralized state. The actual administration of the empire was handled by a vast bureaucracy staffed by Confucian scholars. With this structure in place, for more than 500 years, the autocratic state created by Hongwu governed China's fortunes.

- According to the ancient tradition of Eastern civilization, the emperor was the "son of heaven," a human being designated by heavenly powers to maintain order on earth and blessed to wear the mandate of heaven.
  - o The emperor lived a privileged life within the Forbidden City, with hundreds of concubines and thousands of eunuchs to take care of his every desire. His day was completely orchestrated, and all performances in which he participated carefully choreographed.

  - o Everything about the emperor's person and the institution he represented conveyed a sense of awesome authority. His clothes and personal effects bore designs forbidden to other people, and the written characters of the emperor's name were taboo throughout China.

- Below the emperor and the imperial eunuchs, the day-to-day governing of China was the job of scholar-bureaucrats, the most senior of whom had been personally appointed by the emperor. In the best tradition of Confucianism, these men had earned academic degrees by passing rigorous civil service examinations.
  - o Under the Ming, preparations for the Confucian exams began at an early age. Sometimes, classes in the classics took place in local schools, which (like the exams themselves) were open only to males. However, the fact that wealthy families

employed tutors to help their sons prepare for the exams also made formal education available for girls.

o By the time students were 10 or 11 years old, they had memorized the several thousand Chinese written-language characters that were necessary to deal with Confucian literature, including the *Analects* and all of the Zhou dynasty classics.

o Candidates also studied calligraphy, poetry, and essay writing and had to know a large corpus of commentaries, histories, and literary works that had been written on the classics over the previous 2,000 years.

o The examinations themselves consisted of a series of tests administered at different levels: district, provincial, and metropolitan. Stiff quotas restricted the number of successful candidates in each exam.

o The actual writing of the exam was a grueling process. For three days and two nights, candidates wrote essays in eight sections. There were no interruptions and no communication between candidates; if a candidate died during the exam, his body was wrapped in straw and tossed over the compound walls for his family to come and collect!

o Of course, the possibility of high bureaucratic service (with rich financial and social rewards) meant that despite the grueling nature of the exams, competition for degrees was ferocious at all levels. Those who passed only the district-level exams usually spent their careers as teachers or private tutors. But those who passed the metropolitan exams could at least hope for powerful positions in the imperial bureaucracy.

o By opening the door to the possibility of honor, power, and rewards, the exam system encouraged the serious pursuit of higher education. China under the Ming was undoubtedly the most highly educated society that had ever existed to this point in world history.

- o The system also molded the personal values of those who governed China by ensuring that the ethical philosophy of Confucianism remained at the heart of Chinese education and government, as it had done off and on for more than 2,000 years.

- By driving out the Mongols, Ming China was able to control its own affairs throughout the early modern era; in so doing, it avoided the sort of turmoil that afflicted the Americas and Africa after the arrival of the Europeans.

- As we'll see in the next lecture, for several decades in the early 15th century, the government provided state support for an astonishing burst of naval expeditions, but after that, later Ming emperors moved to restrict foreign expeditions and the access of foreign merchants and missionaries to China.

Suggested Reading

Dardess, *Confucianism and Autocracy.*

Ebrey, *The Cambridge Illustrated History of China*, chapter 8.

Questions to Consider

1. How did the Ming centralize power in the hands of the emperor, and what was the impact of this on later imperial Chinese politics?

2. In what way did the civil service exam system practiced by the Ming ensure that the ethical philosophy of Confucianism remained at the heart of Chinese education and government, as it had done off and on for more than 2,000 years before the Ming?

The Rise of the Ming
Lecture 37—Transcript

Hello everyone, and welcome to this, the first of two lectures on the Ming dynasty of China; a dynasty perhaps best known to you for its famous porcelain and other artistic achievements, but a dynasty that should also be recognized for the remarkable job it did in stabilizing Chinese fortunes and in preserving many of the foundational elements and ideas of Eastern civilization when they threatened to unravel. However, as I also want to argue in this pair of lectures and the following two actually on the Qing dynasty, this stabilization and preservation came at an enormous cost, and resulted ultimately in the surrendering of Chinese power, innovation, and global leadership to the new and rising power of world history: the Europeans.

As we've just seen, during the 13th and 14th centuries China experienced the trauma of rule by detested outsiders: the Yuan dynasty of the Mongols. The Mongols largely ignored Chinese political and cultural traditions; they dismantled the Confucian exam system, for example; and they replaced many Chinese bureaucrats with Central Asian, Persian, and other foreign administrators, many of whom were Muslims. When the long Yuan reign was finally ended and the Mongols had been driven back to the steppes, the Ming emperors who followed attempted in turn to erase all signs of Mongol influence and restore traditional forms of culture and governance to China. In order to do this, they looked back to the great Chinese dynasties that had preceded the Mongols for inspiration. Like the Tang dynasty in particular, the Ming built a powerful and centralized imperial state; they revived the ancient Confucian civil service exam and the whole idea of the scholar-bureaucrat; and they promoted Confucian values, values that had first emerged 2,000 years earlier in the Late Zhou dynasty, at the expense of any and all outside ideas.

As we'll see in the subsequent pair of lectures, the rulers of the Qing dynasty that followed the Ming, although they themselves were Manchus of nomadic origin and thus technically also outsiders, nonetheless also worked hard to promote these traditional Chinese ways. So both the Ming and Qing dynasties were deeply conservative; their focus was on maintaining stability and tradition in a huge agrarian society, and to a certain extent on isolating and protecting China from "unwholesome" outside influences. By adopting policies that favored these classical Chinese traditions, these two dynasties collectively maintained a successful and stable state for half a millennium, something that was certainly appreciated by Chinese intellectuals and by the common people at the time. But modern historians have come to view the Ming and the Qing as dynasties that ultimately acted like a dead weight to slow Chinese innovation and entrepreneurship just when real global competition from European states was about to appear. It's a profound irony that at the same moment tiny European countries like Portugal began to send their fleets into the India Ocean and eventually on to China, the Ming government was attempting to actively withdraw their fleets from the seas, as we'll shortly see. Just as Europeans began putting Chinese inventions like printing, gunpowder, and the compass to very good use, China let its technological superiority slip and gave up its position of global scientific leadership. Undoubtedly, the Ming dynasty preserved peace within China and much of East Asia for centuries, an achievement for which they deserve enormous credit; but ultimately, the peaceful and conservative stagnation of China under the Ming was to have disastrous consequences for China under the succeeding Qing dynasty, as we'll shortly see.

Let's pick up our story with the end of Mongol rule in China. After the Yuan dynasty collapsed in the mid-14th century—you'll remember because of internal dissent and also enormous pressure from peasant uprisings—the Ming dynasty moved quickly to restore native rule to China. Hongwu, the leader of the uprising against the Yuan, ruled as the first Ming emperor for 30 years, from 1368–1398. As founder of the dynasty, he chose the name Ming, which means "brilliant," for the new dynasty; and after driving the Mongols out, he set to work to build a tightly centralized Chinese-run state. Hongwu was the third of only three peasants ever to become leader of China, by the way; part of a very select group. As emperor, Hongwu decided to make extensive use of a new class of bureaucrat called mandarins. These were imperial government officials whose job was to travel throughout the land and supervise the implementation of government policies; a sort of eyes and ears for the emperor and the court. Hongwu also decided to place great trust in eunuchs; men, I'm sure you might remember from previous lectures, who'd been castrated, usually at a young age. Because this meant they couldn't generate families and therefore couldn't build power bases that would challenge imperial authority, eunuchs were trusted with a variety of sensitive positions within government; but this was a trust that many eunuchs learned to abuse.

Three of the most famous—infamous perhaps—eunuchs in China's long history served the imperial court during the Ming dynasty. One of these, deservedly famous, was the great Muslim admiral, seven-foot-tall Zheng He, about whom I'll have quite a bit to say in our next lecture. Another was Liu Jin, who served Prince Zhu Houzhao when the prince was quite young. After the Prince became emperor, Liu Jin was promoted to the position of leading eunuch in the court. He then used his power to control access to the emperor, and is said to have had 56 ethical Confucian officials removed from their positions. His corrupt behavior is blamed by many Chinese historians today for seriously undermining the credibility of the dynasty. The third famous—or in this case definitely infamous—eunuch of the Ming was Wei Zhongxian, a former illiterate hoodlum who used the art of flattery to get close to Emperor Wanli. Despite being a eunuch, Wei was apparently able to maintain an intimate relationship with the nanny of the emperor's grandson Zhu Youjiao, who later became Emperor Xizong. After Zhu Youjiao was proclaimed emperor, eunuch Wei Zhongxian became the real power behind the throne, jailing and killing his enemies and leading the monarchy, which towards the end of the Ming was being totally manipulated by these eunuchs, to the brink of collapse.

Let's leave this sorry tale of corruption for a moment and concentrate on the vigorous and successful rule of the early Ming period, including one of Hongwu's finest successors, Emperor Yongle, who ruled from 1403–1424. Yongle is renowned for launching a series of naval expeditions that sailed throughout the Indian Ocean basin and that showed Chinese colors as far away as East Africa, expeditions led by the eunuch Admiral Zheng He. But Yongle's successors discontinued these expensive maritime expeditions, although they did maintain the tightly centralized state that Hongwu had established. I promise to tell you more about the world historical ramifications of this decision to end the naval expeditions in our next lecture.

One of the reasons the expeditions were stopped is because the Ming emperors were determined to prevent new invasions of China; in particular, they were very concerned about the Mongols, who, although they'd been driven back to the steppes, remained very active and dangerous just to the north of the Great Wall. Because of this concern, in 1421 Yongle decided to move the early Ming capital from Nanjing in the south back to Beijing in order to keep a closer watch on the Mongols and also other nomadic peoples of the steppes; as I mentioned last time I think, Beijing has remained the capital of China ever since, for almost the last 600 years. The early Ming emperors did indeed command powerful armies that were able to keep the Mongols under tight military control; but later emperors were far less able and far less efficient, and by the mid-15th century Ming military forces had lost much of their effectiveness. Powerful Mongol forces actually massacred several Chinese armies in the 1440s, and in 1449 they captured the Ming emperor himself, a clear demonstration of the lack of prowess of the Ming military.

The later Ming emperors, in their desperation to protect their realm from Mongols and other militarized nomads, decided to invest much of their resources into rebuilding and extending new fortifications in the ancient Great Wall system. I'm sure you remember from earlier lectures in the course that it was the first emperor Qin Shi Huangdi who way back in the 3rd century B.C.E. had first connected many of those smaller Zhou dynasty Warring States Period walls together into the first Great Wall system. Various dynasties since then, particularly the Han during the Silk Roads era, had maintained and extended the fortifications; but these ancient walls had largely fallen into ruin by the period of the Southern Song. In their desperation to keep out the Mongols and in the context of an increasingly less effective military, the Ming administration made the reconstruction of the Great Walls a major defensive priority. Hundreds of thousands of workers were employed to labor mightily throughout the late 15th/early 16th centuries to build a truly formidable stone and brick barrier that in the end ran for some 1,550 miles. The Ming Great Wall was a lot more standardized in its construction than its ancient predecessors. It averaged generally between 33 and 50 feet in height; it included watch and signal towers at regular intervals along the wall; it included accommodation for troops, of course, stationed along this very extensive border. If you've been fortunate enough to walk on any of the sections of the Great Wall near Beijing, then you've definitely walked on part of the Ming Great Wall.

These military defeats and subsequent defensive policies pursued by the Ming rulers were part of a larger determination not just to eradicate Mongol and indeed any foreign cultural influence from China, but also to create instead a stable society in the image of the classical Chinese past. With Ming government encouragement, individuals now gave up the Mongol names and the dress that they'd adopted during the Yuan dynasty. The government also sponsored the study of Chinese cultural traditions that the Mongols had suppressed or ignored, especially (no surprise) Confucianism; and they provided financial support for the establishment of imperial academies and regional colleges all over China to teach the foundational ideas and philosophies of Eastern civilization. Most importantly, the Ming restored the ancient civil service exam system that the Mongols had dismantled; this is a subject I'll turn to in a little more detail in just a moment in this lecture.

But the vigor of the early Ming emperors like Hongwu and Yongle didn't survive beyond the mid-16th century, after a series of problems combined to weaken the dynasty. One of the most difficult challenges the government had to deal with was an outbreak of vicious piracy in the Yellow and South China seas. Indeed, for several decades between the 1520s and the 1560s, pirates and smugglers, mostly based in Japan, operated almost at will up and down the entire east coast of China. The Ming navy and coastal defenses proved woefully ineffective in dealing with this outbreak, and conflicts with pirate gangs severely disrupted coastal regions, sometimes well into the interior as well. Let me give you one graphic example for which we have clear and indisputable literary evidence: In 1555, a gang of 67 pirates went on a three-month rampage, looted a dozen cities in three different coastal provinces, and killed more than 4,000 people. Ultimately, it took more than 40 years to suppress the pirates.

We can see further evidence of this ineptitude in the fact that the later Ming emperors lived more and more extravagantly in the Forbidden City, a vast imperial enclave built in the heart of the capital Beijing. The Forbidden City was built over a 14-year period between 1406 and 1420, and modern engineers estimate it probably required the labor of 1 million conscripted laborers to construct. When completed, the complex contained 980 separate buildings and covered an area of close to 8 million square feet. Perhaps many of you have also visited this extraordinary imperial enclave, which was proclaimed a UNESCO world heritage site in 1987 because it houses the largest collection of ancient wooden structures anywhere in the world. If you've walked through the Forbidden City as I have, it's easy to imagine the Ming emperors living their sheltered lives deep inside this vast imperial complex, only receiving news about the outside world through eunuchs and servant administrators, news that was heavily filtered and heavily censored.

Most later Ming emperors adapted to this situation by frankly ignoring government affairs, often for decades, while satisfying their various appetites for wine, women, and other pleasures. The real reason that it took more than 40 years to suppress the pirates, I think we have to say, was because the government was increasingly inept and disinterested. Another example of this ineptitude is that when a series of famines struck China in the early 17th century, the government proved itself incapable of organizing relief efforts. As the famine worsened, as no aid was forthcoming from Beijing, the desperate peasants were so hungry they had to resort to eating grass roots and tree bark. By the 1630s, angry peasants were organizing revolts, and as they gathered momentum city after city withdrew its loyalty from the Ming. At the same time, Manchu invaders in north decided to seize this opportunity to invade China, but also by joining forces with the peasants to make a concerted attack upon the Ming. By the early 1640s, the combined rebel and Manchu forces controlled much of China, and they turned finally in a calculated pincer movement towards the capital Beijing.

But the last emperor of the Ming was so sheltered from the bad news by court eunuchs and mandarins that he had no idea of the seriousness of the situation, nor even of the location of the rebel forces, until it was far too late; almost until they were actually climbing over the walls of the Forbidden City. In April, 1644, with the forces of rebel leader Li Zicheng about to capture Beijing, the last Ming emperor Chongzhen organized a feast and invited all members of the imperial household except his sons to attend. Then, using his sword, he killed all of them to prevent them falling into rebel hands, except for his second daughter Princess Chang Ping who warded off the sword blow but lost her arm in the process. Then, still wearing his glorious imperial costume, he ran to the eastern foot of Jingshan Hill inside the Forbidden City and hanged himself from a Japanese pagoda tree, many of which had been planted inside this imperial enclave. The forces of Li Zicheng then captured the inner city. The original pagoda tree no longer exists, by the way, but a replacement tree with an historical storyboard attached to it has been erected in the Forbidden City for tourists, perhaps you've seen it, to explain the final days of the Ming era of Chinese history. But the explanation is simple enough: As rebels prepared to capture the imperial quarter, the emperor and his family essentially committed suicide, and the Ming dynasty came to its tragic end.

Let me return now to the system of imperial administration that operated under the Ming. Both the Ming and the later Qing dynasties attempted, at least in their early days, to create and then preside over a well-organized and tightly centralized state. The actual administration of the empire, of course, was handled by a vast bureaucracy staffed by Confucian scholars. With this structure in place for more than 500 years, the autocratic state created by Hongwu effectively governed China's fortunes. At the head of the state was the emperor; not quite a god perhaps, but certainly way above any mere mortal. As we've seen from really the earliest lectures in this course, according to the ancient traditions of Eastern civilization, the emperor was the "Son of Heaven," a human being designated by heavenly powers to maintain order on earth, blessed to wear the Mandate of Heaven. The emperor lived a privileged life within the Forbidden City, with hundreds, sometimes thousands, of concubines and certainly thousands of eunuchs to take care of his every desire. His day was completely orchestrated and all performances in which he participated, all rituals, were carefully choreographed; that included audiences, inspections certainly, banquets, whatever. Everything about the emperor's person and the institution he represented conveyed a sense of this awesome authority. His clothes and personal effects bore designs forbidden for other people to wear, and even the written characters of the emperor's name were taboo throughout China. Any individual with the rare privilege of meeting the emperor personally had to kowtow, which meant three kneelings on the floor and then nine solid head knockings on the floor. Even minor offences in the vicinity of the emperor would be severely punished. The highest official in the land could have his bare buttocks flogged with bamboo, a Legalist punishment so brutal it sometimes caused death and reminding us of this long tradition of Legalist punishments in China.

Below the emperor and the imperial eunuchs, the day to day governing of China was the job of the scholar-bureaucrats, the most senior of which had been personally appointed by the emperor. These were mostly gentlemen from the class of well-educated and highly literate men known as the scholar-gentry, a class we've seen, we've met, we've discussed many times before in this course. In the best tradition of Confucianism, at least since the days of the Early Han dynasty, these men had earned academic degrees by passing rigorous civil service examinations. You remember that this is something Confucius himself had argued for way back in the Late Zhou dynasty; this idea that education in the Zhou classics could create leaders—the *junzi*, the princelings—who'd attained a high level of ethical and intellectual cultivation. These were the men who dominated China's political, intellectual, and social life for more than 2,000 years.

Under the Ming, preparations for the Confucian exams began at a very early age. Sometimes classes in the classics took place in local schools, which, like the exams themselves by the way, were only open to males. It's interesting, the fact that wealthy families employed tutors to help their sons prepare for the exams had a positive spinoff effect for women, because the presence of these professional tutors within these households also made formal education more widely available for girls during the Ming. By the time students were 10 or 11, they'd memorized the several thousand Chinese written language characters that were necessary to deal with the Confucian literature, including the *Analects*, of course, and all of the Zhou dynasty classics. The candidates also had to study calligraphy, poetry, and essay writing; and students had to know a very large corpus of commentaries now; also histories and literary works that had been written on these Zhou classics over 2,000 years; they had to know all of this before sitting the exam.

The examinations themselves consisted of a series of tests administered at different levels: There's the district exam; then the provincial exam; and finally, the most rigorous, the metropolitan exam. Stiff official quotas restricted the number of successful candidates in each exam. The quota insisted, for example, that only 300 students could pass the final metropolitan exam each year; so we know from various sources that students frequently took the exam several times before they finally earned a degree. The actual writing of the exam was a grueling process; I remind my students about this all the time. At the appointed hour, candidates would present themselves at the examination compound carrying with them a water pitcher, a chamber pot, their bedding, their food, an inkstone, ink, and calligraphy brushes. After they were verified and then searched—for cheat sheets, that is—the candidates were led through narrow corridors to small cells that contained a bench, a bed, and a desk. For the next three days and two nights, they spent their time writing essays in eight distinct sections on questions that were posed to them by the examiners. There were no interruptions; there was no communication between the candidates; even if a candidate died during the exams, his body was wrapped in straw and tossed over the compound walls for his family to come and collect.

But, of course, the possibility of high bureaucratic service, with rich financial and social rewards, meant that despite the grueling nature of the exams, competition for degrees was ferocious at all levels. We have evidence from the period that demonstrates that the exam system wasn't perfect; sometimes cheating candidates and corrupt examiners did compromise the entire Confucian system. Even so, obtaining a degree didn't necessarily ensure employment. During the Qing dynasty, for example, historians of that period estimate there were around one million degree holders—at all the various levels, of course—at any one time, and all of them were competing for about 20,000 government bureaucratic jobs. Those who only passed the district level exams usually spent their careers teaching in local schools or as private tutors for these wealthy families; but those who passed the metropolitan exams could at least hope for powerful positions in the imperial bureaucracy.

By opening the door to the possibility of honor, power, and rewards, the exam system also encouraged the serious pursuit of formal, higher education. China under the Ming was undoubtedly the most highly educated society that had ever existed to this point in world history. The Confucian exam system also provided an avenue of upward social mobility because the exams, at least in theory, were open to all males regardless of age or class. But in reality, the cost of private tutors and the expense of traveling to the examination sites meant that wealthy families had a distinct advantage. The system also molded the personal values of those who governed China by ensuring that it was the ethical philosophy of Confucianism that remained at the heart of Chinese education and Chinese government, as it had done off and on now for more than 2,000 years.

But let me begin to conclude this first lecture on the Ming dynasty by noting again that by driving out the Mongols, China was able to control its own affairs throughout the early modern period, and in so doing avoid the sort of turmoil that afflicted the Americas, for example, and certainly Africa after the arrival of the Europeans. The rulers of the Ming dynasty built a powerful centralized state and worked hard to eradicate all vestiges of Mongol rule; and as we've just seen, they restored traditional values of Eastern civilization by reviving Chinese political institutions, particularly the ancient Confucian exam system. What I want to show you in the next lecture is that for several decades early in the 15th century, the government also provided state support for a quite astonishing burst of naval expeditions; but as I mentioned, after the later Ming emperors moved to restrict foreign expeditions, and also the access of foreign merchants and missionaries to China, things changed dramatically.

Next time, we're going to go to sea. We're going to explore these great naval voyages; we're going to see the period when Chinese fleets ruled the oceans of the Eastern Hemisphere. We'll also look at the attempts by Jesuit missionaries to bring Catholicism in a very serious, intentional way into China. I look forward to seeing you soon.

Great Treasure Fleets of the Ming
Lecture 38

As we saw in the last lecture, after driving out the Mongols, the Ming dynasty built a powerful centralized state and worked to restore the traditional values of Eastern civilization. In this lecture, we'll pick up the story in the early 15th century, when Chinese fleets ruled the oceans of the Eastern hemisphere. We will explore the impact of these voyages and the ramifications of the decision made by later emperors to disengage from exploration at precisely the same moment that Europeans were stepping out on the world stage. We'll conclude the lecture with a few remarks about the verdict Chinese and world historians have delivered on the ultimate impact of the Ming on both Eastern civilization and global history.

Ming Maritime Expeditions
- Between 1405 and 1433, the eunuch admiral Zheng He sailed on seven maritime expeditions.
  - Zheng He was born in Yunnan province to Chinese Muslim parents who named him Ma He. Captured by a Ming army attempting to put down a provincial uprising, Ma He was castrated and placed as a servant in the household of the current emperor's fourth son, Prince Zhu Di.

  - Because eunuchs were unable to father children and, thus, establish their own powerful families, they were trusted with sensitive government positions. Ma He proved himself to be an exceptionally competent assistant and military adviser to the prince, who renamed him Zheng He.

  - When Prince Zhu Di came to power as Emperor Yongle in 1403, he became intrigued by the possibility of extending Ming prestige throughout the region by sponsoring diplomatic and exploratory maritime expeditions.

- The emperor authorized Zheng He to oversee the construction of a fleet of massive "treasure ships" and to plan the expeditions.

- The first expedition embarked in July 1405 from Liujia Harbor near Suzhou. Its mission was threefold: to establish relations with foreign countries, to expand trade contacts, and to look for exotic treasures for Yongle and the imperial court.

- Under the command of Admiral Zheng He was a fleet of 62 ships manned by more than 27,800 men, including sailors, clerks, interpreters, officers and soldiers, artisans, medical men, meteorologists, and others.
  - The fleet included ships that carried nothing but horses and others that carried water, along with supply ships, troop transports, naval fighting ships, and a host of other specialized vessels.

  - The cargo was so extensive that it had to be broken down into more than 40 different categories: silk goods, porcelain, gold and silver ware, copper utensils, iron implements, cotton goods, mercury, umbrellas, straw mats, and more.

- This massive fleet sailed ponderously south along the coast of Fujian, then visited Vietnam, Java, and Malacca. From there, Zheng He crossed the eastern Indian Ocean to visit Sri Lanka and several trading cities on the south coast of India.

- Wherever his ships sailed on this expedition, and the six that followed, they collected rare treasures to bring back to China and demanded that local rulers recognize the power and dominion of the Ming dynasty and Emperor Yongle.

- On the return journey, the fleet sailed back across the Indian Ocean to the islands of Indonesia but was held up there for several months battling pirates near Sumatra. The fleet returned triumphantly to the port of Nanjing in 1407, after a voyage of two years.

- Over a period of 28 years between 1405 and 1433, Zheng He eventually led seven separate maritime expeditions to some 30 different countries and regions to the south and west of China. Subsequent voyages traveled to Yemen, Arabia, the Persian Gulf, Mecca, and many ports along the East African coast.

- Zheng He intervened in local conflicts in Sumatra and Ceylon, suppressed piracy in Southeast Asia, intimidated local authorities in Arabia and Africa, and generally made China's presence strongly felt throughout the Indian Ocean. He may have traveled as far south as the Cape of Good Hope, but there is no evidence that he crossed the Pacific to the Americas.

- After the reign of Yongle, Zheng He's faction fell out of favor in court, and the Ming government decided to withdraw its support for expensive maritime expeditions, partly because some scholar-bureaucrats argued that they violated the principles of Confucianism.
    - The government ultimately moved to suppress all knowledge of the fleet and its expeditions. Zheng He probably died on his last voyage and was buried at sea.

    - Conservative Confucian factions in the Ming government even tried to ban Chinese merchants from dealing with foreign people, and eventually, the Qing government tried to outlaw maritime travel altogether!

- With the end of the voyages, the world lost the chance to see how differently global history might have played out if the Chinese rather than the Portuguese had come to dominate Indian Ocean trade or what might have happened if the Chinese had reached the Americas before Columbus!

Continuing Maritime Trade
- Even though official support for Zheng He's expeditions dried up, maritime trade continued to play a significant role in the Chinese economy. Indeed, despite the objections of conservative Confucian

officials during the Ming and early Qing dynastic eras, burgeoning global trade brought tremendous prosperity to China.

- To feed an insatiable demand for Chinese exports, Chinese workers labored to produce vast quantities of silk, porcelain, lacquer ware, and tea for consumers in the Indian Ocean basin, the Islamic world, and even Europe. The volume of imports was much lower than that of exports.

- Payment for Chinese exports was usually demanded in the form of silver bullion, which supported a silver-based economy. As we will see in our lectures on the Qing dynasty, this insistence on silver bullion for payment led to a global Chinese monopoly on silver, which increased resentment on the part of foreign merchants at the one-sided nature of the trade. This resentment would have disastrous consequences for China in the 18th and 19th centuries.

- All this commercial growth and expansion took place in an atmosphere of tight government control, but of course, as we have seen, once China began to connect with the world, it was impossible to control the flow of ideas into the state. Among the foreign ideas coming from Europe was Christianity.

Christianity in China
- As we have seen, Christianity had been in China for a long time before the Ming dynasty came to power, but it had disappeared after the collapse of the Yuan dynasty with the Ming's insistence on promoting core Chinese ideologies. Thus, when Roman Catholic missionaries returned in the 16th century, they had to start more or less from scratch in their efforts to reestablish a Christian community.

- The most prominent missionaries of the Ming period were the Jesuits, who worked hard to strengthen Catholicism in Europe and to spread the faith abroad. The founder of the Jesuit mission to China was the Italian Matteo Ricci, who had declared the goal of converting all of China to Christianity, beginning at the top with then-emperor Wanli. To this end, he spent almost 20 years studying the Chinese language and Confucian texts.

- Ricci and his colleagues dazzled their hosts in China with both their intellects and their mastery of European science and technology. The Jesuits were able to correct Chinese calendars that consistently miscalculated solar eclipses. They prepared accurate maps of the world with China at the center and even supervised the casting of high-quality bronze cannons for both the Ming and Qing dynasties.

- Of course, the ultimate goal of the Jesuits was to win converts to Christianity. To facilitate this, they portrayed Christianity as a high faith similar to the greatest achievements of the Eastern cultural tradition. Matteo Ricci wrote a treatise called *The True Meaning of the Lord of Heaven*, in which he argued that the doctrines of Jesus and Confucius were similar. He

The Italian Jesuit Matteo Ricci spent almost 20 years immersing himself in Chinese-language and Confucian texts; he became a popular figure in the Ming court.

further suggested that the adoption of Christianity would represent a return to a purer and more original form of Confucianism.

- The Jesuits held their Christian services in the Chinese language and allowed converts to continue the practice of ancestor worship, but ultimately, they attracted few converts to Christianity, at least partly because the Chinese disliked the "exclusive" nature of Christianity. Like Islam, Christianity claimed to be the only true religion; thus, conversion implied that other creeds, such as Buddhism or Daoism, were wrong, an idea most Chinese were unwilling to accept.

- Ultimately, it wasn't the failure to attract converts that brought an end to the Roman Catholic mission to China but competition for converts and squabbles among the Jesuits, Dominicans, and Franciscans. In response to the pope's commands that all missionaries suppress ancestor worship and conduct services in European languages, the Qing emperor Kangxi ordered an end to the preaching of Christianity in China. By the mid-18th century, the Christian missions had all but disappeared.

- Even though the Roman Catholic mission to China did not convert large numbers of Chinese, it did have important cultural and historical ramifications, for both Europe and China.
    o Besides making European science and technology known in China, the Jesuits also made China known to Europe. In letters, reports, and other writings distributed widely throughout Europe, the Jesuits described China as an orderly and rational society.

    o The Confucian civil service exam system attracted the attention of European rulers, who began to design their own civil service bureaucracies in the 18th century.

    o The rational moral philosophy of Confucius, first translated into Latin by Jesuits, also appealed to the Enlightenment philosophers of Europe, who began to seek alternatives to Christianity as the foundation for ethics and morality.

Conclusions about the Ming
- The Ming period tends to be judged harshly by both Chinese and Western historians today, who struggle to find any significant achievements or "historical heroes" from the period.

- Historians argue that Ming government suffered because of tensions in the bureaucratic system between absolute monarchs and their advisers and surrogates, divisions that reached a point that effectively demobilized the government.

- From a global perspective, the Ming period is viewed not only as weak and inefficient but as a dead weight that slowed Chinese innovation and entrepreneurship just when real global competition from Europeans was about to surface.

- Still, it's important to note that the arbitrary behavior of emperors and eunuchs did little to affect village life. The Chinese population in general grew and became more literate through the widespread dissemination of printed materials; this tended to strengthen the ties of common beliefs, shared history, and core ideologies within the village and town communities.

- At the same time, various new regions, such as Yunnan and Guizhou, were also effectively absorbed into the enormous Chinese state. And we should not forget that the Ming preserved peace within and outside China for more than two centuries—no mean feat in an increasingly hostile world.

Suggested Reading

Hook and Twitchett, eds., *The Cambridge Encyclopedia of China.*

Hsia, "The Catholic Mission and Translations in China, 1583–1700."

Plaks, *Four Masterworks of the Ming Novel.*

Spence, *The Memory Palace of Matteo Ricci.*

Questions to Consider

1. Why did the Ming attempt to withdraw from international affairs and return China to a state of relative isolation, and how successful were they?

2. Despite the efforts of brilliant Jesuit missionaries, such as Matteo Ricci, why did Christianity ultimately fail to attract significant numbers of converts in China?

Great Treasure Fleets of the Ming
Lecture 38—Transcript

In the early 15th century, Ming emperor Yongle set out to establish a Chinese presence in the Indian Ocean basin by sponsoring a series of massive maritime expeditions. Led by the seven-foot-tall eunuch Admiral Zheng He, this Chinese fleet was enormous: up to 62 vessels manned by some 28,000 men; and four of these ships were gigantic, measuring 400 feet long by 160 feet wide. Welcome to this second lecture on the glittering world—perhaps we should say brilliant world—of the Ming dynasty, which will begin with an exploration of these extraordinary naval expeditions.

Last time we noted that after driving out the Mongols, the Chinese were back in control of their own affairs. The Ming dynasty then built a powerful centralized state and worked hard to restore the traditional values of Eastern civilization by reviving Chinese political institutions such as the ancient Confucian exam system. In this lecture, we pick up the story in the early 15th century, when Chinese fleets ruled the oceans of the Eastern hemisphere. We'll explore impact of these voyages, and also the ramifications of the decision made by later emperors to disengage from exploration at precisely the same moment that Europeans were stepping out onto the world stage. One example of this European engagement with the world that did directly affect China was the attempt by Jesuit missionaries to convert the Chinese people to Catholicism during the Ming period. We'll also take a look at this Jesuit attempt in this lecture because it's very instructive, I think, about the ability of the core concepts of Eastern civilization to withstand the influence of even the most powerful, even the most persuasive foreign ideologies. We'll conclude with a few brief remarks again about the verdict that both Chinese and world historians have delivered on the ultimate impact of the Ming on both Eastern civilization and global history.

But first then to these seven remarkable maritime expeditions that sailed between the years 1405 and 1433, led by the eunuch admiral Zheng He, who's frankly an absolutely fascinating character. Zheng He was born in Yunan province in Southern China to Chinese Muslim parents who actually named him Ma He, Ma being short for Muhammad. The Mongols, you might remember, had tolerated Islam and indeed tolerated all the religions in

China during the reign of the Yuan dynasty; but the Ming with their renewed focus on core Chinese ideologies launched a series of persecutions against Muslims, and Ma He's parents were killed in a Muslim uprising in Yunan province. When Ma He was about 11 years old, he and many other children were captured by a Ming army who'd been sent to the south to attempt to reestablish control in Yunan. At the age of 13, Ma He and the other boys were castrated, and Ma He was then placed as a servant in the household of the current emperor's fourth son, Prince Zhu Di. As I've mentioned several times now, because eunuchs were unable to father children and thus establish their own powerful families, they were trusted with all sorts of sensitive government positions. They were court servants, high officials in many cases, even advisors to the emperor, as we've seen; or as members of the imperial choir, and, of course, guardians in the imperial harems. Ma He proved himself to be an exceptionally competent assistant and military advisor to the prince, who renamed him Zheng He after the eunuch's horse was killed in battle outside the city of Zhenglunba.

When Prince Zhu Di came to power as the Emperor Yongle in 1403, he was captivated to hear Zheng He recount seafaring stories that he'd heard from his grandfather. His grandfather was a Persian who'd served as an administrator in the previous Mongol Yuan dynasty, one of many Persian administrators brought in by the Yuan. During his lifetime, he'd traveled to Mecca by sea to undertake the *hajj*, the holy Moslem pilgrimage. Yongle became intrigued by these stories, and also by the possibility of extending Ming prestige throughout the region by sponsoring diplomatic and exploratory maritime expeditions. The emperor decided to authorize Zheng He to oversee the construction of a fleet of massive treasure ships, as they were called, and begin to plan a series of maritime expeditions. Zheng He, who as I said was said to be seven feet tall, a giant of a man, was certainly the first eunuch in China's long history to be given such an important diplomatic and military position.

After construction, fitting out, and manning of this enormous fleet, the first expedition embarked in July, 1405 from Liujia harbor near Suzhou. The agenda for this first voyage was threefold: to establish relations with foreign countries, to expand trade contacts, and also to look for exotic treasures for Yongle and the imperial court. Under the command of Admiral Zheng He was a fleet of 62 ships manned by more than 27,800 men; this included sailors, of course, but also clerks, interpreters, officers and soldiers, artisans, there were medical men, meteorologists, and so on. Four of these ships, as I mentioned, were truly huge: 400 feet long and 160 feet wide. By way of comparison, Columbus's flagship the Santa Maria, in which he sailed from Spain to the Americas nearly a century later, measured a mere 85 feet in length by perhaps 20 feet in width. The great Ming fleet included horse ships that carried nothing but horses; it included water ships that carried fresh water for the crew and for the horses, supply ships, various troop transports; there were naval fighting ships, and a host of other specialized vessels. The cargo carried on board by the fleet was so extensive it needed to be broken down into more than 40 different categories: There were silk goods, of course; Ming porcelain that you'll find today in all the great museums of the world; gold and silver ware; there were copper utensils; iron implements; cotton goods; mercury was carried; umbrellas; straw mats; you get the picture.

This massive fleet sailed ponderously south along the coast of Fujian province, and then visited Vietnam, then the island of Java, and Malacca. From here, Zheng He crossed the vast Eastern Indian Ocean to eventually visit Sri Lanka and a number of trading cities around the south coast of India. Given the overwhelming size of this fleet, we can only imagine the awe it must've inspired as the 62 ships came over the horizon and turned into the harbors of these great port cities. Wherever his ships sailed on this expedition, and the six that followed, they collected rare treasures to back to China; they also demanded that local rulers recognize the power and dominion of the Ming dynasty and Emperor Yongle. On the return journey, the fleet sailed back across the Indian Ocean to the islands of Indonesia but was actually held up there for several months battling pirates near the island of Sumatra, before returning triumphantly, with the pirate captain in captivity, to the port of Nanjing in 1407 after a voyage of two years.

Over a period of 28 years between 1405 and 1433, Zheng He eventually led seven of these magnificent, massive maritime expeditions, visiting at least 30 different countries and regions to the south and west of China. Every single time, he commanded a massive fleet and a staff of tens of thousands. On subsequent voyages they flew the Ming flag in Yemen, in Arabia, inside the Persian Gulf; they visited Mecca and many ports along the East African coast including Mogadishu. He presented gifts of gold, porcelain, and silk to foreign dignitaries; and collected all manner of treasure and exotic items to take back to the emperor, including ostriches, zebras, camels, and a giraffe that was considered so extraordinary by the Chinese when it arrived back in the court that they took this animal as proof that heaven itself had sanctioned these voyages. Zheng He intervened in local conflicts in Sumatra and Ceylon; as I've just said he suppressed piracy all around the waters of Southeast Asia; he intimidated local authorities with a show of massive strength in Arabia and these various African port cities; and he generally made China's presence strongly felt throughout the Indian Ocean. Some scholars believe Zheng He may actually have traveled as far south down the coast of Africa as the Cape of Good Hope; but while this is certainly plausible, I should tell you that there's absolutely no evidence to support the argument advanced in a recent very popular book that Zheng He's fleet crossed the Pacific to the Americas, no evidence whatsoever.

Here's how Zheng He himself described his voyages and achievements on a tablet he had erected in Fujian Province in 1432; let me quote from Zheng He:

> We have traversed more than 100,000 li of immense water spaces and have beheld in the ocean huge waves like mountains rising in the sky, and we have set eyes on barbarian regions far away hidden in a blue transparency of light vapors, while our sails, loftily unfurled like clouds day and night, continued their course [as rapidly] as a star, traversing those savage waves as if we were treading a public thoroughfare...

After the reign of Yongle, however, Zheng He's faction fell out of favor in court and the Ming government eventually decided to withdraw its support for expensive maritime expeditions, partly because some scholar-bureaucrats argued that in some way they violated the principles of Confucianism. The government ultimately moved to suppress all knowledge of the fleet and its expeditions; and Zheng He probably died on his last voyage, to be buried at sea. Conservative Confucian factions in Ming government even tried to ban Chinese merchants from dealing with foreign people, again to eliminate unwholesome foreign influences on the core Chinese values; and eventually, as we'll see next time, the Qing government tried to outlaw maritime travel altogether.

All this leads to a critical question that's often asked now by world historians: How might subsequent global history have been different if the voyages hadn't been so abruptly curtailed by this change of government policy? Would Chinese influence in the Indian Ocean have countered and even surpassed that of Portugal, for example? The expeditions of Zheng He absolutely dwarfed those of the Portuguese navigator Vasco de Gama, who began his voyage to India in 1497, nearly a century after Zheng He's first voyage. De Gama had only four small ships compared to Zheng He's vast fleet of enormous vessels; but ironically, it was this tiny Portuguese voyage that had a much deeper impact on world history than those of the Chinese. Certainly Zheng He's expeditions brought back exotic treasures and won him many friends in the Ming court; but the voyages didn't bring in enough revenue to justify their enormous cost and this, along with renewed threats from the Mongols that we discussed and also these concerns of some of the Confucian scholars, is why the government stopped supporting them. Soon after Emperor Yongle's death the voyages came to an end; and the world lost the chance to see how differently global history might've played out if the Chinese had come to dominate Indian Ocean trade rather than the Portuguese and what might've happened if the Chinese had reached the Americas before Columbus.

Even though official support for Zheng He's expeditions did dry up, maritime trade did continue to play a significant role in the Chinese economy. Indeed, despite the objections of these conservative Confucian officials, during the Ming and on into the Early Qing dynastic eras, burgeoning global trade brought tremendous prosperity into China. To feed an insatiable demand for Chinese exports, Chinese workers labored to produce vast quantities of silk, glorious Ming porcelain, lacquer ware, and tea for customers all over the Indian basin, the Islamic world, and even on into Europe. The silk industry was particularly well organized during this period. Employees worked in very well-managed workshops that paid regular wages for the production of high-value products like fine satins and brocades for export. Chinese silk exports were extensive in volume; we know of one Spanish galleon in the late-Ming period that sailed from China to the Americas carrying 50,000 pairs of silk stockings. Chinese imports, on the other hand, were relatively few: some spices, exotic birds, animal skins; some woolen textiles from Europe also made their way into China, but these were much lower in volume than the levels of export.

Payment for the Chinese exports was usually demanded by Chinese merchants in the form of silver bullion, which supported a silver-based economy in China. China was effectively importing vast quantities of silver bullion and silver coin that was being dug out of mines in Spanish-controlled Peru and Mexico, famous mines like Potosí, and then sent via Manila in the Philippines back into China. As I'm going to show you in our next pair of lectures on the Qing dynasty, this insistence on silver bullion for payment led to effectively a Chinese monopoly of global silver; and this in turn led to increasing resentment on the part of foreign merchants, particularly English merchants, at what was a very one-sided trade. This resentment had enormous consequences, indeed disastrous consequences, in the end, particularly for China in the 18th and 19th centuries, as we'll see in our next pair of lectures.

All this commercial growth and expansion of trade took place in an atmosphere of tight government control, which partly explains the government's sponsorship of this series of expensive naval expeditions. But, of course, as we've consistently seen in this course, once China began to connect with the world in various ways, it was impossible to control the flow of ideas back into the state. China's participation in trans-Eurasian trade during the Han dynasty, and now their involvement in genuinely global trading systems from the 16th century on, meant that it wasn't only foreign goods that entered China but, of course, also foreign ideas. Under the Ming, many of these foreign ideas now came from Europe, most notably Christianity.

Of course, as we've seen, Christianity in one form or another had been in China for a long time before the Ming dynasty came to power. We've noted several times that the Nestorian version of Christianity had established churches in China as early as the seventh century of the Common Era; and I mentioned in our lectures on the Mongols that Catholic communities were quite prominent in China under the Yuan dynasty. We know of several

Christian missionaries—I mentioned them in the previous lecture—who journeyed from Europe to visit the Mongol courts. One of the most famous was John of Plano Carpini, who was sent by Pope Innocent IV to visit the court of the Great Khan in 1246. John, or Giovanni to use his proper Italian name, had been a companion and disciple no lesser Christian luminary than Saint Francis of Assisi, and as part of this important Catholic mission to the Mongols, was one of the first Europeans to actually enter the court of a Great Khan. He and his companions rode some 3,000 miles in just over 100 days; and although they barely survived the rigors of this journey, John was still strong enough to try and convert Guyuk Khan to Christianity, an invitation the Great Khan refused. But Christianity then disappeared from China after the collapse of the Yuan dynasty because of the Ming's insistence on promoting core Chinese ideologies. This meant that when Roman Catholic missionaries started returning in the 16th century, they had to start more or less from scratch in their efforts to reestablish a Christian community.

The most prominent missionaries of the Ming period were the Jesuits, who worked hard to strengthen Catholicism in Europe and also to spread their faith abroad. The founder of the Jesuit mission to China was the great Italian Matteo Ricci, who had the declared and ambitious aim of converting all of China to Christianity, beginning at the top with the then-emperor Wanli. Ricci was a learned, brilliant, and polished individual who became a very popular figure in the Ming court, as indeed did many of his Jesuit colleagues. After arriving in the Portuguese trading colony of Macau in the south in August, 1582, Ricci then delayed his journey into Ming China proper in order to immerse himself in Chinese language and Chinese texts. By the time he was invited by the emperor to attend the Ming Court in Beijing almost 20 years later in 1601, he was so adept at the language that he could write learned Classical Chinese and he could converse at the highest intellectual level with the Confucian scholar-bureaucrats.

Ricci's expertise in Chinese language and Chinese ideology opened doors for the Jesuits, who literally dazzled their hosts with both their intellects but also their mastery of European science and European technology. Ricci and his colleagues—all of whom who had an advanced mathematical and scientific education—were able, for example, to correct Chinese calendars that had been consistently miscalculating solar eclipses. The Jesuits then prepared accurate maps of the world with China in the center; maps whose accuracy was based on the knowledge that European explorers and European cartographers had now been accumulating for a century by this stage. The extraordinarily practical Jesuits even supervised the casting of high quality bronze cannons for both the Ming and the Early Qing dynasties. They introduced their hosts to finely ground glass prisms that became immensely popular because of the way they refracted sunlight into the component parts; this is a 16th-century version of a kaleidoscope, and it was an enormous hit in the court of the Ming. European harpsichords were also of great fascination to the Chinese court, and the skilled Jesuit musicians dazzled the court with compositions written specifically for, and about, their hosts. The Jesuits then played on Chinese curiosity for mechanical devices. The most popular device of all was what the Chinese called the "self-singing bells"; these are spring-driven mechanical clocks that kept accurate time and chimed the hours, sometimes even the quarter hours, another great hit in the Ming court.

But, of course, the Jesuits were using all this technological wizardry simply to capture Chinese attention. That wasn't their true reason; their ultimate goal was to win converts to Christianity. In order to facilitate this, they adopted some of the ideas that Buddhists had used centuries before: They portrayed Christianity as a high faith similar to the greatest achievements of the Eastern cultural tradition. Matteo Ricci even wrote a treatise called *The True Meaning of the Lord of Heaven* in which he argued that the doctrines of Jesus and Confucius were actually very similar. He further suggested that the adoption of Christianity would represent a return to a more pure and original form of Confucianism. The Jesuits decided—not without much discussion, I can assure you—to hold their Christian services in the Chinese language rather than Latin, and this allowed converts to continue the practice of ancestor worship. But in spite of all this—their linguistic and scientific skill, their genuine respect for their hosts, and their ideological flexibility— the Jesuits ultimately attracted few converts to Christianity. We have some pretty good statistical evidence of this actually from a census taken in the mid-18th century during the succeeding Qing dynasty: Chinese Christians numbered about 200,000 out of a total population of 225 million.

The heart of the problem was that the Chinese disliked the exclusive nature of Christianity. For centuries they'd honored and reconciled various spiritual ideologies including, as you folks know, Confucianism, Daoism, and Buddhism, none of which was mutually exclusive. But Christianity, like Islam, claimed to be the only true religion; so conversion implied that all these other creeds were all wrong, an idea most Chinese were simply unwilling to accept. But ultimately it wasn't the failure to attract converts that brought an end to this Roman Catholic mission to China; it was squabbles between the Jesuits, the Dominicans, and the Franciscans who all competed with each other for converts in China. Jealous of the influence of the Jesuits in the Ming court, their rivals began to complain to the Pope about the fact that the Jesuits were conducting services in Chinese and were even encouraging ancestor worship. In the ultra-politicized environment of the Vatican, the Pope became convinced to side with the Jesuit's critics, and he issued proclamations ordering all missionaries to suppress ancestor worship and to conduct services now in European languages. In response to this demand, the Qing emperor Kangxi ordered an end to the preaching of Christianity in China, and by the mid-18th century the Christian missions had all but disappeared.

But even though the Roman Catholic mission to China didn't convert large numbers of Chinese, it did have important cultural and historical ramifications, both for Europe and for China. Besides making European science and technology known in China, the Jesuits also made China known to Europe. In letters, reports, and other writings distributed widely throughout Europe, the Jesuits described China as an enormous orderly and rational society. The Confucian civil service exam system attracted the attention now of European rulers, who also began to design their own civil service bureaucracies in the 18th century. The rational moral philosophy of Confucius, first translated into Latin by the Jesuits, also appealed to the Enlightenment philosophers of Europe, who began to seek alternatives to Christianity as the foundation for ethics and morality. Indeed, for the first time since Marco Polo, and on a much, much larger scale, the Jesuits made firsthand observations of China available to Europeans, which stimulated an enormous and ongoing European interest in China and indeed all East Asian societies.

Let's begin to conclude this lecture now by noting that the Ming period tends to be judged harshly by historians today—and I'm talking about both Chinese and Western historians—who frankly struggle to find any significant achievements or even historical heroes from the period. Historians argue that Ming government suffered because of tensions in the bureaucratic system between the absolute monarchs and their inner court of advisors and surrogates; divisions that reached a point that effectively demobilized the government. We've seen in this course many exceptional emperors in Chinese history; many great emperors who were able to manage the imperial system and these tensions with great skill, getting officials like eunuchs and mandarins to perform their tasks efficiently without letting them take over and serve their own interests. But the Ming offers no such examples, Hongwu and Yongle perhaps as exceptions. Apart from these two early emperors, most later Ming emperors delegated these management chores to officials like eunuchs with, as we've seen, highly variable results; and several emperors simply opted out of their responsibilities altogether, giving themselves over to wine, women, and other pleasures.

From the perspective of the world historian, the Ming dynasty doesn't come off much better. Global historians view the Ming not only as weak and inefficient but, as I mentioned at the beginning of the first lecture, as a dead weight that slowed Chinese innovation and Chinese entrepreneurship just when real global competition from Europeans was about to surface. At the same moment that European countries began to send their fleets into the Indian Ocean and on to China, the Ming were attempting to withdraw from the sea altogether, at least officially. Just as Europeans were putting Chinese inventions like printing, gunpowder and the compass to good use, China was letting its technological superiority slip and giving up its position of global scientific leadership.

But having said all that, we need to remember that the arbitrary behavior of emperors and their eunuchs did little to affect village life, and the millions of Chinese people were largely left to run their own affairs. The Chinese population grew, more and more people became literate through the widespread dissemination of printed materials, and this tended to strengthen the ties of common beliefs, of a long shared history, and of core ideologies within the villages and the town communities. At the same time, various new regions such as Yunan and Guizhou were also effectively absorbed into the enormous Chinese state. Let's not forget that the Ming preserved peace within and outside China for more than two centuries, which is no mean feat in itself in an increasingly hostile world.

But as we'll see in our next two lectures on the Qing dynasty, the last dynasty destined ever to rule China, the peaceful stagnation of China under the Ming was to have disastrous consequences for Chinese sovereignty.

The Qing—Nomads Return from the North
Lecture 39

The Manchus were descended from the pastoral nomads who had had such a profound impact on Chinese and Korean history. There had been frequent clashes over the centuries between Chinese and Manchus over land and resources along the borderlands of southern Manchuria and northern China, with the Chinese generally having the upper hand. But during the late 16th century, an ambitious chieftain named Nurhachi unified the Manchu tribes and changed the name of his people from Hou Jin ("later Jin") to Qing ("clear"). During the 1620s and 1630s, the Manchu army began launching small-scale invasions into northern China, and by 1644, the Qing Manchus had captured Beijing and seized the throne of China for themselves.

Emergence of the Qing

- In the 1630s, after a series of famines in China, angry peasants began organizing revolts; as they gathered momentum, city after city withdrew its loyalty from the Ming. The Qing Manchus from the north decided to seize the moment and join forces with the peasants in a concerted attack on the Ming government.

- By the early 1640s, the combined rebel and Manchu forces controlled much of China and turned to the capital, Beijing, for their final assault. After the last Ming emperor killed most of his family and himself, the Manchus quickly overwhelmed the remaining Chinese forces—including their peasant allies.

- After seizing control of Beijing, the Manchu forces began a long campaign aimed at the complete subjugation of all China under Manchu hegemony. By the early 1680s, they had achieved this goal and were intent on creating an enormous empire based on the ancient Chinese model.

- The establishment of the Qing dynasty was a product of Ming ineptitude and the formidable military prowess of the Manchus but also partly of the support of many Han Chinese for the Manchu invaders. In fact, we know of several Chinese generals who deserted the Ming dynasty in the 1630s and 1640s because of its corruption and inefficiency.

  o Confucian scholar-bureaucrats also worked against the Ming because they detested the eunuchs who had dominated the imperial court, and they hoped that the Qing would restore scholars to their formerly favored position in government.

  o At the same time, the Manchu ruling elites were well schooled in the Chinese language and Confucianism; because of this and their generally respectful attitude toward the ancient traditions of Eastern civilization, the Qing elites enjoyed more respect from scholar-bureaucrats than did the Ming emperor or his administration.

- Although certainly respectful of Chinese traditions, the Manchus were also careful to preserve their own ethnic and cultural identity. They outlawed intermarriage between Manchus and Chinese, for example, and forbade Chinese from traveling to Manchuria or learning the Manchurian language.

- Despite these measures aimed at separating ethnic Han and Manchu, until the 19th century, the strong imperial leadership practiced by the Qing rulers muted any outbreaks of ethnic tension between Manchu leaders and their Chinese subjects.

Emperors Kangxi and Qianlong

- The long reigns of two particularly effective rulers—Kangxi (r. 1661–1722) and his grandson Qianlong (r. 1736–1795)—brilliantly illustrate the ability of the Manchus to maintain their hold on China through potent leadership. During the reigns of these two emperors, Qing China reached the height of its power, prosperity, and size.

- Kangxi was a superb scholar and an enlightened ruler, well versed in the finest traditions of Eastern civilization. He had studied the Confucian classics and genuinely tried to apply their teachings to his policies.

  o As well as being a scholar, poet, and ethical ruler, Kangxi was also a military leader and conqueror; it was under him that the Qing constructed its vast empire.

  o Kangxi conquered the island of Taiwan, where Ming loyalists had retreated after their expulsion from southern China, and absorbed it into the empire. Then, like the Han and Tang emperors before him, he tried to head off problems with militarized nomads by extending Chinese influence deep into Central Asia. Eventually, his conquests in Mongolia and Inner Asia extended almost to the Caspian Sea.

The Qing emperor Kangxi generously patronized Confucian schools and academies, and many important studies of Chinese history, literature, philosophy, and philology were published during his reign.

© Qingprof/Wiki Commons/Public Domain.

  o Kangxi then turned Tibet into a Chinese protectorate, defeating a coalition of Mongolian tribes there known as the Dzungars.

- Kangxi's grandson Qianlong continued to expand Chinese influence in Central Asia. He sought to consolidate Kangxi's conquests in Central Asia by establishing military garrisons in Turkestan (the modern province of Xinjiang). He also encouraged Chinese merchants to settle in Central Asia in the hope that they would stabilize the region and help spread Chinese culture and language.

o   In Tibet, Qianlong supported and backed the Dalai Lama and placed a Qing garrison in Lhasa to protect his legitimacy and power.

o   Not content with these Central Asian conquests, Qianlong also made Vietnam and Nepal vassal states of the Qing, although a war against Burma ended in complete failure for the Chinese.

o   Overall, Qianlong's military expansion nearly doubled the size of the already vast empire and brought into the fold many non-Han Chinese peoples. But these campaigns were tremendously expensive enterprises; virtually all the funds in the imperial treasury had to be put into military expeditions.

o   Though the wars were successful, they were not overwhelmingly so, and the army's efficiency declined noticeably in the face of some challenging enemies; by the end of the various frontier wars, the army was considerably weakened. Despite this, most historians still regard Qianlong's reign as the high point of the Qing dynasty.

o   Like his grandfather, Qianlong was a sophisticated and learned man. He was a major patron of the arts and saw himself as an important "preserver and restorer" of Chinese culture. Qianlong was also a poet and a writer of prose, but at the same time, he sought to destroy all writings that were anti-Qing or that might incite rebellions.

o   During Qianlong's long, stable, and prosperous reign, China was an incredibly wealthy state. The imperial treasury contained so much wealth that on at least four different occasions, the emperor canceled all tax collections for the year!

o However, toward the end of his reign, Qianlong began paying less attention to imperial affairs and delegated many government responsibilities to his favorite eunuchs. He ultimately resigned the throne at age 85, although he retained power until his death four years later.

Population Growth and Economic Development

- For most of its incredibly long history, China has been a predominantly agricultural country, which fits well with Confucian, Daoist, and Legalist ideas about the land and farming. The Qing emperor reinforced the central importance of agriculture by personally plowing the first furrows of the farming season.

- Yet only a fraction of China's land is suitable for farming; thus, farmers were forced to rely on intensive and productive market-garden agriculture. Still, on this strong farming foundation, China was able to build the most commercialized farming economy of the preindustrial world. By intensively cultivating every parcel of land, Chinese peasants were able to increase their annual yields of rice, wheat, and millet well into the 17th century.

- From the mid-17th century on, just as farmers were reaching the upper limits of agricultural productivity using native crops, Spanish merchants from the Philippines began to introduce American food crops, such as maize, sweet potatoes, and peanuts, into China. Chinese farmers were able to grow these crops on land that wasn't suited to indigenous crops. The increased food supply, of course, led to higher populations.

- Scholars estimate that the population of China in 1500 was around 100 million; by 1750, despite intervening plagues and war, it had reached 225 million, and by the early 1800s, it was a staggering 360 million. This demographic explosion set the stage for dynamic economic growth, but it also created economic and social problems, because agricultural growth could not keep pace over the long term.

- Although a growing population placed pressure on Chinese resources, particularly food, the expanding commercial market also offered opportunities for entrepreneurs. Further, after the mid-16th century, the Chinese economy benefited substantially from the influx of Japanese and American silver, which stimulated trade and financed expansion.

- In the 17th century, in attempting to pacify southern China, the Qing government made an abortive attempt to end all maritime activity; however, small Chinese vessels continued to trade actively with Japan and Southeast Asia. When southern China was finally pacified in the 1680s, the strictest measures were rescinded, but Qing authorities closely supervised the activities of all foreign merchants in China.

- As well as limiting the activities of foreign merchants, the Qing also discouraged the organization of large-scale commercial ventures by Chinese merchants; this was ultimately the longest-lasting and most significant result of both Ming and Qing isolationist policies.
  - Without government approval, it was impossible to maintain shipyards that could construct large vessels, like the massive ships that Zheng He had sailed across the Indian Ocean.

  - It was also impossible to organize large trading companies like the English East India Company or the Dutch VOC, which put Chinese merchants at a considerable global disadvantage.

  - We have evidence that thousands of Chinese merchants continued to link China into the global trading network, albeit without the government's approval and, thus, at a significant disadvantage to their European competitors.

- Much of the Chinese economic expansion took place in the absence of technological innovation. As we have seen, under the Southern Song, engineers produced a flood of extraordinary inventions, and China was the world's leader in science and technological innovation. But under the Ming and Qing, innovation slowed, and the Chinese started borrowing ideas from the West.

o Under the Song, the imperial government had encouraged innovation as the foundation for military and economic strength.

o But both the Ming and Qing governments and the Confucian scholar-bureaucrats at the heart of their administrations favored political and social stability over innovation, which they feared would lead to unsettling change.

o The abundance and ready availability of cheap, skilled workers also discouraged technological innovation. If employers wanted to increase production, it was cheaper to hire more workers than to make large investments in new technology.

o In the short term, this maintained relative prosperity in China and helped keep employment rates high. But in the long term, the ultimate result of these developments was that China lost technological ground to the Europeans, who embarked on a round of stunning innovations beginning in the mid-18th century. The essential conservatism of the Ming and Qing dynasties caused China to withdraw from the world at precisely the same moment that the Western powers were aggressively engaging in it!

Suggested Reading

Chen, *China and the West*.

Naquin and Rawski, *Chinese Society in the Eighteenth Century*.

Questions to Consider

1. How, under such emperors as Kangxi and Qianlong, were the Qing able to construct the greatest empire China ever possessed?

2. Why did technological and intellectual innovation in China slow under the Ming and Qing?

The Qing—Nomads Return from the North
Lecture 39—Transcript

Hello and welcome to the first in a pair of lectures on the last dynasty ever to rule China: the Qin dynasty.

The Manchus who established the Qing dynasty in 1644 were descended from pastoral nomads, although most Manchus had long before adopted a sedentary agricultural lifeway in the rich farmlands of southern Manchuria. They were direct descendants, in fact, of the Jurchen tribes who'd ruled northern China as the Jin dynasty between 1115 and 1234, when they were defeated by the Mongols. The remote ancestors of the Manchus had traded with China for a couple of thousand years before this, ever since the Qin dynasty had ruled China way back in the third century B.C.E. As such, the Manchu were part of the great tradition of pastoral nomads who, as we've seen repeatedly in this course, had such a profound impact on Chinese and Korean history for millennia. There had been frequent clashes over the centuries between Chinese and Manchu over land and resources along the borderlands of southern Manchuria and northern China, with the Chinese generally having the upper hand. But during the late 16th century, an ambitious Manchu chieftain named Nurhachi unified the Manchu tribes into a centralized confederation.

Much like Chinggis Khan of the Mongols, Nurhachi then promulgated a code of laws and organized the Manchus into a powerful and very well-organized military force. He then changed the name of his people from Hou Jin, which means the "Later Jin," to Qing, a word that means "clear," in 1636. During the 1620s and 1630s, the Manchu army expelled Ming garrisons in Manchuria, they captured parts of northern Korea and Mongolia, and they began launching small-scale invasions of northern China. By 1644, the Qing Manchus, now under the control of a new six-year-old emperor named Shunzhi who was guided by his uncle the Regent Dorgon, had captured Beijing, crushed their rebel allies, and seized the throne of China for themselves. The Qing then slowly extended their authority throughout the rest of China, although it took them almost 40 years to defeat the final pockets of Ming loyalists and other rebels way to the south in southern China.

But these events remind us of the last days of their predecessors, the Ming dynasty. You might remember that when a series of famines struck China in the early 17th century, the government was so inept that it was incapable of organizing relief efforts. As the famine worsened, the desperate and starving peasants were forced to resort to eating grass roots and tree bark. In the 1630s, angry peasants began organizing revolts; and as they gathered momentum, city after city withdrew its loyalty from the Ming. This was precisely the opportunity that the Qing Manchus had waited for; they decided to seize the moment and join forces with the peasants in a concerted attack upon the Ming government. By the early 1640s, the combined rebel and Manchu forces controlled much of China, and they turned to the capital Beijing for their final assault on the government. As I'm sure you remember, on March 17, 1644, the last Ming Emperor personally killed with his sword most of his family, then fled to a pagoda tree in the Forbidden City and hanged himself, bringing to a tragic end the Ming dynastic era of Chinese history. The victorious Manchus quickly overwhelmed the remaining Chinese forces—including their erstwhile peasant allies, by the way—and after seizing control of Beijing, they began a long campaign aimed at the complete subjugation of all of China under Manchu hegemony. The victors proclaimed a new dynasty—the Qing or "Clear" dynasty—that would go on to rule China from 1644 until 1912, when the last emperor ever to rule the Middle Kingdom abdicated.

By the early 1680s, the Qing were in control of all of China and were intent upon creating an enormous empire based on the ancient Chinese Confucian model. The establishment of the Qing dynasty was a product of Ming ineptitude and also the formidable military prowess of the Manchus; but also partly because of the support of many Han Chinese for the Manchu invaders. We actually know of several Chinese generals who during the 1630s and 40s deserted the Ming dynasty because of its corruption and because of its inefficiency. Confucian scholar-bureaucrats also worked against the Ming because they detested the eunuchs who had for so long dominated the imperial court and they hoped that the Qing would restore them to their formerly favored position in government. At the same time, the Manchu ruling elites were very well schooled in Chinese language and philosophy, particularly Confucianism; and because of this and their generally respectful attitude towards the ancient traditions of Eastern civilization, the Qing elites enjoyed more respect from the scholar-bureaucrats than did the Ming emperor or his administration.

But the Manchus, although certainly respectful of Chinese traditions, were also careful to preserve their own ethnic and cultural identity. After coming to power, they outlawed intermarriage between Manchus and Chinese, for example; they even forbade Chinese from traveling to Manchuria or learning the Manchurian language. Qing authorities also forced Chinese men to shave the front of their heads and grow a Manchu-style queue, which is a long plaited braid worn down the neck and back, as a sign of submission to the dynasty. The Manchus also worked to preserve their own ethnic traditions and nomadic origins, so they continued to practice the skills of horsemanship obviously and also archery at which all pastoral nomadic people had been so adept for millennia. Indeed, archery became so important in Qing China that it was incorporated into the Imperial Military Examination. Although the Qing practiced archery in deference to their nomadic ancestry, archery also had a long tradition in China; it was even mentioned way back in the Shang oracle bone inscriptions, and it was revered, for example, under the Tang dynasty. To this day, archery remains incredibly popular and still a revered sport.

Despite these measures aimed at separating ethnic Han and Manchu, until the 19th century the strong imperial leadership practiced by the Qing rulers muted any outbreaks of ethnic tension between Manchu leaders and their Chinese subjects. The long reigns of two particularly effective rulers—Kangxi, who ruled for 61 years between 1661 and 1722, and his grandson Qianlong, who ruled for 59 years from 1736 until 1795—brilliantly illustrate the ability of the Manchus to maintain their hold on China through very effective leadership. During the reigns of these two emperors, Qing China reached the height of its power and prosperity, as well as an enormous size. Even today, and given the size of China today, the Qing Empire is still recognized as the largest contiguous empire in all of China's incredibly long history.

Let me say something briefly about these two great emperors now to give you some sense of how these outsiders almost epitomized the best ideals of a Confucian leader. Kangxi, for example, was a superb scholar and an enlightened ruler, well versed in the finest traditions of Eastern civilization. He was a great reader; he wrote excellent poetry in the best traditional style. He studied the Confucian classics and genuinely tried to apply their teachings, their philosophy to his policies. For example, he several times organized major flood control and very expensive irrigation projects during his reign, inspired by the Confucian ethical idea that a ruler's first job is to look after the welfare of his subjects. Kangxi also generously patronized Confucian schools and academies, and many important studies of Chinese history, Chinese literature, philosophy, and philology were published during his reign.

But as well as being a great scholar, a poet, and certainly an ethical ruler, Kangxi was a great military leader and a conqueror. It was under him that the Qing constructed its vast empire. Kangxi, for example, conquered the island of Taiwan where Ming loyalists had retreated (fled, frankly) after their expulsion from Southern China and absorbed it back into the empire. Then, like the Han and Tang emperors before him, he tried to head off problems with militarized nomads by extending Chinese influence deep into Central Asia. Eventually his conquests in Mongolia and Inner Asia extended almost as far as the Caspian Sea. Kangxi then turned Tibet into a Chinese protectorate in a foreshadowing, I think, of the policy of the modern Chinese government that you'll remember annexed Tibet in the 1960s; although this earlier conquest of Tibet was only possible after an extended conflict with yet another group of Central Asian nomads known as the Dzungars, a very powerful coalition of tribes from Mongolia. The Dzungars actually invaded Tibet in 1717, taking control of the fabled city of Lhasa with a 6,000-strong army. They held onto the city for two years, and soundly defeated the first Qing army that was sent to the region in 1718. Eventually the Qing did take control of Lhasa in 1720, when Kangxi sent a larger force there to defeat the Dzungars.

In the 1650s meanwhile, in another foreshadowing of more recent tensions between the People's Republic of China and the Union of Soviet Socialist Republics 300 years later, the Qing Empire began to engage the Russian Empire in a series of border conflicts in the Amur Basin region, which ended also in victory for the Qing. After a series of battles and negotiations, both sides ultimately signed the Treaty of Nerchinsk in 1689; and as a result, the border was fixed between these two expansionist empires, and the Amur River valley was given to the Qing Empire.

Kangxi's grandson Qianlong continued to expand Chinese influence in Central Asia. Qianlong, who ruled from 1735–1796, was the sixth emperor of the Qing dynasty and the fourth to rule over a unified Qing Chinese empire. Qianlong sought to consolidate Kangxi's conquests in Central Asia by establishing military garrisons in Turkestan, which is the present-day province of Xinjiang in modern China. Indeed, it was Qianlong who first renamed the western regions Xinjiang—this literally means "western region," and is the name by which they're still known today—after he finally defeated and destroyed the power of the Dzungars. Qianlong also encouraged Chinese merchants to settle in Central Asia in the hope that they'd stabilize the region, and help spread Chinese culture and Chinese language deep in the heart of Asia. In Tibet meanwhile, in an ironic reversal of the policy of modern Chinese governments, Qianlong supported and backed the Dalai Lama, and placed a Qing garrison in Lhasa to protect his legitimacy and power. Not content with these Central Asian conquests, Qianlong also made Vietnam and Nepal vassal states of the Qing, although a war against Burma ended in complete failure for the Chinese.

Despite this one setback in the south, overall the Qianlong emperor's military expansion nearly doubled the size of the already vast empire and brought into the fold many non-Han Chinese people, including Uyghurs, Kazhaks, Kyrgyzs, even Mongols. But these campaigns were tremendously expensive enterprises; virtually all the funds in the Imperial Treasury had to be put into these military expeditions. Although the wars were successful, they weren't overwhelmingly so; and indeed the army's efficiency declined noticeably in the face of some particularly challenging enemies. By the end of the various frontier wars, the army was considerably weakened. But despite this, most historians still regard Qianlong's reign as the high point of the Qing dynasty.

Like Kangxi, his grandson was a sophisticated and learned man. Qianlong was a major patron of the arts, and he saw himself as an important preserver and restorer of Chinese culture. He also had an insatiable appetite for collecting, and personally acquired much of China's great private collections frankly by any means necessary, and then reintegrated their treasures back into the imperial collection. More than any other Qing emperor, Qianlong lavished this imperial collection of historical artifacts and glorious Chinese art with his personal attention and effort. Like his grandfather, Qianlong was also a poet; he reportedly composed more than 40,000 poems and 1,300 prose texts during in his lifetime, and he was a great connoisseur of painting and calligraphy. But we must also note that Qianlong is remembered by historians as a great burner of books. Some 2,300 works were listed for total suppression and another 350 for partial suppression by his administration. The emperor's aim was to destroy all writings that were in any way anti-Qing or inciting of rebellions, including those texts that insulted previous barbarian (as in foreign) dynasties, or that dealt with frontier or defense problems.

During Qianlong's long, stable, and prosperous reign, China was an incredibly wealthy state. We can demonstrate this extraordinary wealth—and despite the cost of the campaigns, by the way—by noting that the imperial treasury contained so much money during his reign that on at least four different occasions, the emperor cancelled all tax collections for the year. Imagine that happening anywhere in the modern world. Throughout the almost six decades of Qianlong's reign then, China remained a wealthy, well-organized, powerful imperial state, undoubtedly one of the great powers of the world. But towards the end of his reign, Qianlong began paying less attention to imperial affairs, and in the manner of his Ming predecessors decided to delegate many government responsibilities to his favorite eunuchs. Qianlong ultimately resigned the throne at the age of 85 in the 60th year of his reign to his son, the Jiaqing emperor, in 1795. For the next four years, he held the title of Retired Emperor, although he continued to hold on to power and the Jiaqing emperor ruled in name only. He never moved into his retirement suites in the Qianlong Garden, and he died in 1799 at the venerable age of 89.

But rather than model themselves on the behavior of Kangxi or the young Qianlong, Qianlong's successors adopted the practices of the emperor's later years, devoting themselves more to hunting and to their harems than to affairs of state. This meant that during the 19th century, the Qing dynasty faced serious difficulties. But I want to wait until the next lecture to really unfold the story of these difficulties to you, and of China's fall from global power. Let me instead devote the rest of this lecture to economic matters, with a particular focus on population growth and economic development during the Qing dynasty in China.

For most of its incredibly lengthy history, China has been a predominantly agricultural country; and this, of course, fit very well with the Confucian idea that the land was the source of everything worthwhile in a state. Actually, this idea also fits very well with Daoist and Legalist notions of the importance, indeed the centrality, of the land and of farming for the health of the state. It's no surprise that the Qing emperor himself reinforced this central importance of agriculture by personally plowing the first furrows of the farming season. But it's important to note that only a fraction of China's land is actually suitable for farming. Even today with modern technology, modern fertilizers, and intensive farming techniques, only about 11 percent of China's enormous area is productive agricultural land. If you've flown over China's vast western regions as I have, you will have been struck by just how arid and unproductive much of this land is. To feed the country's enormous population, farmers were forced to rely on intensive and productive market-garden agriculture.

These small-scale Chinese horticulturalists did this very well, of course; and on this strong and successful intensive farming foundation, China was able to build the most commercialized farming economy of the pre-industrial world. By intensively cultivating every parcel of land, Chinese peasants were able to increase their annual yields of rice, wheat, and millet well into the 17th century. Then, from the mid-17th century on, just as farmers were reaching the upper limits of agricultural productivity using native crops, Spanish merchants from the Philippines began to introduce American food crops into China. Crops that had first been domesticated thousands of years ago in South America and Central America—crops like maize (corn), like sweet potatoes, like the peanut—allowed Chinese farmers to grow crops in soils that had previously been uncultivated because they were unsuited to Chinese indigenous crops.

This, of course, led to an increased food supply and consequently higher populations. In fact, despite regular epidemics of the plague, which killed millions, China's population rose rapidly through the early modern period. These are the best demographic estimates we have; let me give you some idea of this population increase: In 1500, the population of China was somewhere around 100 million. By 1600, a century later, it had risen to 160 million. In 1650, it actually fell perhaps to 140 million because of war and rebellion;

but 50 years later, by 1700, it had returned to 160 million. By 1750, at the height of the successful reign of Qianlong, China's population had surged to 225 million people; that's a 40 percent increase in just 50 years. By the early 1800s, China's population had reached a staggering 360 million people, which was considerably more than the population of the United States today. This demographic explosion set the stage for dynamic economic growth; but, of course, it also created all sorts of economic and social problems because agricultural growth could barely keep pace long term. These problems didn't become really acute until the 19th century as we'll see, although per capita income was already declining during the reign of Qianlong.

While a growing population placed pressure on Chinese resources, particularly food resources, the expanding commercial market also offered opportunities for entrepreneurs. Because of this demographic expansion, for example, entrepreneurs had access to an enormous labor force that was occupationally and geographically mobile so that they could recruit workers at very low cost. As we saw in our last two lectures on the Ming dynasty, after the mid-16th century, the Chinese economy also benefited substantially from the influx of Japanese and American silver, which stimulated trade and financed further expansion.

You'll remember, of course, the great eunuch admiral Admiral Zheng and his seven massive maritime expeditions across the Indian Ocean basin. You'll also remember how after the reign of Emperor Yongle, the Ming withdrew its support for expensive maritime expeditions and they even tried to prevent Chinese subjects from trading with foreigners. In order to try and pacify Southern China in the 17th century, the Qing took this policy a step further when the government made an abortive attempt to try and end maritime activity altogether. An extraordinary and frankly unenforceable imperial edict of 1656 forbade, and I quote, "even a plank from drifting to sea." In 1661, Kangxi also ordered an evacuation of the southern coastal regions in an attempt to end "illegal" maritime activity and bring the region more firmly under Beijing's control.

Yet these policies had only a limited effect. Despite the passing of these laws, we know that small Chinese vessels continued to trade actively with Japan and certainly with Southeast Asia; and because these laws were ultimately unenforceable and thus ineffective, when Qing forces finally did pacify Southern China in the 1680s, the government authorities rescinded the strictest measures. But from then on, suspicious Qing authorities closely supervised the activities of all foreign merchants in China; and this was to lead to tremendous resentment amongst these international merchant communities, as I want to show you in the next lecture. The Qing allowed the Portuguese to operate only in the port of Macau, for example; British agents had to deal exclusively with the official merchant guild in Guangzhou.

As well as limiting the activities of foreign merchants, the Qing also discouraged the organization of large-scale commercial ventures by Chinese merchants; and this, I think, was ultimately the most significant and the most long-lasting result of both Ming and Qing isolationist policies. Without government approval, it was impossible to maintain shipyards that could construct vessels like the massive nine-masted ships that Zheng He had sailed in across the Indian Ocean. Even more importantly, it was also impossible to organize large trading companies like the English East India Company or the Dutch VOC, and this put Chinese merchants at a considerable global disadvantage. But despite these government policies, we have evidence that thousands of Chinese merchants did continue to link China into the global trading network, albeit without their government's approval and thus again at a significant disadvantage to their European competitors.

Nonetheless, Chinese merchants were especially prominent in Manila in the Philippines, where they exchanged silk and porcelain for American silver that was coming across the Pacific Ocean in the Manila galleons. Chinese merchants were also active at the Dutch colonial capital of Batavia, where they supplied the Dutch VOC with silk and porcelain in exchange for silver and Indonesian spices. Under the Qing, then, and with no support from the government, merchants still established a substantial Chinese presence throughout Southeast Asia and indeed further afield. We know that Chinese merchants were active in the Philippines, in Borneo, Sumatra, Malaya, and Thailand where they sought a range of exotic tropical products in these regions for their Chinese consumers.

But again, much of this economic expansion took place in the absence of technological innovation. As we've seen, under the Southern Song dynasty Chinese engineers produced a flood of extraordinary inventions, and China was by far the world's leader in science and technological innovation. But under the Ming and the Qing, innovation slowed and the Chinese started borrowing ideas from the West instead. One clear example of this is that imperial Qing forces began adopting European cannons and European firearms for their own use, thus re-borrowing both advanced iron manufacturing and gunpowder technology that had originated in China but been refined in the more warlike and competitive environment of early modern Europe.

Indeed, there was little innovation in either agricultural or industrial technologies under the Qing dynasty. Part of the reason for this slowdown was the government's emphasis on stability. Under the Song, the imperial government had encouraged innovation as the foundation for military and economic strength; but both the Ming and Qing governments, and the Confucian scholar-bureaucrats who were at the heart of their administrations, favored political and social stability over innovation, which they feared would lead to unsettling change. The abundance and ready availability of cheap skilled workers also discouraged technological innovation. If employers wanted to increase production, it was actually cheaper to hire more workers rather than make large investments in new technology. In the short term, this did maintain relative prosperity in China and helped keep employment rates high; but in the long term, the ultimate result of all these developments was that China lost technological ground to the Europeans, who embarked on a round of stunning innovations beginning in the mid-18th century during a period historians call the Industrial Revolution.

As we'll see in our next lecture, these developments were to have disastrous consequences for Chinese sovereignty. At the heart of the problem facing China with the death of Emperor Qianlong on the eve of the 19th century was the essential conservatism of the Ming and Qing dynasties, which had caused China to withdraw from the world at precisely the same moment that Western powers were aggressively engaging in it.

The Qing—The Last Emperor of China
Lecture 40

In 1759, Emperor Qianlong of the Qing dynasty moved to restrict European commercial presence in the great southern port city of Guangzhou, which had been home to thousands of foreign merchants for about 1,000 years. Qing authorities were determined to bring the activities of foreign merchants more closely under government control and to more tightly regulate the terms of trade, which had become increasingly independent of Qing authority. By the late 18th century, seeking ways to increase their profits and in response to these restrictive Chinese trade practices, officials of the British East India Company began to look for alternatives to silver to exchange for Chinese goods. They settled on a profitable but highly illegal drug: opium.

The Opium Trade

- In the late 18th century, British merchants began to purchase cheap opium from India and ship it to China, using the drug as a substitute for silver to buy Chinese products. The trade in opium was illegal, of course, but it continued unabated for decades because the Chinese made little effort to enforce the law. The lack of enforcement stemmed partly from the fact that Chinese officials also benefited enormously from the trade and partly because no one in the Qing government wanted to risk an all-out confrontation with the British merchants.

- By the late 1830s, the Chinese government was acutely aware that the opium trade was draining massive amounts of silver bullion from China and was having major social consequences, particularly in southern China, where addiction was widespread.

- When Qing government officials took tentative steps to stop the illicit trade in 1838, British merchants immediately started losing money.
  - Qing efforts were stepped up the following year, when an incorruptible official named Lin Zexu was put in charge of

attempts to destroy the opium trade altogether. He confiscated and destroyed 20,000 chests of British-owned opium and arrested 1,600 foreign merchants and Chinese accomplices.

- o Outraged by Chinese action against them, British commercial agents pressed their government for a military response. The ensuing conflict is known as the Opium Wars.

- In the opening stages of the conflict, British naval gunboats demonstrated their clear superiority, but even so, the Chinese refused to sue for peace. In June 1842, British forces broke the stalemate with an armada of 70 ships heading up the Yangtze River. By the time it arrived at the intersection with the Grand Canal, the Chinese had sued for peace.

- China experienced similar military setbacks throughout the remainder of the 19th century, against Britain and France in the 1850s, France again in the 1880s, and Japan in 1894 and 1895. In the wake of these defeats, the Qing government was forced to sign several humiliating treaties that curtailed Chinese sovereignty.
  - o The most famous of these treaties was forced on the Qing by the British, the Treaty of Nanjing. Under this treaty, China agreed to cede the island of Hong Kong to Britain, to open five ports to British commerce and residence, to grant most-favored-nation status to Britain, and to pay reparations to merchants whose chests of opium had been burned.

  - o Later, France, Germany, Denmark, the Netherlands, Spain, Belgium, Austria-Hungary, the United States, and Japan all reached similar unequal treaties with China.

  - o Collectively, these treaties legalized the opium trade, permitted the reestablishment of Christian missions throughout China, opened treaty ports, and prevented the Qing government from levying tariffs on imports of foreign goods.

The Taiping Rebellion

- This humiliating debilitation of the Chinese empire in the late 19th century was as much due to internal problems as it was to foreign intrusion and demands. Large-scale rebellions in the 19th century reflected the people's increasing poverty and discontent with the government. The most dangerous of all the peasant uprisings was the Taiping Rebellion, which lasted from 1851 to 1864 and brought the Qing dynasty to the brink of collapse.

- The catalyst for this rebellion was a schoolteacher named Hong Xiuquan, who became convinced that he had been sent to earth by God to expel the Manchu Qing from China. In 1851, Hong's call for the destruction of the Qing dynasty and the radical transformation of Chinese society appealed to millions.

- The Taiping reform program called for the abolition of private property, communal wealth to be shared according to need, prohibitions on foot-binding and concubinage, free public education, establishment of democratic political institutions, and more.

- After sweeping through southeast China, Hong and his followers captured Nanjing in 1853 and made it the capital of their Taiping ("great peace") kingdom. From Nanjing, they campaigned vigorously throughout China, and as they passed through the countryside, whole villages and towns joined them, sometimes voluntarily, sometimes under coercion.

- By 1855, 1 million armed Taipings were poised to attack Beijing, but Qing forces repelled them. The Taipings then turned their attention to the south, and by 1860, firmly entrenched in the Yangtze Valley, they threatened Shanghai. Ultimately, the Qing created regional armies of Chinese soldiers, led by Confucian scholar-bureaucrats and aided by European military advisers, that gradually overcame the Taipings.

- In June 1864, Hong committed suicide, and the Taiping stronghold of Nanjing fell a few months later. Government forces slaughtered 100,000 rebels in the bloody retribution that followed.

The Taiping Rebellion was over, but it had cost somewhere between 20 and 30 million Chinese lives and caused massive declines in agricultural production.

The Self-Strengthening Movement

- Dealing with aggressive foreign powers and surveying lands ravaged by domestic rebellion, the Qing rulers finally realized that reform was necessary if their empire was to survive. Thus, from 1865 to 1895, Qing authorities tried to recreate an efficient and benevolent Confucian government in an attempt to solve their social and economic problems and, at the same time, adopted foreign technology to strengthen state power.

- The most imaginative reform was called the Self-Strengthening Movement. Funded by money from the Qing authorities, local leaders across China were encouraged to raise troops, levy taxes, and establish modern military forces. Movement leaders tried to blend traditional Chinese culture with modern European industrial technology.

- Although the Self-Strengthening Movement ultimately laid the foundations for Chinese industrialization later in the 20th century, it brought only superficial change in the late 19th.

- A key player in the failure of the attempts at reform was the Empress Dowager Cixi (1835–1908). Cixi was a former concubine who became the consort of Emperor Xianfeng. After his death, she manipulated the succession, effectively making herself the true ruler of China during the last 50 years of the Qing dynasty. Cixi was a conservative and bitterly opposed to reform.

- Further evidence of the failure of the Self-Strengthening Movement is that foreign powers maintained their firm hold on Chinese affairs. Indeed, the imperial states of Europe effectively dismantled the Qing Empire in the decade between 1885 and 1895.
  - In 1885, France incorporated Vietnam into its colonial Indochinese empire; the following year, Britain incorporated

Burma into its empire; and in 1895, Japan forced China to grant independence to Korea, Taiwan, and parts of Manchuria.

○ By 1898, foreign powers had carved the Chinese homeland itself into various spheres of economic interest; it was only mistrust among the foreign governments that prevented the total dismemberment of China!

Ironically, the funds used by the Empress Dowager Cixi to build the Marble Boat at the Summer Palace were diverted from money set aside to modernize the Chinese Navy.

The Hundred Days of Reform

- These humiliating setbacks sparked one last ambitious but ultimately abortive attempt to save China from further subjugation: the Hundred Days of Reform in 1898.

- Two liberal Chinese scholars—Kang Youwei and Liang Qichao—published treatises reinterpreting Confucianism and justifying radical change in the imperial system. Their intention was to remake China as a powerful, modern industrial state.

- Impressed with their ideas, the young Qing emperor Guangxu launched a sweeping series of reforms to try to transform China into a constitutional monarchy. His agenda included guaranteeing civil liberties, eliminating corruption, remaking the educational system, encouraging foreign influence in China, modernizing the military, and stimulating economic development.

- However, the young emperor's aunt, Empress Dowager Cixi, staged a coup to stop the reforms. She nullified the decrees, imprisoned the emperor in the Forbidden City, and executed six leading reformers. Cixi then threw her support behind an anti-foreign uprising known as the Boxer Rebellion and even declared war against all foreign powers.

The Boxer Rebellion

- The Boxer Rebellion was headed by militia groups who called themselves the Society of Righteous and Harmonious Fists. In 1899, the movement went on a rampage to rid China of foreigners, Chinese Christians, and any Chinese who had ties to foreigners.

- In the summer of 1900, 140,000 Boxers besieged foreign embassies in Beijing, but a heavily armed force of British, French, Russian, U.S., German, and Japanese troops quickly crushed the Boxer movement. The Chinese government was then forced to pay a punitive indemnity and allow foreign troops to be permanently stationed in China, not only at embassies but also along all major routes to the sea.

- Because Cixi had supported the Boxers, many Chinese saw their government as morally bankrupt. New revolutionary movements broke out and gained widespread support, including from conservatives.

- Cixi herself died in November 1908, one day after the mysterious death of Emperor Guangxu. Modern tests have revealed that the emperor died of arsenic poisoning. It is intriguing to wonder how the course of modern Chinese and, indeed, world history might have been different had Guangxu been able to carry out his reforms and turn his country into a constitutional monarchy.

The Republic of China

- Just before the deaths of the emperor and his aunt, the Qing court issued the Outline of Constitution, which contained a blueprint for the transformation of China into a constitutional monarchy, complete with a statement on the rights and responsibilities of the people.

- It was all too late, of course. In her last act, Cixi appointed the two-year-old Puyi to the imperial throne, in the hope that he would continue to rule as an old-style emperor.

- But revolution broke out again in the fall of 1911, which resulted in the founding of a new government: the Republic of China. On February 12, 1912, the last Qing emperor, Puyi, abdicated his throne, bringing to an end 4,000 years of dynastic rule in China.

- As we have noted, it was Ming and Qing conservatism that caused China to withdraw from the world at precisely the same moment that Western powers and the Japanese were aggressively engaging in it. The problem facing China and the other East and Southeast Asia nations at the beginning of the 20th century was how to respond to European imperialism.

- Ultimately it would take an industrial revolution in Japan, a communist revolution in China, and two global wars before East Asian states were able to once again gain control of their own destinies!

Suggested Reading

Esherick, *The Origins of the Boxer Uprising.*

Kuhn, *Rebellion and Its Enemies in Late Imperial China.*

Questions to Consider

1. Why did the British force the Chinese to accept opium as payment for exports, and how did this lead to the loss of Chinese sovereignty under the Qing?

2. Why were attempts at reform late in the Qing dynasty frustrated, bringing to an end 4,000 years of dynastic rule in China?

The Qing—The Last Emperor of China
Lecture 40—Transcript

In 1759, Emperor Qianlong of the Qing dynasty moved to try and restrict European commercial presence in the great southern port city of Guangzhou, which had been home to thousands, often tens of thousands, of foreign merchants for about a thousand years to this point. Qing authorities were determined to bring the activities of foreign merchants more closely under government control, and also to more tightly regulate the terms of trade that had become increasingly independent of Qing authority. The Qing government passed a series of laws that insisted that foreign merchants could now deal only with specially licensed Chinese firms known as *cohongs*. Not only was this inconvenient for the European merchants, but they also had to cope with a market in which, as we noted last time, there was little demand for European products; this trade was very much one-way. Because there was such small demand for European imports into China, European merchants had been forced to pay for Chinese silk, porcelain, lacquer ware, and tea mainly with silver, which was dug out of the mines of Central and South America.

By the late 18th century, seeking ways to increase their profits, and in response to these restrictive Chinese trade practices, officials of the British East India Company began to look for alternatives to silver to exchange for Chinese goods. They settled on a profitable but highly illegal drug called opium; here was a product that the Chinese themselves didn't produce, but for which there was a tragically ever-increasing demand. Under the auspices of the British East India Company, British merchants now purchased the cheap opium that was growing in the great poppy fields of India and they shipped this on to China. British company officials, particularly those working for companies such as Dent, Jardine, and Matheson, then used this opium instead of the silver to buy Chinese products in the port city of Guangzhou. This meant that silver coin, which the Qing merchants had demanded as payment for Chinese exports, now began to flow back out of China and into the coffers of British merchants.

One set of statistics demonstrates just what a reversal of the former arrangement this new opium policy was: In the decade of the 1830s, for example, only $7 million worth of silver flowed into China, while some

$27 million worth of silver coin and silver bullion now flowed out of China. Obviously this was an incredibly profitable arrangement for the British merchants, and the opium trade expanded rapidly. We have some statistical evidence of this, too: In 1820, the number of 150-pound chests of this narcotic imported into China by British merchants was around 9,700 chests for the year. But in 1835, an astonishing 35,445 chests of opium entered China in that one year to satisfy the habits of a vast and growing number of drug addicts. With the help of all this opium, the British mercantile companies were soon able to pay for luxury Chinese products without using any silver whatsoever.

The trade in opium was illegal, of course; but it continued unabated for decades because the Chinese made little effort to enforce the law, partly because corrupt Chinese officials also benefited enormously from the situation, and partly because no one in the Qing government wanted to risk an all out confrontation with the British merchants. But by the late 1830s, the Chinese government was acutely aware that this was causing a major economic, as well as drug addiction, problem. Opium trade was draining massive amounts of silver bullion from China, but it was also having major social consequences, particularly in Southern China where addiction was widespread. Chinese officials estimated that some 4 million of their countrymen were addicted to opium by the late 1830s; but a British doctor based in Canton in Southern China suggested the number was probably closer to 12 million.

When Qing government officials took tentative steps to try and stop the illicit trade in 1838, British merchants immediately started losing money. Qing efforts were stepped up the following year: In 1839, an incorruptible official named Lin Zexu was put in charge of attempts to destroy the opium trade altogether. Commissioner Lin was well aware of the financial and social costs that widespread Chinese addiction to opium was causing. He's quoted as saying: "If we continue to allow this trade to flourish, in a few dozen years we will find ourselves not only with no soldiers to resist the enemy, but also with no money to equip the army." Lin Zexu acted quickly, confiscating and destroying 20,000 chests of British-owned opium and arresting 1,600 foreign merchants and their Chinese accomplices. Ultimately, this uncompromising policy ignited a war that ended in humiliating defeat for China and made it obvious where the new balance of global power now lay.

Outraged by Chinese action against them, British commercial agents pressed the British government for a military response. The ensuing conflict has been known to historians ever since as the Opium Wars. In the opening stages of the war, British naval gunboats demonstrated their clear superiority. Equipped only with swords and knives, and occasionally muskets, Chinese coastal towns couldn't defend themselves against gunboats and well-trained English military forces armed with rifles. Even so, the Chinese refused to sue for peace, so British forces broke the stalemate by attacking China's jugular with steam powered gunboats that headed directly for the ancient Grand Canal of China. In June, 1842, a British armada of 70 ships advanced up the Yangtze River; and by the time it arrived at the intersection with the Grand Canal, the Chinese had sued for peace.

China experienced similar military setbacks frankly throughout the remainder of the 19th century against Britain and France in the 1850s, France again in the 1880s, and then against Japan, as we'll see, in 1894 and 1895. In the wake of these defeats, the Qing government was forced to sign several humiliating, unequal treaties that curtailed Chinese sovereignty and effectively guided Chinese relations with foreign states right through until the end of the Second World War. The most famous of these treaties was the first one, forced upon the Qing by the British: the Treaty of Nanjing, signed on August 29, 1842. As a result of this unequal treaty, China agreed to cede the island of Hong Kong to Britain for what ended up being a period of 156 years; also to open five ports, including Guangzhou and Shanghai, to British commerce and British residence; to grant most favored nation status to Britain, and ensure that British residents would no longer be subject to Chinese law; and to pay nine million dollars in reparations to merchants whose chests of opium had been burnt. Later, France, Germany, Denmark, the Netherlands, Spain, Belgium, Austria-Hungary, the United States, and Japan all forced the Chinese to conclude similar unequal treaties with them; how the mighty Qing had fallen.

Collectively these treaties legalized the opium trade; they permitted the reestablishment of Christian missions throughout China, banned, you might remember, earlier in the Qing dynasty; they opened the treaty ports; and they prevented the Qing government from levying tariffs on imports of foreign goods. Christian missions were now reestablished all over China in the wake of these treaties, all the way from the imperial court to the provinces. We also have some statistics on this, too: By the end of the 19th century, there were around 750 Catholic and 1,300 protestant missionaries in China, who between them had converted around 200,000 Chinese to Christianity. By the first year of the 20th century, alongside this proliferation of Christian missionaries, some 90 Chinese ports were also firmly under foreign control, foreign merchants controlled much of China's economy, and foreign gunboats patrolled Chinese waters.

Of course, as is generally the case in world history, this humiliating debilitation of the Chinese empire in the late 19th century was as much due to internal problems as it was to foreign intrusion and foreign demands. Large-scale rebellions in the 19th century reflected the people's increasing poverty and discontent with the government. China's population continued to explode; between 1800 and 1900, the population rose from 330 to a staggering 475 million people, which placed an incredible strain on resources. The concentration of arable land in the hands of elite families, the corruption of government officials, and, of course, the increasing drug addiction throughout China because of the opium trade all led to widespread peasant discontent. Rebellions broke out in Nian between 1853 and 1868, a very lengthy rebellion; and a Muslim rebellion in the Yunan province lasted from 1855–1873, almost 20 years. But the most dangerous of all the peasant uprisings was the Taiping Rebellion, which lasted for 13 violent years between 1851 and 1864, and which brought the Qing dynasty to the brink of collapse.

The catalyst for the rebellion was actually a schoolteacher named Hong Xiuquan, and there's an interesting connection with the renewed Christian missionary activity and also with the United States here. Having failed the provincial-level civil service exam, Hong became involved with a Baptist missionary from Tennessee. Hong became convinced he was actually Jesus Christ's younger brother who'd been sent to earth by God to expel the foreign devils—namely the Manchu Qing—from China. Hong began calling for the destruction of the Qing dynasty and for the radical transformation of Chinese society, and this was a cry that appealed to millions of Chinese in

1851. By now, many Chinese despised the Manchu ruling class as foreigners anyway, and the Taiping reform program contained features that appealed to the discontented masses. Let me give you a partial list of the demands made by Hong and the Taipings; demands that in some cases seemed to call for the abandonment of many of the ideals of traditional Chinese society, but in other cases seemed to reinforce some of these ancient ideals of Eastern civilization. For example, they called for the abolition of private property; for communal wealth to be shared according to need; for the prohibition of foot binding and concubinage; for free public education; for simplification of the written language and for increased literacy for the masses; for the establishment of democratic political institutions; for the building of a modern industrial society; and for the equality under law of men and women.

After sweeping through Southeast China, Hong and his followers captured the great southern city of Nanjing in 1853 and made it the capital of their Taiping, which means "Great Peace," kingdom. From Nanjing, they campaigned vigorously throughout much of the rest of China; and as they passed through the countryside, whole villages and towns flocked to them to join them, sometimes voluntarily, sometimes under coercion. By 1855, one million armed Taipings were poised to attack Beijing, but Qing forces were able to repel them. The Taipings turned their attention to the south instead; and by 1860, firmly entrenched in the Yangtze River valley, the Taipings threatened Shanghai itself.

The conservatives in Chinese society, determined to preserve classical Chinese culture, naturally sided with the government. After imperial forces of Manchu soldiers failed to defeat the Taipings, the Qing then created a series of regional armies of Chinese soldiers led now by these conservative Confucian scholar-bureaucrats. With the aid of European military advisors, these regional armies gradually overcame the Taipings. In June, 1864, Hong committed suicide, and the Taiping stronghold of Nanjing fell just a few months later. Government forces slaughtered 100,000 rebels in the bloody retribution that followed. The Taiping Rebellion was over, but it had cost somewhere between 20 and 30 million Chinese lives and caused massive declines in agricultural production. Starving peasants were so desperate they were forced to resort to eating grass, and there's even evidence of cannibalism, just to survive.

But although ultimately unsuccessful, the Taiping Rebellion changed the course of Chinese history. Dealing with aggressive foreign powers and surveying lands ravaged by domestic rebellions, the Qing rulers finally came to realize that reform was now absolutely necessary if their empire was to survive. For three decades following the end of the Taiping Rebellion, from 1865–1895, the Qing authorities tried to recreate an efficient and benevolent Confucian government in an attempt to solve their social and economic problems, while at the same time adopting foreign technology to strengthen state power. The most imaginative reform was called the "Self-Strengthening Movement" of the 1860s to the 1890s. Funded by money from the Qing authorities, local leaders all over China were encouraged to raise troops, to levy local taxes, and to establish modern military forces. Using a fascinating slogan "Chinese learning at the base; Western learning for use"—so Chinese learning at the base of this, but Western learning for use to reform—the Self-Strengthening Movement leaders tried to blend traditional Chinese culture, Eastern civilization if you like, with modern European industrial technology. While maintaining the great ancient Confucian values that had now been guiding China's fortunes for some 2,500 years, the leaders also wanted to build modern shipyards, modern railways, modern weapons factories, steel mills, and academies now of science and technology.

Although the Self Strengthening Movement did ultimately lay the foundations for eventual Chinese industrialization later in the 20th century, it brought only superficial change in the late 19th century. The Movement wasn't able to introduce enough industrialization to bring real economic and military strength to China; and it was based on two contradictions, frankly: one was that somehow industrialization could bring social change to what was still essentially an agrarian land; and the other was that, despite claims to the contrary, it was inevitable that education in European curricula would undermine Confucianism. At this point in our story, we need to introduce another key player in the failure of these attempts at reforms, another of the extraordinary women that we've seen throughout this course: This is the Empress Dowager Cixi, who lived from 1835–1908.

Cixi was a former concubine who became the consort of Emperor Xian Feng and who gave birth to his successor Tongzhi in 1856. After Xian Feng's death in 1861, Cixi set herself up as the sole regent over the five-year-old boy-emperor. When Tongzhi died in 1875 with no heir, Cixi named her three-year-old nephew Guangxu to the throne. All of this manipulation of the throne meant that it was Empress Dowager Cixi who was effectively the true ruler of China during the last 50 years of the Qing dynasty. Cixi was a conservative; she was bitterly opposed to reform. One example of this, quite extraordinary, is that she personally diverted funds from the Self-Strengthening Movement that had been intended to be used to modernize the navy to build instead a magnificent ornamental pavilion, known ever since as the "marble boat," to grace the lake in the Old Summer Palace in Beijing; perhaps some of you have seen it there as I have. The original stone and wood structure had been erected by Emperor Qianlong back in 1755, but had been destroyed by the British during the Opium Wars. Cixi now had it rebuilt in 1893. Like its predecessor, it's actually made of wood; but the wood has been painted to look like marble. It's a supreme irony that the funds used to build this traditional Chinese pleasure pavilion were diverted from the money that had been set aside to modernize the navy. Actually, Prince Chun's appointment as controller of the admiralty had been arranged by the Empress Cixi, so the prince probably had no choice other than to go along with this embezzlement.

Further evidence of the failure of the Self-Strengthening Movement is that foreign powers maintained their firm hold on Chinese affairs despite these attempts at reform. Indeed, the imperial states of Europe effectively dismantled the Qing Empire in the decade between 1885 and 1895. In 1885, as we saw in an earlier lecture on Southeast Asia, France incorporated Vietnam into its colonial Indochinese empire; the following year Britain incorporated Burma into its empire; and in 1895, Japan forced China to grant independence to Korea, to Taiwan, and to parts of Manchuria in the north; more on this in a subsequent lecture. By 1898, foreign powers had effectively carved the Chinese homeland itself into various spheres of economic interest. It was only mistrust amongst the foreign governments that prevented the total dismemberment of China. Powerless to resist foreign demands, the Qing government was forced to grant exclusive rights for railway and mineral development to Germany in the Shandong Province, to France in the southern border regions north of Vietnam, to Britain in the wealthy Yangtze River valley, to Japan in the Southeastern coastal provinces, and to Russia in Manchuria.

These humiliating setbacks sparked one last ambitious but ultimately abortive attempt to save China from further subjugation: the so-called Hundred Days of Reform in 1898. Two liberal Chinese scholars, Kang Youwei and Liang Qichao, published treatises reinterpreting Confucianism now and justifying radical change in the imperial system. Their intention was nothing less than an attempt to remake China as a powerful, modern industrial state, precisely the same way the Japanese were doing under the Meiji government, as we'll also see in a lecture very soon. Impressed with their ideas, the young Qing emperor Guangxu launched a sweeping series of reforms to try and transform China into a constitutional monarchy. His reform agenda included guaranteeing civil liberties, eliminating corruption, remaking the educational system, encouraging foreign influence in China, modernizing the military, and doing whatever they could to stimulate economic development. But the young emperor's aunt, Dowager Empress Cixi, staged a coup to stop these reforms. She nullified the decrees, she imprisoned the emperor deep in the Forbidden City, and she executed six leading reformers while the scholars Kang and Liang fled to Japan.

Cixi then threw her support behind an anti-foreign uprising known as the Boxer Rebellion, and even declared war against all foreign powers. The movement was headed by militia groups who called themselves the Society of Righteous and Harmonious Fists; they were actually called "The Boxers" by foreign newspapers. In 1899, the movement went on a rampage to rid China of "foreign devils," killing foreigners, killing Chinese Christians, and killing any Chinese who had ties to foreigners. In the summer of 1900, 140,000 Boxers besieged all the foreign embassies in Beijing. But a heavily armed force of British, French, Russian, U.S., German, and Japanese troops quickly crushed the Boxer movement in bloody retaliation. The Chinese government was forced to pay a punitive indemnity; was forced to allow foreign troops to be permanently stationed in China, not only at the embassies but also along all the major routes to the seaports.

Because Cixi had supported the Boxers, many Chinese now saw their government as completely morally bankrupt. New revolutionary movements broke out and gained widespread support throughout the country, including now from the conservatives. In 1905, the ancient Confucian exam system was abolished and thousands of Chinese students actually were sent abroad instead to study Western technology, Western philosophy. Cixi herself died in November, 1908, one day after the mysterious death of the emperor himself; and therein is a fascinating tale. Court officials immediately declared that Emperor Guangxu had died of natural causes; but, of course, rumors of foul play swirled about the Forbidden City, especially after Cixi herself died just 22 hours later. Rumors were all that historians had to go on until a very recent scientific analysis of the emperor's hair and bones took place, and this revealed that the emperor had died of arsenic poisoning. In 2008, on the 100th anniversary of the Emperor Guangxu's death, the director of the National Committee for the Compilation of Qing History announced that on one 10-inch-long hair of the emperor, scientific tests had discovered arsenic content 2,400 times higher than normal. Suspicion falls on Cixi, who was concerned that Emperor Guangxu would undoubtedly carry out modern reforms if he'd outlived her. Anecdotal evidence also pointed to a court eunuch of Cixi's, surely the last in a long line of infamous eunuchs that, as we've seen, repeatedly had so influenced Chinese history. This eunuch was seen coming out of her quarters carrying a bowl of yogurt with instructions to take it to the emperor; and two hours later, he was dead.

Of course, it's intriguing to wonder how the course of modern Chinese history, indeed the course of world history, might've been different had Guangxu been able to carry out his reforms and turn his country into a constitutional monarchy. Just before the emperor and his aunt's death, the Qing Court did indeed issue the "Outline of Constitution," which contained a blueprint for the transformation of China into a modern constitutional monarchy complete with a statement on the rights and responsibilities of the people. But it was all too late, of course; and in her last act, Cixi appointed the two-year-old Puyi to the imperial throne in in the hope that he'd continue to rule as an old-style traditional emperor. But revolution broke out again in the fall of 1911, which resulted in the founding of a new government, the Republic of China; and on February 12, 1912, the last Qing emperor—the last emperor ever to rule China—Puyi abdicated his throne at the ripe old age of six. You might remember seeing these events depicted in a magnificent 1987 film directed by the Italian filmmaker Bernardo Bertolucci called *The Last Emperor*. This film accurately follows the life of Emperor Puyi from his ascent to the throne as a small boy, through to his imprisonment and eventual political rehabilitation by the Chinese communist authorities. Puyi eventually died in 1967.

With the abdication of the last emperor of China, 4,000 years of dynastic rule came to an end in 1912. Throughout this series of lectures, we've followed the magnificent course of Chinese imperial and dynastic history all the way from the semi-legendary Xia dynasty, which came to power in perhaps 2200 or 2100 B.C.E., through now to the end of the Qing dynasty early in the 20th century; more than four millennia of dynastic rule, and this makes China undoubtedly the oldest continuous civilization in all of world history. Imagine if the ancient Egyptians or Sumerians were still ruling into the 20th century; imagine if the Romans and their system of government had operated more or less continuously from the 6th century B.C.E. through to the 20th century. Such was the extraordinary longevity of Chinese history; the extraordinary longevity of Eastern civilization.

As we've noted, it was Ming and Qing conservatism that caused China to withdraw from the world at precisely the same moment that Western powers and the Japanese were aggressively engaging in it. One stark example of the changing face of global power: By the beginning of the First World War in 1914, some 84 percent of the surface of the globe was under the political, military, and economic control of a handful of small industrialized countries. The problem facing China and all the other East and Southeast Asian nations at the beginning of the 20th century was how to respond to European imperialism. Ultimately it would take an industrial revolution in Japan, a communist revolution in China, and two global wars before East Asian states were able to once again gain control of their own destinies.

But before we consider these most recent pages in the epic tale of Eastern civilization, we need to go back to Korea and Japan to also bring the histories of those regions up to the 20th century. Please join me next time as we return to Korea and the 500 year rule of the Choson dynasty.

Korea Choson—Rise of the *Yangban*
Lecture 41

When we last left Korea earlier in the course, it was still under Mongol occupation. But the Koryo king Kongmin (r. 1351–1374) openly opposed the Mongols. When the Ming dynasty was declared in 1368, Kongmin immediately adopted a pro-Ming, anti-Mongol policy. This decision fed into the general chaos that enveloped the final years of Koryo rule, even as the Mongols were being forced out. Two military commanders, Choe Yeong and Yi Song-gye, came to the fore after defeating the Japanese pirates known as the *waegu*. In the aftermath, Yi Song-gye overthrew the last Koryo king and established the Choson dynasty. This dynasty, the subject of this lecture and the next, would rule Korea for more than 500 years.

Emergence of the Choson

- Yi Song-gye borrowed the name Choson ("land of morning calm") for his new dynasty from the most ancient of all Korean kingdoms. He moved the capital to Hanyang (modern Seoul), where it has been ever since, although since the Second World War, Seoul has been capital of South Korea only.

- The Choson elites adopted Neo-Confucianism as their guiding political doctrine and worked for the next 500 years to create a Neo-Confucian state. Although Yi Song-gye had used military power to stage the coup and seize the throne, it was the support of the Neo-Confucian literati class that validated his reign.

- The literati power brokers worked with Yi Song-gye, ruling as King Taejo, to create a new body of administrative law deeply infused with Confucian ideology, which became the blueprint for the Choson system of government. But strong opposition to the Neo-Confucian orthodoxy persisted in certain elite circles, abating only after Taejo's fifth son assassinated the main anti-Confucian critic.

- When King Sejong came to power in 1418, he gave even more status to the Confucian scholar class by establishing an elite academy for the Confucian literati known as the Hall of Worthies.

- After Sejong's death in 1450, the kingship was dominated by the literati for five years, until the throne was seized in 1455 by King Sejo, who went on to rule until 1468. Sejo, determined to reduce some of the power of the Hall of Worthies, killed many opponents.

- Sejo then completed work on the statutory administrative code of the Choson government, which culminated in the production of the national code during his reign. This code clearly delineated the structure of Choson government as a sort of constitutional monarchy, in which the governing process was directed by civil and military bureaucrats.

Choson Government

- The elite political and social bureaucratic class in Choson Korea became known as the *yangban*. These were members of the two orders (military and civil) who, in conjunction with the king, now controlled government. The duties of the *yangban* were to devote themselves deeply to the study of Confucianism, to hold themselves accountable to the highest ethical standards of Confucianism, and of course, to hold elite public office.

- As the super-elite of Choson society, the *yangban* married only members of their own class and lived in separate quarters in Seoul and the villages surrounding it. There were even distinctions within the *yangban*, part of a self-selection process designed to prevent the dilution of their privileges and prestige.

- The highest organ of Choson government was the state council, in which three high state councillors made joint decisions. Below this were six ministries that had direct policy access to the king through the royal secretariat. An office of the inspector-general was also

- created, to act as a surveillance organ that criticized public policy where necessary and as a watchdog against corruption.

- This system of checks and balances was impressive and complex, but it sometimes worked too well, leading to so much internal oversight and strife between the various organs of government that decision making became stagnant.

- To administer the Choson state, Korea was divided into eight provinces, which were, in turn, subdivided into counties. Each province had its own governor and a magistrate to collect taxes. Each province also had its own six-ministry structure, based on the national model.

- Because this sophisticated system of government was so strongly influenced by the Confucian tradition of Chinese government, it was inevitable that a Confucian exam system would be at the heart of official appointments at all levels in the Choson government. In theory, the exams were open to anyone, but in practice, they were monopolized by the *yangban*.

Structure of Choson Society

- By the late 18th century, the *yangban* had acquired most of the traits of a hereditary nobility, except that their status was based on a mixture of family position, access to the Confucian examination system, and their place in the civil service bureaucracy.

- For most of the 500-year-long Choson period, the *yangban* and the king effectively controlled the central government and military. But this was not a tiny elite minority; estimates are that the *yangban* may have constituted as much as 30 percent of the total Korean population by the year 1800.

- At the opposite end of the social spectrum were slaves and others of "low birth," who may have constituted 30 to 40 percent of the total population.

- Slavery was hereditary in Choson Korea but was also used as a form of Legalist punishment. Despite their lowly status, successful slaves could, and often did, own property, and successful private slaves could buy their freedom.

- In the 18th century, with the emergence of new merchant and artisan social classes, the tide of opinion gradually turned against the practice of slavery. In 1801, all government slaves were emancipated by decree, and the institution of slavery was completely abolished as part of the Gabo Reforms of 1894.

- Between the *yangban* and the slaves, most of the remaining 30 to 40 percent of the population were farmers. And because Korean agriculture was efficient and productive, most farming was commercial, not just for subsistence. The middle class, largely made up of free farmers, also included merchants, traders, local government or quasi-governmental clerks, craftsmen and laborers, and textile workers.

- The Choson government regarded most land as belonging to the state, as had several Chinese dynasties. Peasant farmers paid land taxes to the government, as well as taxes to their landlords and local taxes on all manufactured products.

- Along with creating a rigidly stratified social structure, the Neo-Confucian orthodoxy of the Choson state also had serious implications for gender relations. To the *yangban*, the law of nature (and their conservative interpretation of Confucian ideology) explicitly sanctioned female subordination and inferiority.
  - Choson Confucianism drew a clear distinction between the public sphere of men and the domestic sphere of women. As a result, women in Choson Korea were considered to be of very low status.

  - According to the policy of *samjong* ("three obediences"), before marriage, a woman was expected to obey her father; during marriage, a woman must obey her husband; and after the death of her husband, a woman was expected to obey her son.

- o According to another policy governing women's behavior, the *chilgo* ("seven injunctions"), a daughter-in-law or wife could be disowned if she demonstrated any of these behaviors: disobedience to her parents-in-law, inability to bear a male son, adultery, jealousy, having an incurable disease, stealing, or talkativeness.

- Despite the rigid gender and social distinctions, the Choson dynasty remained strong, successful, and vigorous throughout the 14th and 15th centuries. During the long reign of King Sejong (r. 1418–1450) in particular, not only was government stable, but extraordinary advances were made in the arts, science, and technology.

- Sejong was also the monarch who promoted and helped create the unique form of writing for the Korean language, the *Hangul* script. Despite its invention in the mid-15th century, the *Hangul* system came into common usage only in the 20th century, as a response to Japanese colonization.

The Decline of the Choson

- After Sejong, the dynasty fell into the hands of weaker kings and entered a period of decline, characterized by violent succession struggles, bitter division among the *yangban* elites, increasing corruption of the civil service exam, crushing tax burdens on farmers, and raids on Korea by the Japanese in 1592 and 1597 and by the Manchus repeatedly between 1627 and 1636.

- Despite this litany of disasters, the most severe problems of the 16th and 17th centuries were actually caused by the confrontation between two different factions of officialdom.
  - o The *yangban* split into two factions: the Easterners (or Tongin) and Westerners (or Soin). Violent conflict and purges took

place between the two. Eventually, factional politics became bound up with blood lineage.

o The fact that students were also expected to follow the instructions and factional orientations of their teachers helped further factionalize the elite population. This also ensured the entrenchment of a Confucian-style master-disciple relationship that still resonates in both North and South Korean educational institutions to this day.

- These factional problems led to the emergence of a new intellectual movement in Choson Korea, one that advocated for the practical use of human knowledge. Pioneered by Confucian scholar Yi Su-gwang, the Sirhak ("practical learning") movement flourished into the late 18th century, supported by discontented scholars, officials, former bureaucrats, and commoners.

Yi Song-gye ruled the Choson dynasty as King Taejo for only six years, but in his short reign, he worked to create a new body of administrative law influenced by Confucian ideology.

o Sirhak thought advocated a more practical application of the traditional approaches to government and land administration, an increased emphasis on and advocacy for commercial and manufacturing activity, and a renewed interest in Korean history and language.

- In reality, the interests of the Sirhak scholars were many and varied, but they shared a focus on reality and on the practical application of ideas as a way of solving real-life problems, as opposed to obtuse metaphysical speculations.

- One Sirhak school focused on reforming the institutions of the Choson—land policy, education, government, salaries, military service—until eventually, Sirhak had replaced Neo-Confucianism as the dominant school of political thought.

- As the government became less effective in the 19th century, another Western invention—Catholicism—also began to spread more widely through Choson society.
  - Initially, many *yangban* were attracted to Catholicism, but after a series of government persecutions of Catholics, they mostly turned away. Increasingly, converts came from the peasant and artisan classes, attracted to the equality of Catholicism.

  - It was precisely because of this egalitarian message that a brutal persecution was carried out in 1801, but later, Catholicism was less severely suppressed.

- As we will see in our next lecture, attempts by the government to shut out Catholicism were part of a larger movement within the Choson state to keep Korea isolated from outside influences. And despite Western attempts to interfere, Korea was able to remain dormant and relatively isolated, closing itself to outside contacts in the 19th century until the Japanese turned up early in the 20th.

Suggested Reading

Choi, *A Modern History of Korean Philosophy.*

Jeon, *Science and Technology of Korea.*

1. Why did the Choson dynasty in Korea adopt Confucianism as its principal political ideology?

2. Who were the *yangban*, and how was such a tiny elite majority able to control political, military, and social life in Korea for centuries?

Korea Choson—Rise of the *Yangban*
Lecture 41—Transcript

Hello everyone, and welcome to the first of another of our two-lecture mini series in which we return to Korea to bring our story of that region's role in the development of Eastern civilization through from the 14th to the 20th century.

When we last left Korea earlier in the course, it was still under Mongol occupation; but by the mid-14th century the tide was turning against the Mongols actually throughout most of the vast areas of Eurasia that had been under Mongol occupation for more than a century. More recently in the course, we saw how the Ming dynasty in China, under the leadership of Hongwu, was eventually able to drive the Mongols back to the steppes, although they remained a constant threat right throughout the Ming dynasty period. In Korea, it was the Koryo king Kongmin, who reigned from 1351–1374, who was the first ruler to openly oppose the Mongols and who became determined to destroy the power of the families who'd been enriching themselves by working closely with the Mongols. When the Ming dynasty was declared in 1368, the Koryo king Kongmin immediately adopted a pro-Ming, anti-Mongol policy.

His decision fed into the general chaos that enveloped the final years of Koryo rule, even as the Mongols were being forced out. During this chaotic period, King Kongmin was actually assassinated; peasant revolts broke out all over the peninsula (remember the peasants had been bearing a double burden of taxation by the Koryo state and also by the Mongols); and Japanese pirates known as the *waegu* began raiding the Korean coast, devastating the villages. The *waegu* were only lightly armed, but their ability to unexpectedly turn up and raid the coast at will drove many peasants to flee inland and to abandon the rich coastal farmlands. You might remember from one of our lectures on the Ming dynasty that the impact of these pirates on the coastal regions of China was just as severe. Repeated diplomatic representations to the Japanese government failed to end the attacks, so the Koryo decided to launch a major military campaign to try and defeat the pirates.

Two different commanders were appointed to lead the Koryo armed forces: Choe Yong and Yi Song-gye. Their almost immediate success against the *waegu*, which quickly lessened the impact of the devastating raids, resulted in both commanders gaining high status and influence in the Koryo capital. But the two military leaders, colleagues up to this point, soon fell out over the question of whether to attack or support the Chinese Ming dynasty, which had just declared its intention of taking over part of the Koryo's northeastern territory. While Choe Yong was leading an expedition against the Ming forces, Yi Song-gye—who'd adopted a pro-Ming policy and was opposed to the expedition—surprised everyone by suddenly leading his forces into the capital and staging a military coup against both Choe Yong and the king.

Following this overthrow of the last Koryo king, Yi Song-gye quickly established the next dynasty of Korean history: the Choson dynasty. The Choson—the last dynasty to rule Korea and the subject of this pair of lectures—went on to rule for more than 500 years, from 1392 until the August 22, 1910, when, as we'll soon see, Korea was annexed by the rising power of Japan. Yi Song-gye chose the name "Choson" for his new dynasty, which he borrowed from the most ancient of all Korean kingdoms. We discussed this first Korean dynasty much earlier in the course; the name Choson actually means the "land of morning calm," a reflection of the sublime and tranquil landscape of Korea. Yi Song-gye then decided to move the capital to Hanyang, which is modern Seoul, where it's been ever since; although, of course, since the Second World War, Seoul has been capital of South Korea only.

The Chosen elites adopted Neo-Confucianism as their guiding political doctrine and worked for the next 500 years to create a Neo-Confucian state, reminding us once again of the extraordinary longevity and wide political and social influence of Confucian philosophy, which had first emerged 2,000 years earlier in Late Zhou dynasty China. The Choson also worked with the military to expand the area of Korean territory, bringing it close to its present size. The emergence of a new Neo-Confucian literati class in Choson Korea resulted in an intensifying repudiation of Buddhism, by the way, which was now seen as destructive to families and ultimately ruinous to the state. Although Yi Song-gye had used military power to stage his coup and seize the throne, it was the support of the Neo-Confucian literati class that validated his reign. Yi Song-gye ruled the Choson dynasty as King Taejo for only six years, from 1392–1398; but during his short but incredibly effective reign the literati powerbrokers worked with the king to create a new body of administrative law deeply infused with Confucian ideology, and this became the blueprint for the Choson system of government. Not everyone was on board, of course, and strong opposition to this new Neo-Confucian orthodoxy persisted in certain elite aristocratic circles, abating only after Taejo's fifth son assassinated the main anti-Confucian critic. This was just the beginning of a long and bitter struggle between the Neo-Confucian literati and their critics.

When King Sejong came to power in 1418, he gave even more status to the Confucian scholar class by establishing an elite position for the Confucian literati known as the Hall of Worthies. Sejong was a ruler of extraordinary vision, and we'll see shortly why he remains one of the most revered rulers in Korea's very long history.

After Sejong's death in 1450, the kingship was dominated by the literati for five years until the throne was seized in 1455 by King Sejo, who went on to rule until 1468. Sejo was determined to reduce some of the power of the Hall of Worthies and to try and transfer more power back to the kingship, so he killed many opponents. After a plot against him was discovered, he carried out a bloodbath in which the elite six martyred ministers and many other members of the Hall of Worthies were killed. Sejo then completed work on compiling the statutory administrative code of Choson government, which culminated in the production of the National Code during his reign.

This Code clearly delineated the structure of Choson government as a sort of constitutional monarchy in which the governing process was directed by civil and military bureaucrats. This new elite political and social bureaucratic class in Choson Korea became known as the *yangban*. These were members of the two orders, both military and civil, who in conjunction with the king now controlled government. The duties of the *yangban* were to devote themselves deeply to the study of Confucianism, to hold themselves accountable to the highest ethical standards of Confucianism, and, of course, to hold elite public office. The *yangban* didn't perform duties like medical officers, interpreters, astronomers, accountants, or law clerks; these became the hereditary preserve of the *chungin* class, literally the "middle people." The *yangban* were thus the quintessential Confucian scholar-bureaucrats, functioning at the highest levels of government, attempting to fashion an ideal Confucian state through the moral cultivation of the entire society. As the super-elite of Choson society, the *yangban* married only members of their own class, and they lived in separate quarters in Seoul and in the villages surrounding it. There were even distinctions within the *yangban*—the civil order was much more prestigious than the military order, for example—and descendants of *yangban* by their secondary wives found it difficult to gain access to the Confucian exam system, which was similar to the exam system operating in Ming China, but was restricted to elites only; more about this in just a moment.

These limitations and distinctions were part of a self-selection process designed to prevent the dilution of *yangban* privileges and prestige. The highest organ of Choson government was the State Council, in which three High State Councilors—obviously all elite *yangban*—made joint decisions. Below this were six ministries that had direct policy access to the king through the Royal Secretariat. An Office of Inspector-General was also created to act as a surveillance organ that criticized public policy where necessary, and also as a watchdog against corruption that even censured the moral behavior of the king on occasion. This system of checks and balances was impressive and complex; in fact, just as impressive the many complex and well-organized bureaucratic systems of government that we've seen the Chinese put in place, reminding us again of this long and ancient tradition of sophisticated government that's such a hallmark of Eastern civilization. But sometimes the Choson system worked too well, leading to so much internal oversight and strife between these various organs of government that decision making became difficult, even stagnant.

To administer the now-expanded Choson state, the Korean peninsula, Korea was divided into eight provinces, and these in turn were subdivided into counties. Each province had its own governor appointed, and also a magistrate whose job was to collect taxes. Each province also had its own Six Ministries structure based on the national model. Because this sophisticated system of government in Choson Korea was so strongly influenced by the great bureaucratic Confucian tradition of Chinese government, it was inevitable that a Chinese Confucian exam system would have to be at the heart of the appointment of officials at all these levels of Choson government.

But one big difference between the Korean and the ideal Chinese model was that in the Choson dynasty access to the exam was restricted to sons of officials of the second *yangban* rank or above, which meant the path to higher office was effectively closed for most Koreans. According to the law, the exams should in theory have been open to anyone; but in practice, they were effectively monopolized by the *yangban*.

The approach to government and the appointment of officials had obviously major implications for the structure of Choson society, and this is a subject I'd like to turn to next. By the late 18th century, the *yangban* had acquired most of the traits of a hereditary nobility, except that their status was based on a mixture of family position, access to the Confucian examination system, and their place in the civil service bureaucracy. For most of the 500-year-long Choson period, the *yangban* and the king effectively controlled the central government and the military. But this wasn't a tiny elite minority; estimates are that the *yangban* may have constituted as much as 30 percent of the total Korean population by 1800. This meant that most *yangban* became gentry of high social status but not necessarily of high income, because access to the top positions in government became increasingly competitive.

At the opposite end of the social spectrum were slaves and other "low born," who may have constituted as much as 30–40 percent of the total population of Choson Korea. Indeed, slavery was hereditary under the Choson; but it was also used as a form of Legalist punishment. The slave class consisted of both government owned and privately owned slaves. Sometimes the government gave slaves to citizens of higher rank as a reward for exemplary behavior. We also have evidence that privately owned slaves could be inherited as personal property. Despite their lowly status, successful slaves could, and often did, own property; and successful private slaves could eventually buy their way to freedom. In the 18th century, with the emergence of a new merchant and artisan social class, the tide of opinion gradually turned against the practice of slavery. In 1801, all government slaves were emancipated by decree, and the institution of slavery was completely abolished as part of the Gabo Reforms of 1894.

Between the elite *yangban* and the slaves, most of the remaining 30–40 percent of the population were farmers; and because Korean agriculture was efficient and productive, most farming was commercial, not just for subsistence. This middle class of free farmers also included merchants and traders, local government or quasi-governmental clerks, craftsmen, laborers, and textile workers. Indeed, given the relatively small size of the freeborn middle class, it's not surprising that individuals often had more than one role in life; they might, for example, have worked as a farmer certainly, but also as a merchant or a textile worker. Similar to the argument advanced by, as we've seen, several Chinese dynasties, the Choson government regarded most land as belonging to the state; so in return for having land to farm, the peasant farmer had to pay a land tax to the government. Originally this was set at 10 percent, but under King Sejong it was lowered to a very reasonable 5 percent of total produce. Although this does sound very generous, we need to remember that as well as his obligation to the state, the peasant farmers also had to pay taxes to their local landlord, plus a local tribute tax—a sales tax, really—on all manufactured products that they purchased: utensils, fabrics, paper, woven mats, and so on. Still, the rapid expansion in the cultivation of cotton in Choson Korea led to the emergence of a thriving cotton textile industry, and this became the principal household industry of the period.

Along with creating this rigidly stratified social structure, the Neo-Confucian orthodoxy of the Choson state also had serious implications for gender relations. The status of women was strongly influenced by the *yangban's* attempts to create an ideal Confucian patriarchal society. To the *yangban*, the law of nature—and their very conservative interpretation of Confucian ideology—explicitly sanctioned female subordination and inferiority; so Choson Confucianism drew a clear distinction between the public sphere of men and the domestic sphere of women. As a result of this careful delineation of spheres and roles, women in Choson Korea were considered to be of very low status indeed. In fact, women weren't permitted to make any major decisions about their own lives. According to the policy of *samjong*, or the "three obediences," before marriage a woman was expected to obey her father; during marriage, a woman must obey her husband; and after the death of her husband, a woman was expected to obey her son. At no point in her life was a woman ever able to make her own decisions about anything. According to another policy governing women's behavior, the *chilgo* or "seven injunctions," a daughter-in-law or wife could be disowned if they demonstrated any of these seven behaviors: disobedience to the parents-in-law; not being able to bear a male son; adultery; jealousy; having an incurable disease; stealing; or talkativeness.

Despite these rigid gender and social distinctions, the Choson dynasty remained strong, successful, and vigorous throughout the 14th and 15th centuries. During the long reign of the fourth monarch in particular, the revered King Sejong who I mentioned a couple of times already in the lecture, who sat on the throne from 1418–1450, not only was government very stable but quite extraordinary advances were made in the arts, science, and technology. Let me just give you a few examples, a sort of list of Choson technological achievements: Korean scientists developed a gauge to accurately measure rainfall in 1442; this is about 200 years before something similar appeared in Europe. Wind streamers were in use in Choson Korea to help gauge the direction and the velocity of the wind. A magnificent and very sophisticated observatory was constructed on the grounds of Kyongbok Palace—perhaps you've seen it there—to make accurate celestial observations. A triangulation device and surveyor's rod were developed to measure land elevations and distances. All kinds of complex, extraordinary astronomical clocks, sundials, water clocks, and so on were designed and built.

Sejong is also the monarch who promoted and helped create the unique form of writing for the Korean language. The creation of Hangul script and an indigenous alphabet for the Korean language was actually a monumental achievement, then, of the early Choson; and King Sejong himself became convinced of this need for a writing system designed specifically to record the language of everyday Korean speech, as opposed to the language of the elite *yangban* that was, of course, written in Classical Chinese. The king himself was the driving force behind this development of a new written language, and he enlisted the services of elite scholars in the Hall of Worthies to help him create the new alphabet. Hangul was thus developed quite explicitly, quite intentionally in this atmosphere of scientific enlightenment that characterized the 15th century, particularly during the rule of King Sejong. The new alphabet was proudly proclaimed by the king in 1446 during his 28th year on the throne. This native writing system of Korea used a phonetic alphabet organized into blocks of syllables, by the way; and each block uses at least 2 of the 24 letters. There are 14 consonants, and 10 vowels. For reasons I'll explain in the next lecture, despite its invention in the mid-15th century, the Hangul system only came into common usage in the 20th century as a direct response to Japanese colonization of Korea; and so it remained largely unused for almost five centuries after it was devised.

Let's begin to conclude this lecture by turning to the decline of the Choson dynasty. After Sejong, the dynasty fell into the hands of weaker kings and entered a period of decline characterized by several violent succession struggles; by bitter division amongst the *yangban* elites; by increasing corruption of the civil service exam; by increasing and crushing tax burdens on farmers; and also by raids on Korea by the Japanese first in 1592, then five years later in 1597, and also by the Manchus repeatedly between 1627 and 1636. Despite this litany of disasters, no surprise here, the most severe problems of the 16th and 17th centuries were internal; they were actually caused by the confrontation between two different factions of officialdom. The *yangban* now split into two factions: the Easterners or Tongin, and the Westerners or Soin; and violent conflict and purges between the two took place. As generation followed generation, resentment was carried over for decades, so that factional politics eventually became bound up with blood lineage, with blood feuds really. The fact that students were also expected to follow the instructions and the factional orientation of their teachers without question helped further factionalize the elite population for all the generations that followed. This also ensured, by the way, the entrenchment of a Confucian-style master-disciple relationship that still resonates in both North and South Korean educational institutions to this day.

These factional problems led to the emergence of a new intellectual movement in Choson Korea, one that began to advocate for the practical use of human knowledge. This movement was pioneered by Confucian scholar Yi Su-gwang. It was called the Sirhak, or "practical learning," Movement, and it was inspired by knowledge of the physical sciences that he'd acquired on official visits to Beijing. The Sirhak Movement flourished well into the late 18th century, supported by discontented scholars, officials, by former bureaucrats, and also by commoners. Of course, continual innovation in science and technology had been one of the hallmarks of Eastern civilization for millennia; but as we've seen in recent lectures, under the Ming and Qing dynasties, China began to give up its position of global technological superiority to the West. In many ways, despite the conservatism of Korean and Japanese cultures, the mantle of practical innovation in Eastern society was transferred now from China to both of her East Asian neighbors during this early modern period.

I guess I could sum up the main tenants of Sirhak thought like this: This was a much more practical application of the traditional approaches to government and to ways of administering the land. There was an increased emphasis on and advocacy for commercial and manufacturing activity; and Sirhak promoted a renewed interest in Korean history and language. In reality, the interests of the Sirhak scholars were many and varied, but they all shared a focus on reality, on the practicality of application of ideas as a way of solving real life problems, as opposed to obtuse metaphysical speculations. The Sirhak movement was determined to use these practical skills to solve the problems facing Korea, and this began to push Choson thinking in new directions. One Sirhak school focused on reforming the institutions of the Choson—they focused on land policy, on education systems, on government and bureaucracy, on salaries, on military service—until eventually Sirhak had replaced Neo-Confucianism as the dominant school of political thought. Other Sirhak scholars focused on science: on researching the varieties of marine life, for example; they studied the smallpox virus; and so on. Knowledge of Western science and technology, acquired by Korean embassies to China where they learned many of the ideas that the Jesuits had introduced (you'll remember our discussion about that from a previous lecture), helped further inspire Sirhak scholars. Some specific examples of Western-inspired advances include the promulgation of a new and much more accurate calendar; the adoption of a complex, extraordinary European pulley mechanism to aid in construction; and also some very advanced studies on the movement of planets in the solar system.

But as Choson government became less and less effective in the 19th century, another Western invention, Catholicism, also began to spread more widely through Choson society. This spread wasn't initially because of the activities of Catholic missionaries, but because native Koreans had converted to the faith while visiting Beijing late in the 18th century and used the texts that they brought back to baptize many of their countrymen. Initially, many *yangban* were attracted to Catholicism; but after a series of government persecutions of Catholics, the elites mostly turned away. But more and more converts came from the peasant and artisan class, attracted to this creed of equality that argued that all humans regardless of class were children of God. It was precisely because of this egalitarian message that a brutal persecution was carried out in 1801; but later in the reign of King Sunjo, who reigned until 1834, Catholicism was less severely suppressed. By the end of the 19th century, specialists estimate that perhaps 20,000 Koreans had converted, French missionaries were certainly active throughout the peninsula, and various Catholic books were also being published. As we'll see in our next lecture, attempts by the government to shut out Catholicism were part of a larger movement within the Choson state to keep Korea isolated from outside influences in a manner not unlike the conservative factions of the Qing dynasty at the same time, as we've so recently seen.

Despite all this, the expansion of Western powers into East Asia in the 19th century was destined to alter the ancient established order of Korean foreign affairs, which can be summed up frankly as essentially the domination of Korea by China. China under the Qing dynasty was now in serious decline, having lost sovereignty and power to Western nations including France, Britain, and Russia. Shortly in the course, we'll consider how Japan responded to European imperialism by modernizing its government and its economy rather than submitting to the West after it was humiliatingly forced to open its ports by Commodore Perry of the U.S. Navy in 1853 and 1854. But as we'll see in the next lecture, despite Western attempts to interfere, Korea was able to remain dormant and relatively isolated, closing itself to outside contacts in the 19th century until the Japanese turned up very early in the 20th.

Next time, we conclude our look at Choson Korea, and we continue our journey through the long and complex story of Eastern civilization.

Korea Choson—The Last Dynasty
Lecture 42

Early in the 19th century, Western nations came knocking at the door of the "hermit nation," determined to establish contact with Korea for trade and other commercial purposes. Of course, the Korean people and the Choson government were only too aware of the fate that had befallen China through the Opium Wars and other clashes with the far more powerful Europeans. In this context, the Choson government decided that its best hope of avoiding a similar fate was essentially to reject all Western overtures for trade and exclude the foreigners. But as the Chinese had experienced, it ultimately proved impossible to keep out the determined and well-armed foreigners.

Conflict with the West and Japan

- Beginning in the 1830s, Korea experienced a series of encounters with British, French, Russian, and American merchant and war ships. In response, the Choson government decided essentially to reject all Western overtures for trade and shut out foreigners.

- In 1866, the Choson government also launched a full-scale campaign against Catholicism. By the time the persecution was over, 9 French missionaries and perhaps 8,000 Koreans had been killed.

- One of the French missionaries who escaped the persecution made his way to China, where he persuaded the commander of the French Asiatic Squadron to take punitive action against the Koreans. A fleet of seven warships entered Korean waters in October 1866. The French clashed with the Koreans, but were ultimately forced to withdraw.

- In 1871, in response to the earlier destruction of an American trading ship, the U.S. Asiatic Squadron was ordered to send a squadron of warships into Korean waters.

- As a result of the French incident five years earlier, the Choson government had worked hard to strengthen Korea's coastal defenses.

  - When the U.S. warships tried to steam through the Kanghwa Straits, between the island and the mainland, shore batteries opened fire. Shocked, the U.S. fleet decided not to engage and instead withdrew to China.

- The failure of these attacks by two modern military fleets only strengthened Korea's isolationist attitude. The failure of the attacks was undoubtedly due, at least in part, to stubborn Korean resistance, but it was also partly due to the fact that the Western powers were too preoccupied at the time to press their military strength on the Choson.

- The Japanese, however, turned out to be a different matter. Having overthrown the Tokugawa shogunate in 1867, the leaders of Japan decided to adopt an increasingly aggressive attitude toward Korea. By 1873, Japanese leaders were publicly calling for an "expedition" against Korea.

Reversal of Korean Isolationism

- In 1875, the Japanese government provoked a naval "incident" as a pretext for direct intervention, then landed a force of warships on the east coast of Kanghwa Island. Choson officials could not resist the heavily armed force and had little option but to sign the Treaty of Kanghwa in 1876. This unequal treaty cleared the way for the increasing involvement of Japan in Korean affairs and attempts to limit interference from China.

- The signing of this treaty produced a sea change in the attitude of the Choson government; faced with the probability of ongoing aggressive Japanese intervention, the Choson decided that it was probably in Korea's best interests to actively engage more closely with the rest of the world as a counter to Japanese interference.

- The first result of this foreign policy change occurred in October 1880, when the Choson sought to establish diplomatic relations with the United States. At the same time, the Koreans sent study missions to China and Japan, with the express aim of learning more about modern weapons technology.

- In 1882, the Korean-American Treaty was signed, which the Choson government hoped would discourage both Russian and Japanese aggression against Korea. Indeed, the treaty included a specific clause implying that the United States would come to Korea's aid under a range of circumstances. Similar treaties with other foreign powers quickly followed.

- But these international outreach efforts sparked pushback from the conservative elements of Korean society, who preferred the old hermit nation approach. Some of the conservative Confucian elites demanded the reinstatement of an isolationist government.

- This reinstatement took place after civil and military unrest broke out, but it was short-lived. Both the Chinese and Japanese governments used the Korean about-face as an excuse to intensify their military interference.
  - Japanese forces had been stationed in parts of the peninsula since the signing of the Treaty of Kanghwa in 1876.

  - In 1882, the Qing dynasty in China quickly dispatched its own force of 4,500 men to the peninsula, and by August, the Chinese troops were firmly entrenched in Seoul.

- After something of a standoff, a treaty was signed that temporarily removed both Chinese and Japanese troops from Korea. This allowed the Chinese to remain the major cultural influence on the country for the next decade, from 1885 to 1894.

- While this competition for Korea was being waged by the Japanese and Chinese, the Russians were also becoming increasingly involved in Korean affairs. The Korean king and queen viewed the involvement of Russia as a third party as an effective means of balancing Chinese and Japanese influence.

- But this pro-Russian attitude immediately provoked suspicion and resentment in China and Japan, particularly after word began to circulate of the signing of a secret treaty between Korea and Russia. As a result, by the late 19th century, the Korean court was deeply split into rival pro-Chinese, pro-Japanese, and pro-Russian factions.

- In 1895, the Japanese ambassador to Korea masterminded nothing less than the brutal assassination of the Choson queen, who had vocally opposed the Japanese-supported politicians in court. The Korean king fled to the Russian legation in Seoul to avoid Japanese plots against him; he publicly rejected Japan and the reform measures being demanded by the pro-Japanese lobby.

Outbreak of War

- These events led to the organization of a massive national campaign, launched by political leaders and intellectuals, to try to gain Korean independence from foreign control. Advocates argued for reform in Korean politics and customs to bring them in line with Western practices.

- At the same time, under the influence of modern education being provided by Protestant mission schools, hundreds of young men held mass meetings in the streets, demanding democratic reforms and an end to Russian and Japanese domination. Conservative (and often pro-Japanese) forces inside Korea responded by jailing reformist leaders.

- In 1894, a major peasant uprising—the Tonghak Rebellion—broke out. The Korean court asked China to send troops to help quell the rebellion. This request, interpreted by the Japanese government as a breach of the recent treaty, gave the Japanese government the pretext it had been waiting for to dispatch troops to Korea. Japan and China were soon at war.

- After six months of continuous Japanese victories, the Qing government was forced to sue for peace, demonstrating not only the total failure of the Qing to modernize its military but also the fact that that the balance of power in East Asia had shifted from China to Japan.

- The victorious Japanese now established complete hegemony over Korea via the Treaty of Shimonoseki, signed in 1895. The treaty dictated to the Korean government a wide-ranging series of measures to prevent further domestic disturbances.

- Throughout this period, Russian influence was also on the rise in East Asia, and of course, Russian expansion was in direct conflict with the Japanese desire for expansion in the same region. In alliance with France and Germany, Russia forced Japan to return the Liaodong Peninsula to China. The Russians then promptly leased the territory back from China, a direct provocation to Japan.

- The secret Sino-Russian treaty signed in 1896 served as a defensive pact between China and Russia in case of Japanese aggression. Despite this, tensions between Japan and Russia continued to increase for the next decade, exploding into open conflict during the Russo-Japanese War of 1904–1905.

Japanese Occupation

- Contrary to expectations among diplomats and military experts around the world, the Japanese easily defeated the Russians in what has been called "the first great war of the 20th century."

- In the wake of this conflict, President Theodore Roosevelt quietly acquiesced to Japanese domination in Korea as part of a quid pro quo arrangement for Japan's recognition of U.S. hegemony in the Philippines.

- The treaty resulting from the Sino-Japanese war acknowledged Japan's right to take appropriate measures for the "guidance, control, and protection" of Korea. Not content with these arrangements, the

Japanese moved to bring Korea even more firmly under their yoke, dissolving the Korean army, installing a resident Japanese general of Korea, suspending Korean newspapers, and ultimately forcing the emperor to step down. The Chosen dynasty came to end on August 22, 1910.

- Japan officially annexed Korea as a colony and began a 35-year period of harsh colonial rule. During the occupation, the Japanese built up the Korean infrastructure but also attempted to eradicate many elements of Korean culture.

- After the outbreak of the Second Sino-Japanese War in 1937, followed by the beginning of World War II in 1939, Japan further stepped up its efforts to eradicate Korea as a unique cultural entity. The observance of virtually any aspect of Korean culture became illegal, and perhaps as many as 70,000 Korean cultural and historical artifacts were either destroyed or taken to Tokyo.

On August 22, 1910, Emperor Sunjong of Korea was forced to issue a proclamation in which he relinquished both his throne and his country, bringing an end to the Choson dynasty of Korea.

© Library of Congress, Prints and Photographs Division, LC-USZ62-80003.

- In the last phase of colonial rule, between 1941 and 1945, the Japanese found themselves increasingly distracted by fighting a war on several fronts. To help bolster its ranks, the Japanese imperial army had started accepting Koreans into the armed forces in 1938; after 1943, a general conscription law was introduced that resulted in thousands of Korean men being drafted into military service for the Japanese.

- At the same time, Korean resistance groups were fighting guerrilla warfare with the Japanese, with the assistance of the Chinese Communist Party. The leader of these anti-Japanese guerilla units was none other than Kim Il-Sung, founder of the Democratic People's Republic of North Korea! Tens of thousands of Koreans also joined the People's Liberation Army and fought the Japanese in China.

- The surrender of the Japanese on August 15, 1945, was a day of jubilation throughout Korea. But after 35 years, Japanese imperial rule had transformed the political ideologies and loyalties of the Korean people. As we will see, political tensions in Korea became mixed up with Cold War geopolitics to create the two Koreas—North and South—that continue to play a critical role in the 21st century.

Suggested Reading

Lee, *A New History of Korea*, chapters 8–12.

Palmer, *Korea and Christianity.*

Questions to Consider

1. Why did Choson Korea attempt to disengage from the world and return to isolationism?

2. What role did the Japanese play in Korean reengagement with the world?

Korea Choson—The Last Dynasty
Lecture 42—Transcript

Early in the 19th century, Western nations came knocking at the door of the hermit nation, as Korea was often described in Western newspapers, determined to establish contact with and a foothold in Korea for trade and other commercial purposes. English merchant and war ships began appearing off the coast in 1832 when the British East India Company ship the Lord Amherst arrived seeking trade. The Choson government was extremely wary of these foreign overtures and described the foreign vessels as "strange looking ships." In June, 1846, three French warships dropped anchor off the coast, left a letter to be forwarded to the Choson court protesting the government's persecution of French Catholic missionaries, and then departed. In April, 1854, two Russian warships sailed along the coast of Hamyong province and interfered with Korean commercial shipping, causing some injuries and deaths amongst the ships they encountered. This incident prompted the Choson government to issue a ban forbidding the people of Hamyong to have any contact with foreigners.

Twelve years later, in August, 1866, an American trading ship, the *General Sherman*, appeared off the coast and sailed brashly up the Taedong River to Pyongyang, where the captain asked permission to trade. Local officials refused the overtures to enter a trade relationship and, in fact, demanded that the *General Sherman* depart immediately. The Americans responded by taking a Choson official hostage and firing their guns into civilians on shore. Not content with this, the crew came ashore to plunder the town of Pyongyang and murdered seven Koreans in the process. In response, the governor of the province ordered his men to attack the ship; in the melee that followed, the *General Sherman* ran aground on a sandbar, the ship was burned to the ground, and the entire crew of 20 was killed.

The government later denied that this was an American vessel that had been destroyed, describing it simply as another of those aggressive "strange looking ships." Of course, the Korean people and the Choson government were only too aware of the fate that had befallen China through the Opium Wars and other clashes with the militarily far more powerful Europeans. This was the context in which the Choson government decided that its best hope of avoiding a similar fate was essentially to reject all Western overtures for trade and try and shut the foreigners out. As I also mentioned in the last lecture, since the 1830s, French missionaries had been actively pursuing converts in Korea, so it was inevitable that this foreign religion would also soon be targeted. Indeed, as Catholicism gained more ground amongst the peasants, the Choson government's attitude hardened until finally a fullscale campaign against Catholicism was launched in 1866. This turned into a bloodbath; by the time the persecution was over, nine French missionaries and perhaps 8,000 Koreans had been killed, or martyred as the Church claimed. Korea's doors were now as tightly closed to foreign ideology as they were to foreign trade and military contacts; but just as the Chinese had experienced, it ultimately proved impossible to keep the determined and well-armed foreigners out.

One of the French missionaries who'd managed to escape the persecution made his way to China, where he persuaded the commander of the French Asiatic Squadron to take punitive action against the Koreans. A fleet of seven warships entered Korean waters in October, 1866, two months after the destruction of the *General Sherman*. The French seized, pillaged, and looted the administrative center on Kanghwa Island; but a contingent of French military forces sent to the mainland was beaten back, and in the end the French squadron was forced to withdraw. This victory earned the jubilant Koreans a reprieve from foreign intervention for five years, until 1871. During that year, in response to the destruction of the *General Sherman* in 1866, the United States Asiatic Squadron was ordered to send a squadron of warships into Korean waters. As a result of the French incident five years earlier, the Choson government had worked hard to seriously strengthen Korea's coastal defenses; so when the U.S. warships tried to steam through the Kanghwa Straits between the island and the mainland, shore batteries opened fire. Shocked, the U.S. fleet decided not to engage and instead withdrew back to China.

The failure of these two attacks by two modern military fleets only strengthened further Korea's isolationist attitude and steely resolve to shut out foreign intervention. The government now did all it could to encourage uncompromising resistance amongst the people, and intellectuals like Yi Hang-no used a sophisticated Confucian argument with the Choson elites to support armed resistance should the foreigners show up again. The failure of the attacks was undoubtedly due, at least in part, to this very stubborn Korean resistance; but it was also partly due to the fact that Western powers were too preoccupied at the time to really press their military strength upon the Choson. But the Japanese turned out to be a very different matter indeed.

Having overthrown the Tokugawa shogunate in 1867 through a revolution known as the Meiji Restoration, events we'll follow in our next pair of lectures in our course, the leaders of Japan decided to adopt an increasingly aggressive attitude towards Korea. Part of the reason for this was the need to find an outlet for the energies of the samurai who, as we'll see, had been banned in Japan but who remained restive and discontented, a constant threat to the Meiji government's stability. But the Japanese were also looking for a market for their manufactured goods in the same way that European imperialist powers were using their colonies all around the world now as captive markets to sell their mass-produced, manufactured goods, products, of course, of the Industrial Revolution. A third reason for the heightened Japanese interest in Korea is that the Japanese government was also determined to try and stop the encroachment of the Russians into East Asian affairs. With these reasons in mind, it's no surprise that by 1873 Japanese leaders were publicly calling for an expedition against Korea.

This leads me to our second subject for this lecture: how Japanese aggression ignited a reversal of previous Korean isolationism and a decision to actively seek reengagement with the world. It was the Japanese military then, not any European or American force, which became the first foreign power to penetrate Korea's defensive wall. In 1875, the Japanese government provoked a naval incident as a pretext for this direct intervention. They followed this up by dispatching a powerful force of warships and soldiers that landed on the east coast of Kanghwa Island. Choson court officials couldn't resist these heavily armed Japanese forces, and they had little option other than to sign the Treaty of Kanghwa in 1876. This unequal treaty cleared the way for the increasing involvement of the Japanese in Korean affairs; and at the same time, it attempted to limit interference from China, which had, of course, historically claimed suzerainty over Korea for most of the previous 2,000 years.

The signing of this treaty produced a sea change in the attitude of the Choson government. Faced with the probability of ongoing aggressive Japanese intervention, the Choson now decided that it was probably in Korea's best interests to actively engage more closely with the rest of the world as a counter to this Japanese interference. The first result of this foreign policy sea change occurred in October, 1880, when the Choson sought to establish diplomatic relations with the United States of America. At the same time, the Koreans sent a study mission to China and to Japan with the express aim of learning more about modern weapons technology. In 1882, the Korean-American Treaty was signed and the Choson government hoped that this would discourage both Russian and Japanese aggression against Korea. Indeed, the treaty included a specific clause that implied that the United States would come to Korea's aid under a range of circumstances. The Choson king reportedly "danced for joy" when the first United States ambassador to Korea arrived in May, 1883, believing that the Americans would be the salvation of his country. Similar treaties with other foreign powers quickly followed: with Britain and Germany in 1883; Italy and Russia a year later, 1884; France in 1886; and even with the Austro-Hungarian Empire in 1889.

But these international outreach efforts sparked a real pushback from the conservative elements of Korean society, who preferred the old hermit nation approach. Some of these conservative Confucian elites became so outraged they demanded a reinstatement of an isolationist government; and this is, in fact, precisely what happened after a violent Soldier's Riot and other civil and military unrest broke out. But the victory for a return to reactionary isolationism was to be short lived, because both the Chinese and Japanese governments used this abrupt about face as an excuse to intensify their military interference in Korea.

With Japanese forces still stationed in parts of the peninsula since the signing of the Treaty of Kanghwa back in 1876, the Qing dynasty in China quickly dispatched its own force of 4,500 men to the peninsula in 1882. By August that year, the Chinese troops were firmly entrenched in Seoul. Eventually after something of a standoff, a treaty was signed that temporarily removed both the Chinese and the Japanese troops from Korea; and this allowed the Chinese to remain the major cultural influence at least on the country for the next decade, from 1885 through to 1894.

While this competition for Korea was being waged by the Japanese and the Chinese the Russians weren't idle and were also becoming increasingly involved in Korean affairs. The Korean king and queen became convinced of the advantages of this Russian interest because they saw the involvement of a third party as an effective means of balancing Chinese and Japanese influence. But this pro-Russian attitude immediately provoked suspicion and resentment within China and Japan, particularly after word of a secret treaty having been signed between Korea and Russia began to circulate. As a result of all this, by the late 19th century, the Korean court was deeply split into rival pro-Chinese, pro-Japanese, and pro-Russian factions. These tensions came to a dramatic and brutal head in 1895.

In that fateful year, the Japanese ambassador to Korea masterminded nothing less than the brutal assassination of the Choson Queen Min, who with her clan was vocally opposing the Japanese-supported politicians in court. The queen was attacked in her palace, dragged outside, and publicly hacked to death by Japanese thugs. This brutal attempt to squash opposition backfired, however. The Korean king immediately and publicly rejected Japan and the reform measures being demanded by the pro-Japanese lobby and turned instead for support to one of Japan's enemies: Russia. The king, in fact, fled to the Russian legation in Seoul to avoid Japanese plots against him and conducted the nation's business from there, protected by diplomatic immunity and by Russian armed forces.

All this led to the organization of a massive national campaign launched by political leaders and intellectuals to try and gain Korean independence from foreign control. Advocates now argued for reform in Korean politics and customs to try and bring them in line with Western practices, and it was in this atmosphere that the ancient and indigenous Korean writing system of Hangul finally gained widespread public acceptance. You'll remember that Hangul had been developed during the enlightened reign of King Sejong back in the mid-15th century as an indigenous alphabet and script explicitly designed to record the speech of everyday Koreans. But the system hadn't been widely used until this critical moment in Korean history, a moment in which nationalists were rejecting foreign intervention and demanding the advancement of indigenous Korean culture. In 1894, the first newspaper to use the Hangul writing system and the vernacular Korean language was published, and it rapidly attracted a growing audience. At the same time, under the influence of modern education being provided by Protestant mission schools, hundreds of young men started holding mass meetings on the streets demanding democratic reforms and an end to Russian and Japanese domination. Conservative and often pro-Japanese forces inside Korea responded by attacking the newspaper's offices and jailing reformist leaders in an attempt to suppress this reform movement.

In the midst of all this general chaos, a major peasant rebellion, the Tonghak Rebellion, broke out and blighted the country between 1894 and 1895; this was a rebellion that had major international repercussions. The peasant Tonghak army gained early victories and the uprising spread quickly from southwest to central Korea, menacing the capital of Seoul. The Korean court felt unable to cope with the rebels and asked China to send troops to help quell the rebellion. This request, interpreted, of course, by the Japanese government as a direct breach of the earlier treaty, gave the Japanese government the pretext it had been waiting for to dispatch troops to Korea, ostensibly to quell the rebellion but really to keep the Chinese forces out. Japan and China were soon at war.

The First Sino-Japanese War was fought between August, 1894 and April, 1895. After six months of continuous Japanese victories, the Qing government was forced to sue for peace, demonstrating not only the total failure of the Qing to modernize their military—and, of course, waste money intended for the purpose of building the navy on building the marble boat, as you'll remember—but it also showed that the balance of power in East Asia had clearly shifted now, for the first time really, from China to Japan. The victorious Japanese now established their complete hegemony over Korea via the Treaty of Shimonoseki, signed in 1895. This treaty dictated to the Korean government a wide-ranging series of measures to prevent further domestic disturbances. During the war and immediately afterwards, the Choson government passed a series of reforms, the Gabo Reforms, aimed at modernizing Korea along Japanese lines; you'll remember, we mentioned these in the context of the abolition of slavery in the last lecture. The reforms included the abolition of the hierarchical class system; the opening up of the exam system and government positions to all men of talent, regardless of class; and a decree that all official documents would now be written in Hangul, not Chinese.

Throughout this entire period, Russian influence was also on the rise in East Asia; and, of course, Russian expansion was in direct conflict with the Japanese desire for expansion in the same region of the world. In alliance with France and Germany, Russia forced Japan to return the Liaodong Peninsula to China, which Japan had seized during the First Sino-Japanese War. The Russians then promptly leased the territory back from China, and this, of course, was a direct provocation to Japan. This secret Sino-Russian treaty signed in 1896 also gave the Russians the right to build and operate the Chinese Eastern Railway across parts of Manchuria in the north, and this served as a link in the enormous Russian Trans-Siberian Railway complex to Vladivostok. The Treaty also served as a defensive pact between China and Russia in case of Japanese aggression. But despite this, tensions between Japan and Russia continued to increase for the next decade, exploding into open conflict during the Russo-Japanese War of 1904–1905.

Contrary to the expectations of all of the diplomats and military experts around the world, who frankly had no idea just how strong and modern the Japanese military had become, the Japanese easily defeated the Russians in a conflict some historians have called "'the first great war of the 20th century." In the wake of this conflict, U.S. President Theodore Roosevelt quietly acquiesced to Japanese domination in Korea as part of a quid pro quo arrangement for Japan's recognition of U.S. hegemony in the Philippines. The treaty resulting from the Sino-Japanese War acknowledged Japan's right to take appropriate measures for the "guidance, control, and protection" of Korea.

But not content with these arrangements, the Japanese moved to bring Korea even more firmly under their yoke. Following the signing of a new agreement forced upon the Koreans in 1907, Japan dissolved the Korean army; and in May, 1910, the Japanese Meiji government appointed General Terauchi Masatake as the new resident general of Korea. Masatake's first order was to dispatch 2,000 Japanese police to be stationed in Korea; his second was the suspension of all Korean newspapers. Finally, on August 22, 1910, Emperor Sunjong of Korea was forced to issue a proclamation in which he relinquished both his throne and his country, bringing to an end the Choson dynasty of Korea.

Japan had now officially annexed Korea as a colony, and a period of harsh colonial rule of Korea by Japan had begun. Korea was occupied and controlled by Japan for 35 long years, from 1910 to the surrender of Japan in August, 1945, at the end of the Second World War. During the occupation, the Japanese built up Korean infrastructure, modernizing the street and railroad systems, for example. Because of this, even today some Japanese historians try and argue that the Japanese occupation was good for Korea; I've heard these arguments promoted myself at conferences in East Asia. But at the same time, as Korean historians like to remind us, the Japanese ruled with an iron fist and attempted to eradicate many—some say all—elements of Korean culture. The Korean people were forced to adopt Japanese names now; they were forced to convert to Shintoism. They were also eventually forbidden to use Korean language altogether in schools and businesses.

Nine years after the initial occupation, a populist Independence Movement emerged in Korea in March, 1919, but it was brutally suppressed by Japanese troops. This crackdown ultimately led to the death of 7,000 protestors, to the maiming and imprisoning of tens of thousands more, and to the destruction of hundreds of churches, temples, schools, and private homes. The movement was actually inspired by U.S. President Woodrow Wilson's great post-First World War speech of 1919 in which, amongst other things, he demanded an end to colonial rule worldwide. But neither Wilson nor the U.S. government ever commented upon the Japanese repression of the independence movement.

The Japanese did build hundreds of schools in the first decade of its rule, and because of this hundreds of thousands of Korean students went to school for the first time. But there were two sets of schools, those for Koreans and those for Japanese; and only 5 percent of Korean students ever moved on past the elementary level. Eventually Japanese language was taught in all schools as the national language; Korean was only now a secondary language, and Korean history was taught with a strong Japanese interpretation of events. Because of these policies, a widespread fear emerged that the Japanese appeared intent on completely eradicating Korean culture; on destroying all

313

traditional elements that thousands of years of Korean history and a close relationship with China had created.

As this fear of cultural genocide spread, anti-Japanese uprisings intensified, and this led to a further strengthening of Japanese military rule in 1931. After the outbreak of the Second Sino-Japanese War in 1937, followed by the beginning of World War II in 1939, Japan further stepped up its efforts to eradicate Korea as a unique cultural entity; or at least, again, this is certainly how the Koreans saw it, and many Korean historians to this day continue to see it. The observance of virtually any aspect Korean culture now became illegal; worship at Shinto shrines was now made compulsory; school curriculum was more radically modified to eliminate teaching in the Korean language and the teaching of Korean history; and as well as use of the Korean language itself being more or less banned now, all Koreans were forced to adopt Japanese names.

But something else was going on at the same time: the large-scale disappearance of Korean historical and artistic artifacts. Indeed, modern Korean authorities have long been aware that something like 70,000 Korean cultural and historical artifacts were either destroyed or taken back by the to Tokyo during the occupation. This remains a source of serious tension between Japan and Korea, although a number of these stolen Korean treasures were recently returned by the Japanese government. In December, 2011, in fact, more than 1,000 royal archives and other historical artifacts were all flown back to Seoul from Tokyo. But even after this goodwill gesture, a study by South Korea's National Institute of Cultural Heritage estimates that still some 61,000 Korean cultural artifacts are probably being held in Japan.

In the last phase of colonial rule, between 1941 and 1945, during the Second World War, the Japanese found themselves increasingly distracted by fighting a war on several fronts. To help bolster their ranks, the Japanese imperial army had started accepting Koreans into their armed forces back in 1938; but after 1943, an increasingly desperate Japanese military introduced a general conscription law that resulted in thousands of Korean men being drafted into military service for the Japanese. But by far the greatest involuntary contribution Koreans made to the Japanese war effort was as forced laborers in the mines and factories of northern Korea, and of Manchuria back in Japan. Labor conscriptions were so severe that historians estimate that by 1944, close to 4 million people—which is about 16 percent of the total population of Korea—were living outside its borders as virtual slave workers. But let's not forget that at the same time, Korean resistance groups were fighting guerrilla warfare with the Japanese in Korea with the assistance of the Chinese Communist Party. The leader of these anti-Japanese guerilla units was none other that Kim Il-sung, founder of the Democratic People's Republic of North Korea. Tens of thousands of Koreans also joined the Peoples Liberation Army and fought the Japanese in China. As well as the huge numbers of men that were conscripted into Japan's military, around 200,000 girls and young women were also conscripted into sexual slavery, with the name "comfort women." Many of the surviving comfort women are still protesting today to the Japanese government for compensation today, as I'm sure you are aware, casting a continuing shadow over the bilateral relations between these two countries.

The surrender of the Japanese on August 15, 1945 was a day of jubilation throughout Korea. But as a result of three-and-a-half decades of Japanese colonial rule, Korean society in 1945 was a chaotic mix of old and new classes, ideologies, and, of course, political factions. Traditional Korean culture had been turned on its head by Japanese imperial rule, which had transformed the political ideologies and loyalties of the Korean people. On the left of the political spectrum were thousands of dedicated communists determined to transform Korea into a more egalitarian society. On the right were landlords, businessman, and many Japanese collaborators determined to preserve their privileged place in Korean society.

In the final few lectures of this course, as we try and wrap everything up, we'll see how these political tensions became mixed up with Cold War geopolitics to create the two Koreas, North and South, which continue to play such a critical role in the world of the 21st century.

Medieval Japan—Samurai and Shoguns
Lecture 43

W hen we were last in Japan, late in the 11th century, we saw that, despite the sophistication of the imperial Heian court, the Japanese countryside was in a state of decline. By the 12th century, the Minamoto clan had claimed the right to rule in the name of the Heian emperor, but they also installed a shogun to take command of the state. The Minamoto established the seat of government at Kamakura and went on to rule Japan for the next four centuries. Thus began the so-called medieval period of Japan's history, which we will explore in this lecture by considering two distinct shogunate eras: the Kamakura and Muromachi shogunates (1185–1465) and the Tokugawa shogunate (1600–1868).

The Kamakura Shogunate

- In 1185, the powerful leader of the Minamoto clan (which instituted the Kamakura shogunate), Yoritomo, forced the emperor to grant him the title of shogun and became supreme military and political commander of Japan.

- Although many historians are uncomfortable applying the term "feudal" to Japanese history, the Kamakura shogunate did introduce a quasi-feudal system. That is, both the Kamakura and subsequent Muromachi shogunates were characterized by a decentralized political and economic system in which provincial lords exercised great power in local regions. It was in this context that the mounted warrior known as the samurai began to play a distinctive and major role in Japanese life.
    - o The origins of the samurai can be traced back to reforms introduced in the 8th century, whereby one in every three or four males was drafted into the military, part of an attempt by the imperial government to establish a Chinese-style professional military.

- These soldiers were expected to provide their own weapons and, in return, were exempted from taxes.

- As part of the same reforms, 12 new classes of bureaucrats were established; those of the sixth class and below were called samurai, which comes from a Chinese word meaning "those who serve the nobility."

- Over the centuries that followed, the term "samurai" was gradually applied to military men, particularly to those warriors who became associated with the powerful clans.

- After the establishment of the Kamakura shogunate, the samurai were given increasing responsibilities by the shogun, until they effectively became the ruling class of medieval Japan.

The Way of the Warrior

- During the Kamakura shogunate, the more refined forms of behavior associated with the samurai in Western consciousness began to appear, in a way not unlike the evolution of chivalry among European knights.
  - It was during a period of violent disturbances in medieval Europe that the Christian church began to form a closer relationship with secular royalty and nobility for protection. This relationship improved the behavior of the nobility and their knights in that it added Christian values to the knightly code of chivalry.

  - The samurai began without any code of chivalry, but this changed and evolved until these warriors attained the level of the military and ethical behavior also being championed by European knights.

  - Undoubtedly, the samurai were professional warriors, skilled in the martial arts and in the use of the bow and arrow and the sword. But they also subscribed to the philosophy of Bushido—the "Way of the Warrior"—not only because it emphasized superb military skills, but because it was seen as a way of attaining great honor.

- o Bushido demanded that the samurai demonstrate an extraordinary degree of loyalty to one another, to their local overlord (*daimyo*), and, ultimately, to the powerless but nonetheless still-respected emperor.

- Interestingly, we know of many samurai women, who were expected to endure the same Spartan hardships as their male consorts and to fight to the death with their husbands. In fact, Japanese elite woman had a long history of learning martial arts and participating in battles well before the Kamakura shogunate.

- The popular image of the samurai suggests that they had no fear of death; they would enter any battle, no matter the odds, because to die in battle would bring honor to one's family and one's lord. However, we know of some cowardly, disloyal, and treacherous samurai who fell far short of the idealized image.

Some historians argue that the early samurai were more like mercenaries and robbers than the elite warriors they became under the Kamakura shogunate.

- Although the samurai were skilled in battle formations and combined assaults, they also sought the opportunity to fight alone,

one on one, rather than as part of a contingent. When a samurai killed his opponent, he often severed the head, which he took back to his base after battle as proof of his victory.

- The only option open to a defeated samurai was death on the battlefield or by a form of ritual suicide called *seppuku* ("stomach cutting"), or disembowelment. This form of suicide was performed under various circumstances: to avoid the dishonor of surrender or capture in battle and to atone for a misdeed or unworthy act.

Mongol Invasions and Civil War

- In 1274 and again in 1281, the Kamakura shogunate and its samurai successfully defended Japan from the Mongols, although the shogunate was weakened in the process. Both invasions failed as much because of the efforts of Mother Nature as the military prowess of the defenders. The sword-wielding samurai were really no match for the invaders, who were armed with superior fighting technology and tactics.

- Despite their fear of the sea, the Mongols landed on the shores of Kyushu after occupying Tsushima and other nearby islands, but gathering typhoon storms called *kamikaze* ("divine winds") forced the Mongols to leave. As we know, the term *kamikaze* was revived nearly 700 years later by suicide-mission fighter pilots in the last stages of World War II.

- The decades following the attempted Mongol invasions saw intermittent civil war in Japan as factions fought the new Muromachi shogunate government, which had replaced the weakened Kamaukura shogun, ostensibly on behalf of the emperor. This increasing fragmentation led in 1467 to full-scale civil war, which lasted more or less for the next century.

- Despite the bitter conflict, the Japanese economy grew quickly after Portuguese missionaries and merchants, followed by other European traders, started arriving in the early 16th century. Thereafter, increasing numbers of European missionaries began to arrive, and by 1600, Japan was known by, and open to, the outside world. That openness ended, however, with the advent of the Tokugawa shogunate, which became determined to return Japan to isolation.

The Tokugawa Shogunate

- Late in the 16th century, a series of leaders in Japan attempted to bring an end to Japan's own "Warring States" era. In 1600, one of these leaders, Tokugawa Ieyasu, established a military government known as the Tokugawa *bakufu* ("tent government"). This temporary government ended up ruling Japan for more than 250 years.

- The principal aim of the Tokugawa was to prevent a return to civil war, which meant curtailing the power of the powerful territorial lords, the *daimyo*. The shoguns also attempted to tightly control relations between Japan and the outside world.

- Once the *daimyo* were under control, political stability returned to Japan, which allowed the Tokugawa to focus on economic growth. Production of rice, cotton, and silk began to increase, and many villages were able to move away from subsistence to market farming for the first time in Japan's history.

- Increased food production led, in turn, to population growth; demographers estimate that during the 17th century, the population of Japan rose to 29 million. But the fear of overstraining resources caused many families to limit population growth, mostly through the practice of infanticide.

Tokugawa Society and Culture

- These economic and demographic developments allowed the Tokugawa to preside over a period of marked social change in Japan. Many of the elites fell into financial difficulty, while merchants became increasingly wealthy and powerful.

- Despite this, Confucianism and Chinese language and culture remained the dominant focus of elite culture throughout the Tokugawa shogunate. At the same time, however, some scholars tried to establish a more distinctive Japanese voice and style in their work. During the 18th century, the "native learning" school publicly scorned both Neo-Confucianism and even Buddhism as alien cultural imports, emphasizing Japanese folk traditions and Shintoism instead. A strong element of nationalism and even xenophobia marked this movement.

- The emergence of a prosperous merchant class led to the development of a vibrant urban culture. In such cities as Kyoto, Edo, and Osaka, Japanese entertainers catered to a sophisticated middle class. At the heart of Tokugawa urban culture were the floating palaces—vast entertainment and pleasure emporiums that contained teahouses, brothels, and public baths. New developments also arose in fiction and theater, including Kabuki and Bunraku.

- From the mid-16th century on, Jesuit missionaries became increasingly vigorous in their conversion efforts in Japan, and by 1615, there were an estimated 300,000 Christians in Japan. But because several *daimyo* had been converted, the Tokugawa sought to restrict Jesuit activities for fear they might allow the *daimyo* to rebuild their former lucrative relationships with European merchants. In a series of violent crackdowns, European Christians were tortured and executed by the government.

Turmoil in the 19th Century

- By the early 19th century, Japanese society was in turmoil. A series of agricultural crises occurred, and harsh taxation led to a general economic crisis and starvation among rural people. Impoverished migrants flocked to the cities, and as the price of food rose, the urban poor also experienced extreme poverty. Even the samurai and *daimyo* faced hardship as they fell into debt to the expanding merchant class.

- The Tokugawa government responded by passing a series of conservative reforms between 1841 and 1843, which included canceling samurai debt and forcing peasants back to the land to grow rice, but the reforms failed.

- Like its East Asian neighbors in the mid-19th century, Japan also came under foreign pressure, particularly from the United States, which was seeking ports for its Pacific merchant and whaling fleets.

- When Japan refused these requests, in 1853 and again in 1854, a U.S. naval squadron under Commodore Matthew Perry trained its guns on the Tokugawa capital and demanded that the shogun sign a treaty with the United States and open Japanese ports to commercial relations. The shogun had no alternative but to agree, and Japan was forced to sign the first of a series of unequal treaties.

- Both the emperor and the *daimyo* bitterly resented the fact that the shogun had signed the treaties. Domestic opposition to the Tokugawa grew rapidly, particularly among the samurai. The Tokugawa responded by imprisoning their samurai critics, but in a brief civil war, opposition armies trained by foreign experts and armed with Western weapons put so much pressure on the Tokugawa that the shogun resigned.

- In January 1868, the young emperor Meiji took power, and as we will see in the next lecture, he went on to rule successfully until 1912.

Suggested Reading

Duus, *Feudalism in Japan.*

Schirokauer et al., *A Brief History of Chinese and Japanese Civilizations,* chapters 11–13.

Varley, *Imperial Restoration in Medieval Japan.*

1. How useful and accurate is the word "feudalism" in describing the political and social organization of Japan during its "medieval period"?

2. What does the famous novel *The Life of a Man Who Lived for Love* tell us about the sophisticated urban lifestyle followed by many Japanese during the Tokugawa period?

Medieval Japan—Samurai and Shoguns
Lecture 43—Transcript

Hello, and welcome to this lecture, the first of a pair of lectures on Japanese history and culture, and Japan's continuing influence on the evolution of Eastern civilization between the 12th and 20th centuries.

When we were last in Japan, we saw how, late in the 11th century, despite the sophistication of life and culture in the Imperial Heian court, the Japanese countryside was in a state of decline. The equal-field system, designed to equitably distribute land to the peasants and the landlords, and as we've seen one of the most ancient economic and social systems of all Eastern civilization, began to fall apart. It was the aristocratic clans that now accumulated most of the land for themselves in a competitive territory grab, backed by their own powerful armies. By the 12th century, the two most powerful clans of all, the Taira and the Minamoto, were engaged in open war, from which, in 1185, the Minamoto emerged victorious.

They claimed the right to rule in the name of the Heian emperor, but they also quickly installed a shogun, or military governor, to take command of the state. The outcome of this new system was that it was the shogun who now exercised real power in Japan, although he was careful to always pay due ceremonial deference to the hereditary emperor. The Minamoto established the new seat of their government at Kamakura, and went on to rule Japan for the next several centuries. Kamakura today is a small regional town about 30 miles south-southwest of Tokyo. It was Yoritomo, the leader of the victorious Minamoto clan in 1185, who chose Kamakura to be the seat of the new government because this was the location of his ancestral family home. Just like the Fujiwara clan that had dominated politics during the late Heian period, the Minamoto didn't seek to abolish imperial authority, but simply claimed the right to rule in the name of the emperor, who was in reality powerless and thus could do nothing to dispute this. The emperor and his imperial court remained at Kyoto, and the shogun ruled now from Kamakura.

Thus began the so-called medieval period of Japan's history, which I would like to explore with you today by considering two distinct shogunate eras. The first of these is the era of the Kamakura and succeeding Muromachi shogunates, a period of almost 300 years from 1185 through to 1465. The second is the era of Tokugawa shogunate, which ruled Japan from Edo Castle near Tokyo between 1600 and 1868, when they were replaced by the Meiji government, beginning a period that historians have called ever since the Meiji Restoration. In between the end of the Muromachi in 1465 and the establishment of the Tokugawa in 1600, Japan essentially experienced its own Warring States era.

Western historians sometimes refer to the Kamakura and Muromachi shogunates as Japan's medieval period; and, indeed, I used that phrase just a moment ago. But the use of the label "medieval Japan," and for that matter the phrase "classical Japan," which is sometimes applied to the Nara and Heian periods, is rejected by other historians because it seems to apply a European chronological periodization scheme to a uniquely East Asian historical process. Those historians who do use the descriptor "medieval" justify this by applying the strict Latin meaning of the word *medieval*, literally "middle age." They see medieval Japan as a middle era falling between the Nara and Heian imperial periods that, as we've seen, were dominated by Chinese cultural influence, and the modern age instigated by the Tokugawa dynasty in the 17th century, which began to introduce a more Western-style centralized and unified government to Japan. Some historians also refer to the medieval period as "feudal"; but the term "decentered" is more commonly used today because "feudalism" also has so many specific and particular associations with European history. What we can say with certainty is that during this medieval period, Japanese culture took on increasingly distinctive characteristics that differentiated it more and more from that of Korea and China. Because of this, many of the foundations of Eastern civilization—including ancient ideas about the mechanism of governance, political philosophy, social structures, and attitudes towards women—were modified and transformed by Japanese shogunate politics and culture.

To the Kamakura shogunate first, which lasted from 1185–1333. The victorious Minamoto clan, which instituted the Kamakura shogunate, is widely celebrated in Japanese books, movies, and TV today. The powerful leader Yoritomo forced the emperor to grant him the title of shogun, and he became supreme military and political commander of Japan. Although the shoguns ruled from Kamakura, they were careful to pay utmost respect to the emperor. Although many historians are uncomfortable applying the term "feudal" to Japanese history, the Kamakura shogunate did introduce a quasi-feudal system; that is, both the Kamakura and subsequent Muromachi shogunates were characterized by a decentralized political and economic system in which provincial lords exercised great power in all the local regions where they controlled the land and the economy. They had little to no respect for the refined conduct that had prevailed at the Chinese-style Heian court; rather, they valued military talent and discipline above courtesy and etiquette. It was in this political and ideological context that the mounted warrior known as the samurai began to play a distinctive and major role in Japanese life.

The origins of the samurai can be traced back to reforms introduced back in the eight century, whereby one in every three or four males were drafted into the military, part of an attempt by the imperial government to establish a Chinese-style professional military force. These soldiers were expected to provide their own weapons, and in return were exempted from taxes. As part of the same series of reforms, 12 new classes of bureaucrats were also established; those of the 6th class and below were called "samurai," which comes from a Chinese word and means "those who serve the nobility." Over the centuries that followed, the term "samurai" was gradually applied to military men, particularly to those warriors who became associated with the powerful clans. Some historians argue that these early samurai were more like mercenaries and robbers, and that until the 14th century it would be more appropriate to describe them as violent mobsters rather than elite warriors.

After the establishment of the Kamakura shogunate, the samurai were given more and more responsibilities by the shogun until they effectively became the ruling class of medieval Japan. It was now that the more refined forms of behavior associated with the samurai in Western consciousness began to appear in a way not unlike the evolution of chivalry amongst European knights. In fact, if I can digress into European history for just a moment, I think there's an interesting comparison to be made here. It was during a period of violent disturbances in medieval Europe—including the invasions by Vikings, Saracens, Magyars, and others—that the Christian church began to form a closer relationship with secular royalty and nobility for protection. It was this relationship that improved the behavior of the nobility and their knights, in that it added Christian values to the knightly code of chivalry. During the early Middle Ages in Europe, the only code of conduct knights accepted was to maintain their military virtue, their prowess in combat, their courage, and their loyalty to each other and their lord. But later chivalry added Christian values and images—the search for the Holy Grail is an obvious example—and also stressed the reverence and protection of women. The samurai in Japan began without any code of chivalry whatsoever, but this also changed and evolved until it attained the level of the military and ethical behavior also being championed by European knights.

Undoubtedly, the samurai were professional warriors; they were skilled in the martial arts and in the use of the bow and arrow and the sword; and, of course, they were also great horsemen. But they also subscribed to the philosophy of Bushido, the "Way of the Warrior," not only because it emphasized superb military skills, but because it was seen as a way of attaining great honor. Bushido demanded that the samurai demonstrate an extraordinary degree of loyalty to each other, to their local overlord known as the *daimyo*, and ultimately to the powerless but nonetheless still respected emperor. In the end, the samurai became, in the main, trustworthy and honest. The same can be said of samurai women, by the way; we know of many who were expected to endure the same Spartan hardships as their male consorts and to fight to the death with their husbands. Japanese elite woman actually had a long history of learning martial arts and participating in battles well before this Kamakura shogunate period; but between the 12th and 19th centuries, many young women of the samurai class became masters of the sword and the *naginata*, a blade attached to a long staff, and rode out to battle with their husbands.

In theory, all samurai lived frugal lives with no apparent interest in riches or material things; they were interested only in military prowess and honor. The popular image of the samurai suggests that they had no fear of death; they would enter any battle no matter the odds because to die in battle would only bring honor to one's family and one's lord. But we do know of some cowardly, disloyal, and treacherous samurai in history who fell far short of this idealized image. Although the samurai were skilled in battle formations and combined assaults, they also sought the opportunity to fight alone, one-on-one, rather than as part of a contingent. An individual samurai, superbly armed and uniformed, would call out his family's name, rank, and accomplishments, seeking an opponent with similar rank to do battle. When the samurai killed his opponent, he often severed his head, which he took back to his base after battle to show proof of his victory. The heads of generals and those of other high ranks were transported back to the capital at Kamakura and displayed there for the officials, for the shogun, to see.

The only way out for a defeated samurai was death on the battlefield or death by a form of ritual suicide called *seppuku*. *Seppuku*, which literally means "stomach cutting," is also known in popular Western culture as *hara-kari*. The first recorded instance of *seppuku* was in 1180 when samurai Yorimasa of the Minamoto clan disemboweled himself after the Battle of Uji rather than suffer the shame of surrender or of falling into enemy hands. *Seppuku* quickly became a fundamental tenet of the samurai Code of Bushido. A samurai would stab a knife or razor-sharp sword into his abdomen and then slowly cut his own stomach open. After the disembowelment, when the samurai was on the brink of death, a colleague would slice off his head. This form of suicide was performed under various circumstances; obviously to avoid the dishonor of surrender or capture in battle, but also to atone for a misdeed or any unworthy act. The bottom line is that a samurai would rather kill himself than bring shame and disgrace to his family name or his *daimyo*.

In 1274, and again seven years later in 1281, the Kamakura shogunate and their samurai successfully defended Japan from the Mongols, although the shogunate was weakened in the process. Both invasions failed as much because of the efforts of Mother Nature as to the military prowess of the defenders. To be absolutely honest, the sword-wielding samurai of Japan were no match for the invaders, who were armed with gunpowder cannons and other superior fighting technology and tactics. Despite their very real fear of the sea, the Mongols did succeed in landing on the shores of Kyushu Island after occupying Tsushima Island and other nearby islands on their way there; but gathering typhoon storms called *kamikaze* or the "divine winds" forced the Mongols to pack up, leave, and head back to Korea. So glorious and significant was this defeat of the Mongols that the term *kamikaze* remained in popular usage and was, of course, revived and used nearly 700 years later by suicide fighter pilots in the last stages of the Second World War, as we'll see in our next lecture.

The decades following the attempted Mongol invasions saw intermittent civil war break out in Japan as factions fought the new Muromachi shogunate government, which had replaced the weakened Kamakura shogun ostensibly on behalf of the emperor. This increasing fragmentation of Japan led in 1467 to full-scale civil war that lasted more or less for the next century. Despite the bitter conflict, the Japanese economy grew quickly after Portuguese missionaries and then merchants arrived, followed by other European traders; they started arriving in the early 16th century. The Portuguese traders quickly transformed the small fishing village of Nagasaki into one of the largest ports in Asia. Before the long, the Spanish had made their own merchant port at Hirado, the English at Nagoya, and the Dutch on Kyushu. Thereafter, increasing numbers of European missionaries began to arrive, particularly our friends the Jesuits, and by 1600 Japan was known by and was very open to the outside world. But all that ended with the advent of the Tokugawa shogunate, which became determined to return Japan to isolation. Let me outline the circumstances for you in the second part of this lecture, which focuses on the period from 1600 through to 1868.

Late in the 16th century, a series of leaders in Japan attempted to bring an end to Japan's long warring states era. In 1600, one of these leaders, a man called Tokugawa Ieyasu who ended up ruling Japan as shogun from 1600–1616, established a new military government known as the Tokugawa *bakufu*, a word that literally means the "tent government" because the Tokugawa *bakufu* was only supposed to be temporary. But this temporary tent government ended up ruling Japan for more than 250 years, from 1600 through to 1868. The principal aim of the Tokugawa was to prevent a return to civil war, which meant curtailing the power of the powerful territorial lords, the *daimyo*. By this stage, each *daimyo* had their own lands, their own military forces (the samurai, of course); they had independent courts and schools; they were even printing their own money. Many *daimyo* had also established close relationships with European traders who helped them financially and taught them how to make and use gunpowder weapons.

From the castle town of Edo, again near modern Tokyo, the Tokugawa shogun used various policies to try and reduce the power of these regional lords, the *daimyo*. Very similar to what we've observed in the foreign policies of both China and Korea during this same period, the shoguns also attempted to tightly control relations between Japan and the outside world. In the 1630s, a series of laws were passed that restricted Japanese relations with foreigners, and even forbade Japanese from going abroad under pain of death. Haven't we seen similar measures passed by governments in Korea and China around the same time? The policy did allow some closely controlled trade to continue and also permitted some Chinese and Dutch merchants to continue to operate in Nagasaki, so Japan was never completely isolated.

Once the *daimyo* were somewhat under control, political stability returned to Japan, and this allowed the Tokugawa to focus on economic growth. Production of rice, cotton, and silk began to increase, and this meant that many villages were able to move away from subsistence to market farming really for the first time in Japan's long history. Increased food production led in turn to population growth; demographers estimate that during the 17th century, the population of Japan rose by 33 percent to 29 million. But the fear of overstraining resources caused many families to limit population growth, mostly through a practice of infanticide, which was euphemistically called "thinning out the rice shoots."

These various economic and demographic developments allowed the Tokugawa to preside over a period of marked social change in Japan. The old Confucian order had ranked the ruling elites—that is, the *daimyo* and the samurai—as the most privileged class, followed by peasants, the artisans, and the merchants at the bottom. But as the *daimyo* and the samurai lost their roles in a more peaceful Japan, many fell into financial difficulty. At the same time, merchants became increasingly wealthy and powerful; and cities and ports also began to flourish—Edo, for example, had a population of 1 million by 1700—and it was the merchants who now controlled most of this new urban wealth.

Despite this, Confucianism and Chinese language and culture did remain the dominant focus of elite culture throughout the Tokugawa shogunate period. Indeed, even as late as the 19th century, elite Japanese scholars were still writing their philosophical, legal, and religious dissertations in classical Chinese. The common people also continued to embrace Buddhism, modified as we saw in an earlier lecture by Shintoism; but at the same time, some scholars were trying to establish a more distinctive Japanese voice and style in their work. During the 18th century in particular, the so-called "native learning" school publicly scorned both Neo-Confucianism and even Buddhism now as alien cultural imports. They emphasized instead the importance of Japanese folk traditions and the indigenous Shinto religion. Undoubtedly, there was a strong element of nationalism, even xenophobia in this native learning movement. Many members of the native learning camp argued that Japanese culture was superior to all others and they sought to glorify some abstract notion of ancient and "pure" Japanese culture, before it had been polluted by Chinese and other foreign influences.

The emergence of this prosperous merchant class also led to the development of a vibrant popular urban culture. In cities like Kyoto, Edo, and Osaka, Japanese entertainers now catered for a very sophisticated middle class. At the heart of the Tokugawa urban culture were the floating palaces. These were vast entertainment and pleasure emporiums that contained tea houses, brothels, and public baths. Entertainment here was secular and satirical, often ridiculing the pompous and ceremonial proceedings of the government. This in turn led to new developments in prose fiction and theater. One example: The prolific poet Ihara Saikaku, who lived between 1642 and 1693, helped create a new genre of prose fiction called "the books of the floating world." In his most famous book *The Life of a Man Who Lived for Love*, Ihara unfolds the experiences of urban men who devote their lives to a quest for sexual pleasure. This is a book about erotic love, not aesthetic, laid out clearly in a series of short episodic stories. His novels appealed to the modern, literate urban resident who had no time or interest in dense Neo-Confucian texts.

During the 17th century, two new forms of drama also became popular in Tokugawa cities. One of these was Kabuki, which consisted of several acts of lively and often bawdy skits, and was delivered using a form of highly stylized acting combined with lyric singing, with dancing, and with very modern and often abstract set designs. The other form of new popular theater was Bunraku, puppet theater, in which the storytellers unfolded a drama by using puppets. With three operators, the puppets could act out the most subtle and intricate of movements.

From the mid-16th century on, Jesuit missionaries became increasingly vigorous in their conversion efforts in Japan, and by 1615 there were an estimated 300,000 Christians in Japan. But because several of the *daimyo* had been converted, the Tokugawa was concerned to try and restrict Jesuit activities for fear that they might allow the *daimyo* to rebuild their former lucrative relationships with European merchants. In a series of violent crackdowns very similar to what we saw happening in Choson Korea, European Christians were tortured and executed by the government. Faced with martyrdom, some missionaries abandoned their faith altogether and became Buddhists, like the Portuguese Jesuit Cristovao Ferreira, who after five hours of brutal torture renounced Christianity, changed his name to Sawano Chuan, and became one of the so-called "fallen priests." Because of these persecutions, by the late 17th century, tens of thousands of Japanese Christians were dead, and thereafter Christianity survived only as an underground sect in Japan.

By the early 19th century, Japanese society was in turmoil. A series of agricultural crises occurred, and harsh taxation led to a general economic crisis and even starvation amongst the rural people. Impoverished migrants now flocked to the cities, and as the price of food rose, the urban poor also experienced extreme poverty and destitution. Even the samurai and the *daimyo* faced hardship as they fell into debt to the wealthy and still expanding merchant class. The Tokugawa government responded to all this by passing a series of conservative reforms between 1841 and 1843, which included cancelling samurai debt and also forcing the peasants back to the land to grow rice; but the reforms all failed.

Like its East Asian neighbors in the mid-19th century, Japan also came under foreign pressure, particularly from the United States, which was seeking ports for its Pacific merchant and whaling fleets. When Japan refused these requests in 1853 and again the following year, a U.S. naval squadron under Commodore Perry trained his guns on the Tokugawa capital and demanded that the shogun sign a treaty with the U.S. and open Japanese ports to commercial relations. The shogun had no alternative but to agree, and Japan was forced to sign the first of a series of unequal treaties like their contemporaries the Qing dynasty in China. This in turn led to a domestic political crisis: Both the emperor and the *daimyo* bitterly resented the fact that the shogun had signed these treaties. Domestic opposition to the Tokugawa grew rapidly, particularly amongst the samurai. The Tokugawa responded by imprisoning their samurai critics; but in a brief civil war, opposition armies trained by foreign experts and armed with Western weapons put so much pressure on the Tokugawa that the shogun resigned. In January, 1868, the young Emperor Meiji took power; and as we'll see next time, he went on rule very successfully for 44 years, until 1912.

If I can sum up this lecture: Through this long "medieval period" of Japanese history, the samurai and the *daimyo* had effectively functioned as the ruling class of Japan, although the first phase of this era degenerated into civil war in the 16th century. But the Tokugawa were able to effectively unify Japan under their leadership, and for a time warfare disappeared and urban life flourished. Late in the Tokugawa era, the government became desperate to modernize and adopt a Western way of political and economic life. This meant that there was no longer any need for the samurai, who were now seen as an anachronism; an embarrassing relic from a bygone era. The samurai and their way of life were officially abolished in the early 1870s, events described in a movie many of you may have seen, *The Last Samurai*. Ultimately, both the samurai and the *daimyo* went the way of the Tokugawa: to extinction.

Next time, we bring our account of Japanese history and culture up to the mid-20th century. I'll see you soon.

Tokugawa and Meiji Japan
Lecture 44

I n the last lecture, we saw that by forcing the Tokugawa shogun to sign an unequal treaty in 1854, the United States provoked a political crisis in Japan. Ultimately, the shogun was forced to resign, and in January 1868, the young emperor Meiji took power, ushering in an era of Japanese history known as the Meiji Restoration. As we will see, the Meiji era led to the complete political, economic, and social reorganization of Japan and was responsible for its dramatic transformation into a modern global military and industrial power. We will look at three aspects of this era: the Meiji Restoration itself, the period of imperialism in Japan, and Japan's role in World War II.

The Meiji Restoration

- The Meiji Restoration brought an end to a series of military governments that had dominated Japan since the Kamakura shogun first claimed power in 1185. Determined to gain equality with foreign powers, a conservative coalition of *daimyo*, nobles, and samurai sought to study and copy the industrial policies of the West.

- In a later stage of modernization, the Meiji government eliminated the old feudal order by removing the *daimyo* from power and abolishing the samurai. In 1889, a new constitution was proclaimed, establishing a constitutional monarchy with a bicameral legislature (the Diet).

- This rapid reorganization of the political structure demonstrates just how determined the Meiji were to cast off the traditional trappings of Chinese-style dynastic government and the semi-feudal structure that had dominated Japan's long middle ages.

- According to the new Western-style constitution proclaimed by the Meiji, the emperor, powerless for centuries, now commanded the armed forces, named the prime minister, appointed the cabinet, and had the right to dissolve the Diet.

After the resignation of the Tokugawa shogun, the new emperor took the name Meiji, meaning "enlightened rule."

- The Meiji then created a modern transport, communication, and educational infrastructure along Western lines and removed all barriers to internal trade. Universities were created to provide advanced technical education. Most enterprises were private, but the government controlled all military industries and did all it could to stimulate industrial development.

  o In the 1880s, the government sold most of the remaining industries under its control to private investors and corporations. This move concentrated economic power in the hands of a small group of powerful capitalist enterprises known as the *zaibatsu*, which literally translates as "wealthy clique."

  o *Zaibatsu* were the equivalent of cartels or trusts and were usually organized around a single family or clan. The four primary *zaibatsu* during this period were Mitsui, Mitsubishi, Sumitomo, and Yasuda.

  o During the first half of the 20th century, the *zaibatsu* grew massively large and wealthy, but they were dissolved by the Allied powers after World War II. In the 1950s, new enterprise groups emerged, many created by companies that had formerly been part of the big four *zaibatsu*.

- By the early 20th century, Japan had joined the ranks of the major industrial powers, but this rapid economic development came at a brutal cost for the peasants, who produced 90 percent of all government revenues during the reform stage and, thus, suffered from an appalling tax burden. Peasant uprisings broke out in 1883 and 1884 and were ruthlessly crushed, as was a growing labor union movement in 1901.

- Still, these radical and painful reforms worked; by 1902, Meiji Japan was strong enough to sign an alliance of equal power with Britain.

Military Ascendance

- As we have seen, Japan displayed its newfound military prowess with rapid victories over China in 1895 and Russia in 1905. These victories were mostly the result of Japan's ability to gain access to modern military technology.
  - When an anti-foreign rebellion broke out in Korea in 1893, the Qing sent a Chinese army to restore order. Because the Meiji government was unwilling to recognize Chinese control over a land so close to Japan, it declared war on China in August 1894 and forced Qing armies out of Korea.

  - The easy Japanese victory startled other foreign powers, especially Russia, which also had ambitions for expansion in East Asia. In 1904, war broke out between Japan and Russia, and the following year, the Japanese navy destroyed the Russian Baltic Fleet. Clearly, Japan had transformed itself into one of the major military and industrial powers of the globe.

- When the First World War broke out in 1914, Japan entered the war on the side of the Allies. It quickly demanded that Germany hand over its leased territories in China to Japan without compensation and that all German warships withdraw from Chinese waters. The Japanese then took control of numerous German possessions in East Asia and the Pacific.

- With the Allies preoccupied by the fighting in Europe, the Japanese also took the opportunity to present a charter of 21 secret demands to the new republican government in China. The Chinese had little option but to accede to some of these demands, and only British support for the Chinese government prevented total capitulation.

- By the end of the Great War in 1918, the Japanese were poised to become not just a leading economic and military force but also a major imperial power.

The Great Depression in Japan
- Throughout the 1920s, Japan's economy surged, but this moment of prosperity was short-lived. Japan, like much of the developed world, suffered badly during the Great Depression.

- The Japanese economy was by now greatly dependent on U.S. markets to sell its manufactured goods, and as demand in the United States fell sharply, unemployment skyrocketed in all export sectors in Japan. By the early 1930s, a frustrated public blamed the government for continuing economic problems.

- Right-wing groups called for an end to party rule, and xenophobic nationalists demanded the preservation of unique Japanese cultural elements and the eradication of all Western influences.

Japanese Imperialism
- Those politicians who supported Japan's continuing role in the international industrial-capitalist system faced increasing opposition from those who favored a militaristic vision of Japan as the dominant imperial power of East Asia.
    - The militarist faction set its sights on China, arguing that political instability there made that vast country an inviting target for Japanese expansion.

    - The nationalists focused particularly on Manchuria, arguing that Japan needed to protect its considerable interests there from the Chinese.

337

- o On the night of September 18, 1931, Japan's military used a staged pretext to launch a military invasion of the region. By 1932, Japanese troops were in control of all of Manchuria.

- In response to the invasion, the leader of the Chinese Guomindang, Chiang Kai-shek, appealed to the League of Nations for assistance to help stop Japanese aggression. The League eventually called for the removal of troops, but the Japanese responded by leaving the League.

- The Japanese military embarked on a series of conquests in East Asia, determined to create an empire. In doing so, they helped spark World War II.

Lead-Up to Global War
- The world's second global conflict really began, not with the Nazi invasion of Poland in September 1939, but some eight years earlier, with Japan's attacks on China in the 1930s. The Japanese conquest of Manchuria between 1931 and 1932 was the first step in a revisionist process of aggressive expansionism that more accurately marks the beginning of the Second World War.

- By the early 1930s, it was clear to the world that civilian politicians in Japan had lost control of the government and that militarists and imperialists were now in charge. Following Japan's withdrawal from the League of Nations, it had no impediment to a continuation of its ultranationalist and pro-military expansionist policy.

- The Japanese government launched a full-scale invasion of China in 1937. After the Battle of Marco Polo Bridge, Japanese troops quickly took control of Beijing and then moved south toward Shanghai and the Nationalist capital of Nanjing. By December 1937, Nanjing and Shanghai had both fallen, and for the next six months, the Japanese forces won repeated victories.

- China became the first nation to experience the horrors of World War II: Chinese civilians suffered death and destruction on a massive scale; tens of thousands of citizens in Shanghai alone died from Japanese bombing of the city.

- In September 1937, the formerly bitterly opposed Chinese Nationalists and Communists agreed to work together, uniting into an army of 1.7 million men and women. Although the Chinese never defeated the Japanese, by 1941, they had tied up half the Japanese army.

- Meanwhile, the Japanese government allied itself with other aggressive states, forming the Axis alliance. In September 1940, the Japanese signed the Tripartite Pact with Germany and Italy. They then cleared the way for further empire building in Asia and the Pacific by signing a pact with the Soviet Union in April 1941.

- As Japanese forces continued their conquests in East Asia, the U.S. government responded by freezing Japanese assets. But the Japanese ignored U.S. demands to withdraw from China and Southeast Asia and became even more intractable after October 1941, when Tojo Hideki became prime minister. The new Japanese government immediately drew up plans for war against Britain and the United States.

- The Japanese hoped to destroy American naval power in the Pacific in a single blow with an attack on Pearl Harbor, but instead, their attack gave the United States the pretext it had been waiting for to declare war on Japan, Germany, and Italy.

- Despite this, the Japanese went from victory to victory, quickly capturing Borneo, Burma, and the Dutch Indies and threatening Australia. The turning point in the Pacific war finally came with the Battle of Midway, fought on June 4, 1942. The Allies took the offensive, hopping from island to island until the United States gradually retook the Philippines and islands close to Japan, such as Iwo Jima and Okinawa.

- The fall of Okinawa, Iwo Jima, and the Saipan islands brought the Japanese homeland within easy reach of U.S. bombers, and in August of 1945, the U.S. government, in an attempt to bring the war to a rapid end, used its revolutionary new weapon—the atomic bomb—against the cities of Hiroshima and Nagasaki at an immediate cost of 200,000 lives.

- Japan surrendered on August 15, utterly humiliated. Ultimately, the role of the United States in Japanese postwar recovery would prove to be decisive, ensuring not only a rapid recovery but also the creation of a stable Western-style democracy based on a robust export economy. This facilitated Japan's complete rehabilitation and reacceptance into the ranks of major nations, where it has remained as a partner of stability and moderation ever since.

Suggested Reading

Totman, *Early Modern Japan.*

Wilson, *Patriots and Redeemers in Japan.*

Young, *Japan's Total Empire.*

Questions to Consider

1. How was Japan able to transform itself into a modern global power under the Meiji government?

2. What was the impact on Eastern civilization of Japanese aggression during the Second World War?

Tokugawa and Meiji Japan
Lecture 44—Transcript

Welcome to this second lecture of a two-part mini series focused on the history and culture of Japan, from the so-called medieval period through to the mid-20th century.

Last time, we saw that by forcing the Tokugawa shogun to sign an unequal treaty in 1854, the U.S.A. provoked a political crisis in Japan. Widespread domestic resentment and opposition to the Tokugawa grew rapidly in response to this, particularly amongst the samurai. The Tokugawa tried to imprison the samurai; but in a brief civil war, opposition armies trained by foreign experts and armed with Western weapons forced the shogun to resign. In January, 1868, the young Emperor Meiji took power, the start of a successful reign that, as we'll see, lasted for more than four decades until 1912. After years of conflict and the bloody civil war with the samurai, hopes ran high in Japan that the resignation of the Tokugawa government and the accession of Emperor Meiji would usher in a new era of peace and expansion for Japan. The new emperor was only a boy when he came to the throne, but he was the first Japanese emperor to rule with any real power since the early Heian era seven centuries earlier. He chose the regal name "Meiji," which means "Enlightened Rule," and took the reigns of power on January 3rd 1868, ushering in an era of Japanese history known ever since as the Meiji Restoration.

As we'll see, the Meiji Era led to the complete political, economic, and even social reorganization of Japan, and was responsible for its dramatic transformation into a modern global military and industrial power. Nowhere in the long pantheon of global history has there ever been such a rapid and dramatic transformation of any society, anywhere. The Meiji Restoration and its imperial and ultimately self-destructive aftermath is the subject for this lecture, and it'll be explored in three separate sections: the Meiji Restoration first, then the period of imperialist Japan, and then concluding with Japan's role in the Second World War.

The first thing we can say about the Meiji Restoration is that it brought to an end a series of military governments that had dominated Japan since the Tokugawa shogun first claimed power way back in 1185. The second thing we can say is that, determined to gain equality with foreign powers, a conservative coalition of *daimyo*, nobles, and samurai were determined to study and essentially copy the industrial policies of the West. In order to achieve this, the Meiji government sent many students and officials abroad to study everything from technology to political constitutions, and they also hired many foreign experts to come to Japan and help facilitate economic development there.

In the next stage of modernization, the Meiji government abolished the old feudal order by removing the *daimyo* from power and abolishing the samurai, who rebelled but were crushed in 1878; again, events outlined in the movie *The Last Samurai*. The Meiji also revamped the tax system by converting the old grain tax that the peasants had been paying for centuries into a monetary tax, which had the immediate effect of forcing inefficient farmers off the land. A new constitution was eventually proclaimed in 1889, and this remained the constitution of Japan until 1947. Written by the government and based closely on European models, the document established a constitutional monarchy with a legislature known as the Diet, consisting of both an upper and a lower house. This rapid reorganization of the political structure demonstrates just how determined the Meiji were to cast off the traditional trappings of Chinese-style dynastic government, and for that matter the semi-feudal structure that had dominated Japan's long middle ages.

While certain of the foundational elements of Japanese culture did remain intact—Shinto religion, for example, and imperial government—the Japanese were much more willing, I think, to abandon other of the core values of Eastern civilization than, as we've seen, the Qing dynasty in China or the Choson dynasty in Korea were prepared to do. During the Meiji, then, we can clearly see an ancient Eastern civilization deliberately turning away from their ancient foundational ideals and explicitly embracing those espoused by an alternative region of the world, by Western civilization, in the hope of competing with aggressive industrialized Western powers on the world stage. The end result was that as China and Korea lost their sovereignty to the West, Meiji Japan was quickly able to take its place as one of the world's leading industrial powers in less than two generations.

According to the new Western-style constitution proclaimed by the Meiji emperor, the emperor, powerless for centuries, now commanded the armed forces; the emperor now named the prime minister; the emperor appointed the cabinet; and he also had the right to dissolve the Diet, the parliament. The Meiji then created a modern transport, communications, and even educational infrastructure very much along Western lines and also removed all barriers to internal trade. For the first time in Japan's history, universal primary and secondary education was introduced, and universities were created to provide advanced technical education. Most economic enterprises were private, but the government controlled all of the military industries and did all it could to stimulate industrial development generally. In particular, the government recruited the help of outside experts, more than 3,000 of whom were brought to Japan as *gaikokujin*, or "hired foreigners." This was in line with the last article of the Meiji Charter Oath of 1868, and let me quote this; it states: "Knowledge shall be sought throughout the world so as to strengthen the foundations of imperial rule"; further evidence, I think, of the desire by the Meiji to look beyond the ideas of Eastern civilization now and seek help and seek inspiration from the West.

In the 1880s, the government sold most of the remaining industries under its control to private investors and corporations, many of whom had close ties to Meiji officials. This had the effect of concentrating economic power in the hands of a small group of powerful capitalist enterprises known as the *zaibatsu*, which literally translates as the "wealthy clique." *Zaibatsu* were the equivalent of modern day cartels or trusts, and were usually organized around a single family or clan. The big four *zaibatsu* during this period were Mitsui, Mitsubishi, Sumitomo, and Yasuda. These four *zaibatsu* owned companies that were active in all the various fields of economic activity in Meiji Japan—in foreign trade, for example; insurance, mining, iron and steel manufacturing, textile production, and food production—and they all owned banks as well to mobilize capital and direct it to wherever it was needed in the corporation.

During the first half of the 20th century, the *zaibatsu* grew massively large and massively wealthy, but they were dissolved by Allied powers after the Second World War. In the 1950s, new enterprise groups emerged, many created by companies that had formerly been part of the big four *zaibatsu*. Cooperation

343

within and between these groups helped drive Japan's remarkable postwar recovery, as we'll see in one of our final lectures.

Through all these initiatives, both government and private, by the early 20th century Japan had joined the ranks of the major industrial powers. As I noted at the top of the lecture, this is quite frankly one of the most extraordinary and dramatic political and economic transformations in the annals of world history. But this rapid economic development came at a brutal cost for the peasants, who produced perhaps 90 percent of all government revenues during this reform stage, and who thus suffered from an appalling tax burden. Peasant uprisings broke out in 1883 and the following year, 1884; but they were ruthlessly crushed, as was a growing labor union movement in 1901. The result was that hundreds of thousands of peasants lived in destitution and starvation in a state that seemed to have no concern for the welfare of its workers.

But these radical and painful reforms worked. By 1902, Meiji Japan was strong enough to be signing an alliance of equal power with Britain; not an unequal treaty, then, but an equal treaty. How extraordinary. As we've seen, Japan then displayed its newfound military prowess with rapid and crushing victories over China in 1895 and 10 years later over Russia in 1905. These victories were mostly due to Japan's ability to gain access to modern military technology; technology that was now being produced by Western innovation rather than Eastern.

As early as 1876, the Meiji began to purchase modern warships from Britain; and as we saw in a recent lecture, they promptly used their naval muscle to force Korea to accept an unequal treaty with Japan. You might remember that when an anti-foreign rebellion broke out in Korea in 1893, the Qing dynasty sent a Chinese army to Korea to restore order. The Meiji were unwilling to recognize Chinese control over a land so close to them, so they declared war on China in August, 1894. The Japanese navy destroyed the Chinese navy in five hours, and the Japanese army forced the Qing forces out of Korea. In the peace treaty that followed, the Chinese acceded Korea to Japanese influence and also gave up control of Taiwan and other East Asian islands.

This easy Japanese victory startled other foreign powers, especially Russia, which, as we've noted on several occasions now, also had ambitions for territorial and diplomatic expansion in various parts of East Asia. Eventually war between Japan and Russia broke out in 1904, and the following year the Japanese navy destroyed the Russian Baltic fleet, which had sailed halfway around the world to support the war effort. This war also ended very quickly; so quickly that it was now absolutely clear to the entire world that by 1905 Japan had transformed itself into one of the major military and industrial powers of the globe.

But when the First World War broke out in 1914, Japan entered the war in August of that year on the side of the Allies. It quickly demanded that Germany hand over its leased territories in China to Japan without compensation, and that all German warships withdraw from Chinese waters. The Japanese then quietly and rapidly took control of numerous German possessions in East Asia and throughout the Pacific. With the Allies preoccupied by the fighting in Europe, the Japanese also took the opportunity to present a charter of 21 secret demands to the new republican government in China; more about this in the next lecture. The Meiji wanted confirmation of the Japanese hold on Chinese lands; they also wanted to establish industrial monopolies in China; they wanted joint Japanese control of the Chinese police force; they wanted a restriction of arms purchasing to Japanese manufacturers only; and an agreement that all Chinese arms purchases had to be approved by the Japanese government first. The Chinese had little option other than to accede to some of these demands, and only British support for the Chinese government and subsequent pressure from Whitehall on Tokyo prevented total capitulation. But Japan was determined to maintain a strong economic presence in Manchuria. They quickly built the Manchurian railway and stationed Japanese troops there to protect it.

All this meant that by the end of the Great War in 1918, the Japanese were poised to become not just a leading economic and military force, but also now a major global imperial power. After the Great War, Japan joined the League of Nations as one of the "big five" global powers; something, of course, that was absolutely inconceivable, impossible for any of the other less economically developed states of East Asia, like Vietnam, Korea, even

China. In 1928, the Japanese government also signed the Kellogg-Briand Pact, which renounced war as an instrument of national policy.

Throughout the 1920s, Japan's economy surged, creating genuine prosperity for most of the Japanese population for the first time in that country's long history. But this moment of economic prosperity was short-lived because Japan, like much of the developed world, suffered very badly during the Great Depression. The Japanese economy was by now greatly dependent on United States markets to sell its manufactured goods; and as demand in the U.S. fell sharply, unemployment in all export sectors in Japan skyrocketed. This had dangerous ramifications for Japanese politics, and public demands for sweeping political and social reform were heard throughout the late 1920s and 1930s. The conservative *zaibatsu* and the Meiji politicians blocked most of these reforms, although they did allow the establishment of universal male suffrage for all men aged over 25 in 1925.

But by the early 1930s, a frustrated public was blaming the government for continuing economic problems. Right-wing groups now called for an end to party rule, and xenophobic nationalists started demanding the preservation of unique Japanese cultural elements like Shinto religion, like the ideals of the samurai, and the eradication of all Western influences. A campaign of murders and assassinations targeting business leaders broke out, culminating in the murder of the prime minister, Inukai Tsuyoshi, in 1932. Those politicians who supported Japan's continuing role in the international industrial-capitalist system faced increasing opposition from those who favored a militaristic vision of Japan as the dominant imperial power of East Asia. This militarist faction set their sights on China, arguing that political instability there made that vast country an inviting target for Japanese imperial expansion.

The nationalists focused particularly on Manchuria. Japan needed to protect its considerable interests in Manchuria from the Chinese, they argued, particularly the Japanese-built Manchurian railway that was still being maintained by the Japanese. On the night of September 18, 1931, Japan's military used a staged pretext—that is, blowing up a section of their own railway in Manchuria and then accusing the Chinese of doing it—to launch a military invasion of the region. By 1932, Japanese troops were in control of all of Manchuria. In response to the invasion, the leader of the Chinese Guomindang—the Nationalist Party that we'll discuss in our next lecture—Chiang Kai-shek appealed to the League of Nations for assistance to help stop Japanese aggression. The League did eventually call for the removal of Japanese troops, but the Japanese responded by leaving the League instead and it appeared that nothing could be done by the global community to halt Japanese imperialism.

The Japanese military now embarked on a series of conquests in East Asia, determined to create their own empire. In so doing, of course, they helped spark the Second World War; and it's Japan's involvement in the war that's the final topic of this lecture. The world's second global conflict really commenced not with the Nazi invasion of Poland in September, 1939, but some eight years earlier with Japan's attacks on China in the early 1930s. It was the Japanese conquest of Manchuria between 1931 and 1932, the first step in a revisionist process of aggressive imperial expansionism, which more accurately actually marks the beginning of the Second World War. By the early 1930s, it was clear to the world that civilian politicians in Japan had lost control of the government; and that militarists and imperialists were now in charge. Following Japan's withdrawal from the League, it had no impediment to a continuation of its ultranationalist and pro-military expansionist policy.

Believing that more territorial expansion was now essential to its very survival, the Japanese government launched a full-scale invasion of China in 1937. After the Battle of Marco Polo Bridge, fought in Beijing in July of that year, Japanese troops quickly took control of Beijing and then moved south towards Shanghai and the nationalist capital of Nanjing. By December, 1937, Nanjing and Shanghai had both fallen, and for the next six months the Japanese forces won repeated victories throughout China. China thus became the first nation in the world to experience the horrors of World War II; and by that I mean brutal total warfare against civilians followed by repressive occupation. Chinese civilians suffered death and destruction on a massive scale; tens of thousands of citizens in Shanghai alone died from Japanese bombing of the city. Once Japanese troops entered Nanjing, inflamed by ultra-nationalism and war passion, they raped at least 7,000 women, they murdered hundreds of thousands of unarmed civilians, and they burned down one-third of all dwellings in the city. The numbers are very difficult to pin down here, but an estimated 260,000–300,000 Chinese lost their lives as Japanese soldiers used them for bayonet practice and machine gunned them into open pits.

As we'll see in one of the final lectures in the course, the Chinese actively resisted the Japanese invaders throughout the war; and Japanese aggression actually reignited slumbering Chinese nationalism, which only grew stronger the longer the war went on. In September, 1937, the formerly bitterly-opposed Chinese Nationalists and Communists—more on this in the next lecture—agreed to work together, uniting into an army of approximately 1.7 million men and women. Although the Chinese never defeated the Japanese, by 1941 they'd tied up half the Japanese army. Meanwhile, the Japanese government allied itself with other aggressive states, forming the so-called Axis Alliance. In September, 1940, they signed the Tripartite Pact with Germany and Italy; this was a 10-year military and economic agreement. Next, they cleared the way for further Japanese empire building in Asia and the Pacific by signing a pact with the Soviet Union in April, 1941. Apart from the Chinese army, Japan didn't face any determined opposition to its ambitions until the United States of America entered the conflict in December, 1941.

Even before the Japanese attack on Pearl Harbor, the U.S.A. had been inching towards involvement in the war. As Japanese forces continued their conquests in East Asia, capturing Vietnam, Laos, and Cambodia, the U.S. government responded by freezing Japanese assets in the United States. But the Japanese ignored U.S. demands to withdraw from China and Southeast Asia, and they became even more intractable after October, 1941, when Tojo Hideki became prime minister. The new Japanese government immediately drew up plans for war against Britain and the United States of America. The Japanese hoped to destroy American naval power in the Pacific in a single blow with their attack on Pearl Harbor. On December 7, 1941, Japanese pilots took off from six aircraft carriers to attack Pearl Harbor. More than 350 Japanese planes sank or disabled 18 U.S. ships, and American naval power in the Pacific was devastated. But, of course, you know this: This ended up being the biggest mistake the Japanese could've made, because it gave the United States government the pretext it had been waiting for to immediately declare war on Japan, Germany, and Italy.

Despite this, the Japanese went from victory to victory. They quickly captured Borneo, Burma, and the Dutch Indies; and Australia, the land of my birth, of course, was now in serious danger of invasion. The frankly humiliating surrender of British-held Singapore dealt a major blow to British prestige and shattered any lingering myths of European invincibility. The slogan under which Japan pursued the war was "Asia for Asians," implying that the Japanese would lead Asian people to independence from European colonialists. This, of course, was a clever piece of Japanese propaganda, because most of East, Southeast, and South Asia really was sick and tired of being under the thumb of Western imperial states, in some cases now for centuries. But continuing Japanese brutality, particularly against conquered Asian peoples, made it obvious to most Asians that the real agenda was "Asia for Japan."

The turning point in the Pacific war came with the Battle of Midway, fought on June 4, 1942. Three Japanese carriers were sunk in five minutes, a fourth later that same the day. Now it was the Allies who took the offensive, hopping from island to island until the United States forces gradually retook the Philippines and eventually islands close to Japan, such as Iwo Jima and Okinawa. The fighting at Iwo Jima and Okinawa was particularly savage. On Okinawa, the Japanese introduced a new war tactic, the *kamikaze*. These were pilots who volunteered to fly suicide missions with just enough fuel to reach Allied fleets before smashing their aircraft into ships. Carrier battles like Midway had inflicted incredible damage on the Imperial Japanese Navy Air Services, and frankly there were very few experienced pilots or undamaged aircraft left by this stage. So the decision was made to send obsolete aircraft and inexperienced pilots into the air, most of whom volunteered to join the *kamikaze* units on these suicide missions against the enemy fleets. It's no surprise, of course— you folks know this now—that the name *kamikaze* was chosen for these units. As I'm sure you remember, this is the name the Japanese had given to the "divine winds" that had twice blown up and prevented the Mongols from invading Japan back in the 13th century. In the two-month battle for Okinawa, the Japanese flew 1,900 kamikaze missions, which sank dozens of ships and killed more than 5,000 U.S. soldiers and sailors.

The savagery of the combat convinced many in the United States government and military that Japan would never surrender. The fall of Okinawa, Iwo

Jima, and the Saipan islands brought the Japanese homelands within easy reach of U.S. bombers, and on August 6 and 9, 1945, the U.S. government, in an attempt to bring the war to a rapid end, decided to use their revolutionary new weapon, the atomic bomb, against the cities of Hiroshima and Nagasaki, at an immediate cost of 200,000 lives. Japan surrendered on August 15, and the war was officially over by September 2. With its utter defeat following the dropping of these two atomic weapons, Japanese humiliation was complete.

The question now was: How quickly would Japan recover from the war, and what sort of social, economic, and political policies would the new government pursue? Would it return to the traditional thinking that had guided Japanese history for thousands of years now; or would it be able to continue to embrace Western political and economic structures and ideas without losing its commitment to these traditional values of Eastern civilization, and also without returning to a militaristic and imperialist mindset? Ultimately, the role of the United States of America in Japanese postwar recovery would prove to be decisive, as we'll see; ensuring not only a rapid recovery, but also the creation of a stable Western-style democracy based on a robust export economy. This facilitated Japan's complete rehabilitation and reacceptance into the ranks of major nations, where it's remained as a partner of stability and of moderation ever since.

In the remaining handful of lectures in the course, we need to try and bring a lot of threads together. Although we've taken our story of Korea and Japan up to 1945, we last left China back in 1912 at the moment of abdication of the last emperor ever to rule there, the boy Puyi. In our next lecture, then, we must return to China to pick up the story from the end of the Qing dynasty and follow Chinese political and cultural history through to the end of the Second World War. That will leave us three final lectures to bring this extensive investigation of the foundations and evolution of Eastern civilization through to a satisfying conclusion. This is a tough job, but we can do it.

The People's Republic of China
Lecture 45

To this point in our course, we have explored the history of the East Asian region by considering a number of foundational themes: ideas about effective forms of government and economic structures; the critical roles of Korea, Japan, and Southeast Asia; and ideas about society and the roles of particular social groups. With this lecture, we will return to these enduring themes and consider the most recent developments in the political, economic, social, and cultural history of the major Eastern nations. We begin by returning to China; when we last left this nation, poor government and Western imperial aggression had led to a loss of sovereignty and the virtual dismantling of the Chinese state by the early 20th century.

Political Upheaval in China

- During the first four decades of the 20th century, China was in a state of almost continuous political upheaval. With the abdication of the child emperor Puyi in 1912, China's dynastic era came to an abrupt end more than 4,000 years after it had begun.

- One year after Puyi's abdication, a leading opponent of the old Qing regime, Dr. Sun Yat-sen, proclaimed the establishment of a Chinese republic. He described his revolutionary manifesto as the Three People's Principles: nationalism, democracy, and the livelihood of the people.

- On October 10, 1911, while Sun was in Colorado raising funds for his Revive China Society, his colleagues, along with soldiers loyal to the movement, rebelled against the Chinese government and captured the city of Hankou. Almost immediately, several Chinese provinces declared their independence from Beijing and the Qing dynasty.

The Chinese Republic

- With the dissolution of central government, the Chinese republic was soon plunged into a state of political and economic anarchy marked by a return of the rule of warlords. No stable government was created, nor did any semblance of political order appear. Foreign imperial powers took advantage of Chinese instability by establishing new "spheres of interest" along the coast of the China Sea.

- This continuing foreign interference fostered a strong nationalist sentiment throughout China. Intellectuals wanted a new democratic form of government, but they also wanted to revive Chinese culture.

- Intellectuals and students looked forward optimistically to the 1919 Peace Conference in Paris as the start of a new era for China, hoping for the termination of the treaty system and the restoration of Chinese sovereignty. But those hopes were shattered when Japan was given approval for increasing interference in Chinese affairs.

- The so-called May Fourth Movement quickly erupted all over China, as citizens protested Japanese interference. Despite these protests, the Treaty of Versailles, signed on June 28, 1919, explicitly sanctioned Japanese control over all its Chinese territories. In response, the May Fourth Movement's leaders pledged to rid China of imperialism and began to seek out radical ideologies that might help them to do so, including communism.

The Chinese Communist Party

- Inspired by the success of the 1917 Bolshevik Revolution in Russia, by 1921, the Chinese Communist Party had been proclaimed in Shanghai, organized along Soviet lines. Among its early members was Mao Zedong, a young man destined to become one of the iconic figures of the 20th century.

- The Communists argued that a Marxist-inspired revolution was the only cure for China's problems. They also questioned many of the foundational social elements of Eastern civilization, championing equality for women, for example, and opposing arranged marriages and foot-binding.

- Sun Yat-sen did not share the Communists' enthusiasm for Marxist ideology. Instead, he promoted his own platform for modernization that included elimination of special privileges for foreigners, national reunification, rapid economic development, and the establishment of a democratic republican government based on universal suffrage. Sun also realized the importance of having a strong military to support his movement; thus, he established a military academy to train troops and appointed Chiang Kai-shek as its head.

- Sun was determined to bring the country under the control of his Nationalist Party (the Guomindang), but this was made more difficult after it was infiltrated by members of the Chinese Communist Party. Advisers from the Soviet Union helped reorganize both parties, hedging their bets in an attempt to ensure that Soviet influence would be strong in China, whoever won the political struggle!

Nationalist Rise to Power
- After the death of Sun Yat-sen in 1925, leadership of the Guomindang fell to General Chiang Kai-shek. He quickly launched a major offensive known as the Northern Expedition that attempted to defeat the warlords and bring China under Guomindang control.

- Initially, Chiang left the Communists alone, but in 1927, he unexpectedly turned against them, brutally suppressing Shanghai's Communist-led labor movement and bringing to a bloody end a period of cautious cooperation between the two parties. The Communists retreated to an isolated region of southeast China, where they tried to reconstitute their forces.

- In 1928, with both the warlords and Communists weakened, Nationalist forces occupied Beijing, established a central government in Nanjing, and declared the Guomindang to be the official government of a unified China. Chiang Kai-shek and the Nationalists ruled China for the next nine years, from 1928 to 1937, as a one-party dictatorship that they claimed was readying the country for democracy.

- Despite some limited success on the international front, the Nationalists never gained the support of the Chinese peasants, who looked to the Communists for relief.

- In September 1931, the Japanese used a pretext of Chinese sabotage of the Manchurian railway to invade parts of northern China, where they declared a puppet government. The Communists, meanwhile, tried to rebuild their strength, despite repeated military campaigns sent against them by Chiang Kai-shek. In October 1934, the Communist Red Army was defeated in Jiangxi province.

The Long March
- Mao Zedong and the remnants of the Red Army managed to escape a Nationalist blockade and begin a strategic retreat, known as the Long March. As the march continued, Mao broke from his colleagues, who favored a more traditional approach to military strategy, and advocated for the adoption of guerilla tactics.

- By the time the Communists had reached Guizhou province, Mao was widely recognized as the leader of the movement. The marchers continued toward Shaanxi province by a harrowing and dangerous route. Some 86,000 Red Army members had begun the march, but only 8,000 survived the journey to Shaanxi, where the new Communist headquarters was established.

- As a result of the Long March, Mao Zedong was now the undisputed leader and principal theoretician of the party, with Zhou Enlai as his loyal deputy, a situation that changed little over the next 40 years.

- Mao articulated the Chinese version of Marxism (soon called Maoism), which argued that oppressed peasants, rather than the urban proletariat, were the true foundations of a successful Communist revolution. China was on the brink of an unknown future, but with the Second World War about to intervene, it would be another 14 years before that future would be determined.

Japanese Invasion and Aftermath
- The Chinese mounted staunch resistance to the Japanese invasion of China. By September 1937, the Nationalists and Communists had agreed to work together against the Japanese. Although the Japanese had naval and air superiority, by 1941, the ragtag Chinese forces had managed to tie down half the Japanese army.

- The tenuous coalition of Nationalists and Communists threatened to tear apart many times throughout the war, and there were numerous military clashes between the two. But the Communists' guerilla tactics against the Japanese captured the loyalty of millions of Chinese peasants. By the end of the war, the Communists were poised to take control.

- With the defeat of Japan in 1945, civil war in China immediately resumed. In 1948, the momentum swung to the Communists after the People's Liberation Army inflicted heavy defeats on the Nationalists.

- Chiang Kai-shek and about 2 million Nationalists fled the mainland to the island of Taiwan, where they proclaimed themselves China's legitimate government. Meanwhile, on the mainland, Mao Zedong proclaimed the establishment of the People's Republic of China on October 1, 1949.

Mao's Leadership
- Mao Zedong set out to reorganize China by imitating the organizational structure of the Soviet Union. A new constitution was declared in 1954, which stipulated a national assembly chosen by popular election. But in reality, political power was monopolized by the central committee and politburo chaired by Mao.

- To protect its authority, the party orchestrated campaigns to remove from power individuals likely to be a threat, particularly those affiliated with the old Nationalist government. In 1951 alone, tens of thousands were executed and many more sent to labor camps.

- The economy of China was utterly transformed when land ownership was declared collective and rapid industrialization was instituted. Radical social reforms also quickly eliminated many Chinese traditions that had been in place for centuries.

- Moscow and Beijing worked closely during the early years of the Cold War; both saw the United States as their common enemy. But cracks soon appeared in this relationship, and Mao embarked on a series of programs to distinguish Chinese from Soviet communism.

From the 1920s until his death, Mao Zedong was the global epitome of a great revolutionary leader, a larger-than-life character in the vein of the charismatic and autocratic emperors of Chinese history.

- The Great Leap Forward (1958–1961) was an attempt to have the Chinese economy match that of more developed nations by collectivizing all agriculture and industry. But the abolition of private ownership had a disastrous impact on agricultural production, and a deadly famine ensued.

- After this disaster, Mao tried in 1966 to reignite the revolutionary spirit of China with a Cultural Revolution, designed to root out revisionists. Millions of people—particularly teachers, professionals, managers, and intellectuals—were singled out by the Red Guard for humiliation, persecution, and death.

- During the early 1970s, political struggles within the party gradually undermined Mao's power. When he died in September 1976, four of the most influential supporters of the Cultural Revolution—the so-called Gang of Four—staged a coup and tried to seize control of the party, but the gang was arrested and the Cultural Revolution was finally over.

- The Chinese people have been able to reconcile the complex personality of Mao Zedong by treating him as a split personality: a "good Mao" and a "bad Mao." In a later lecture, we will see how the next generation of Chinese leaders would deal with Mao's cultural, political, and economic legacy.

Suggested Reading

Dirlik, *The Origins of Chinese Communism.*

Salisbury, *The Long March.*

Sheridan, *The Republican Era in Chinese History, 1912–1949.*

Snow, *Red Star over China.*

Questions to Consider

1. Why did the Communists succeed and the Nationalists fail in the chaotic race for control of China during the first half of the 20th century? How significant was the role of Mao Zedong?

2. What impact did the Cultural Revolution have on many of the foundational elements of Chinese civilization?

The People's Republic of China
Lecture 45—Transcript

Hello folks, and welcome to this lecture; number 45, if you can believe that, in our 48-lecture course. We're rapidly approaching the end of what's been an epic and I trust rewarding journey through the great sweep of Eastern civilization and the foundations it was built upon. Through 44 lectures now, we've explored the rich and fascinating history of the East Asian region, from ancient times through to the 20th century. We've done this by considering a number of key foundational themes, which collectively have defined what we mean by Eastern civilization. These have included ideas about the most effective form of government; the best way of organizing an economy; the critical role of Korea, Japan, and Southeast Asia in Eastern civilization; and, of course, changing ideas about society and the roles of different groups within East Asian social structures that have occupied great thinkers for thousands of years. It's this scheme, I think, which provides a roadmap for the best way to conclude our course. That is, we need now to return to these enduring themes and consider the most recent developments in the political, economic, social, and cultural history of the major Eastern nations; developments that, it goes without saying, have turned that region into one of the most dynamic zones on earth.

In this particular lecture, I want to return to Chinese ideas about government and political organization; ideas that, as we've seen in this course, have occupied government officials and intellectuals for so many thousands of years; ideas that have profoundly influenced the development of governance throughout most of the Eastern Hemisphere. Early in our course, we looked at the very first cultures of China and we saw the emergence of leaders who'd learned to combined shamanistic and secular power through the use of ritual. The Shang dynasty, for example, used both human sacrifice and oracle bone divination as mechanisms for effective governance. We followed this with a consideration of the Mandate of Heaven first promoted by the Zhou dynasty; the extraordinary idea that an impartial heaven sits in judgment of affairs on earth and bestows its mandate upon a new dynasty when the old one has lost its legitimacy. This was a political ideology that lasted for more than 3,000 years, right through to the 20th century. Let's not forget that the three great and enduring philosophies of Eastern civilization that all emerged during the chaotic Later Zhou dynastic period—I'm talking, of course, about Confucianism, Legalism, even Daoism in this way—were each at their core ideologies about the best practices of governing people, and also of social organization.

Consider also the great parade of powerful autocratic emperors we've met in this course, each of whom had to essentially decide which of these three political ideologies, or what combination of them, would be his, and in just one case her, philosophy of government. For the first emperor, Qin Shi Huangdi, it was Legalism; for Wudi, the great "Martial Emperor" of the Early Han dynasty, it was Confucianism, with a dash of Legalism and Daoism thrown in. Following the Age of Disunity, rulers of the Sui and Tang dynasties used a mixture of homegrown and imported philosophies, particularly Buddhism now, to try and restore unity and effective government to China. During the Song dynasty, you remember, Buddhism and Confucianism competed for the attention of rulers and intellectuals alike, even as the government was focused more pragmatically on economic growth and innovation. Later, after the external imposition of somewhat disinterested and inefficient rule by the Mongol emperors of the Yuan dynasty, it was the often naïve and corrupt rulers of the Ming and Qing, who opted to be kept isolated from the real world of politics by their eunuchs and by their Mandarins, which led to China's demise in the 18th and 19th centuries, and to the domination of that great nation by Western powers.

This was the situation when we last left China in this course: Poor quality government and Western imperial aggression had led to a loss of sovereignty and the virtual dismantling of the Chinese state by the early 20th century. Let's pick up the story again now in 1912. In the decades that followed, we'll see the appearance of new experiments in Chinese governance; experiments like Republicanism, Nationalism, and, of course, Communism. We'll see also the emergence of a group of new leaders who vied for power over the vast Chinese state and its untold millions; men like Sun Yat-sen, like Chiang Kai-shek, and the young communist revolutionary Mao Zedong.

The first thing we need to say is that during the first four decades of the 20th century, China was in a state of almost continuous political upheaval. With the abdication of the child emperor Puyi in 1912, the last emperor of the

Qing, China's dynastic era came to an abrupt end more than 4,000 years after it had begun. Four thousand years of rule by more or less the same dynastic system of government is just another example of the extraordinary longevity of both the Chinese state and also of this concept we've been trying to define throughout our course as "Eastern civilization." Can you think of any other political structure devised by humans that's lasted virtually without interruption for four millennia?

One year after Puyi's abdication, a leading opponent of the old Qing regime, Dr. Sun Yat-sen—better known in China, by the way, by his revolutionary name of Sun Zhongshan—proclaimed the establishment of a Chinese Republic. Sun Yat-sen is a fascinating figure in modern Chinese political history, and actually an individual who had close ties to the United States. At the age of 13, Sun moved to Hawaii to live with an older brother; he studied English in a private Christian missionary school on the island of Oahu. After returning to China, he studied Western medicine, but he was soon swept up in the ferment of revolutionary politics that swirled about China during the last decades of the Qing dynasty. In 1894, Sun organized the "Revive China Society," then spent the next several years working tirelessly raising funds and promoting his revolutionary cause in Southeast Asia, in Japan, and certainly back in North America. Some historians argue that Sun was inspired by Abraham Lincoln's famous description of government as being of the people, by the people, for the people when he described his own revolutionary manifesto as the "Three People's Principles": nationalism, democracy, and the livelihood of the people. Sun later gained U.S. citizenship, apparently by using a forged birth certificate that showed he'd been born in Hawaii.

On October 10, 1911, while Sun was in Denver, Colorado raising funds, his colleagues in the Revive China Society, along with soldiers loyal to the movement, rebelled against the Chinese government and captured the city of Hankou. Almost immediately, several Chinese provinces declared their independence from Beijing and from the Qing dynasty. The abdication of the last emperor was actually part of a negotiated agreement between the revolutionaries and the Qing government. A Qing general, Yuan Shikai, was appointed president in the emperor's place. So the old dynasty was dead; but it would be a very long time indeed before a durable structure would appear to take its place. Declaring a republic is one thing; but achieving stability through political revolution is quite another, of course.

With the dissolution of central government the republic was soon plunged into a state of political and economic anarchy marked by a return of the rule of warlords; how many times have we seen this occur in China's history? The central government managed to run a few agencies from Beijing—like the Post Office, for example—but the warlords reestablished themselves as the new provincial rulers. With warlords in control, irrigation was neglected, the opium trade was revived, and the Chinese economy began to collapse. No stable government was created, nor did any semblance of political order appear. Sun Yat-sen and his president Yuan Shikai soon fell out, which didn't help matters any more. Even after the general died in 1916, Sun and his revolutionaries were unable to restore any order. With the warlords in control of various parts of the country, the relationship between foreign powers and the Chinese state also disintegrated. As we've seen, it was a series of unequal treaties that had effectively guided Chinese relations with the industrialized world during much of the previous century. Foreign control of China had prevented economic development, and their privileged status had obviously impaired Chinese sovereignty. Now, in the first decades of the 20th century, the foreign imperial powers took full advantage of Chinese instability by establishing new "spheres of interest" along the coast of the China Sea.

But this continuing foreign interference actually fostered a strong nationalist sentiment throughout the country. Intellectuals wanted a new democratic form of government, but they also wanted to revive traditional Chinese culture. Peking University became a hotbed now of intellectual activity amongst students and faculty, with increasing demands made for modern government, for the introduction of scientific principles, and for the modernization of the Chinese written script. These same intellectuals and students looked forward optimistically to the 1919 Peace Conference in Paris as the start of a new era for China, hoping for the termination of the treaty system and the restoration of Chinese sovereignty. But these hopes were shattered when Japan was given approval for increasing interference in Chinese affairs, a situation we discussed in a previous lecture.

The so-called May Fourth Movement quickly erupted all over China, as citizens protested against Japanese interference. Despite these protests, the Treaty of Versailles, signed on June 28, 1919, explicitly sanctioned Japanese control over all its Chinese territories. In response, the May Fourth Movement's leaders pledged to rid China of imperialism and began to seek out radical ideologies that might help them to do so; and one such ideology, of course, was Communism. Disillusioned by the cynical self-interest of the United States and the European powers, one group of Chinese radical intellectuals became increasingly interested in Marxist-Leninist thinking. Inspired by the success of the 1917 Bolshevik Revolution in Russia, by 1921 the Chinese Communist Party had been proclaimed in Shanghai, organized very much along Soviet lines. Among its early members was Mao Zedong, a young man destined to become one of the iconic figures of the 20th century.

Mao had been born in Hunan province in 1893. His father was a poor peasant who made good and became a successful farmer and a wealthy grain dealer. The young Mao divided his time between working on his father's farm but also acquiring first a provincial elementary and then a secondary education. After a brief period as a member of the Revolutionary Army, Mao gained employment as an assistant librarian at Peking University, where he attended the lectures that were being given by these key revolutionary intellectuals; those who were demanding political, economic, and cultural reform in China. On July 23, 1921, the now-27-year-old and married Mao attended the first ever session of the National Congress of the Communist Party of China; and within two years, Mao had been elected as one of the five commissars of the Central Committee.

The Communists argued that a Marxist-inspired revolution was the only cure for China's problems. They also questioned many of the foundational social elements of Eastern civilization, championing equality for women, for example, and opposing arranged marriages and foot-binding. Sun Yat-sen, still the most prominent Nationalist leader, didn't share the Communists' enthusiasm for Marxist ideology. Instead, he promoted his own platform for modernization: the elimination of special privileges for foreigners, national reunification, rapid economic development, and the establishment of a democratic Republican government based on universal suffrage. Sun also realized the importance of having a strong military force to support his movement, so he established a military academy to train loyal troops. The man appointed head of this academy was a young solider also destined to play a key role in this chaotic period: Chiang Kai-shek.

Sun was determined to bring the country under the control of his Nationalist Party, called the Guomindang; but this was made more difficult after it was infiltrated by members of the Chinese Communist Party. Advisors from the Soviet Union helped reorganize both parties, really hedging their bets in an attempt to ensure that Soviet influence would be strong in China whoever won the political struggle. After the death of Sun Yat-sen in 1925, leadership of the Guomindang fell to the now General Chiang Kai-shek. Chiang Kai-shek quickly launched a major offensive known as the Northern Expedition that attempted to defeat the warlords and bring China under Guomindang control. Initially, he left the Communists alone; but in 1927, he unexpectedly turned against them, brutally suppressing Shanghai's Communist-led labor movement and bringing to a bloody end a period of cautious cooperation between the two parties. The Communist forces retreated to an isolated region of Southeast China where they tried to reconstitute their forces.

In 1928, with both the warlords and Communists weakened, Nationalist forces occupied Beijing, established a central government in Nanjing in the south, and declared the Guomindang to be the official government of a reunified China. Chiang Kai-shek and the Nationalists ruled over China for the next nine years, from 1928 through to 1937, as a one-party dictatorship that they claimed was readying the country for democracy. Despite some limited success on the international front—including, for example, regaining Chinese control of trade tariffs and revoking many of the more humiliating foreign concessions—the Nationalists never gained the support of the Chinese peasants whose lives didn't improve and who looked instead to the Communists for relief.

In September, 1931, as we've seen, the Japanese used a pretext of Chinese sabotage of the Manchurian railway to invade parts of northern China where they declared a puppet government, ironically under the leadership of the last emperor of the Qing, Puyi. The Communists, meanwhile, tried to rebuild their strength despite repeated military campaigns sent against them by Chiang Kai-shek. One such campaign occurred in October, 1934, a relentless attack by the Nationalist forces that used 700,000 soldiers to surround the Communist forces and trap them in Jiangxi province. The result was the death of about 1 million people, most of them Communist sympathizers, and the defeat of the Communist Red Army. Mao Zedong and the 86,000 remnants of the army managed to escape the military blockade and begin a strategic retreat known ever since as the "Long March." During the first three months, as the Red Army marched north, it was bombarded and decimated by the Nationalists. As the march continued, Mao broke from his colleagues who favored a more traditional approach to military strategy, and Mao advocated instead for the adoption of guerilla tactics. By the time the Communists had reached Guizhou province, Mao was widely recognized as the leader of the movement. With Mao at the helm, the Communists continued towards Shaanxi province by a harrowing and dangerous route.

By the time the Red Army ended its long march, it had crossed 18 mountain ranges and 24 rivers in a journey of 12,500 kilometers, almost 8,000 miles. These statistics, by the way, which have passed into historical lore, have been challenged by modern historians who estimate the march to have only been some 6,000 kilometers in length; but the Chinese media has stuck by Mao's figures, making them now an indelible part of the historical record. One other set of statistics reinforces the compelling tale of the Long March: Although some 86,000 Red Army members began the march, only 8,000 survived the journey to Shaanxi, where the new Communist headquarters were established. As a result of the Long March, Mao Zedong, who later uttered the famous lines "the longest march begins with the first step," was now the undisputed leader and the principal theoretician of the party, with Zhou Enlai as his loyal deputy; a situation that changed little over the next 40 years. Mao now began to articulate a Chinese version of Marxism, soon called "Maoism," which argued that oppressed peasants rather than the urban proletariat were the true foundations of a successful Communist revolution, particularly in China. China was now on the brink of an unknown future; but with the Second World War about to intervene, it would be another 14 years before that future would be determined.

The Chinese mounted staunch resistance to the Japanese invasion of China because, as I mentioned in our previous lecture, Japanese aggression further ignited Chinese nationalism. By September, 1937, the Nationalists (reluctantly) and the Communists had agreed to work together against the Japanese, forming a combined army of some 1.7 million fighters. As I mentioned last time, although the Japanese had naval and air superiority, this ragtag Chinese army managed to tie down half of the Japanese army by 1941. Of course, the tenuous coalition of Nationalists and Communists threatened to tear apart many times throughout the war, and there were numerous military clashes between the two. The Nationalists tended to shy away from direct confrontation with the Japanese and kept their government alive by moving inland to Chongqing. But the Communists carried out full-scale guerilla warfare against the Japanese from their mountain bases, sabotaging bridges and railroads and harassing Japanese troops. These tactics captured the loyalty of millions of Chinese peasants, and by the end of the war the Communists were poised to take control.

With the defeat of Japan in 1945, civil war in China immediately resumed. Between August 1945 and December 1946, Communists and Nationalists fought each other and raced to take over areas previously occupied by the Japanese. In 1948, the momentum swung to the Communists after the People's Liberation Army inflicted very heavy defeats on the Nationalists. With the writing now on the wall, Chiang Kai-shek and about 2 million Nationalists fled the mainland and sought refuge on the island of Taiwan, where they proclaimed themselves China's legitimate government. On the mainland, meanwhile, on October 1, 1949, Mao Zedong proclaimed the establishment of the People's Republic of China. This brought to an immediate end the long era of imperialist intrusion in China and led to the establishment of a close relationship with the U.S.S.R. To further cement this relationship, Mao actually traveled outside of China for the first time in his life in December, 1949 to meet with his Soviet counterpart Joseph Stalin in Moscow.

Mao Zedong now set out to reorganize China by imitating the organizational structure of the Soviet Union. A new constitution was declared in 1954, which stipulated a national assembly chosen by popular election; but in reality, political power was now monopolized by the central committee and politburo chaired by Mao. To protect its authority, the party orchestrated campaigns to remove from power individuals likely to be a threat, particularly those who'd been affiliated with the old Nationalist government. In 1951 alone, tens of thousands were executed, and many more were sent to labor camps. At the same time, the economy of China was utterly transformed when land ownership was declared collective and rapid industrialization instituted; more about this in a subsequent lecture. Radical social reform also quickly eliminated many Chinese traditions that, as we've seen, had been in place for centuries, in some cases millennia; more about this, too, in our last couple of lectures.

Moscow and Beijing worked closely together during the early years of the Cold War; both saw the U.S.A. as their common enemy, of course. But as we'll see in our next lecture, cracks soon began to appear in this relationship. By 1964, the CCP was declaring the U.S.S.R. under Nikita Khrushchev to be "revisionist" for pursuing a policy of peaceful coexistence with the U.S.A.; and the Soviets were calling Mao a dangerous "left-wing adventurist" because he insisted war between communism and the West was inevitable. Mao then decided to embark upon a series of programs to try and distinguish Chinese communism from Soviet communism. The Great Leap Forward between 1958 and 1961 was an attempt to have the Chinese economy match that of more developed nations by collectivizing all of agriculture and industrial production. But the abolition of private ownership had a disastrous impact on agricultural production, and a deadly famine ensued. Between 1959 and 1962, up to 20 million Chinese died from starvation.

After this disaster, Mao tried in 1966 to reignite the revolutionary spirit of China with a Cultural Revolution designed to root out revisionists. Millions of people now—particularly teachers, professionals, managers, and intellectuals—were singled out by the Red Guard for humiliation, persecution, and death. Victims were beaten and killed, jailed, or sent to labor camps in the country. The Cultural Revolution cost China years of stable development and gutted the education system. Although the Ninth Party Congress in April, 1969 ended the most radical phase of the Cultural Revolution, it didn't completely die down until Mao's death in 1976. During the early 1970s, political struggles within the party gradually undermined Mao's power. When he died in September, 1976, four of the most influential supporters of the Cultural Revolution—the so-called "Gang of Four," which included Mao's wife—staged a coup and tried to seize control of the party, but the gang was arrested and the Cultural Revolution was finally over.

From the 1920s until his death, Mao Zedong was the global epitome of a great revolutionary leader; a larger-than-life character very much in the vein of the charismatic, inspirational, and even autocratic emperors of Chinese history. Remember Mao's two extraordinary swims across the Yangtze River that we discussed way back at the very beginning of the course, symbolic of the power of nature certainly, but also of Mao's ability to inspire his people by pitting himself against one of the greatest rivers on earth. Even today, despite the excesses of the Cultural Revolution, Mao Zedong remains one of the iconic figures of the 20th century, still widely respected in China today. His image looks down upon Tiananmen Square, I'm sure many of you have seen this; his tomb is one of the most visited tourist sites in the country; and Mao hats, Mao badges, and the Little Red Book are ubiquitous at shops throughout the country. The Chinese people have been able to reconcile the complex personality of Mao Zedong by treating him as a split personality; I've had many educated Chinese tell this to me personally: There's a good Mao and there's a bad Mao, but the good clearly outweighs the bad.

It remains for us to see how the next generation of Chinese leaders would deal with the cultural, political, and economic legacy left by Mao Zedong following his death in 1976. But first, please join me next time as we investigate the tragic impact of the Cold War on East Asia, including the ramifications of the fateful split between the People's Republic of China and the U.S.S.R., and the outbreak of bloody conflicts in Korea and Vietnam.

Isolation and Cold War Conflicts

Lecture 46

As we have seen throughout this course, for thousands of years, Eastern civilization had evolved in relative geographical and geopolitical isolation from the rest of the world. But from the 18th century on, it had become impossible to ignore the involvement of a host of foreign players in East Asian affairs, and this forced interconnectedness of the world increased exponentially during the Cold War. Thus, in this lecture, we will take a closer look at the impact of the Cold War and the general trend toward globalization on Eastern civilization during the 20th century.

China and the Soviet Union

- Throughout most of the 1950s, China was happy to recognize the Soviet Union as the undisputed authority in world communism, and China received Soviet weapons and economic aid in return. For their part, the Soviets worked diligently in the UN to have the Chinese seat in the Security Council transferred from the Nationalists in Taiwan to the Chinese Communist Party in Beijing.

- But cracks started to appear in the partnership late in the decade when China realized it was receiving less aid from the Soviets than noncommunist Egypt and India were. It was also in the 1950s that tensions between China and India broke out over the question of the sovereignty of Tibet. The Soviets infuriated the Chinese by outwardly remaining neutral in the conflict yet secretly giving a huge loan to India.

- By the early 1960s, occasional border clashes occurred between Soviet and Chinese troops in Central Asia. China's successful nuclear weapons test in 1964 escalated the tensions.

- This deteriorating relationship between two major nations was played out in the even larger context of the Cold War, which became a truly global phenomenon in the 1950s. In military terms, the Cold War passed through several distinct phases.

o In the late 1940s and 1950s, when the United States held a distinct advantage in weaponry, the Soviets or Chinese could not risk a major clash.

o When U.S. allies Britain (in 1952) and France (in 1960) also developed nuclear capacity, NATO published its doctrine of "overwhelming retaliation," a further disincentive to the outbreak of any major military conflict.

o But the Cold War became hot twice, and in both cases, these wars were fought in East Asia: in Korea between 1950 and 1953 and in Indochina, where defeated French troops gave way to Americans in 1954, dragging the United States into the Vietnam War, which lasted until 1975.

The Division of North and South Korea

• As we have seen throughout this course, Korea has a long history of division between north and south, and the roots of this division had remained deep, even during periods of Japanese occupation.

• Korea was liberated from Japanese hegemony on August 15, 1945, but after three and a half decades of Japanese colonial rule, Korean society was a chaotic mix of old and new classes, ideologies, and political factions.

o On the left of the political spectrum now were thousands of dedicated communists, many of whom had waged guerilla warfare against the Japanese for years and were determined to transform Korea into a more egalitarian society.

o On the right were landlords, businessmen, and former Japanese collaborators who were determined to preserve their privileged place in society.

• Following the defeat of the Japanese, the United States and the Soviet Union agreed to a proposal to jointly occupy the Korean peninsula as a trusteeship, with an agreed-upon division between the two along the 38th parallel. Originally, the arrangement was to be temporary.

- In February 1946, a provisional government was established north of the parallel by communist leader and anti-Japanese guerilla hero Kim Il-Sung. This government was known as the North Korean People's Provisional Committee.

- As mistrust grew between the United States and the Soviet Union, the United States sought UN involvement in the question of Korea's future, but the Soviets boycotted the discussions.

- With dwindling hopes for reunification, the Republic of Korea was declared in the south on August 15, 1948. And on September 9, 1948, the Democratic People's Republic of Korea was declared in the north, with Kim Il-Sung as its first prime minister.

- Almost immediately, the relationship between the two Koreas degenerated into a series of bloody skirmishes along the 38th parallel, escalating into full-scale war in 1950.

The Korean War
- On June 25, 1950, North Korean forces, equipped with Soviet weapons, suddenly invaded the South. They took Seoul in three days, and by early August, virtually all of the peninsula was under their control.

- The United States (under UN auspices) quickly came to the aid of the South Koreans, and General MacArthur succeeded in splitting the North Korean army in two with a successful amphibious assault on the port of Inchon, near Seoul. A rapid U.S./UN counteroffensive then recaptured Seoul and forced the North Koreans back past the 38th parallel.

- At that moment, the Chinese Red Army came to the aid of the communist North. Chinese troops drove the UN forces back past the

38th parallel; on January 4, 1951, Seoul fell for a second time. UN forces managed to recapture the city in March 1952, but thereafter, a stalemate developed between the two sides.

- The real potential that this conflict could escalate into nuclear war finally ended with an armistice that restored the border between the Koreas near the 38th parallel and created the Demilitarized Zone, a 2.5-mile-wide buffer zone between the two Koreas that is still in place today.

The Vietnam War

- Vietnam also has a long history of division between north and south, based on geography, cultural and linguistic differences, and its long and complex relationship with the Chinese and French.

- During the 18th and 19th centuries, the French had assembled a colonial empire in Indochina that included Vietnam, Laos, and Cambodia.
  - o Much of Indochina was then occupied by the Japanese in the Second World War, with a puppet Vichy-style French colonial administration left in charge.

  - o Late in the war, Japan replaced this French regime with a pro-Japanese Vietnamese emperor named Bao Dai, who immediately proclaimed independence from France.

- During the war, as was the case in Japanese-occupied China and Korea, a communist guerilla force, the Viet Minh, formed the most effective anti-Japanese resistance movement. The Viet Minh were particularly strong in the north, close to their bases just across the border in China.

- When Japan surrendered, the leader of the Viet Minh, Ho Chi Minh, moved quickly to fill the power vacuum and proclaimed an independent Democratic Republic of Vietnam. The French reoccupied the major cities with the indirect assistance of British forces.

The U.S. government believed that war was necessary to prevent the communist takeover of South Vietnam, while the North Vietnamese government saw U.S. involvement as an extension of the colonial war it had just successfully waged against France.

- The first direct confrontation occurred at Haiphong harbor in November 1946, when the Viet Minh fired on a French warship. In the brutal retaliation that followed, 6,000 Vietnamese were killed, leading to the outbreak of a guerilla war against the French.

- The initial phase of the war, from 1947 to 1949, resulted in a stalemate. But with the success of the Communist revolution in China in 1949, the Viet Minh gained a powerful ally and, with Chinese military assistance, drove the French out of North Vietnam the following year.

- From 1952 onward, the United States agreed to cover the cost of the colonial war for the French. The 1954 Geneva Accords that followed the French defeat at Dien Bien Phu partitioned Vietnam into two zones, with the hope that this would be a temporary measure until national elections could reunite the two halves. The north was now ruled by the Viet Minh as the Democratic Republic of Vietnam, and the south was known as the State of Vietnam.

- The U.S. government saw the situation in Vietnam as a test case for the containment of communism. U.S. military advisers started arriving in Vietnam in the 1950s, troop levels tripled in 1961 and 1962, and combat units were deployed beginning in 1965. U.S. military involvement peaked in January 1968 at the time of the Tet Offensive.

- With support for the war eroding and bitter divisions in the administration of President Lyndon Johnson, U.S. ground forces were gradually withdrawn. But despite the Paris Peace Accords signed by all parties in January 1973, fighting continued for two more years. In April 1975, the North Vietnamese captured Saigon just as the last U.S. personnel were withdrawn, an event that marked the real end of the Vietnam War.

- North and South Vietnam were reunified the following year and, unlike Korea, have stayed united up to the present day, under the control of a communist government in Hanoi.

Diplomatic Rapprochement

- As both the Vietnam War and the Cold War dragged on, the U.S. government decided it was time to try something new to take advantage of the tense split between the Soviets and Chinese.

- In 1972, President Richard Nixon visited the aging Chairman Mao Zedong in China, a diplomatic coup that had the immediate effect of bringing China back into what had been an essentially bipolar world. Nixon's visit was followed by several trips by Henry Kissinger. It wasn't long before liaison offices opened in Beijing and Washington DC, and formal diplomatic relations were inaugurated in 1979.

- As a direct result of the establishment of this relationship between China and the world, the Soviets felt under increasing pressure to stabilize their European flank. This led quickly to a major breakthrough in the lessening of Cold War tensions: the Helsinki Conference, which ran from 1972 to 1975.

- With Nixon's visit to China and the end of the Vietnam War, the Cold War had entered a new phase that saw China reassume an important geopolitical position. But even with these diplomatic breakthroughs, China was still mired in the Cultural Revolution and trying to deal with a failing economy. In the next lecture, we'll see how China's economy revived under Mao's successor, Deng Xiaoping.

Suggested Reading

Karnow, *Vietnam: A History*.

Meisner, *Mao's China and After*.

Rees, *Korea: The Limited War*.

Questions to Consider

1. How did the globalization of the Cold War affect the relationship between the Soviet Union and China, resulting in the emergence of different ideological visions in each country?

2. Why were the only "hot wars" during the entire Cold War period both fought in East Asia?

Isolation and Cold War Conflicts
Lecture 46—Transcript

Today I want to continue our exploration of the transformation of the key political, economic, social, and cultural foundations of Eastern civilization that occurred during the 20th century, a century at least partly characterized by Cold War and globalization.

Last time, we saw how, following the collapse of the ancient dynastic system of government in 1912, China had to endure almost four decades of civil war plus a brutal invasion by the Japanese until some semblance of political stability was reestablished. But this stability came with a high price: the division of China into two rival states ruled by two competing governments. In 1948, you'll remember, Chiang Kai-shek declared a Nationalist democratic government on the island of Taiwan; and the following year, on October 1, 1949, Mao Zedong declared the establishment of the People's Republic of China on the mainland. The existence of two Chinas—and ironically also of two Koreas and two Vietnams, as we'll see later in this lecture—reflected the wider division of virtually the entire world into two bitterly opposed and heavily armed camps following the end of the Second World War. These two camps, one led by the United States of America, the other by the Union of Soviet Socialist Republics, were both bristling with nuclear weapons. They remained bitterly divided for much of the second half of the 20th century by political ideology.

For this reason, the history of Eastern civilization in the decades after the Second World War must of necessity be unfolded in the context of the global reality of the Cold War. As we've seen throughout this course, for thousands of years, Eastern civilization had evolved in relative geographical and geopolitical isolation from the rest of the world. But from the 18th century on, it had become impossible to ignore the involvement of a host of foreign players in East Asian affairs; foreigners who dragged most of East Asia into their colonial empires and spheres of interest. But this forced interconnectedness of the world increased exponentially during the Cold War. After the Second World War, there was really nowhere on the planet that was isolated anymore. Affairs in one part of the world could potentially have a devastating impact on another region thousands of miles away. In this lecture, we take a closer look at the impact of the Cold War, and also the more general trend towards globalization, on Eastern civilization during the 20th century. We'll do this by exploring the theme of division in several ways: of an initially close but later bitterly divided relationship between China and the Soviet Union first; then the outbreak of two bloody "hot" wars that divided both Korea and Vietnam in two, the former permanently, the latter for 30 years. In our very last lecture, we'll also touch briefly upon the future of the two Chinas: How long will Taiwan and Beijing remain unreconciled? Will we see a restoration of unity in our lifetimes?

Let's pick up our story now with the evolving relationship between the People's Republic of China and the U.S.S.R., a subject that we touched upon in our last lecture. With the success of the communist revolutions in Russia in 1917 and China in 1949, by 1950 the communist camp contained roughly half the world's population. Delighted with their success, Moscow and Beijing worked closely together during the early years of the Cold War, united by their common commitment to communism and against their common enemy, the U.S.A. and her allies. The Chinese were particularly incensed by the American rehabilitation of their former enemy Japan, and also by U.S. support for the ancient Chinese client states of South Korea and Taiwan. Throughout most of the 1950s, China was happy to recognize the U.S.S.R. as the undisputed authority in world communism, and China received Soviet weapons and Soviet economic aid in return. For their part, the Soviets worked diligently in the United Nations to have the Chinese seat in the Security Council transferred from the Nationalist government in Taiwan to the CCP government in Beijing. But cracks started to appear in the partnership late in that decade when China realized it was receiving less aid from the Soviets than non-communist Egypt and India were. It was also in the 1950s that tensions between China and India, along with military skirmishes high in the Himalayas, broke out over the question of the sovereignty of Tibet. In the midst of this tense standoff between the two most populous states on earth, India and China, the Soviets infuriated the Chinese by outwardly remaining neutral in the conflict, yet secretly giving a huge loan to India. By the early 1960s, occasional border clashes were occurring between Soviet and Chinese troops in Central Asia; and by 1964, both countries were publicly engaging in name calling.

As I mentioned last time, the CCP declared the U.S.S.R. under Khrushchev to be "revisionist" because it was pursuing a policy of peaceful coexistence with the U.S.A. The Soviets responded by declaring Mao a dangerous "left-wing adventurist" because he insisted that war between communism and the West was inevitable. When the Chinese successfully tested their own nuclear weapons in 1964, this only served to further increase tensions in the communist world. As we also noted last time, Mao then embarked upon a series of social and economic programs to try and distinguish Chinese communism from Soviet communism. The Great Leap Forward, between 1958 and 1961, was an attempt to have the Chinese economy catch up, even match those of the more developed nations by collectivizing all agriculture and industry. But, as I mentioned last time, the abolition of private ownership led to failed harvests and a deadly famine that resulted in the deaths of perhaps 20 million Chinese by 1962.

This deteriorating relationship between two major nations was playing out in the even larger context of the Cold War, which became a truly global phenomenon in the 1950s. The globalization of the war was really the inevitable outcome, I think, of a confrontation that pitted the dominant power of the Eurasian landmass, the Soviet Union, against a power that could project forces all over the world by land, by sea, by air, the United States of America. The Cold War also pitted one block aimed at worldwide communist revolution against another block committed to democracy, capitalism, and free trade. Tensions were fueled by related global processes, particularly decolonization and most particularly in Africa, which left a string of unstable, ex-colonial countries open to Cold War competition; and also by rivalry over oil resources in the Middle East.

The globalization of the Cold War became absolute with the invention of Inter-Continental Ballistic Missiles, which placed every corner of the earth in constant danger of nuclear attack. In military terms, the Cold War passed through several distinct phases. In the late 1940s and 50s, when the U.S.A. held a distinct advantage in weaponry, the Soviets or the Chinese couldn't dare risk a major clash. When U.S. allies Britain in 1952 and France in 1960 also developed their nuclear capacity, NATO was able to publish its doctrine of "overwhelming retaliation," a further disincentive to the outbreak of any major military conflict. But the Cold War did become hot twice, and in both cases these wars were fought in East Asia: in Korea between 1950 and 1953, and then in Indo-China, where defeated French troops gave way to Americans in 1954, dragging the U.S.A. into the long and bloody Vietnam War that lasted until 1975.

Let's leave the deteriorating relationship between China and the Soviet Union for a moment and turn to those two "hot" conflicts, both of which occurred in countries that had been powerfully influenced for millennia by the foundational ideas of Eastern civilization. As we've seen throughout this course, Korea actually has a long history of division between north and south. Remember the Three Kingdoms period way back during the first centuries of the Common Era? North Korea was then under the control of the powerful Koguryo kingdom, while the south was divided between Silla and Paekche. The relationship between these three kingdoms was one of constant warfare and shifting alliances, with the Chinese playing a key role. Even after Silla was able to unify the south under its hegemony in the seventh century, the North remained under the control of a separate Parhae dynasty. During their 500-year reign, the Choson dynasty was able to maintain rule over a unified Korea; but the roots of this cultural division between north and south remained deep, even during the period of Japanese occupation.

This reminds me that we last visited Korea on August 15, 1945, the date upon which Korea was liberated from Japanese hegemony, a day of jubilation throughout the country. But as a result of three-and-a-half decades of Japanese colonial rule, Korean society in 1945 was a chaotic mix of old and new classes, ideologies, and political factions. The core cultural elements of Korean culture—by that I mean dynastic governance, a rigid social hierarchy as we've seen, the ancient values of Confucianism and Buddhism, and a penchant for isolation from the world—had all been turned on their heads by Japanese imperial rule, which had severely shaken up the ideals and loyalties of intellectuals and ordinary folks alike. On the left of the political spectrum now were thousands of dedicated communists, many of whom had waged guerilla warfare against the Japanese for years, and who were now determined to transform Korea into a more egalitarian society, as their communist comrades in China were in the process of doing at that very moment. On the right were the landlords, the businessman, and many former Japanese collaborators who were determined to try and preserve their privileged place in society. It's easy to see how these political tensions, coupled with this long history of division, would become mixed up with Cold War geopolitics to create the two bitterly divided Koreas of today.

Following the defeat of the Japanese, the United States and the Soviet Union agreed to a proposal—opposed by most Koreans, by the way—to jointly occupy the peninsula as a trusteeship, with an agreed upon division between the two along the 38th Parallel. Although this arrangement was supposed to be temporary, the Soviets repeatedly postponed elections in their northern sector, which led ultimately to the establishment of a communist state under Soviet auspices in the north and a pro-Western democratic state in the south. Even this trusteeship arrangement forced upon the country by external powers has deep historical precedents in Korea, given the various periods of occupation the peninsula had suffered since ancient times, as we've seen, by outside powers like China and the Japanese.

There's an interesting story behind the decision to make the 38th Parallel the dividing line between north and south, by the way: In August, 1945, two young American officers were asked by the U.S. government to quickly establish an appropriate line of demarcation between the Soviet and U.S. trusteeships in Korea. Coincidentally, one of the two young U.S. officers was Dean Rusk, who later became U.S. Secretary of State under both President John Kennedy and President Lyndon Johnson. Working quickly and completely unprepared for this task, the officers used an old *National Geographic* map to select the 38th Parallel, mainly because it would leave the Choson capital of Seoul in the Western-aligned democratic south. Although no Koreans were consulted about this, the decision was quickly written into General Order Number 1 for the administration of postwar Japan.

North of the parallel, a provisional government was established in February, 1946 by communist leader and anti-Japanese guerilla hero Kim Il-sung called the North Korean People's Provisional Committee. As mistrust grew between the U.S. and the U.S.S.R., the U.S. sought United Nations involvement in the question of Korea's future, but the Soviet's boycotted the discussions. With dwindling hopes for reunification, the Republic of Korea was declared in the south on August 15, 1948; and on September 9 of that same year, the Democratic People's Republic of Korea was declared in the north with Kim Il-sung its first prime minister. Almost immediately, the relationship between the two Koreas degenerated into a series of bloody skirmishes along the 38th Parallel, skirmishes that escalated into full-scale war in 1950.

The Korean War that ensued was a bitter military conflict between the Republic of Korea in the south, supported by the United Nations, and the Democratic People's Republic of Korea in the north, supported by the Soviet Union and the People's Republic of China. The war began on June 25, 1950, and an armistice wasn't signed until just over three years later, on July 27, 1953. The tense military skirmishes along the 38th Parallel escalated into full-scale, open warfare when North Korean forces suddenly invaded the south on June 25, in what was the first significant armed conflict of the Cold War. The well-trained and well-armed North Korean forces, equipped with Soviet weapons, took Seoul in three days and swept on to the south, until by early August virtually all of the peninsula was under their control. The United States, under U.N. auspices, quickly came to the aid of the South Koreans; and General Douglas MacArthur succeeded in splitting the North Korean army in two with a successful amphibious assault on the port of Inchon, near Seoul. A rapid U.S./U.N. counteroffensive then recaptured Seoul and forced the North Koreans back past the 38th Parallel. But at that moment, the Chinese Red Army came to the aid of the communist North. There's a long history here, too, of course, of Chinese military alliances with various Korean factions, and even several military invasions of Korea, as we've seen several times in this course. Hundreds of thousands of Chinese troops drove the U.N. forces south again, back past the 38th Parallel. On January 4, 1951, Seoul fell for a second time. U.N. forces managed to recapture the city in March, 1952; but thereafter, a stalemate developed between the two sides.

The very real potential that this conflict could escalate into nuclear war finally ended with an armistice that restored the border between the Koreas near the 38th Parallel and created the Korean Demilitarized Zone, a 2.5-mile-wide buffer zone between the two Koreas that, of course, is still in place today. The war cost the lives of 2 million combat personnel and civilians, including 37,000 U.S. dead. Politically, it solved nothing and brought ruin to both halves of the country; although, as we'll see, with the aid of the United States the economy of South Korea soon staged a remarkable recovery. Even

380

today, of course, as so often in its past, the Korean peninsula, the "land of morning calm," remains bitterly divided. The real legacy of the Korean War has been to instill a sense of fear and insecurity that still blights the two Koreas in both their internal development and, more particularly, in the relationship between the two halves. So one ancient division of an East Asian society continues through to the present; and so also could have been the fate of Vietnam as a result of another brutal Cold War conflict there.

Vietnam also has a long history of division between north and south; divisions, as we've seen, based on geography, cultural and even linguistic differences, and in its long and complex relationship with the Chinese and with the French. During the 18th and 19th centuries, the French had assembled a colonial empire in Indo-China, which included Vietnam, Laos, and Cambodia. Much of Indo-China was then occupied by the Japanese during the Second World War, with a puppet Vichy-style French colonial administration left in charge. Late in the war, Japan replaced this French regime with a pro-Japanese Vietnamese emperor named Bao Dai, who immediately proclaimed independence from France. During the war, as was the case in Japanese-occupied China and Korea—and indeed much of Nazi-occupied Europe—it was a communist guerilla force known as the Viet Minh in Vietnam that formed the most effective anti-Japanese resistance movement. The Viet Minh were particularly strong in the north, close to their bases just across the border in southern China. When Japan surrendered, the leader of the Viet Minh, Ho Chi Minh, moved quickly to fill the power vacuum and quickly proclaimed an independent Democratic Republic of Vietnam.

But the French were determined to reassert their control of the region. They reoccupied the major cities with the indirect assistance of British forces that had been sent to assist with the surrender of the Japanese. The first direct confrontation between the French and the Viet Minh occurred at Haiphong harbor in November, 1946, when the Viet Minh fired on a French warship. In the brutal French retaliation that followed, 6,000 Vietnamese were killed, leading to the outbreak of a guerilla war against the French. The initial phase of the war, from 1947–1949, resulted in stalemate; but with the success of the communist revolution in China in 1949, the Viet Minh gained a powerful ally, and with Chinese military assistance they were able to drive the French out of North Vietnam the following year. The cost of maintaining this colonial war was now too much for the French government. From 1952 onwards, the United States of America agreed to cover cost of the war. The French did make one last dramatic attempt to defeat the Viet Minh by enticing them into what they hoped would be a decisive confrontation at Dien Bien Phu. But the 15,000 French soldiers sent to Dien Bien Phu were quickly surrounded by the Viet Minh; and following a six-month-siege—from November, 1953 through to May, 1954—the French garrison was forced to surrender. This defeat marked the end of French colonial ambitions in Indo-China.

The 1954 Geneva Accords that followed Dien Bien Phu partitioned Vietnam into two zones, but the hope was this would be only a temporary measure before national elections could reunite the two halves. The North was now ruled by the Viet Minh as the Democratic Republic of Vietnam; the South was known as the State of Vietnam. The United States government, of course, saw the situation in Vietnam as a test case for the containment of communism; and this resolve led to the outbreak of a second and much more bloody conflict known to Western historians ever since simply as the Vietnam War. The United States government believed it was essential to prevent the communist takeover of South Vietnam. The North Vietnamese government, on the other hand, saw U.S. involvement as an extension of the colonial war they'd just successfully waged to drive out the French. The North dismissed the new State of Vietnam, later known as the Republic of Vietnam, in the south as nothing more than a U.S. puppet state.

U.S. military advisors started arriving in Vietnam quite quickly in the 1950s. Troop levels then tripled in 1961 and 1962, and combat units were deployed beginning in 1965. U.S. and Australian military involvement peaked in January, 1968 at the time of the Tet Offensive, when in a well-coordinated move, 80,000 Viet Minh troops captured around 100 towns and cities. Although United States troops and their allies recaptured much of the lost territory, the brutal battles at Hue and Khe Sanh shook the U.S. military and also shook the U.S. public, which had been led to believe that the communists were incapable of such tactics and would be easily defeated. With this profound erosion of support for the war, and with bitter divisions in the administration of President Lyndon Johnson, United States ground forces were gradually withdrawn. But despite the Paris Peace Accords signed by all parties in January, 1973, fighting continued for two more years. In April, 1975, the North Vietnamese captured Saigon just as the last U.S. personnel were withdrawn, an event that marked the real end of the Vietnam War.

North and South Vietnam were reunified the following year, and unlike Korea they've stayed united up to the present day under the control of a communist government in Hanoi. This second brutal East Asian Cold War conflict also exacted a tragic human toll: Somewhere between 3 and 4 million Vietnamese from both sides were killed, as were 2 million Laotians and Cambodians, and 58,159 U.S. service personnel.

Let me try and begin to wrap up this lecture now by returning to the global vicissitudes of the Cold War, particularly as it played out in East Asia into the 1970s. As both the Vietnam and Cold Wars dragged on, the United States government decided it was time to try something new; time to try and take advantage of this tense split between the Soviets and the communist Chinese. In 1972, President Richard Nixon visited the aging Chairman Mao Zedong in China, a diplomatic coup that had the immediate effect of bringing China back into what had been for the past quarter century an essentially bipolar world. Nixon was greeted by Chinese Premier Zhou Enlai when Air Force One touched down in Beijing, a city then still known in the West as Peking, and a historic handshake took place at the foot of the gangway. In the background was a huge anti-imperialism poster quoting the words of Chairman Mao: "Make trouble, fail. Make trouble again, fail again, until their doom. This is the logic of imperialism and reactionaries the world over." President Nixon visited the Forbidden City and the Great Wall, of course; and at a farewell banquet in Shanghai found himself involved in a series of heads back, swallow it whole toasts with the Chinese leadership. Needless to say, the trip was a great success, as were several follow up trips by Henry Kissinger.

It wasn't long, in fact, before liaison offices opened in Beijing and Washington, DC; and formal diplomatic relations were later inaugurated in 1979. In fact, during the 1970s, Communist China established full diplomatic relations with several other major Western powers and also with Japan. As a direct result of the establishment of this relationship between China and the world, the Soviets felt under increasing pressure to try and stabilize their

383

European flank. This led quickly to a major breakthrough in the lessening of Cold War tensions: the Helsinki Conference, which ran from 1972–1975.

With Nixon's visit to China and the end of the Vietnam War, the Cold War had entered a new phase that saw China reassume an important geopolitical position as one of the great global powers; a position frankly that, as we've seen repeatedly in this course, China had occupied for much of world history. But let's not forget that even with these diplomatic breakthroughs, China in the mid-1970s was still mired deep in the Cultural Revolution and desperately trying to deal with a failing economy.

In our next lecture, it seems appropriate that we turn to another of those enduring themes of the course: economics. We'll see how, under the leadership of Mao's successor Deng Xiaoping, the ancient Chinese economy was revived so spectacularly that within one generation China was boasting one of the largest and most vibrant economies on the planet. It wasn't only China that staged a remarkable recovery, of course. We'll also return to Japan and see how that country quickly rehabilitated itself after the horrors of World War II to rejoin the ranks of the leading economies of the modern world, and to inspire a similar economic revolution in South Korea and all the other so-called Little Tigers of East Asia. See you soon.

The Rise of the East Asian Tigers
Lecture 47

In 1981, five years after the death of Mao Zedong, Deng Xiaoping assumed complete control of both the Chinese Communist Party and the People's Republic of China. Deng immediately moderated Mao's commitment to economic self-sufficiency and brought China into the international trading and financial system. This decision to pursue a quasi-capitalist model would undoubtedly have surprised the sociologist Max Weber, who had argued that Confucianism and Daoism were essentially incompatible with capitalism. As we will see, this tension between the necessity of adopting imported models to ensure modernization and economic success while retaining ancient ideals that had long sustained Eastern civilization has been played out repeatedly in all the nations of East Asia in the 20th and 21st centuries.

The Four Modernizations

- Deng Xiaoping's program of introducing the principles of market capitalism to China was dubbed the Four Modernizations. Essentially, this meant that China needed to make significant progress in agriculture, industry, science and technology, and defense.

- To facilitate his program, and realizing how desperately China needed to educate its managerial class after the anti-education policies of the Cultural Revolution, Deng sent tens of thousands of Chinese students to foreign universities to build a modern professional base.

- Along with attempts to build a more educated workforce, Deng and the party also focused on another modernization: reforming the agriculture sector, a challenge faced by every Chinese government from the ancient Shang dynasty onward.
  - Abandoning Mao's commitment to communes, production teams of 30 or 40 families were contracted to produce a certain quantity of crops on land allotted to them. These communities could plan together to maximize production because they had

an incentive: If they produced more than their quota, they could keep the overage and sell it.

o This policy, along with the reinstatement of private markets, had immediate success in increasing national food production.

- Deng and the party also opened manufacturing up to foreign trade and new technology and welcomed international investment. As local entrepreneurs were able to concentrate on the production of consumer and export goods, foreign exports exploded. This increased both private and public income and led to surging development, particularly in those coastal areas that already had a long history of involvement in foreign trade, such as Hong Kong.

Hong Kong

- The manner in which the Chinese government handled the British return of Hong Kong in 1997 is a further example of pragmatism and economic rationality under Deng Xiaoping.

- Hong Kong had long been part of Chinese sovereign territory, but under the Qing dynasty, the British had used "gunboat diplomacy" to force the Chinese to cede Hong Kong to Britain for about a century and a half. During the Second World War, Hong Kong was occupied by the Japanese from 1941 until it was liberated by British and Chinese troops in August 1945.

- A flood of labor from the mainland into Hong Kong in the 1950s transformed the territory into a major industrial manufacturing center. In the 1960s, as mainland China struggled economically, traditional Chinese values were increasingly challenged in Hong Kong by its booming capitalist economy. By the 1970s, Hong Kong was arguably the major tourism and commercial center of Southeast Asia.

- But as the fateful year of 1997 approached—the year in which, according to the treaty, the British government had agreed to hand Hong Kong back to Chinese control—many worried residents left

Under its "special status," Hong Kong has continued to thrive; new buildings are constantly being added to an already impressive skyline.

the island. After the handover of sovereignty, Hong Kong was designated by the government as a region of "special status," and very little happened to change its position as a major tourism and economic hub.

Entering the 21st Century

- As the end of the 20th century approached, China could look back on 50 years of tumultuous change since the declaration of the People's Republic of China in 1949 by Mao Zedong.

- The leadership of Deng Xiaoping had steered China away from the Legalist excesses of Maoism and toward a successful and stable economic future based on equitable ownership of agricultural land and the creation of an educated workforce to better manage the manufacturing and export sectors of the economy.

- The bloodshed in Tiananmen Square in 1989 had stained Deng's reputation, but the peaceful return of Hong Kong not only added a wealthy commercial center to the Chinese state but also demonstrated China's ability to govern with greater tolerance.

- As Deng's health deteriorated before his death in 1997, President Jiang Zemin and other members of his generation gradually assumed control of the day-to-day functions of government. This "third-generation" leadership was determined to take China into the 21st century as a stable, prosperous, and more moderate economic powerhouse.

The Economy of Japan

- The economies of China, Japan, South Korea, and other so-called Asian tiger nations underwent dramatic growth in the 20th century. Despite what some have called the Cocacolonization of the world, there has been a genuine commitment in these nations to embrace those Western ideologies that are critical for survival in the globalized village without completely abandoning the traditional cultural ideas that have sustained them for so long.

- After its defeat in 1945, Japan's economic revival was jumpstarted by policies promoted by the United States. So effective was the alliance between U.S. aid and Japanese industriousness that by 1949, the Japanese economy was already back to prewar output levels!

- In the same way that European postwar recovery benefited directly from the injection of cash and technology funneled through the Marshall Plan, the Japanese economy also receive a "blood transfusion" in the form of $2 billion in investment aid from the United States. Further, no restrictions were placed on the entry of Japanese goods into the U.S. market.

- The United States then signed a mutual defense treaty in 1960, stipulating that Japan could never spend more than 1 percent of its gross national product (GNP) on defense. (Earlier treaties had formalized Japan's relationship with the United States and its role in the international arena.) In essence, the United States took care of Japanese defense, allowing Japan to invest virtually all of its GNP income back into the economy.

o The U.S. military commitment to Japan continues to the present day, with more than 35,000 military personnel and 5,000 civilians still stationed on bases in Japan.

o This continuing U.S. military involvement in Japan has many opponents.

- In the 1950s, Japanese economic planners decided to focus on pursing export-driven economic growth, supported by low wages.
  o Japanese workers were prepared to work long hours for low wages during this initial period of recovery as part of a typically East Asian collectivist approach to solving their nation's problems.

  o Although Japan had to import raw materials, the low cost of labor ensured price-competitive production and export.

- During the 1950s, the Japanese economy churned out labor-intensive manufactured goods, such as textiles and steel. But by the 1960s, Japanese companies had generated such significant profits that they were able to invest in more capital-intensive manufacturing, producing higher-value consumer products, such as radios, televisions, motorcycles, and automobiles.

- In the decades that followed, Japanese corporations took advantage of what had by now become a highly skilled workforce to shift their resources to technology-intensive products, such as memory chips, LCDs, and CD-ROM drives. By the 1980s, the label "Made in Japan" signified state-of-the-art products of the highest quality.

- As their economy continued to grow, the Japanese government and financial institutions began to assume an increasingly prominent voice in global affairs. But in the 1990s, it became clear that Japanese growth rates were not sustainable, and the nation's economy sputtered into a recession that lasted into the 21st century. Still, however, Japan has the third-largest economy in the world today.

Recent Economic Situation in East Asia

- The earliest and most successful imitators of the Japanese model were Hong Kong, Singapore, South Korea, and Taiwan, and by the 1980s, these four "little tigers" had each become a major economic power.

- All four suffered from similar problems: a shortage of capital, few natural resources, and overpopulation. But like Japan a generation earlier, they transformed these disadvantages into advantages by focusing on export-driven industrialization. Indeed, the four quickly became serious competitors to Japan by imitating Japanese products and undercutting them with cheaper versions because of lower labor costs. Before long, Indonesia, Thailand, and Malaya had also joined the "tigers club"!

- As we have seen, it was also in the 1980s that Chinese leaders reversed Mao's economic plans and, instead, actively sought foreign investment and foreign technology. A new generation of highly educated managers and entrepreneurs was created, who used the incentives now built into the system to achieve spectacular levels of growth in all sectors. With the economy surging, the government officially signaled in 1992 that China had embraced a "socialist market economy."
  o The role of government was transformed from central planner to an entity that provided a stable but competitive environment.

  o In December 2001, China joined the World Trade Organization and officially became a global economic superpower!

- President Hu Jintao succeeded Jiang Zemin as the top leader of what was then the fourth-generation leadership of the People's Republic of China. His low-key and reserved leadership style was a further example of China's transition of leadership from old, hard-core communists to younger, more pragmatic economic technocrats.

- o Hu reinstated some controls on the economy that had been relaxed by previous administrations, and he and his colleagues were also highly conservative in their attitude toward political reform.

- o But in foreign policy, Hu and his colleagues pursued an approach that has been termed "China's peaceful development," using soft power in international relations.

- o These policy approaches seem certain to continue under the new president, Xi Jinping.

- When the global financial crisis hit in 2008, China immediately launched an economic stimulus plan to deal quickly with the crisis and ward off potential recession. The plan focused on increasing affordable housing, easing credit restrictions for mortgages, lowering taxes on real estate sales and commodities, and pumping more public investment into infrastructure development. It has been a spectacular success.

- Today, China seems poised to move from export dependency to further development of its own massive internal market, particularly in the face of instability in the European economy. Some economic experts have predicted that China could become the world's largest economy by as early as 2030, although others see this as unlikely. There is, however, every reason to believe that China will dominate the technology economy in the very near future.

Suggested Reading

Dower, *Embracing Defeat.*

Haiwang Yuan, ed., *This Is China*, chapter 4.

Meisner, *Mao's China and After.*

Tanner, *China: A History*, chapter 16.

1. Should Deng Xiaoping ultimately be credited with saving Chinese communism and preserving Chinese civilization?

2. What role did the United States play in the postwar economic recovery of Japan?

The Rise of the East Asian Tigers
Lecture 47—Transcript

Five years after the death of Mao Zedong in September, 1976, following a bitter power struggle within the upper echelons of the Chinese Communist Party, Deng Xiaoping assumed complete control of both the party and the People's Republic of China in 1981. Deng immediately moderated Mao's commitment to economic self-sufficiency and isolation—the sort of isolation that so many Chinese leaders before him had attempted to pursue over the millennia—and brought China into the international trading and financial system.

This new economic policy direction was facilitated by the normalization of relations between China and the U.S.A. that had begun, as we saw, with President Nixon's 1972 visit to Beijing; a diplomatic coup for which Nixon deserves enormous credit, I think. In his desire to push for more rapid economic development, Deng decided to walk something of a tightrope: to open up the nation to capitalist market principles without surrendering any of the control the CCP exercised over the state. This decision to pursue a quasi-capitalist economic model in China would no doubt have surprised the late-19th, early-20th sociologist Max Weber. In two of Weber's classic works, *The Protestant Ethic and the Spirit of Capitalism* and *The Religions of China: Confucianism and Taoism*, Weber had argued that the core ideologies of Confucianism and Daoism were essentially incompatible with capitalism. Weber argued that actively working to acquire wealth was frowned upon by the Confucian ethic, which was focused more on self-restraint, on the acquisition of status through intellectual and ethical cultivation, and an emphasis on communal rather than individual values. Because of this, Weber believed that capitalism could never develop in China. Certainly one of the classic sayings of Confucius in the *Analects* seems to support Weber's interpretation; you might remember this saying from an earlier lecture: "The noble man does what is right, the lesser man does what is profitable."

But perhaps Weber wouldn't have been so astounded by Den Xiaoping's embrace of capitalism and China's extraordinary economic success in the 20th century. He'd probably point out that this development was precisely because China had intentionally turned away from its ancient Confucian values and adopted many of the ideals of the West. This tension, this tightrope walk, between the necessity of adopting imported models and ideals to ensure modernization and economic success, while at the same time not letting go of the ancient models and ideals that had sustained unique Eastern civilization for so long, has been played out over and over again in all the nations of East Asia in the 20th and 21st centuries, as we've seen and as we'll see.

Deng Xiaoping's program of introducing the principles of market capitalism to China was dubbed the "Four Modernizations." Essentially this meant that China needed to make significant progress in the agriculture sector, in industry, in science and technology, and in defense. To facilitate this, and realizing how desperately China needed to educate its managerial class after the anti-education policies of the Cultural Revolution (during which slogans like "Red over Expert" had abounded), Deng sent tens of thousands of Chinese students to foreign universities to build a modern professional base to help him achieve the four modernizations.

Thinking again of the continuing relevance of Confucianism just for a moment, we've seen repeatedly in this course that one of the really enduring ideas of Eastern civilization has been this commitment to advanced education for the people; something Confucius himself argued for 2,500 years ago and an idea pursued by all the leading dynasties of China ever since, right through the Confucian exam system. But an educated populace can also be more difficult to manage by governments, so we've also seen periods in which a more Legalist distrust of education was embraced by the state, beginning with the Qin dynasty and more recently during the Cultural Revolution. As large numbers of students were sent overseas by the government—and, by the way, I remember them turning up at my former university in Sydney, Australia—they undoubtedly gained a high quality technical education, but they were also exposed to democratic ideals as they studied at universities in Australia and in the United States of America. It was this exposure that led directly to the outbreak of pro-democracy demonstrations in Beijing's Tiananmen Square in 1989, an event we'll consider in our final lecture.

Along with attempts to build a more educated workforce, Deng and the party also focused on another modernization: reforming the agriculture sector; a challenge frankly faced by every Chinese government from the ancient Shang dynasty onwards. Abandoning Mao's commitment to communes, production teams of 30 or 40 families were now contracted to produce a certain quantity of crops on land allotted to them by the government. You remember, of course, the equal-field system first tried by the Sui and Tang dynasties 1,300 years earlier? There are definite similarities here. These communities could now plan together to maximize production because they had an incentive: If they produced more than their quota, they could keep it and they could sell it. This policy, along with the reinstatement of private markets—the sort of markets that have dominated village life in China for 8,000 years now—had an immediate success in increasing national food production, which was Deng's first great triumph.

Turning to the industrial sector next, Deng and the Party opened manufacturing up to foreign trade and to new technological ideas, and they also began to welcome international investment. As local entrepreneurs with more autonomy were able to concentrate now on the production of consumer and export goods, foreign exports exploded. This increased both private and public income and led to surging development, particularly in those coastal areas that already had a long history of involvement in foreign trade. One such region in southern China was the island of Hong Kong; and the manner in which the Chinese government handled the British hand back of Hong Kong in 1997 is a further example, I think, of the pragmatism and economic rationality of the People's Republic of China under Deng Xiaoping.

Hong Kong had long been part of Chinese sovereign territory, having been initially incorporated into China way, way back during the Qin dynasty, in the third century B.C.E. During the Tang dynasty in the eighth century C.E., the island and surrounding territory had developed into a thriving commercial hub, a status that it had maintained into the modern period. But under the Qing dynasty, the British used what's euphemistically known as "gunboat diplomacy" to force the Chinese to cede Hong Kong to Britain for about a century and a half as part of the first unequal treaty signed between the two nations; you remember the circumstances. During the Second World War, Hong Kong was occupied by the Japanese from 1941 onwards, until it was liberated by British and Chinese troops in August, 1945. A flood of labor from the mainland into Hong Kong in the 1950s transformed the territory into a major industrial manufacturing center. In the 1960s, as mainland China struggled economically, traditional Chinese values were increasingly challenged in Hong Kong by its booming capitalist economy, in which enormous numbers of Chinese found work in Western-style manufacturing and Western financial industries. By the 1970s, Hong Kong was arguably the major tourism and commercial center of Southeast Asia; I remember being astonished by Hong Kong when I first visited there as a child.

But as the fateful year of 1997 approached, the year in which, according to the treaty, the British government had agreed to hand Hong Kong back to Chinese control, many worried residents left the island. True to their word, the last British governor of Hong Kong, Chris Patten, supervised a peaceful and orderly handover of sovereignty on July 1, 1997, and the world waited to see what would happen next. Surprisingly to many, very little happened to change Hong Kong's position as a major tourism and economic hub. The People's Republic of China designated Hong Kong as a region of "special status," governed by a Provisional Legislative Council elected by a selection committee whose members were initially appointed by the People's Republic of China government. Under this special status, Hong Kong has continued to thrive, and new buildings are constantly being added to an already extraordinary and impressive skyline.

As the end of the 20th century approached, then, China could look back on 50 years of tumultuous change since the declaration of the People's Republic of China in 1949 by Mao Zedong. The leadership of Deng Xiaoping had steered China away from the Legalist excesses of Maoism, and towards a successful and stable economic future based on equitable ownership of agricultural land and the creation of an educated workforce to better manage the manufacturing and export sectors of the economy. The bloodshed in Tiananmen Square in 1989—and again, this is something we'll talk about more in our next lecture—had stained Deng's reputation; but the peaceful hand back of Hong Kong not only added a wealthy commercial center to the Chinese state, it also allowed China to demonstrate its ability to govern with greater tolerance. As Deng's health deteriorated prior to his death in 1997, President Jiang Zemin and other members of his generation gradually assumed control of the day-to-day functions of government. This third generation leadership was determined to take China into the 21st century as a stable, prosperous, and more moderate economic powerhouse. But before we consider China's continuing growth during the past decade and a half, let's turn next to the economies of the other major nations of East Asia.

This is a topic of enormous world historical importance, of course, because there can be no doubt that the surge towards globalization and worldwide economic integration that so characterized the latter part of the 20th century benefited enormously from economic developments throughout all of East and Southeast Asia. This is because the economies of not only China but also Japan, South Korea, and all the other so-called "Asian tiger nations" underwent dramatic growth in this age of market globalization.

Some might argue that what was lost in this tidal wave of globalization were many of the core cultural ideologies that had sustained Eastern civilization for so long, because it was Western-style economic and cultural ideas that were now adopted by the nations of East and Southeast Asia. But as we've seen, despite what some have called the "Cocacolonization" of the world, there's been a genuine commitment in China, Korea, Japan, and Southeast Asia to embrace those Western ideologies that are critical for survival in the globalized village, but at the same time not completely abandon the traditional cultural ideas that had sustained these states for so long. How much longer this delicate cultural balancing can be maintained will be something incredibly interesting for us all to watch in the years ahead.

It was policies promoted by the United States, policies obviously influenced by Cold War politics, which jump started Japan's economic revival after its defeat in 1945; and so effective was this alliance between United States aid and Japanese industriousness that by as early as 1949, the Japanese economy was already back to its prewar output levels. In the same way that European postwar recovery benefited directly from the injection of cash and technology funneled through the Marshall Plan, the Japanese economy also receive a blood transfusion in the form of $2 billion in investment aid from the United States government. As a further and perhaps even more valuable form of assistance to this new U.S. Cold War ally, no restrictions whatsoever were placed on the entry of Japanese goods into the U.S. market. The United States then signed a mutual defense treaty in 1960 that stipulated that Japan could never spend more than 1 percent of its GNP on defense; so in essence, the United States took care of Japanese defense, allowing Japan to invest virtually all of its GNP income back into the economy. It was the Treaty of San Francisco and the associated Security Treaty, both signed in 1951, that formalized Japan's relationship with the U.S. and its role in the new international arena. By the time the treaties went into effect on April 28, 1952, Japan was a free nation and a very close ally of the United States of America.

Following the Japanese surrender in 1945, the Japanese Imperial Army and Navy had been decommissioned, and, as I mentioned, all of the Japanese military bases taken over by U.S. Armed Forces. The U.S. imposed a constitution on Japan that included a no-armed-force clause in 1947; and the later Treaty of San Francisco made the U.S., as I mentioned, legally responsible for the defense of Japan. The U.S. military commitment to Japan continues through to the present day, of course; more than 35,000 military and 5,000 civilian personnel still stationed on bases in Japan today. The base at Yokosuka is home to the U.S. Seventh Fleet; the 3rd Marine Expeditionary Force is based in Okinawa; and about 130 U.S. Air Force fighters are stationed at the Misawa and Kadena Air Bases. But this continuing U.S. military involvement in Japan has many opponents within that country. Some object to what they see as a continuing U.S. "occupation" of their country and others object for social reasons. Evidence of social concerns was seen at a 2009 protest in Okinawa that denounced the presence of U.S. Marines after Japanese police had arrested a Marine for the rape of a 14 year old Japanese girl.

After the 1951 treaties were signed, Japanese economic planners decided to focus on pursuing export-driven economic growth, supported by very low wages. Japanese workers were prepared to work long hours for very low wages during this initial period of recovery as part I think of a typically East Asian collectivist approach to solving their nation's problems. This, of course, gave Japanese manufacturers a competitive cost advantage over international rivals who were paying much higher wages; this is very much like the advantage Chinese manufacturers have enjoyed over recent decades, of course. Although Japan had to import its raw materials, the low cost of labor assured price competitive production and export. During the 1950s, the Japanese economy churned out labor-intensive manufactured goods like textiles and steel. But by the 1960s, Japanese companies had generated such significant profits that they were able to invest in more capital-intensive manufacturing, producing higher-value consumer products now like radios, televisions, motorcycles, and automobiles. In the decades that followed, Japanese corporations took advantage of what had by now become a highly skilled workforce to shift their resources to technology-intensive products like memory chips, LCDs, CD-ROM drives, and so on; and by the 1980s, the label "Made in Japan" signified state-of-the-art products of the highest quality. Will we see something similar happening with the "Made in China" label in the decades ahead, I wonder?

That question brings me to my next topic for this lecture: a brief consideration of the economic situation in East Asia over the past couple of decades. As their economy continued to grow, the Japanese government and Japanese financial institutions began to assume an increasingly prominent voice in global affairs. By the 1980s, it was even conceivable that Japan could overtake the United States as the world's largest economy. But in the 1990s, it became clear that these surging growth rates weren't sustainable, and the Japanese economy sputtered into a recession that lasted into the 21st century. Let's not forget, however, that Japan still has the third largest economy in the world today, just marginally behind China. Japanese success also served as an inspiration for other East and Southeast Asian countries. The earliest and the most successful imitators of the Japanese model were Hong Kong, Singapore, South Korea, of course, and Taiwan; and by the 1980s, these four so-called "little tigers" had each become a major economic powerhouse. All four suffered from similar problems: a shortage of capital, few natural resources, and overpopulation. But like Japan a generation earlier, they transformed these disadvantages into advantages by focusing on export-driven industrialization. Indeed, the four quickly became serious competitors to Japan by imitating Japanese products and then undercutting them with cheaper versions because of their lower labor costs. Before long, Indonesia, Thailand, and Malaya had also joined the "tigers club."

As we've seen, it was also in the 1980s that Chinese leaders reversed Mao's economic plans and instead actively sought foreign investment, and foreign technology was imported on a large scale. A whole new generation of highly educated managers and entrepreneurs was created now, who used the very real incentives built into the system to also achieve spectacular levels of growth in all sectors. With the economy surging, the government officially signaled in 1992 that China had embraced a "socialist market economy." Under the third generation leadership, the centrally-planned economic system of the past had given way to a genuine market economy now, where demand for goods and services drove production and drove price. The role of government was now transformed from central planner to an entity that provided a stable but competitive environment. To do this, the government sought and received massive foreign investment because of the attractions of low labor costs and a vast market of over one billion consumers. In December, 2001, China joined the World Trade Organization and was officially a global economic superpower.

President Hu Jintao succeeded Jiang Zemin as the top leader of what was then the fourth generation leadership of the People's Republic of China. Until his retirement at the end of 2012, Hu Jintao served as General Secretary of the Communist Party of China, as President of the People's Republic of China, and as Chairman of the Central Military Commission. His lowkey and reserved leadership style was a further example of China's transition of leadership from old, hardcore communists to younger, more pragmatic economic technocrats. In some ways, he represented a sort of blended Confucian-Legalist approach to government, similar to the approach that many of his ancient predecessors had espoused. For example, Hu reinstated some controls on the economy that were relaxed by the previous administration, and he and his colleagues were also highly conservative in their attitude towards political reform. But in foreign policy, Hu and his colleagues pursued an approach that's been termed "China's peaceful development," using soft power in international relations. Under Hu, for example, China's global influence in Africa, Latin America, and other developing countries increased dramatically. These policy approaches seem certain to continue under the new president of the People's Republic of China, Xi Jinping, only the fifth leader of China now since 1949.

What can we say about the future of the Chinese economy? As I mentioned a moment ago, in mid-2011, the economy of the People's Republic of China, with a GDP of over $5 trillion, surpassed that of Japan to become the world's second largest economy after the United States of America. (Just to put that in perspective, though, despite the 2008 recession, the U.S.A. still boasts a massive GDP of about $14.25 trillion.) But there's no denying that China is the world's fastest growing economy, with average annual growth rates of close to 10 percent for the last 30 years. China is also the second largest trading nation in the world after the U.S.A.; China is the largest exporter, of course, but also the second largest importer in the world.

As the global financial crisis hit in 2008, China immediately launched an economic stimulus plan to deal quickly with the crisis and ward off potential recession. This plan focused on increasing affordable housing; on easing credit restrictions for mortgages; on lowering taxes on real estate sales and commodities; and on pumping more public investment into infrastructure development, such as the rail network, roads, and ports as a stimulus to development. The plan was a spectacular success: By the end of 2009, as the rest of the world was deep in a slump, the Chinese economy was already showing signs of recovery, so much so that "managing inflation expectations" was added to the list of economic objectives for the plan.

Today, China seems poised to move from export dependency to further development of its own massive internal market, particularly in the face of the instability in the European economy. Wages are rapidly rising all over the country; Chinese leaders are all calling for an increased standard of living. Some economic experts have predicted that China could become the world's largest economy by as early as 2030; although, to be honest, most others see this as unlikely.

But there's certainly every reason to believe that China will dominate the technology economy in the very near future. Patrick Thibodeau, who's a technology and IT journalist with particular knowledge of China, has pointed to five very valid key reasons why he believes that Chinese domination of the world of technology is inevitable: First, China's leadership deeply understands engineering and technology. At the time of writing this lecture, eight of the nine members of the Standing Committee of the Political Bureau in 2012, including Hu Jintao himself, had engineering degrees. It's worth noting here that in 2009, China awarded more than 350,000 engineering degrees, compared to just 137,000 in the United States. Second, the Chinese government has made technological innovation their leading goal in almost everything, including clean energy. In 2009, for example, the Chinese invested close to $35 billion in clean energy, nearly double the investment of the United States. Third, China now has a massive pool of highly skilled technical labor; I've met many highly trained engineering and technology people in China myself in casual conversations on airplanes, and also chemists, physicists, and geologists. Fourth, the United States is falling way behind China in science and math education at all levels. In China, 42 percent of all college undergraduates earn science or math degrees, compared to something like 10 percent in the United States of America. Finally, China is dominating virtually all technology manufacturing industries everywhere; this means everything from TVs to supercomputers. I'm sure I don't need to remind us all that China is also one of the world's two largest creditor nations, along with Japan, and owns over 25 percent of U.S. Treasury Bonds.

Now we have one final lecture to try and wrap up this epic course. We've spent some time in these last lectures considering two of the key foundational themes that we've pursued from the very beginning: politics and the economy. We've seen continuing experiments in government, including the triumph of a modified form of Marxist-Leninist ideology, in the success of the People's Republic of China. We've seen extraordinary economic growth and advanced technological innovation that reminds us very much of the technologically advanced and wealthy China that we've met so many times in this course before decline under the Qing dynasty. We've also noted the economic and political success of many other smaller nations of East Asia, including Japan obviously, South Korea, and the many other "little tigers." All this success was despite, and in some ways because of, the tense Cold War geopolitical situation that dominated most of the world for much of the second half of the 20th century, an example of East Asia's complete integration now into the globalized world of today.

In our final lecture, I want to come back to the people of East Asia; to their societies, to their lives, to the billionaires and the peasants, the lives of men and women. How many of the ancient ideas about ethical relationships and the role of the individual in maintaining a harmonious communal society still resonate in contemporary East Asia today, particularly in China? Please join me next time as we bring our epic exploration of Eastern civilization to its conclusion.

The Enduring Ideas of Eastern Civilization
Lecture 48

Throughout this course, we have explored the evolution of ideas across vast areas of geographical space and through eons of historical time, as we followed in the footsteps of great adventurers, warriors, rulers, peasants, and some of the greatest minds of all time. We have examined the development of the philosophy, science, religion, economics, politics, and social life of China, Japan, Korea, and Southeast Asia and have measured their influence on other Eastern states, as well as their legacy in the contemporary world. In this final lecture, we will return to our definitions of key terms from the first lecture and then conclude by considering two foundational themes we have seen throughout the course: social and gender relationships.

Definitions Revisited
- In the first lecture of this course, we tried to unpack three key terms: foundations, Eastern, and civilization.

- We fixed the geographical scope of our course on China, Korea, Japan, and Southeast Asia, although as we have seen repeatedly, to truly understand events in these regions, it has been necessary to trace connections between the Eastern Hemisphere and the rest of the world.
  - As a direct result of the expedition of Zhang Qian, the brave Han dynasty envoy who first breached the barriers of China's western frontier in his journey to Central Asia, China was linked into the great trading system of ancient Eurasia, and the Silk Roads began to flourish.

  - This connection made possible the spread of Buddhism out of India and into China, then on to Korea, Japan, and Southeast Asia. Buddhist monks from all these countries later undertook journeys back to India to seek knowledge and inspiration.

- o Later, the Mongols connected East Asia into a vast trans-Eurasian empire that made possible the transmission of many Eastern technological and intellectual inventions to the West, where they had a profound impact on subsequent world history.

- o In the later stages of our course, we traced the often torturous connections that developed between all East Asian countries and the imperializing nations of the West.

- In our first lecture, we also came up with another interpretation of the word "Eastern"—as referring to those regions of the world that have been profoundly influenced by the culture of China. We traced this influence through language and writing, ideas about governance and administration, philosophy, social organization, economic management, and technological inventions. And we learned that despite the size and power of China, the other states of East Asia constructed their own societies that were much more than mere carbon copies of China.

- In our first lecture, we saw that most historians are wary of the word "civilization." In its original Latin context, the word simply pertains to cities and their citizens—and we have certainly visited some splendid cities in this course: Changan, Beijing, Seoul, and others. But we also saw the dangers in the classical use of the word "civilization" when it is used to make a value judgment.

- We considered a third way of understanding "civilization": as a concept that describes the entire culture of a complex society, the complete set of ideas, customs, and arts that make that culture distinctive, even unique.
  - o Thus, we can talk about "Chinese civilization" as a genuine cultural entity, and we can define those characteristics that collectively add up to Chinese civilization: Confucian, Daoist, Legalist, and Buddhist ideology; imperial dynastic government; a strong emphasis on education; a collectivist as opposed to individualistic mindset; particular types of food and clothing; and so on.

- o We can also, as we have done throughout this course, talk about "Eastern civilization" as the sum total of all the complex societies that emerged in the region—the complete set of ideas, customs, and arts of China, Korea, Japan, and Southeast Asia that make Eastern civilization so unique.

- The last term we discussed in our introductory lecture was "foundations." Here, we attempted to identify, define, and trace the development of all the significant cultural axioms, ideas, and principles that emerged within the construct that we defined as "Eastern civilization." And then we tried to see how these core foundational ideas, principles, and technologies went on to influence the development of society and civilization within the East Asian region and, eventually, around the world.

- In the last three lectures, we have been intent on bringing our discussion of the evolution of all these ideas up to the present day.
  - o We focused on government and politics in China and elsewhere in the 20th century; we returned to the theme of global connections as we traced the impact of the Cold War on the states of East Asia; and we looked at economic developments in the region since the Second World War.

  - o At other places in the course, we commented on the continuing relevance of Confucianism in China today, an idea that has received strong support even from within the highest echelons of the Communist Party.

  - o We have discussed developments in language and written script, such as the adoption of *Hangul* in Korea as a direct response to Japanese occupation and the development of Pinyin in mainland China after the Communist revolution.

  - o We have also had quite a bit to say about the development of rich streams of art and literature throughout the course, from the ancient Zhou dynasty classics and magnificent Tang poetry, through to Kabuki drama and even early-modern erotic novels in Japan.

Tiananmen Square, 1989

- Demonstrations in Tiananmen Square began on April 14, 1989, during a momentous year that saw the rapid collapse of communist governments around the world. The protests in Beijing were sparked by the death of Hu Yaobang, a Chinese government official known for tolerating dissent.

- On the day of Hu's funeral, 100,000 people gathered in Tiananmen Square, including many who were against the government's authoritarianism. Demonstrations quickly spread in the streets around the square, and large-scale protests broke out in other cities throughout China, including Shanghai.

- The protests lasted seven weeks until the government, driven by concerns for stability and, perhaps, a fear of being overthrown, decided to pursue a classic Legalist response by sending troops into the square on June 4.

- The number of deaths that ensued is not known; no video footage or written evidence of violence in the square has ever surfaced. Intelligence reports received by the Soviet Politburo estimated that 3,000 protesters were killed, but this number is impossible to verify. The government followed up the military assault by conducting widespread arrests of protesters and their supporters.

- China continues to grapple with the question of human rights, of course, with regular demands being made by individuals within the country and around the world for more participatory government and greater individual freedom. Commentators debate whether China will eventually democratize or remain a totalitarian one-party state under the control of the Chinese Communist Party.
  - Some argue that democracy itself might ultimately be undermined by the success of China and smaller communist countries. They point out that China is becoming a model

of booming development, political stability, affordable housing, successful social welfare, and more, all of which will have been achieved under the control of an authoritarian, nondemocratic regime.

o Many other China watchers argue that a second Tiananmen Square uprising is inevitable, because of such problems as increasing inequality, land ownership rights, environmental degradation, and corruption among officials.

o Certainly, the government has adopted many policies to try to solve these problems and improve the lives of the people: increasing spending in rural areas, abolishing taxes, cracking down on corruption, and attempting to increase the standard of living for all sectors of China's vast population. Some of these policies are remarkably similar to those adopted by many of China's ancient dynasties.

The One-Child Policy and Gender Roles

- China's one-child policy restricts the growth of urban families, although there are many exemptions for rural couples and minorities. The government claims that this policy has prevented more than 250 million births between 1978 and 2000.

- The policy is often criticized in the West for encouraging abortion and female infanticide, for creating a serious gender imbalance in China, and for a dramatic increase in female adoptions in the West. But a 2008 Pew Center survey of a large sample of the Chinese population showed that some 76 percent of the Chinese people support the policy.

- The gender imbalance is seen as a serious problem. According to 2010 statistics, with sex-specific abortions, 119 boys are being born for every 100 girls; projecting these figures forward shows that, by 2020, 24 million men of marrying age will have no chance of finding a female partner.

Under communist rule, women in China are now more empowered to work outside the home, and foot binding, child marriages, prostitution, and arranged marriages have all been banned.

- Quite recently, the head of China's National Population and Family Commission announced the introduction of a series of measures to correct the gender imbalance of the policy, particularly a crackdown on illegal prenatal gender tests and selective abortions. The government also recently announced that the policy would remain in place until 2015 and would then be reassessed.

- Gender roles and relationships are changing in China and the rest of East Asia today. The success of the Communist revolution led to a significant reevaluation of women's roles, although the inherent contradiction between a woman as reproductive agent and a woman as equal partner and worker in society has hardly been resolved. Still, under communist rule, the social status of women, particularly educated urban women, in China has improved considerably.

The End of Our Journey

- China has enjoyed one of the longest and most continuous histories of any society on the planet, and traditions that emerged thousands of years ago continue to guide and influence Chinese development to the present day.

- At the same time, other East and Southeast Asian societies have developed their own fascinating and unique cultural traditions, partly in response and even resistance to the powerful influence of China.

- Our course has been a rich and diverse story of triumph and tragedy without parallel in world history—a story of emperors and peasants, princesses and concubines, Confucians and Legalists, Daoists and Buddhists, camels and silkworms, revolutions, war, and peace. Who can say how the story will continue to unfold in the 21st century? Whatever happens, it is sure to be just as rich and fascinating as the story of all the previous millennia of Eastern civilization.

Suggested Reading

Feigon, *China Rising*.

Haiwang Yuan, ed., *This Is China*, chapter 4.

Wolf, *Revolution Postponed*.

Questions to Consider

1. What do the events in Tiananmen Square in 1989 and the ongoing one-child policy tell us about the complex relationship between the Chinese government and its people?

2. What is the future of Eastern civilization?

The Enduring Ideas of Eastern Civilization
Lecture 48—Transcript

Hello friends, and welcome to our final lecture of the course. We have made our way through 47 lectures, nearly 24 hours, in this exploration of the rich and fascinating history and culture of East Asia; or, I guess I should more accurately say, our exploration of the entity we attempted to define in our very first lecture as Eastern civilization. Perhaps you remember some of the challenges we encountered in that initial lecture when we tried to unpack the three key words in the name of the course: foundations, Eastern, and civilization. We were able, after some discussion, to fix the geographical scope of our course on China, Korea, Japan, and Southeast Asia. But as we've repeatedly seen over the past 47 lectures, to truly understand events in these regions it's been necessary to frequently trace connections between the Eastern Hemisphere and the rest of the world. I'm sure you remember Zhang Qian, the brave Han dynasty envoy who first breached the formidable barriers of China's west in his journey to Central Asia. He was captured by the Xiongnu twice, he was rejected by the Yuezhi, but he still managed to make his way back to the court of Han Wudi and encourage the emperor to begin to expand Chinese interests westwards. As a direct result of that expedition, China was linked into the great trading system of ancient Eurasia and the Silk Roads began to flourish.

This connection in particular made possible the spread of Buddhism out of India and into China, and then on to Korea, Japan, and Southeast Asia. Buddhist monks from all these countries later undertook their own journeys back to India, seeking knowledge, seeking inspiration. The Tang dynasty monk Xuanzang who undertook his *Journey to the West* in the company of an extraordinary collection of characters—Pigsy, Monkey, Sandy, and the Dragon King—is just the best known of these traveling monks. Later again we saw how the Mongols connected East Asia into a vast trans-Eurasian empire that made possible the transmission of many Eastern technological and intellectual inventions to the West, where they had a profound impact upon subsequent world history. Would the Europeans have been able to create their vast global empires without Chinese inventions like gunpowder, the rudder, and the compass, do you think? There's another perhaps surprising connection to the Americas here: The Italian navigator Christopher

Columbus claimed to have been inspired to become an explorer after reading Marco Polo's epic account of his visit to China and the Mongol Yuan court of Kublai Khan. In the later stages of our course we traced the often torturous connections that developed between all East Asian countries and the imperializing nations of the West. Despite the fact that our geographical interpretation of "Eastern" has been fixed upon China, Korea, Japan, and Southeast Asia, this has also been a course about Eastern civilization in a global context.

In our first lecture, we came up with another interpretation of the word *Eastern*: those regions of the world that have been profoundly influenced over thousands of years by the culture of China. We traced this influence in all sorts of ways: through the powerful influence of Chinese language and writing on the language and writing systems of Korea, Japan, and Vietnam, for example; or the impact of early Chinese ideas about governance and administration that were soon picked up by all the other states of the region. We've seen the overwhelming influence of Chinese philosophy on the entire region, particularly Confucianism, an influence just as profound in shaping Eastern civilization as Classical Greek philosophy was in shaping civilization in the West. The same is true with Chinese ideas about social organization, economic management, technological inventions; the impact of China has been profound in so many ways.

But we've also seen that despite the size, power, and wealth of China, the other states of East Asia constructed their own impressive societies that were a lot more than mere carbon copies of China. The Korean, Japanese and Vietnamese peoples all managed to resist being swamped by a Chinese cultural tidal wave, to develop their own unique ideas and customs: Chan Buddhism, Shintoism, the samurai tradition, and so on. But I don't want to retreat from the essential premise that China has been the cultural giant of the region; and it's because of this we can talk with justification, I think, about an Eastern Hemisphere, unified for thousands of years by common cultural ideas, practices, and customs that first emerged in China and that continue to bind the region together through to the present day.

We also had some fun in that first lecture trying to unpack a word that most historians are extremely wary of today: that word is *civilization*. We know that in its original Latin context the word simply pertains to cities and their citizens; so strictly speaking, when we use the word *civilization* we're describing regions of the world in which cities are the largest and most important communities. Haven't we visited some splendid cities in this course, by the way; particularly the great imperial capital of Changan? We first became aware of this extraordinary city when Qin Shi Huangdi was constructing his vast mausoleum there, and later when Han Wudi had the first ever Confucian college constructed inside the city. By the time the Tang dynasty came to power, Changan had already been an imperial capital for 2,000 years. During the reign of Xuanzong in the ninth century, you'll remember that we entered Changan through the southern gate. We walked together along the huge central avenue—four miles long, 500 yards wide—all the way to the imperial palace and the lavish, cultured court of the emperor. Home to 2 million residents, foreign dignitaries from all over Asia, students from Korea and Japan, Buddhist missionaries from India, Muslim merchants and their Bactrian camels; imagine the noise, the color, and the atmosphere in what was undoubtedly the largest and most splendid city on earth. Changan, now called by its modern name of Xian, is still one of the most extraordinary cities on earth, home to over 10 million people. Perhaps, like me, you've wandered through this extraordinary metropolis, full of so many ghosts and memories from China's ancient past.

But, of, course there have been so many other extraordinary cities: Beijing with its labyrinthine Forbidden City; Seoul under the Choson dynasty, with its magnificent palaces occupied by the elite Yangban scholars; the court city at Nara in Japan, where we found, we explored, one of the greatest collections of Eurasian art ever assembled in the log cabin Shoso-in; and the Todaiji Temple, which housed the gigantic bronze Buddha cast from thousands of bronze mirrors that the ladies of the court had donated. So cities and the power structures that sustain them have certainly been a major focus of our exploration of the civilization of the East; but we also discussed some of the dangers of the classical use of the word *civilization*, where it was used to make a value judgment to suggest that these particular people were civilized, but these other people weren't; they were backward, they were barbaric. Historians run a mile from those sorts of judgments today. Who are we to value the achievements of one human community over another; to suggest one is civilized, the other uncivilized; one superior, the other inferior?

We also considered a third way of understanding *civilization*: as a concept that describes the entire culture of a complex society; the complete set of ideas, customs, and arts that makes that culture distinctive, even unique. We can talk about "Chinese civilization" as a genuine cultural entity, and we can define those characteristics that collectively add up to Chinese civilization: Confucian, Daoist, Legalist, and Buddhist ideology; imperial dynastic government; a strong emphasis on education; a collectivist as opposed to an individualistic mindset; particular types of food and clothing; and so on. We can also, as we've done throughout this entire course, talk about "Eastern civilization" as the sum total of all the complex societies that emerged in the region; the complete set of ideas, of customs, and arts of China, Korea, Japan, and Southeast Asia that make Eastern civilization so special and so unique.

The last thing we did in that introductory lecture was to consider the meaning of our third key word, *foundations*. We talked about foundations as axioms or principles upon which something stands; the principles of geometry, of mathematics. We talked about foundations as the underlying base or support of something tangible; the foundations of a building. But in the end, I think a vaguer definition has been more useful for us; one that emerges from both these ideas. In our search for the foundations of Eastern civilization, we attempted to identify, define, and trace the development of all these significant cultural axioms, ideas, and principles that emerged within this construct that we defined as "Eastern civilization." Then we tried to see how these core foundational ideas, principles, and technologies went on to influence the development of society and civilization within the East Asian region and eventually right around the world, including inventions like gunpowder, printing, the compass, and silk.

You folks know what these foundational elements are now; essentially, the same core axioms or principles that have defined all civilizations throughout history. But while many of these foundational elements have been common to all civilizations, the peoples of East Asia thought about them differently. They faced the same big challenges that all civilizations face, the same enormous questions, but they answered them from their own unique environmental and cultural context, resulting in a radically different and fascinating set of solutions. These big ideas of Eastern civilization emerged so many thousands of years ago, but they endured and they shaped the long history of these regions all the way through to the present. My great joy—and I mean that sincerely—has been to explore these ideas with you, the evolution of ideas across vast areas of geographical space and through eons of historical time as we followed in the footsteps of great adventurers, of warriors and emperors, peasants and exotic women, and some of the greatest minds of all time.

In the last three lectures, we've been intent on bringing our discussion of the evolution of all these ideas up to the present day. In Lecture 45, we focused on government and politics: on the chaotic period in China following the collapse of the Qing dynasty; on the civil war between Nationalists and Communists; on the triumph of the Communists; of the split between the People's Republic of China and Taiwan; on Mao Zedong and his successors. In Lecture 46, we returned to our theme of global connections but also of bitter division as we traced the impact of the Cold War on all the states of East Asia, including the outbreak of bloody wars in Korea and Vietnam, the only time the Cold War ever turned hot. In our penultimate lecture, we focused on the economy: on the development of a surging socialist market economy in China; on Japan's spectacular economic rehabilitation after the Second World War; on Korea and all the other economic "little tigers" that emerged during this same period; and on the prospects for continuing economic and technological growth in the future.

At other places throughout the course we've commented upon philosophy; upon the continued relevance of Confucianism in China today, for example, an idea that's received strong support even from within the highest echelons of the Communist Party. We've discussed developments in language and written script, such as the adoption of Hangul in Korea as a direct response to Japanese occupation; and to the development of Pinyin in mainland China after the Communist revolution as a script for all the people. We've had quite a bit to say about the development of rich streams of art and literature all the way through the course, from the ancient Zhou dynasty classics, the magnificent poetry of the Tang, through to Kabuki drama, and even the early modern erotic novels of Japan.

In what remains of this lecture, I'd like to return to two other linked foundational themes that have occupied us often throughout this course, the themes of social and gender relationships; for as much as this has been a course about powerful dynasties and emperors, it's also been about the ordinary people: their lives, their hopes, their relationships. In the brief time left to us, what can we say about society in East Asia, particularly in China, today? Are people content or unhappy? How do they feel about living under a one party government, for example? How do they feel about the ancient traditions that have shaped their societies for so many thousands of years? In seeking answers to these questions, perhaps a brief consideration of the events that occurred in Beijing's Tiananmen Square in 1989 might be useful. What can we learn about the relationship between the individual and the collective society of which he or she is a part, and about the attitudes of well-educated young Chinese towards the ancient notions of filial piety, for example, respect for elders, particularly respect for government officials from the events in Tiananmen? The demonstrations actually began on April 14, 1989, during a momentous year in world history that saw the rapid collapse of communist governments around the world. But unlike many European governments, the collapse of the communist government of the People's Republic of China wasn't to be the ultimate outcome of the protests in Tiananmen Square during that same extraordinary year.

The protests in Beijing were sparked by the death of Hu Yaobang, a People's Republic of China official known for tolerating dissent, whose death students and intellectuals wanted to mourn. Of course, many of these students were part of the same cohort that, as we saw in our last lecture, had been sent to study at universities in Australia and the United States as part of Deng Xiaoping's modernization program. On the day of Hu's funeral, 100,000 people gathered in the vast Tiananmen Square in the heart of Beijing, including many liberal reformers who were against the government's authoritarianism. Demonstrations quickly spread to the streets around the square, and large-scale protests also broke out in other cities throughout China, including Shanghai. The protests lasted seven weeks until the government, driven by concerns for stability and perhaps also a very real fear of being overthrown, decided to pursue a classic Legalist response by sending troops into the square on June 4.

The number of deaths that ensued isn't known; no video footage or written evidence of violence in the square has ever surfaced, although we've all seen the iconic scenes of lone individuals standing defiantly in front of Red Army tanks. Intelligence reports received by the Soviet politburo estimated that perhaps 3,000 protesters were killed, but this number is impossible to verify. The government followed up the military assault by conducting widespread arrests of protesters and their supporters. They also cracked down on the other protests around China, they banned the foreign press, and they strictly controlled coverage of events in the Chinese press. Those members of the Party who'd publicly sympathized—in a way, like good Confucian leaders—with the protesters were purged, with several high-ranking members placed under house arrest. Widespread international condemnation (I'm sure you'll remember this) of the PRC government's use of force against the protesters quickly followed; but Deng Xiaoping and the Chinese government toughed it out and made little official reference to the event, which is known in China today as the "June 4th incident," by the way.

Of course, China continues to grapple with the question of human rights of course, with regular demands being made by individuals within the country and around the world for more participatory government and greater individual freedom. Commentators debate whether China will eventually democratize or remain a totalitarian one-party state under the control of the CCP. Some even argue that the very idea of democracy itself might ultimately be undermined by the success of China and by other smaller successful communist countries like Vietnam. They point out that China is becoming a model of booming development, political stability, affordable housing, successful social welfare and nationalized medicine, and also of sustainable technology, a gradually cleaner environment, and widespread prosperity, all of which is being achieved under the control of an authoritarian, non-democratic regime. This is something like the classic model of a benevolent dictatorship promoted by so many philosophers from Plato to Hegel as a better system of government than democracy; and frankly this isn't that different to China's long history of Confucian dynastic government. As we've seen many absolute emperors—none of whom was ever elected, of course—adopted an explicitly Confucian commitment to governing for the benefit of the people whose care they're morally expected to pursue through policies of benevolence. Of course, as a result of U.S. involvement during the Cold War, democracy remains strong in South Korea, Japan, and Taiwan; the peoples of these states seem absolutely committed to the maintenance of their participatory political system. North Korea, on the other hand, is an entirely different story.

But many other China watchers argue that a second Tiananmen Square uprising is probably inevitable because of problems like increasing inequality in China, land ownership rights, environmental degradation, and corruption amongst officials. Certainly the government has adopted many policies to try and solve these problems and to try and improve the lives of the people: for example, increasing spending in rural areas, abolishing onerous taxes, cracking down on corruption, and attempting to increase the standard of living for all sectors of China's vast population. These policies, too, are remarkably similar to those adopted by many of China's ancient dynasties—reforms to the tax system as we've seen many times, the equal-field system, establishing ministries to root out corruption, and so on—demonstrating the continuing relevance of so many foundational ideas, even in Communist China today.

In thinking of China's huge population, and also of attempts to improve its standard of living, perhaps we should also briefly mention now the "One Child Policy," first introduced back in 1978 as the latest in a long history of attempts to control and care for the largest population on the planet. The policy restricts urban families to just one child; there are many exemptions for rural couples and minorities, by the way. The government claims that the policy has prevented more than 250 million live births between 1978 and 2000; and this is pretty significant because at the time of writing this lecture, China's population stands at a whopping 1.34 billion people. The policy is often criticized in the West for encouraging abortion and female infanticide, for creating a serious gender imbalance in China, and for a dramatic increase in female adoptions to the West. But interestingly, a 2008 Pew Center survey of a pretty large sample of the Chinese population showed that some 76 percent of the Chinese people actually support the policy. The gender imbalance is seen as a serious problem because sex-specific abortions mean that, according to 2010 statistics, 119 boys were being born for every 100 girls, which projected forward would mean that 24 million men of marrying age would have no chance of finding a female partner by 2020. But just a month or so before I completed this lecture, the head of China's National Population and Family Commission announced the introduction of a series of measures to correct the imbalance, particularly a crackdown on illegal prenatal gender tests and selective abortions. The government also recently announced that the policy would remain in place until 2015 and then be reassessed. In conversations I personally have had with people in China, I've actually found fairly widespread support amongst educated urban dwellers for the policy, but also some very real frustrations with the complexities of the system.

Gender roles and relationships are also changing in China and frankly the rest of East Asia today. In our course, we've often looked at the influence of Confucianism on attitudes towards women; attitudes that stressed morality, cleanliness, womanly duties you'll remember, and proper and differentiated roles for men and women. Later conservative Neo-Confucians used their interpretation of the philosophy, and also of yin and yang ideals, to argue for female subordination, which was partly responsible for the practice of foot binding. The success of the Communist revolution led to a significant reevaluation of women's roles, although frankly the inherent contradiction between a woman as reproductive agent and a woman as equal partner and worker in society has hardly been resolved. But I think it's fair to say that under communist rule in China, the social status of women has considerably improved. Women are more empowered to work outside the home; foot binding, child marriages, prostitution, and arranged marriages have all been banned. China has also seen a decrease in domestic violence due to government-supported grassroots programs to counter these practices. But women in rural areas still remain largely uneducated, and in the cities employers are often reluctant to hire female workers because Chinese law requires that employers cover the costs of maternity leave and even childbirth. But certainly for educated Chinese women living in the great metropolises like Beijing, Shanghai, and Guangzhou, including many students and educated professional women that I've met, there are far more opportunities available today than at any previous time in China's history.

Our investigation of the foundations of Eastern civilization has come a very long way since we began our course 47 lectures ago. Together, we've explored many thousands of years of history and culture; actually millions of years if you include our discussion of the migration of hominids like *Homo erectus* and *Homo habilis* to East Asia. China has enjoyed one of the longest and most continuous histories of any society on the planet, and traditions that emerged thousands of years ago continue to guide and influence Chinese development to the present day. At the same time, we've seen other East and Southeast Asian societies develop their own fascinating and unique cultural traditions, partly in response and even resistance to the powerful influence of China. This is a story rich and diverse; this is a story of triumph and tragedy without parallel in world history; this is a story of emperors and peasants, princesses and concubines, Confucians and Legalists, Daoists and Buddhists, camels and silk worms, of revolutions, war, and peace. Who can say with any certainty how the story will continue to unfold into the 21st century? Whatever happens, I'm sure it'll be just as rich and fascinating as the story of all the previous millennia of Eastern civilization.

As we finish our journey, my greatest hope is that this story will continue to resonate with you for the rest of your lives. Ultimately, perhaps your greatest reward from this course will be a much deeper understanding, appreciation, and curiosity for this long and rich history of Eastern civilization, and also some enhanced insight into how and why the story might develop into the future. I hope that when you read a fascinating article about China or Korea, or you hear in the news about some extraordinary event in Japan or Vietnam, you might say, "Aahhh, I know where that story comes from; I hear in that event the echo of thousands of years of struggle, discovery, war, triumph, isolation, and finally engagement." Thanks for being such wonderful friends on this long journey. I wish you well, and I hope that we might all get to meet again in the future. Goodbye for now.

Bibliography

Aldiss, S., ed. *Zen Sourcebook: Traditional Documents from China, Korea and Japan.* Indianapolis: Hackett Publishing, 2008. A superb collection of the traditional writings of the masters of the Zen Buddhist tradition.

Allen, S. *The Shape of the Turtle: Myth, Art and Cosmology in Early China.* Albany: State University of New York Press, 1991. A well-written examination of Shang dynasty cosmology and Zhou dynasty myths.

Asia Society. "Studies of Japanese Art by Period." http://www.asiasocietymuseum.org/region_results.asp?RegionID=6&CountryID=14&ChapterID=38. A superb online collection of Japanese art organized by historical period.

Barfield, T. *The Perilous Frontier: Nomadic Empires and China, 221 BC to AD 1757.* Oxford: Blackwell Publishers, 1989. A superb, sweeping overview of China's relationship with militarized nomads over 2,000 years.

Barnes, G. L. *China, Korea and Japan: The Rise of Civilization in East Asia.* London: Thames and Hudson, 1993. Now a classic, this was one of the first books written by a distinguished archaeologist to offer a synthesis of archaeological discoveries throughout the region and provide a unified account of the origins of common cultural traditions.

Baum, R. *Burying Mao: Chinese Politics in the Age of Deng Xiaoping.* Princeton: Princeton University Press, 1994. Fascinating account of the power struggles and soul searching within the Chinese Communist Party following the death of Mao Zedong.

Benjamin, C., and S. Liu, eds. *Walls and Frontiers in Inner Asian History.* Silk Roads Studies, vol. VI. Turnhout, Belgium: Brepols Publishers, 2002. A fascinating collection of papers and articles presented at the Australasian Society for Inner Asian Studies Conference in 2000.

Benjamin, C. "The Kushans in World History." *World History Bulletin* XXV, no. 1 (spring 2009): 30–32. A neat and readable overview of the importance of the Kushan Empire to Eastern civilization and world history.

———. "A Nation of Nomads? The Lifeway of the Yuezhi in the Gansu and Bactria." In *Toronto Studies in Central and Inner Asia*, edited by M. Gervers and G. Long, vol. VII, pp. 93–122. Toronto: University of Toronto Press, 2005. A discussion of the complex relationship between early Chinese dynasties and the various nomadic confederations that dwelt along the borders.

———. "The Kushans." In *Berkshire Encyclopedia of World History*, 2nd ed., edited by W. McNeill, J. Bentley, D. Christian, D. Levinson, H. Roupp, and J. Zinsser, vol. 3, pp. 1090–1093. Great Barrington, MA: Berkshire Press, 2010. Brief and readable account of the importance of the Kushans to world history.

———. "'The great deliverer, the righteous, the just, the autocrat, the god, worthy of worship': Kanishka I, Kushan Dynastic Religion, and Buddhism." In *Toronto Studies in Central and Inner Asia*, edited by M. Gervers and G. Long, vol. IX. Toronto: University of Toronto Press, 2012. An article exploring the relationship between the great Kushan king Kanishka and Buddhism.

———. "Hungry for Han Goods? Zhang Qian and the Origins of the Silk Roads." In *Toronto Studies in Central and Inner Asia*, edited by M. Gervers and G. Long, vol. VIII, pp. 3–30. Toronto: University of Toronto Press, 2007. A readable account of the expedition of Zhang Qian, sent by Han Wudi to attempt to forge an alliance with the Yuezhi against the Xiongnu.

———. *The Yuezhi: Origin, Migration and the Conquest of Northern Bactria.* Turnhout, Belgium: Brepols Publishers, 2007. My own study of the origin and important migration of the Yuezhi nomadic confederation following its defeat by the Xiongnu and the impact this had on the subsequent establishment of the Silk Roads.

Bodde, D. *China's First Unifier: A Study of the Ch'in Dynasty as Seen in the Life of Li Ssu.* Leiden: E. J. Brill, 1938. A classic in every way—the first insightful study of the life and legacy of the first emperor of China, Qin Shihuangdi.

Boxer, C. R. *The Christian Century in Japan.* Berkeley: University of California Press, 1951. Classic account of the interaction between early Christian missionaries and Japanese elites in Japan.

Buell, P. D. *The A to Z of the Mongol World Empire.* New York: Rowman and Littlefield, 2010. A new and thoughtfully organized history of the impact of the Mongols.

Chang, K. C. *The Archaeology of Ancient China.* 4th ed. New Haven: Yale University Press, 1986. A classic study of the archaeology of ancient China by one of China's leading archaeologists.

Chapuis, O. *A History of Vietnam: From Hong Bang to Tu Duc.* Contributions to Asian Studies No. 5. Westport, CT: Greenwood Press, 1995. Comprehensive and erudite study of the long and fascinating history of Vietnam.

Chen, J. *China and the West: Society and Culture, 1815–1937.* Bloomington: Indiana University Press, 1979. A well-written and accessible study of the complex relationship between the Qing dynasty and various Western powers during the 19th and early 20th centuries.

Choi, Min-hong. *A Modern History of Korean Philosophy.* 3 vols. Seoul: Seong Moon Sas, 1980. A monumental and comprehensive history of the major philosophical periods in Korean history.

Christian, D., and C. Benjamin, eds. *Realms of the Silk Roads: Ancient and Modern.* Silk Roads Studies, vol. IV. Turnhout, Belgium: Brepols Publishers, 2000. A fascinating collection of papers and articles presented at the Australasian Society for Inner Asian Studies Conference in 1998.

————, eds., *Worlds of the Silk Roads: Ancient and Modern.* Silk Roads Studies, vol. II. Turnhout, Belgium: Brepols Publishers, 1998. A fascinating collection of papers and articles presented at the Australasian Society for Inner Asian Studies Conference in 1996.

Church, P. *A Short History of Southeast Asia.* Singapore: John Wiles and Sons, 1986. A concise but surprisingly inclusive history of the major states and nations of Southeast Asia from ancient times to the present.

Confucius. *The Analects of Confucius.* Translated and with notes by Simon Leys. New York: W.W. Norton, 1997. A modern, fluent, and readable translation of the classic work of Confucius.

Dardess, J. *Confucianism and Autocracy: Professional Elites in the Founding of the Ming Dynasty.* Berkeley: University of California Press, 1983. A thorough study of the elites closest to the throne in the complex transition from the Yuan to the Ming dynasties.

De Bary, T., and R. Lufrano, eds. *Sources of Chinese Tradition.* 2 vols. New York: Columbia University Press, 2000. A superb collection of primary sources with commentary focused on the origins and evolution of Chinese culture.

di Cosmo, N. *Ancient China and Its Enemies: The Rise of Nomad Power in East Asian History.* Cambridge: Cambridge University Press, 2002. Probably the finest and most erudite book available on the relationship between ancient China and its militarized nomadic neighbors, particularly between the Han dynasty and the Xiongnu.

Dien, A., ed. *State and Society in Early Medieval China.* Stanford: Stanford University Press, 1990. An excellent sampling of recent scholarship on the Age of Disunity.

Dirlik, A. *The Origins of Chinese Communism.* New York: Oxford University Press, 1989. A detailed and intellectually compelling account of the origins and rise to power of the Chinese Communist Party.

Dower, J. W. *Embracing Defeat: Japan in the Wake of World War II*. New York: W. W. Norton, 1999. A thoughtful account of the changing mindset in Japan following defeat in World War II, which facilitated the extraordinary postwar recovery of Japan.

Duus, P. *Feudalism in Japan*. New York: Alfred P. Knopf, 1969. A classic history of the "feudal" period of Japanese history.

Ebery, P. *The Inner Quarters: Marriage and the Lives of Chinese Women in the Song Period*. Berkeley: University of California Press, 1993. One of the first—and still one of the best—studies of the lives of women in China.

————. *The Cambridge Illustrated History of China*. Cambridge: Cambridge University Press, 2000. This book contains a splendid collection of images, but it is the author's erudition and command of her subject that makes this one of the finest resources available on Chinese history and culture.

Eckert, Carter J., Ki-Baik Lee, Young Ick Lew, Michael Robinson, and Edward W. Wagner. *Korea Old and New: A History*. Cambridge, MA: Harvard University Press, 1990. Written by a team of Korean history specialists, this is an excellent attempt to meet the need for a general history of Korea, with a particular emphasis on the 20th century.

Economy, E. C. *The River Runs Black: The Environmental Challenge to China's Future*. Cornell: Cornell University Press, 2004. A gripping and depressing account of the many environmental challenges facing modern China.

Esherick, J. W. *The Origins of the Boxer Uprising*. Berkeley: University of California Press, 1987. A well-researched study of the rebellion that brought the Qing dynasty to its knees.

Feigon, L. *China Rising: The Meaning of Tiananmen*. Chicago: Ivan Dee, 1990. A compelling account of the democracy movement in China and the 1989 events in Tiananmen Square.

Franck, I. M., and D. M. Brownstone. *The Silk Roads: A History*. New York and Oxford: Oxford University Press, 1986. A sweeping and dynamic overview of the Silk Roads throughout world history.

Fung Yulan. *A History of Chinese Philosophy*. Translated by D. Bodde. Princeton: Princeton University Press, 1993. A thorough survey of the origins and evolution of the main philosophical traditions of China.

Haiwang Yuan, ed. *This Is China: The First Five Thousand Years*. Great Barrington, MA: Berkshire Publishing, 2010. A superb and concise overview of the history and culture of China, from the early culture to the present.

Henthorn, W. E. *A History of Korea*. New York: Free Press, 1971. A concise and readable general history of Korea from ancient times through to the 19th century.

Hinch, B. *Women in Early Imperial China*. New York: Rowman and Littlefield, 2002. A recent, well-researched, and engaging account of the lives of women during the early imperial dynasties of China.

Hoefer, H. J. *Insight Guides: Korea*. Hong Kong: APA Productions, 1981. A superbly written and beautifully illustrated guide to Korean history and culture.

Hook, B., and D. Twitchett, eds. *The Cambridge Encyclopedia of China*. 2nd ed. Cambridge: Cambridge University Press, 1991. This is probably the best single-volume reference work available on the history of China.

Hsia, R. Po-chia. "The Catholic Mission and Translations in China, 1583–1700." In *Cultural Translation in Early Modern Europe*, edited by P. Burke and R. Po-chia Hsia. Cambridge: Cambridge University Press, 2007. Fascinating study of the Catholic mission to Ming China.

Hurst, G. C. Jr. "The Structure of the Heian Court." In *Medieval Japan: Essays in Institutional History*, edited by J. W. Hall and J. P. Mass. New Haven: Yale University Press, 1974. A useful collection of scholarly essays focused on the history of political and other institutions in early Japanese history.

Jagchid, S., and V. J. Symons. *Peace, War and Trade along the Great Wall: Nomadic Chinese Interaction through Two Millennia.* Bloomington: Indiana University Press, 1989. A sweeping study of the interaction between sedentary Chinese states and dynasties and the various nomadic confederations that dwelt along the northern and western frontiers of ancient China.

Jeon, Sang-woon. *Science and Technology of Korea: Traditional Instruments and Techniques.* Cambridge, MA: MIT Press, 1974. A pioneering and high-standard analysis of the history of Korean innovation in science and technology.

Joe, W. J. *Traditional Korea: A Cultural History.* Seoul: Chungang University Press, 1972. A comprehensive cultural history of Korea from antiquity to the 19th century.

Karnow, S. *Vietnam: A History.* London: Penguin Books, 1984. Best-selling history of the origins, conduct, and aftermath of the Vietnam War.

Kristoff, N., and S. WuDunn. *China Awakes: The Struggle for the Soul of a Rising Power.* New York: Random House, 1994. A well-written account by leading journalists covering the 1989–1993 period in China.

Kuhn, P. *Rebellion and Its Enemies in Late Imperial China.* Cambridge, MA: Harvard University Press, 1970. An excellent study of the many rebellions that marked China in the 19th century and attempts to suppress them by Qing authorities.

Lee, Ki-baik. *A New History of Korea.* Cambridge, MA: Harvard University Press, 1984. Translated by E. W. Wagner and E. J. Schultz. The first English translation of Professor Lee's famous and detailed political and cultural history of Korea.

Lee, P. H., and W. T. de Bary. *Sources of Korean Tradition.* New York: Columbia University Press, 1997. A superb and comprehensive collection of early Korean source materials.

Loewe, M. *Everyday Life in Early Imperial China*. Indianapolis: Hackett Publishing Company, 2005. A lively and well-illustrated account of the lives of peasants, townsfolk, and the elite during the Han dynasty of ancient China.

McKnight, B. *Law and Order in Sung China*. Cambridge, MA: Harvard University Press, 1992. A detailed and fascinating account of the police system and penal institutions involved with catching and punishing criminals in Song China.

Meisner, M. *Mao's China and After: A History of the People's Republic*. New York: Free Press, 1986. A flowing and exciting narrative account of the post-1949 period in China.

Morgan, D. *The Mongols*. Cambridge, MA: Basil Blackwell, 1986. Classic book on the origins, history, and long-term influence of the Mongols.

Mote, F. W. *Intellectual Foundations of China*. New York: McGraw-Hill, 1989. A classic account of the origins of Chinese philosophy, demonstrating a deep understanding of the intellectual underpinnings of Confucianism, Daoism, and Legalism.

Moule, A. C., and P. Pelliot. *Marco Polo: The Description of the World*. London: Routledge and Sons, 1938. Still regarded as one of the best translations of the diary of Marco Polo.

Naquin, S., and E. Rawski. *Chinese Society in the Eighteenth Century*. New Haven: Yale University Press, 1987. A superb introduction to the history, culture, and society of the Qing dynasty.

Nelson, S. M. *The Archaeology of Korea*. Cambridge: Cambridge University Press, 1993. A richly detailed and insightful study of the archaeology of Korea, from the early Paleolithic era through to the Three Kingdoms Period.

Owen, S. *The Great Age of Chinese Poetry: The High Tang*. A superbly translated and edited collection of classic Tang poetry, by some of the greatest poets in world history.

Palmer, S. J. *Korea and Christianity: The Problem of Identification with Tradition.* Seoul: Royal Asiatic Society, Korea Branch, 1967. A thoughtful account of factors in Korean society that help explain the remarkable success Protestant Christianity has achieved there.

Pearson, R. *Ancient Japan.* New York: Arthur Sackler Gallery, 1992. A fascinating and well-illustrated account of the early stages of Japanese culture.

Plaks, A. *Four Masterworks of the Ming Novel.* Princeton: Princeton University Press, 1987. A masterful study of the development of the novel in Ming dynasty China.

Rees, D. *Korea: The Limited War.* New York: St. Martin's Press, 1964. Useful because it includes an extensive bibliography, a comprehensive collection of sources, and fascinating statistical material about the Korean War.

Saburo Ienagi. *Japanese Art: A Cultural Appreciation.* New York: Weatherhill, 1979. This book, which represents some of the best scholarship of the Japanese on their own artistic and cultural traditions, offers deep and invaluable insight into the interpretation of Japanese art and archaeology.

Salisbury, H. *The Long March.* New York: Harper and Row, 1995. A readable and fascinating account of Salisbury's retracing of the Long March in the early 1980s, enlivened by interviews with survivors.

Schirokauer, C., Miranda Brown, David Lurie, and Suzanne Gay. A Brief History of Chinese and Japanese Civilizations. 3rd ed. New York: Thomson Wadsworth, 2006. Written by a team of experts, this is a sweeping overview of the history of Chinese and Japanese culture, with a particular emphasis on art, religion, philosophy, and literature.

Sheridan, J. *The Republican Era in Chinese History, 1912–1949.* New York: Free Press, 1975. An accurate and able survey of the turbulent republican era, from the collapse of the Qing through to the declaration of the People's Republic of China.

Snow, E. *Red Star over China.* New York: Random House, 1938; reprint, New York: Grove Press, 1968. A classic firsthand account of the experience of the Communists, particularly Mao Zedong, in the 1930s.

Song Nan Zhang. *The Ballad of Mulan.* Union City, CA: Pan Asian Publications, 1998. A modern version of the classic "Ballad of Mulan," lavishly illustrated by Song Nan Zhang.

Spence, J. D. *The Memory Palace of Matteo Ricci.* New York: Viking, 1984. A readable and accurate account of Matteo Ricci's mission to the Ming court in China.

Tanner, H. M. *China: A History.* Indianapolis: Hackett Publishing Company, 2009. A readable yet rigorous overview of the political and social development of Chinese civilization, from ancient times to the present.

Tarling, N., ed. *The Cambridge History of Southeast Asia.* Cambridge: Cambridge University Press, 1999. An exhaustive multivolume history of Southeast Asia; includes contributions from many of the leading specialists in the region.

Totman, C. *A History of Japan.* Oxford: Blackwell, 2000. A comprehensive and up-to-date survey history of Japan from ancient times to the present.

———. *Early Modern Japan.* Berkeley: University of California Press, 1993. Comprehensive account of the history and culture of the early modern period in Japanese history.

Tsunoda, R., and L. Carrington. *Japan in the Chinese Dynastic Histories.* Kyoto: Perkins Oriental Books, 1968. A useful collection of source references to early Japanese history as recorded in the annals of ancient Chinese dynasties.

Tyler, R., trans. "Introduction." In The Tale of Genji, written by Murasaki Shikibu. New York: Penguin, 2001. Tyler's introduction is a welcome addition to this excellent translation of Genji.

Varley, H. P. *Imperial Restoration in Medieval Japan.* New York: Columbia University Press, 1971. A thoughtful account of the Kamakura and Muromachi periods of Japanese history.

Vietnam-Culture.com. "Vietnam History." http://www.vietnam-culture.com/zones-25-1/Vietnam-History.aspx. Comprehensive online history of Vietnam from ancient times to the present. An accessible and easy-to-navigate site with neat summaries of the key periods in Vietnamese history.

Watson, B. *Ssu-Ma Ch'ien: Grand Historian of China.* New York: Columbia University Press, 1958. A thoughtful and sympathetic biographical and historiographical interpretation of the great Han dynasty historian, Sima Qian.

———. *Records of the Grand Historian of China.* 2 vols. New York: Columbia University Press, 1961. A classic translation of Sima Qian's great work, the *Shiji.*

Wilson, G. M. *Patriots and Redeemers in Japan: Motives in the Meiji Restoration.* Chicago: University of Chicago Press, 1992. One of the best books available explaining the extraordinary transition of the Meiji Restoration period in Japan.

Winchester, S. *The River at the Center of the World.* Toronto: Harper Collins, 2004. A beautifully written account of the author's journey up the Yangtze River, from mouth to source, packed full of fascinating history and cultural insights.

Wolf, M. *Revolution Postponed: Women in Contemporary China.* Stanford: Stanford University Press, 1985. An excellent account of the fate of women and women's rights in modern China.

Wriggins, S. *The Silk Road Journey with Xuanzang.* New York: Basic Books, 2003. A modern, readable, and enjoyable account of the journey of Xuanzang by an author who retraced the great Buddhist pilgrim's journey from China to India.

Wright, A., and D. Twitchett, eds. *Perspectives on the Tang.* New Haven: Yale University Press, 1981. A useful and readable collection of essays on the history and culture of the Tang dynasty.

Xinru Liu. *The Silk Roads.* New York: Bedford. St. Martin's, 2010. A compelling narrative and interesting primary documents on the early history of the Silk Roads.

Young, L. *Japan's Total Empire: Manchuria and the Culture of Wartime Imperialism.* Berkeley: University of California Press, 1998. Detailed and erudite analysis of the imperial and militaristic culture that appeared in Japan in the 1930s.

Zhiqun Zhu. *Global Studies: China.* 14th ed. New York: McGraw-Hill, 2010. A concise collection of essays and journal and newspaper articles exploring many of the contemporary political, social, and economic issues facing China today.

Zurcher, E. *The Buddhist Conquest of China: The Spread and Adaptation of Buddhism in Early Medieval China.* Leiden: E. J. Brill, 1959. A thorough, fascinating, and highly scholarly account of the spread of Buddhism in China from the end of the Han to the Tang.

Notes